I0762151

**You will get close to cracking open, in fact you will see inside, really inside.**

"ALMOST THE NEXT DAY," DATE: Unknown (see p. 246)

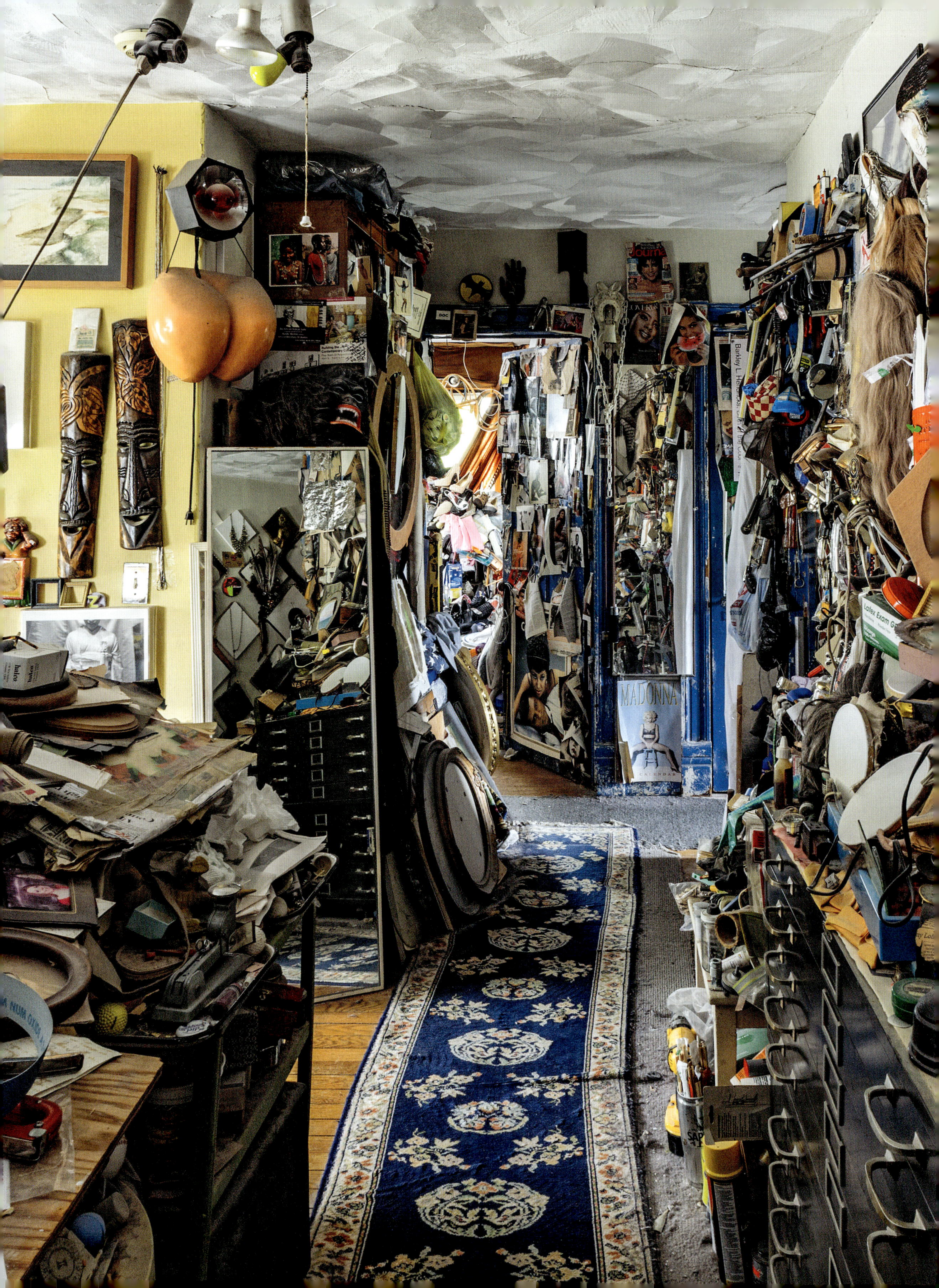
MADONNA

**It will be beautiful and terrifying at the same time.**

“ALMOST THE NEXT DAY,” DATE: Unknown (see p. 246)

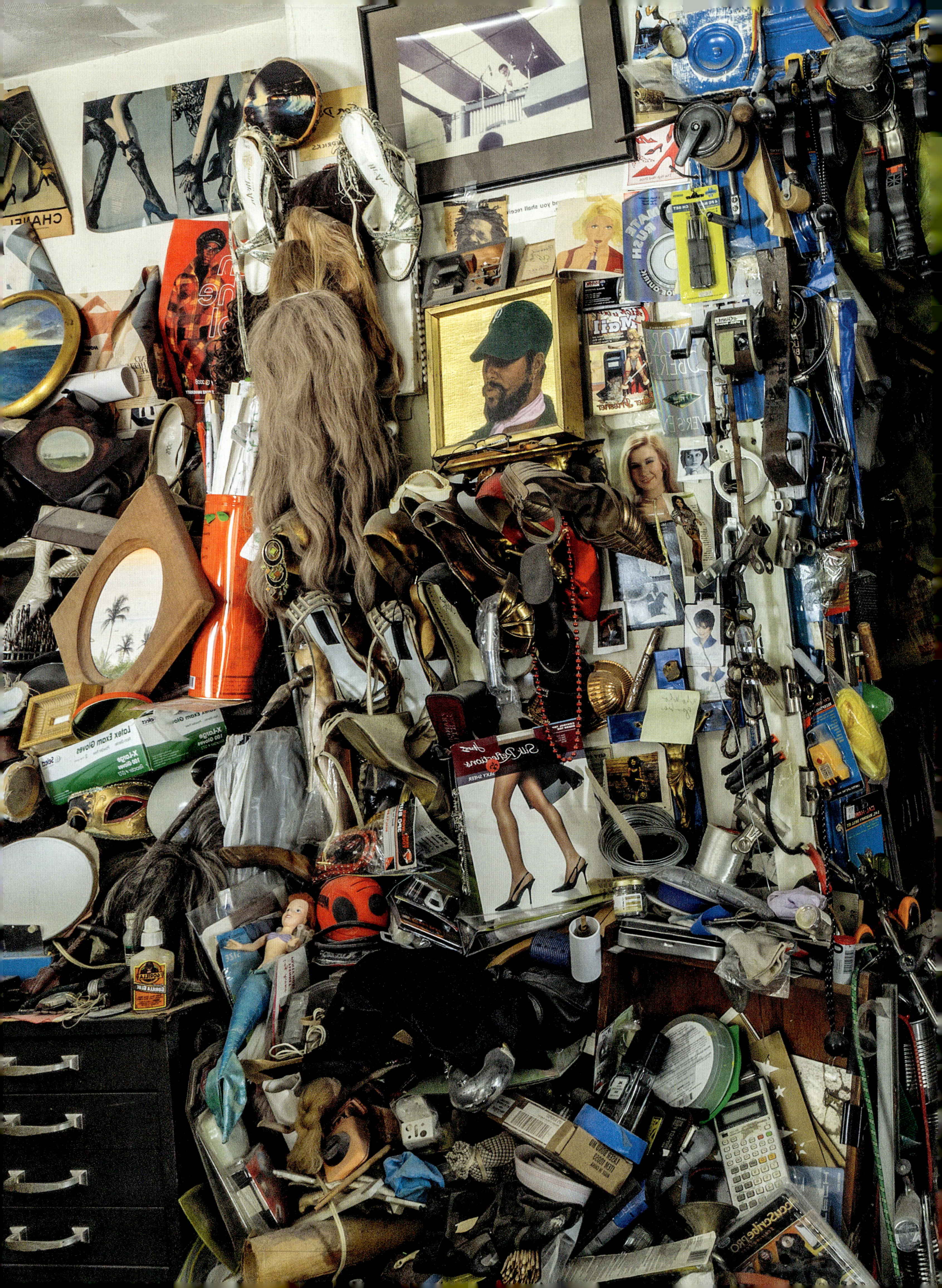

CHANEL
Latex Exam Gloves
GORILLA GLUE

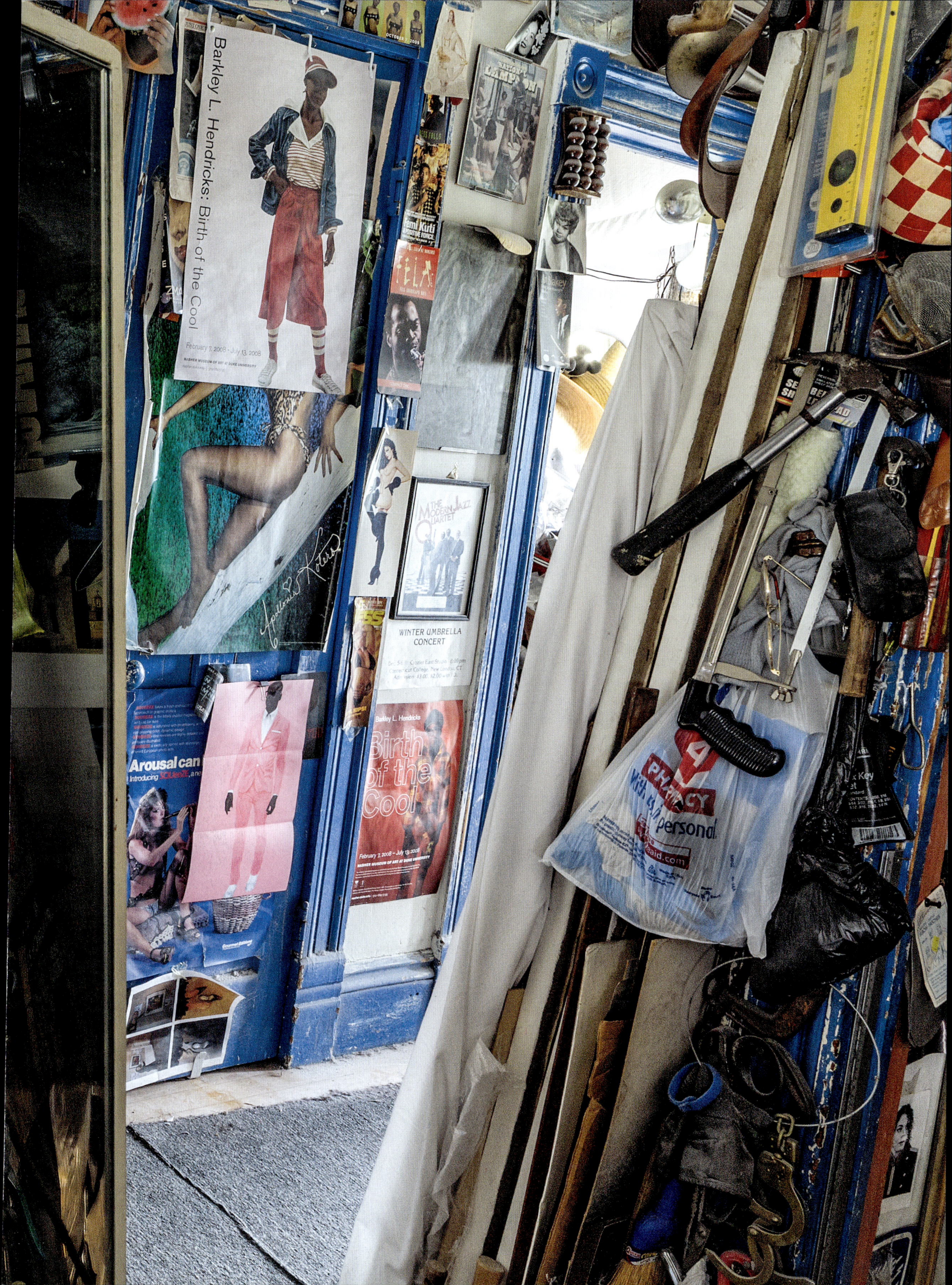
Barkley L. Hendricks: Birth of the Cool
February 7, 2008 – July 13, 2008
WINTER UMBRELLA CONCERT
Barkley L. Hendricks
Birth of the Cool
Arousal can

**After that things will be cool.**

**Really laid back.**
**For a long, long time.**

“ALMOST THE NEXT DAY,” DATE: Unknown (see p. 246)

Published by Hirmer Publishers
Bayerstraße 57-59
80335 Munich, Germany
www.hirmerpublishers.com

Design: Shiffman&Kohnke, Tracey Shiffman with James Ihira
Copyediting and proofreading: Rosamond Decker
Senior Editor: Elisabeth Rochau-Shalem
Project Manager: Rainer Arnold

Lithography and pre-press: Reproline Mediateam, Unterföhring
Printing and binding: Printer Trento s.r.l.
Paper: Magno Volume, 170 gsm
Fonts: New Spirit, Pitch



ISBN: 978-3-7774-4602-8

Library of Congress Control Number: 2025908681

Printed in Italy

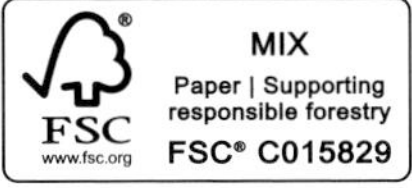


HIRMER

# Barkley L. Hendricks

# Piles of Inspiration Everywhere

Susan Hendricks
David Katzenstein

## Contents

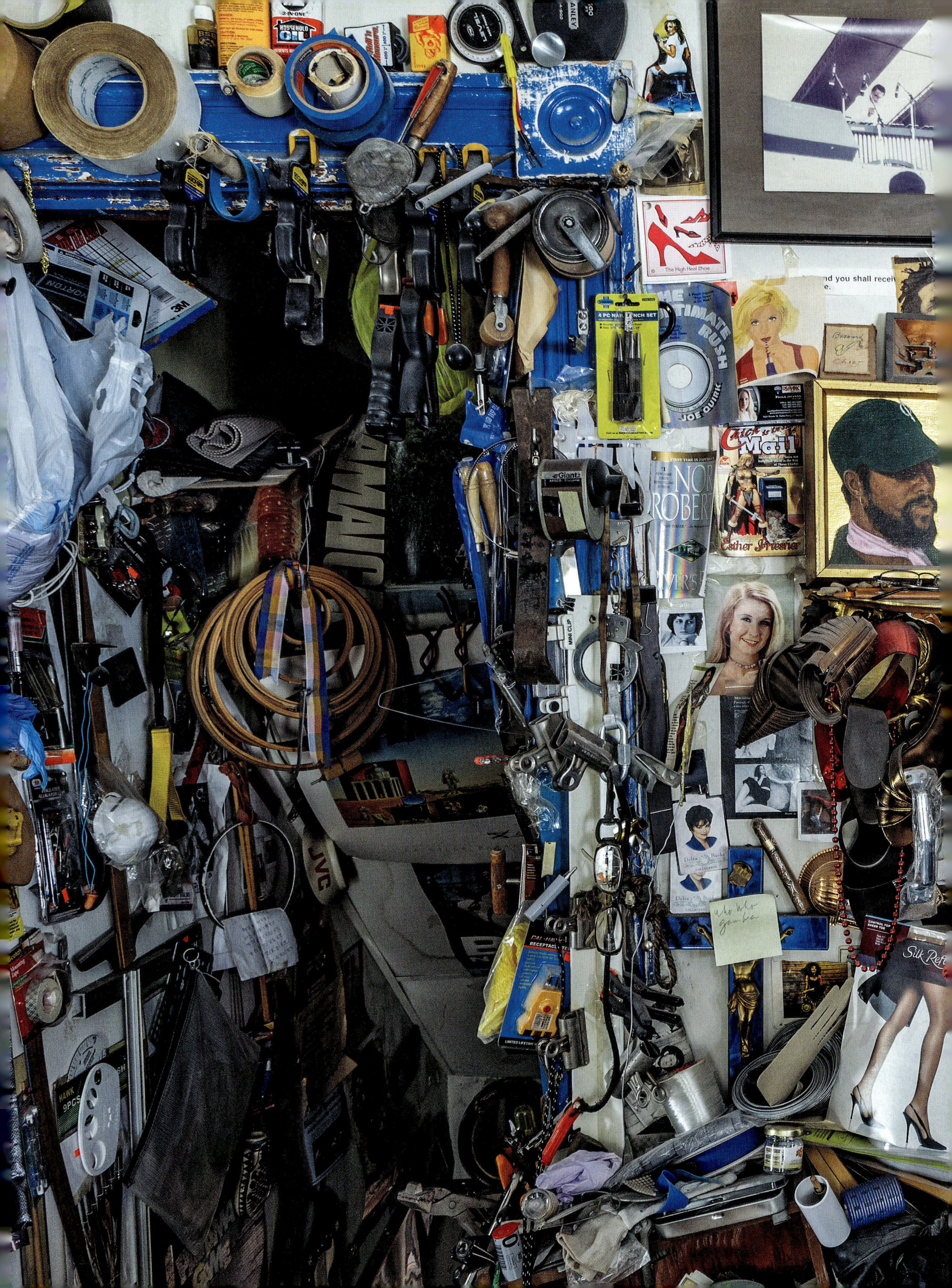
3-IN-ONE
HOUSEHOLD OIL
The High Heel Shoe
THE ULTIMATE RUSH
JOE QUIRK
Esther Friesner
MINI CLIP
JVC
HAWK
9PCS

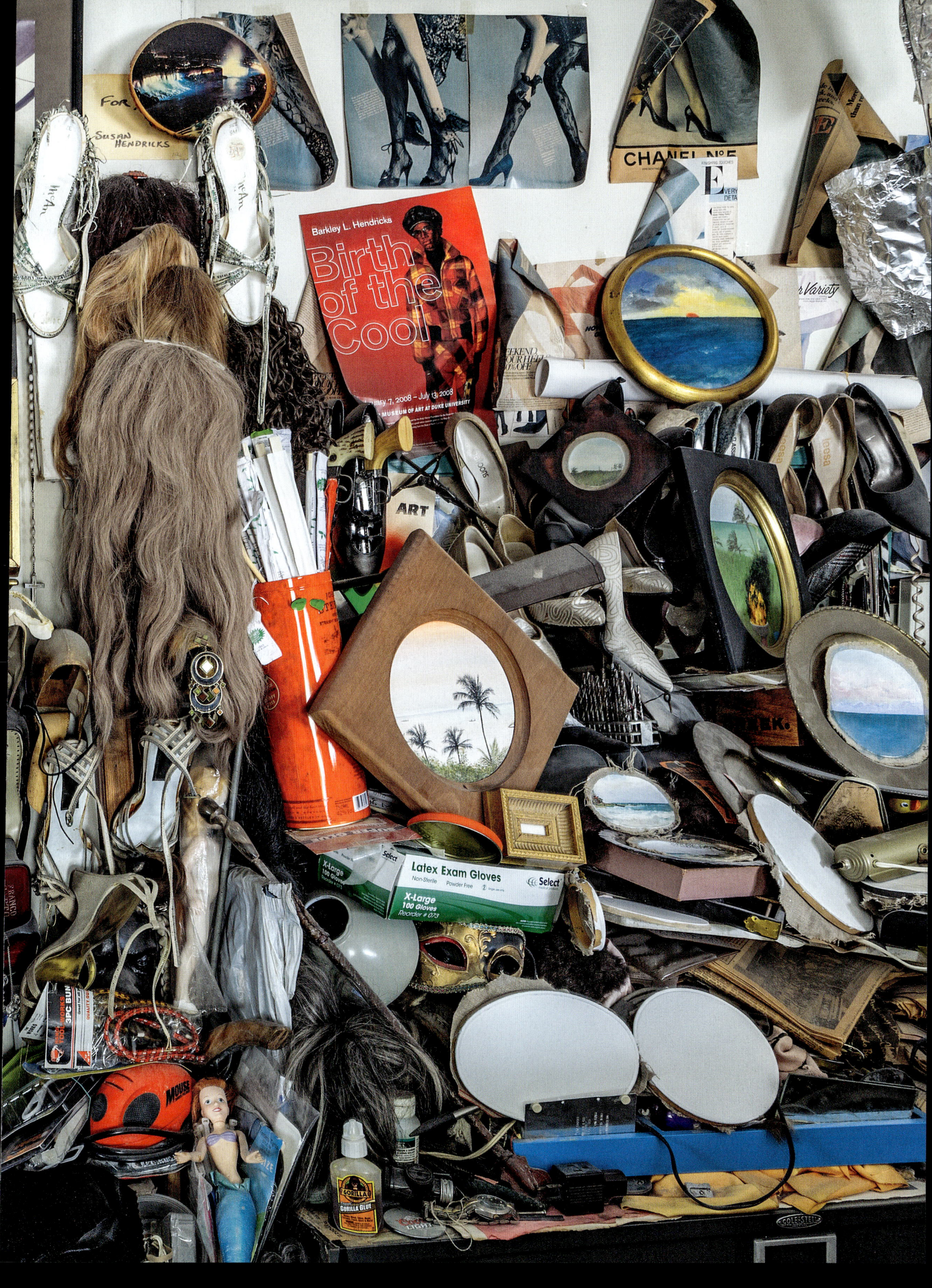

FOR
SUSAN HENDRICKS
CHANEL N°5
Barkley L. Hendricks
Birth of the Cool
MUSEUM OF ART AT DUKE UNIVERSITY
ART
Latex Exam Gloves
Non-Sterile
Powder Free
Select
X-Large
100 Gloves
Reorder # 073
GORILLA GLUE

**“Much too late to speculate”**

**Which is what I have been doing a lot of lately. Or have I?**

# Barkley L. Hendricks: Piles of Inspiration Everywhere

# A Conversation with Susan Hendricks and David Katzenstein

DK: David Katzenstein
SH: Susan Hendricks

**DK:** Susan, you and I have embarked on a project to create a book about the life of Barkley Hendricks through his environment, telling his story through the place where he lived with you and where he worked for decades. It's a home that is filled with stuff, all of which was inspirational on a daily basis to the artist as he walked through the spaces and worked in his studio.

**SH:** After Barkley passed in April of 2017, you approached me about visiting our home in New London, Connecticut—which also served as Barkley's studio—so we could begin to document the different parts of the house where he worked and where we lived.

**DK:** Recently, when you and I went through all the photographs I took for this project, I noticed that the first ones were taken on May 1st, 2017, which was just two weeks after Barkley passed on April 18th. He had not been sick, and his death was very unexpected.

**SH:** Those first few weeks after he passed, I was still kind of shell shocked, and it never occurred to me that, before I started trying to wade through things, it would probably be a good thing to have the space documented. But I thought that you had a valid point that once I started moving stuff, it was never going to be the way he left it. So when you suggested the idea, I said okay.

**DK:** I know Barkley was very private, both as an individual and as an artist.

**SH:** Over the span of the 35 years that we lived together in the house, no one coming to visit ever went into Barkley's studio on the second floor. No curators, and not even our gallerist. Certainly I could be there, I lived here with him, but the studio was his space, and I respected that. It was where he created, and it wasn't, in his mind, open to questions or exploration. So you were really the first person to come in and document his space.

When you first came up and spent the better part of the day photographing on your own all over the house, that was the beginning of this project, and a number of the photographs that we show from that first day are literally piles of everything everywhere. It might not be a stacked pile, it might be a horizontal pile, it might be things on a wall layered on top of each other. There might be vertical and horizontal piles of things in the studios, but I would say pretty much every picture in the book is some sort of a reflection of the title.

**DK:** What was it like day to day, living in this home environment where so much creativity emanated everywhere?

**SH:** It was thrilling, infuriating, and heartbreaking. Those are my three words. Always thrilling. Artistic expression and creativity were everywhere I looked. There was always something to look at, even if it was in a pile. It could be, you know, difficult sometimes living in an environment that is so full. It was, and it is. It's like living in an art wonderland. Barkley's art and visual inspirations surrounded us everywhere—a drawing he did, a magazine clipping tacked to the wall, record covers to inspire him—there are literally images everywhere. It's just a cacophony of visuals.

Having said that, the person who hung most of the stuff and created most of the things isn't here anymore. So that's very difficult after spending 35 years together in this home. There's a big hole there.

**DK:** Can you talk a little about the evolution of the space over time?

**SH:** Barkley purchased the house in the early 1980s and renovated the entire interior. He even did all the plastering and refinished all of the woodwork of this beautiful Victorian home. The majority of the second floor became his studio. In late 1982, once I moved in (we were married in April 1983), we divided up parts of the first floor, which also included the kitchen. So we each had our own space in addition to his office on the second floor and his studio space, which was most of the second floor.

In those early years Barkley had already completely inhabited the studio. When I moved in, it didn't look like it does in these photographs you made, but it was certainly already full. Over the years, it became even more full as Barkley absorbed and acquired and bought and collected more stuff to inspire him to paint and photograph and draw.

It evolved to the point where—in the middle of the music room, you can see in one of the photographs—he had created a little space to sit on the sofa that was about as big as his hips, and he was completely surrounded by his drumming set and his pictures and piles of books and his trumpet and his saxophones, so he was sitting in this tiny corner of the couch and everything else in the room was just overflowing with stuff.

On occasion, I would roll my eyes about having to walk through certain rooms sideways: there was a path through the stuff, and I would literally have to walk through sideways. Barkley would sort of shrug and point around the room, whichever room we were in, and say it was just "piles of inspiration everywhere." It's also a quote from one of his journals, and I think that is a perfect summation of everything I knew about him, especially since he actually said it.

**DK:** Another quote of Barkley's is displayed on the cover of the book: "I am part of a very fascinating drama which I record in the mediums of my desire." I think that this is a great starting point to discuss his life and his work.

**SH: You and I have talked over the years since he left about how you had asked him if you could take his portrait in the studio and he declined. He liked to be the person behind the camera. He did not want to be the subject unless he was painting himself in a self-portrait. He took many self-portrait photographs of himself, but he didn't think of himself as the subject of somebody else's photographic work. So it still saddens me that you were not able to capture him on film.**

**Recently I went into the studio; when I do visit, I don't usually spend a lot of time. I don't sit in the spot where Barkley always sat when he was reviewing what he just painted. But I do go in and commune for a little bit, you know, ten or 15 minutes. But this time I wound up spending more time because I looked around much more closely and I spotted a variety of things in the room that I didn't remember seeing before. Some new things jumped out at me. Piles of inspiration—new to me.**

**DK:** I've found that too. I've seen new things as I've come back to photograph the house over the years.

**SH: You came back to the house three or four or five times, right?**

**DK:** More. After the first visit in May of 2017 I returned a few times that year to continue to photograph, and then there were visits in 2018, 2019, and the beginning of 2020, before Covid shut things down. At that point, we were still just working to document the space where Barkley and you lived and worked. Then in 2024, when you and I decided to create this book, I came up a couple of times again, because at that point, we had an idea of what still needed to be photographed.

**SH: Can you describe the evolution of the book project, from your perspective?**

**DK:** It was a process. As I came up every so often to continue to explore the different areas of the house and to see where things had changed as you began to organize, it gradually developed into an idea for telling the story of his life through those things that inspired him. I thought of it as an 'archeological site' being excavated over time. As areas were uncovered, new things appeared that I could photograph. This project really developed out of that process. You and I began working together in the spring of 2017 shortly after Barkley passed, with the plan of visually documenting his home studio, and then I ended up exploring the entire house, making regular trips up to New London, Connecticut from New York City to spend a day at a time photographing what I could find in each part of the house.

After working on this project for a few years, I built up a large library of photographs, and we both thought that the images really told the story of the life of this artist. And at that point, we discussed the possibility of creating a book around these photographs, and also around the writings of Barkley Hendricks that you had collected, and had begun to go through, at your home.

**SH: As I was looking at your photographic output, it became more and more fascinating, especially when you would focus in on, for example, the reflection in a mirror of a pile of stuff that was in the background, but also reflected in a mirror. Or, a closeup photo of woodwork that had a variety of things—from a Renaissance painting, to the cover of a Fela Kuti album, to some calligraphic scrawl that Barkley had done.**

**I was fascinated by the vast cacophony of visuals. It just seemed like it would be really cool to look at everything all together. And I'd never really seen anything like that. Probably the closest thing were some photographs I saw once of Francis Bacon's studio, which was even messier than Barkley's. I thought that these photographs**

**could serve as the vehicle that would make it possible for people who knew Barkley's work to see how and where he created it.**

**DK:** As I photographed, I began to notice the smaller details that make up what you describe as the "vast cacophony of visuals." I started focusing more on some of the elements within those larger spaces.

**SH: In the book, there is a section with a series of photographs of small objects, and a section with photographs of Barkley's collection of cameras. How did those ideas materialize?**

**DK:** When I came across a number of small objects collected by Barkley that were strewn around his work spaces, I decided to try to photograph them, using his original drawing table as the constant background. The worn paper surface that remains on his table today served as a perfect backdrop for the series, and I used the diffuse natural light that exists in the space.

For the second series, I asked you to collect all of his cameras. I then decided to create a mini set outdoors on the front porch of the house, and placed each camera that Barkley had used on a white sheet of his drawing paper. I remembered you telling me that since you met Barkley, whenever he left home he was never without a camera hanging over his shoulder.

**SH: That's correct. Photography was always important to him, beginning when he was at the Pennsylvania Academy in the mid to late 60s, until he passed. Barkley used to say, "I was a photographer before I was a painter." Whenever he left the house he always had a camera or two around his neck, and usually a point and shoot in his pocket. Often there were three or four mediums that he was working on simultaneously: oil paintings, works on paper, sketches or drawings, and photography.**

**DK:** And then there were his journals, his writings. When we started to think about the idea of using Barkley's actual words as text for the book, you began to delve into his day journals and his papers. Tell me your process for deciphering all of Barkley's writings.

**SH: As you and I continued to work on documenting the house over time, I simultaneously started to go through the many, many composition books and yellow legal pads that Barkley used as journals to create a compilation of his thoughts. I started finding things that I thought would be really interesting to somehow incorporate into the story and that might work well with the visuals that you were creating. For example, in some of the journal entries Barkley wrote about a Fela Kuti concert he'd attended. I thought how cool it would be to juxtapose that writing with an image on a particular blue door jam where he had mounted a picture of Fela from one of his CDs. I thought it was really interesting to delve into Barkley's written documentation using the context of some of the photographs you had taken.**

**And then at some point, you proposed the idea of photographing the journals themselves. How did you come up with the idea of where and how to do that?**

**DK:** I asked you if we could do a test of photographing some of these pages, with the idea of possibly using them in the book itself. I located a spot in the sun room on the first floor, in an area near the sliding door to the outside, with wonderful natural light, where there was a vintage rag rug on the floor. I placed a few of the pages onto it. These test photographs turned out beautifully, so I scheduled a visit to return when you were finished going through some more of Barkley's writings.

What I love about this process is that text was lifted from the selected pages and used typographically throughout the book, and then we also reproduced those pages at the end of the book in full. It was special to take Barkley's words from the original pages where he wrote and photograph them in a place in his home where he spent a lot of time.

**SH: Interestingly, the place on that rug where you photographed was where, at one point, Barkley's exercise bicycle was. So he was actually using that very rug for a different purpose, and there is an image in the book of three small unframed landscape paintings that he had set up on a pile of stuff between the table and the back of a chair so that as he was riding the bike and exercising, he could look down and see his own beautiful landscapes that he had painted in Jamaica. Inspiration everywhere!**

**DK:** Let me just say that as I photographed this long-term project all over the house and in his studio, I always kind of had a sense that Barkley was there with me, looking over my shoulder. And hopefully he was happy with what I was doing, because he lived throughout the whole house and worked throughout the whole house. I felt that he was always with me while I was doing this project.

**SH: David, please tell me about your first encounters with Barkley.**

**DK:** I first met Barkley when I was a sophomore at Connecticut College, studying art and history. At that time at the college, there was no full time professor of photography in the art department. So I had taken a number of introductory art classes with different professors and had also studied photography independently with two or three of the senior faculty in the department, but they were either print makers or painters—not photographers. And then I met Barkley.

I think I met him in the spring of my sophomore year, and I asked him if I could study with him independently the next semester. He was a new, young professor at the time. I think that he was 29 years old, and I was 20 years old. So, in the fall of my junior year, I began studying with him individually, and we continued doing this for four straight semesters until I graduated in 1976. Those four courses that I took independently with him over the course of two years were, for me, a groundbreaking experience.

When we began our studies, I was already a fully formed photographer. I had become serious about photography at age 13, and had begun work in a darkroom in my home outside of Boston a few years after that. So I didn't need any technical training with my craft—my goal with Barkley was to learn about composition. As my independent studies progressed I came to realize that Barkley was a master of composition from his own artwork. This experience was instrumental in my creative development as a young artist, to get to be in the same room every week with someone who I could actually share my compositional thoughts with and who was already a master.

**SH: I've always appreciated your art of composition, whether you are photographing people or landscapes or anything that's a little more abstract. And I was always taken with Barkley's photographic composition. I find it interesting that sometimes with his compositions the frame might be much more full of stuff or people or background compared with his paintings of people, which are pristine, with usually a single subject, and sometimes a couple, who are presenting themselves to the viewer with no background at all.**

**DK:** While Barkley was working in his studio, did he ever bring pieces he was working on out into other parts of the house? I'm interested in his work process.

**SH: If Barkley was working on paintings, they usually stayed on the easel until they were completed. Before moving into our house, he lived from 1972 to 1980 in a loft studio space on State Street in New London. It had a huge studio space to the front, which had the light, and a smaller living space to the rear. The studio space allowed him to work on six or eight paintings at a time—this was his super prolific Portrait Painting period. When he moved into the house, he might work on two paintings at a time, but they were one behind the other. He didn't really have the room to spread out like in the original studio. At that time, he tended to work on one single painting until it was done.**

**During this prolific period of his life, he was very busy working in different mediums simultaneously, from huge paintings to collage works on paper, to drawings, to photographs. Throughout this whole period, he was also always with a camera, he was painting, and during that same time, he was also creating the really interesting and clever and fun Works on Paper on standard 20" x 30" watercolor paper.**

**DK:** Working on this project with you has been an honor. Thank you for allowing me into the space you and Barkley shared, the private domain of a man, artist, and teacher whom I admired so deeply. Gaining insight into his thoughts and artistic process through the medium of the space where he lived and worked—it has been invigorating, eye-opening, and immensely rewarding.

**SH: It's thrilling and at the same time heartbreaking—I miss Barkley. Every day of my life is now devoted to carrying on his legacy. Everywhere I look in our shared home, I see the things that Barkley chose to surround himself with. Hence the title of the book: *Piles of Inspiration Everywhere*.**

# 1st Floor

# Front Hallway, Sun Room, Music Room, Kitchen

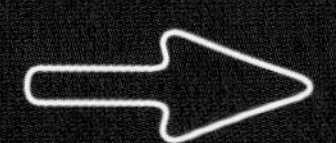

# I am part of a very fascinating drama which I record in the mediums of my desire.

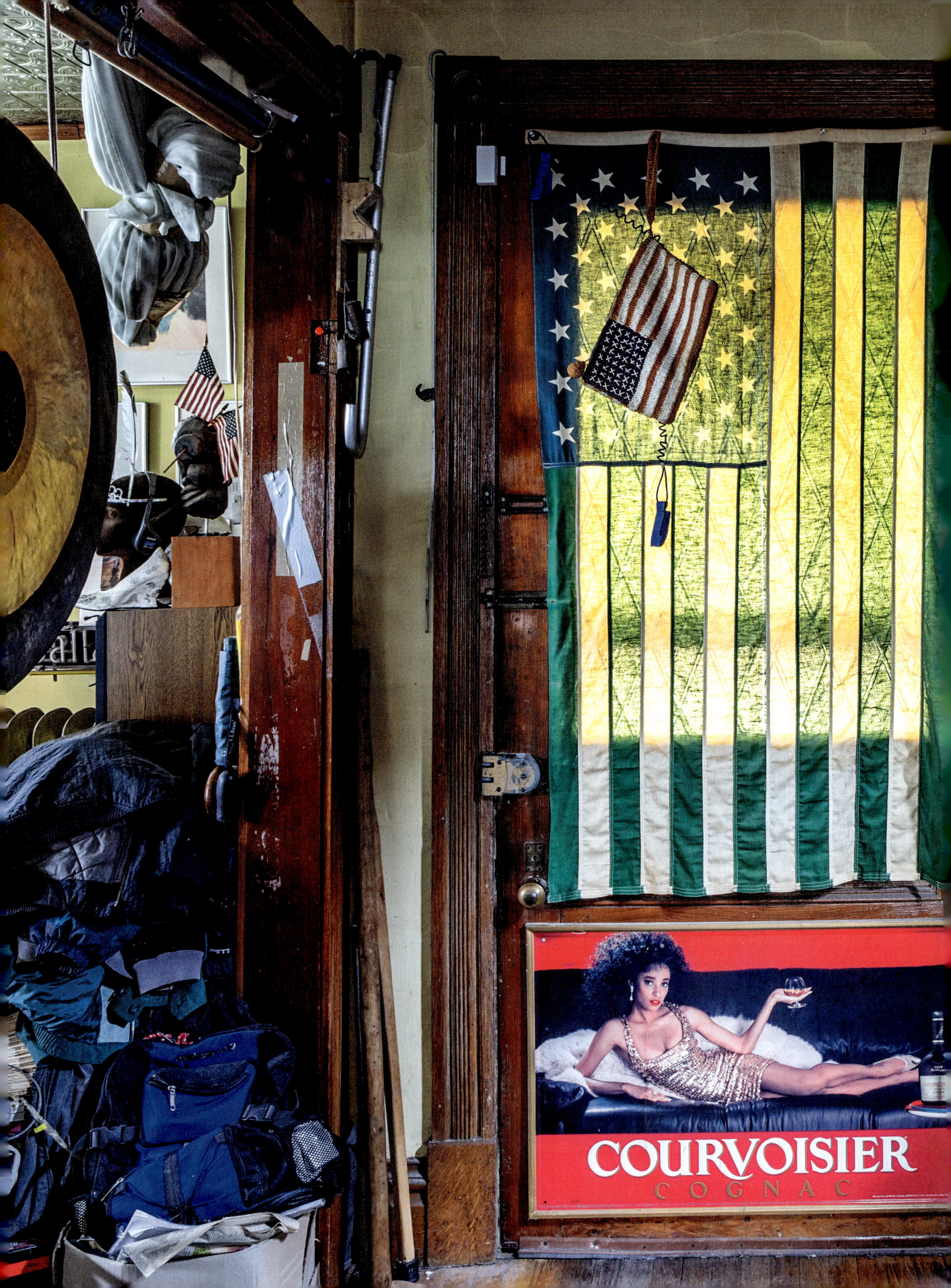
COURVOISIER
COGNAC

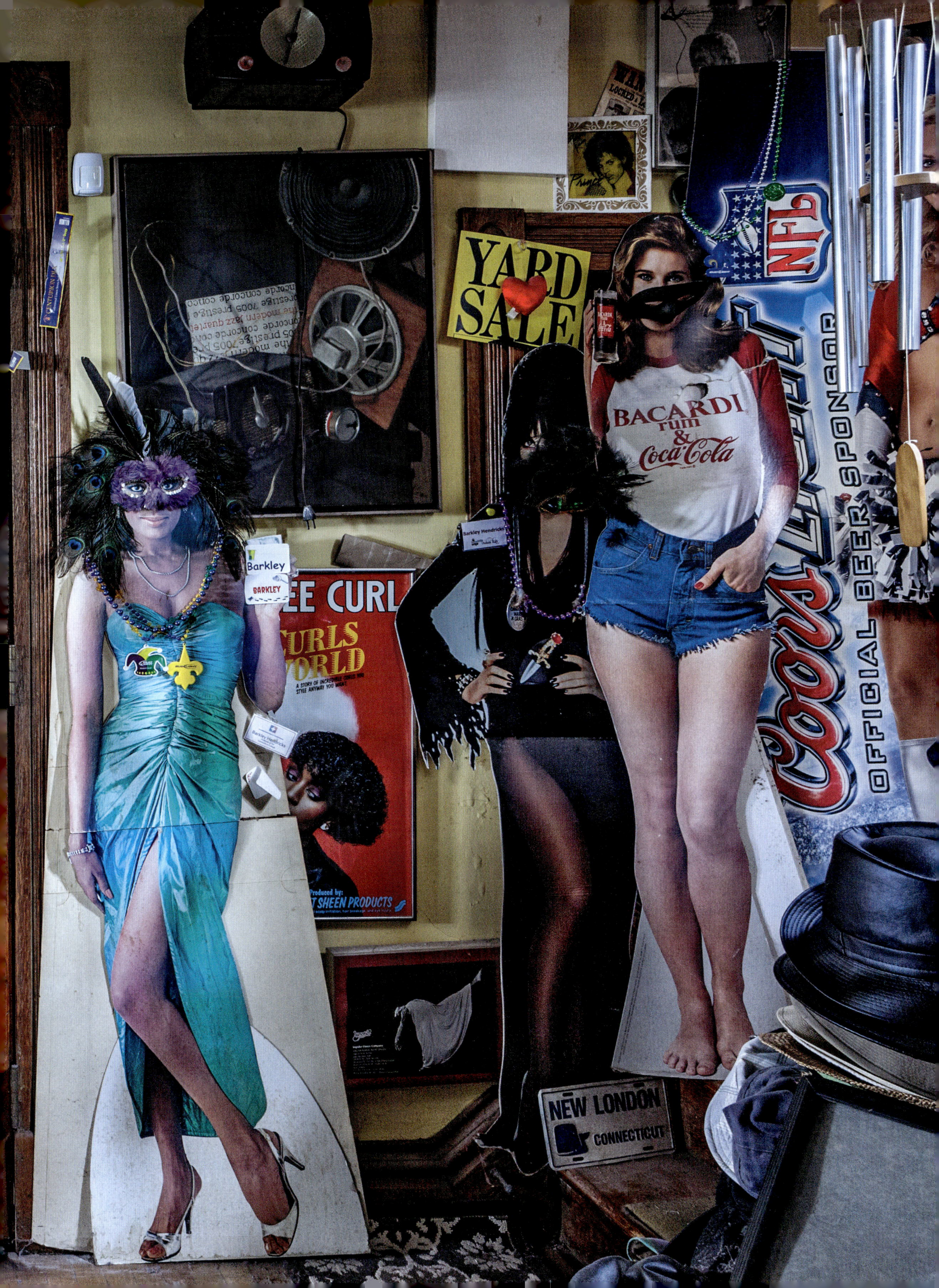
YARD SALE
NFL
BACARDI rum & Coca-Cola
Coors
OFFICIAL BEER SPONSOR
Barkley
BARKLEY
EE CURL
CURLS WORLD
Produced by:
SHEEN PRODUCTS
NEW LONDON
CONNECTICUT

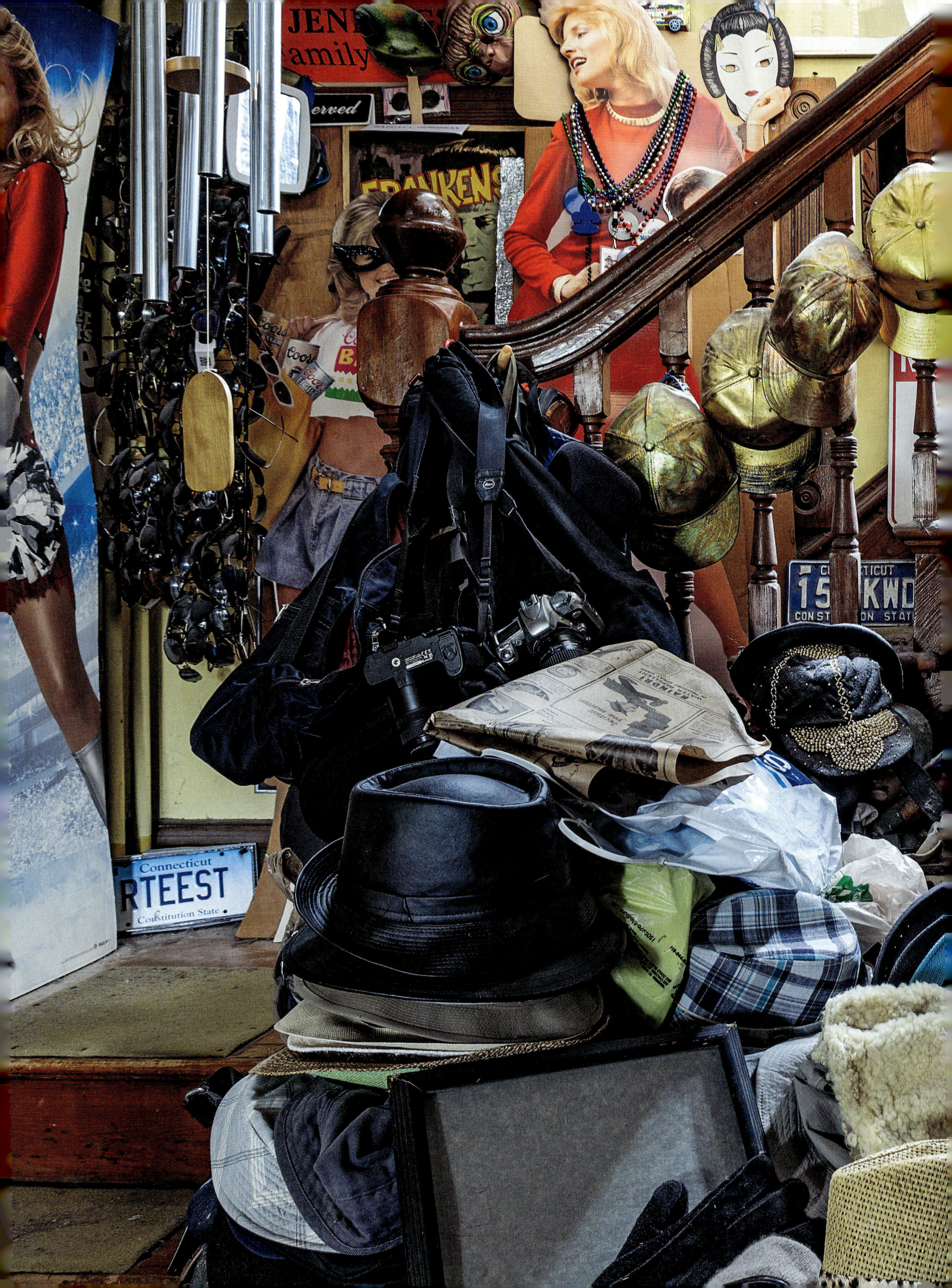
Connecticut
RTEEST
Constitution State

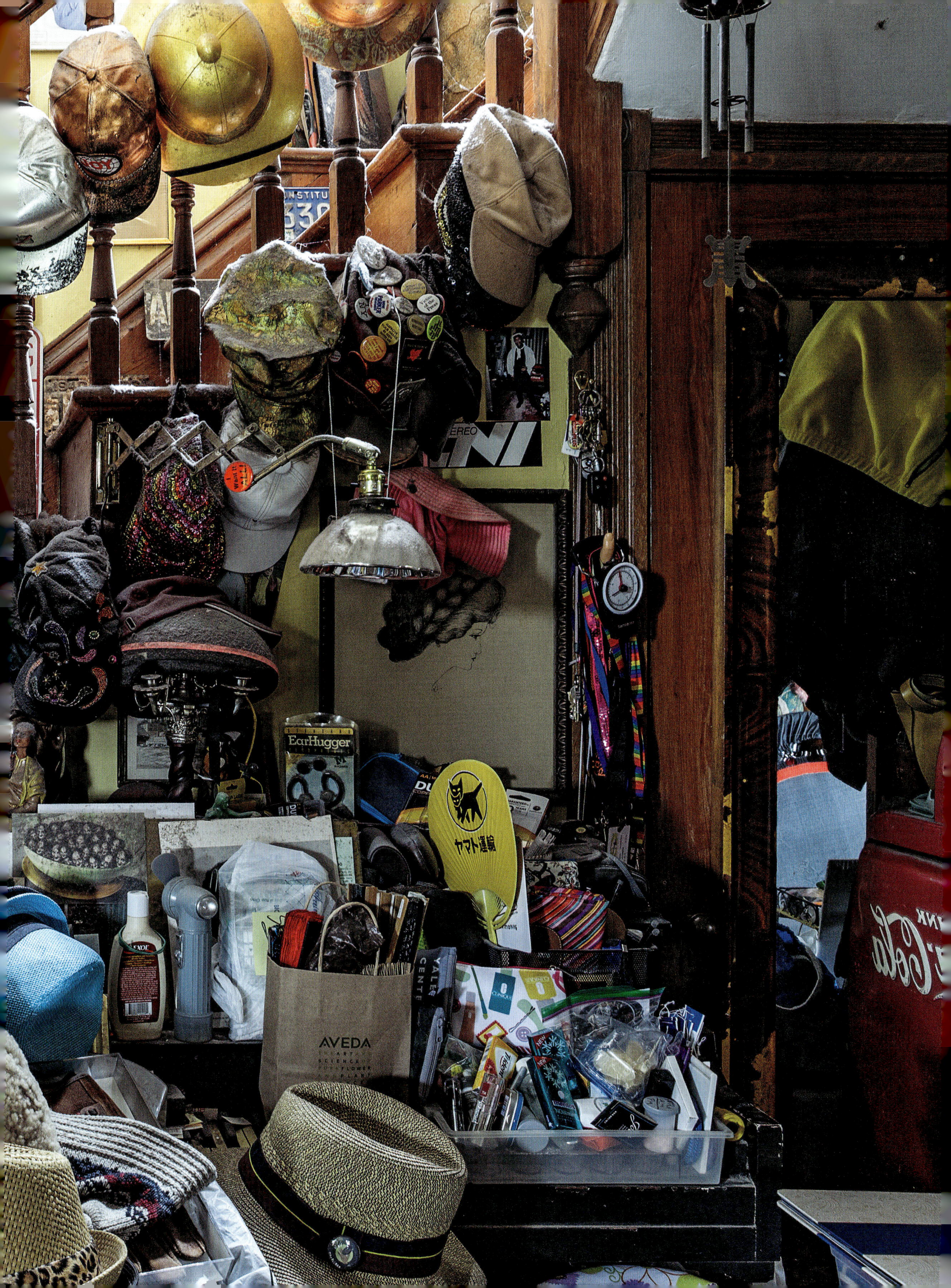
EarHugger
ヤマト運輸
AVEDA

# I feel I'm into everything. More arms than I have, all reaching. Energy! Energy! Energy!

"OCTOPUS," Sept 28, 1977 (see p. 253)

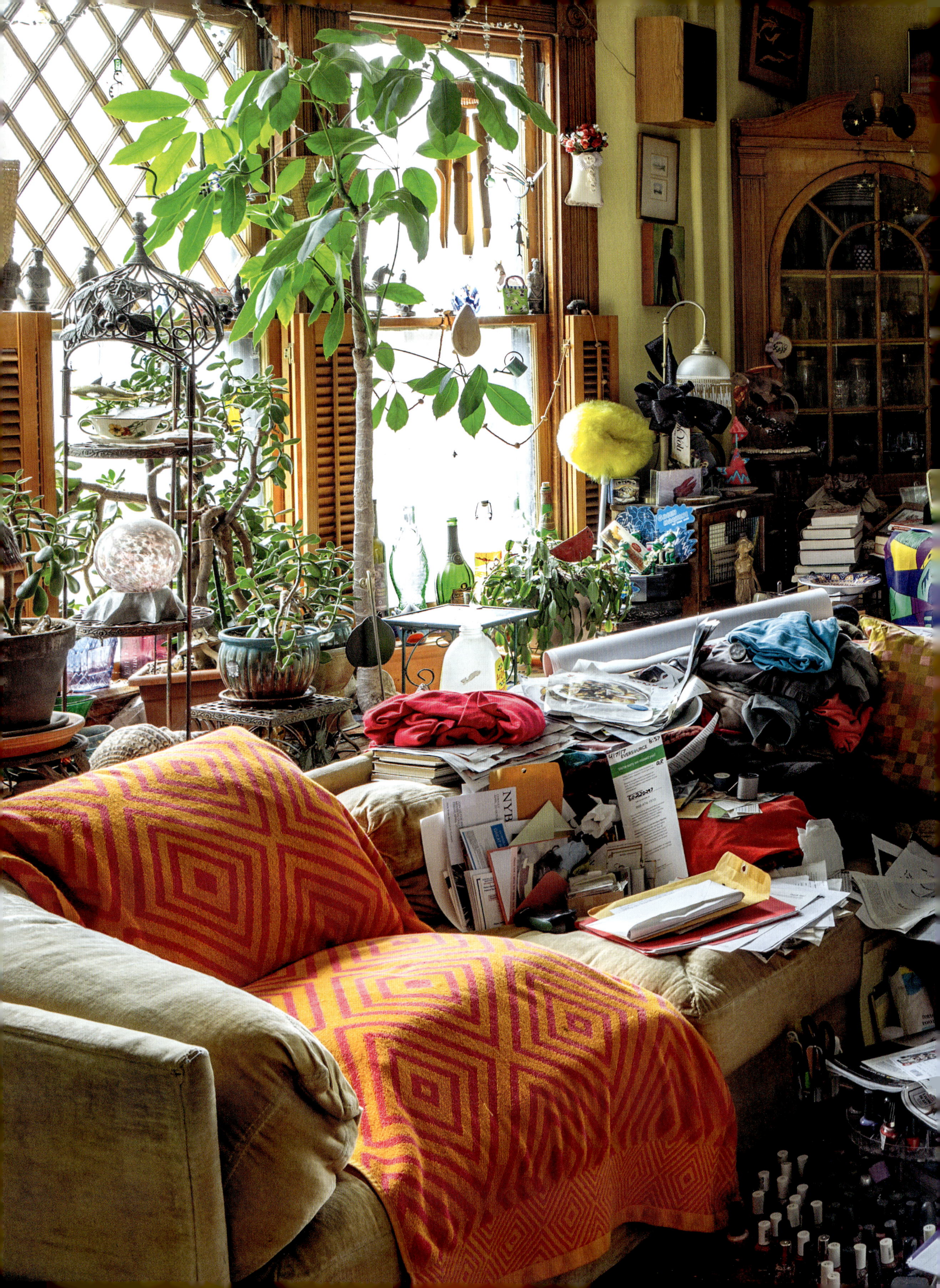

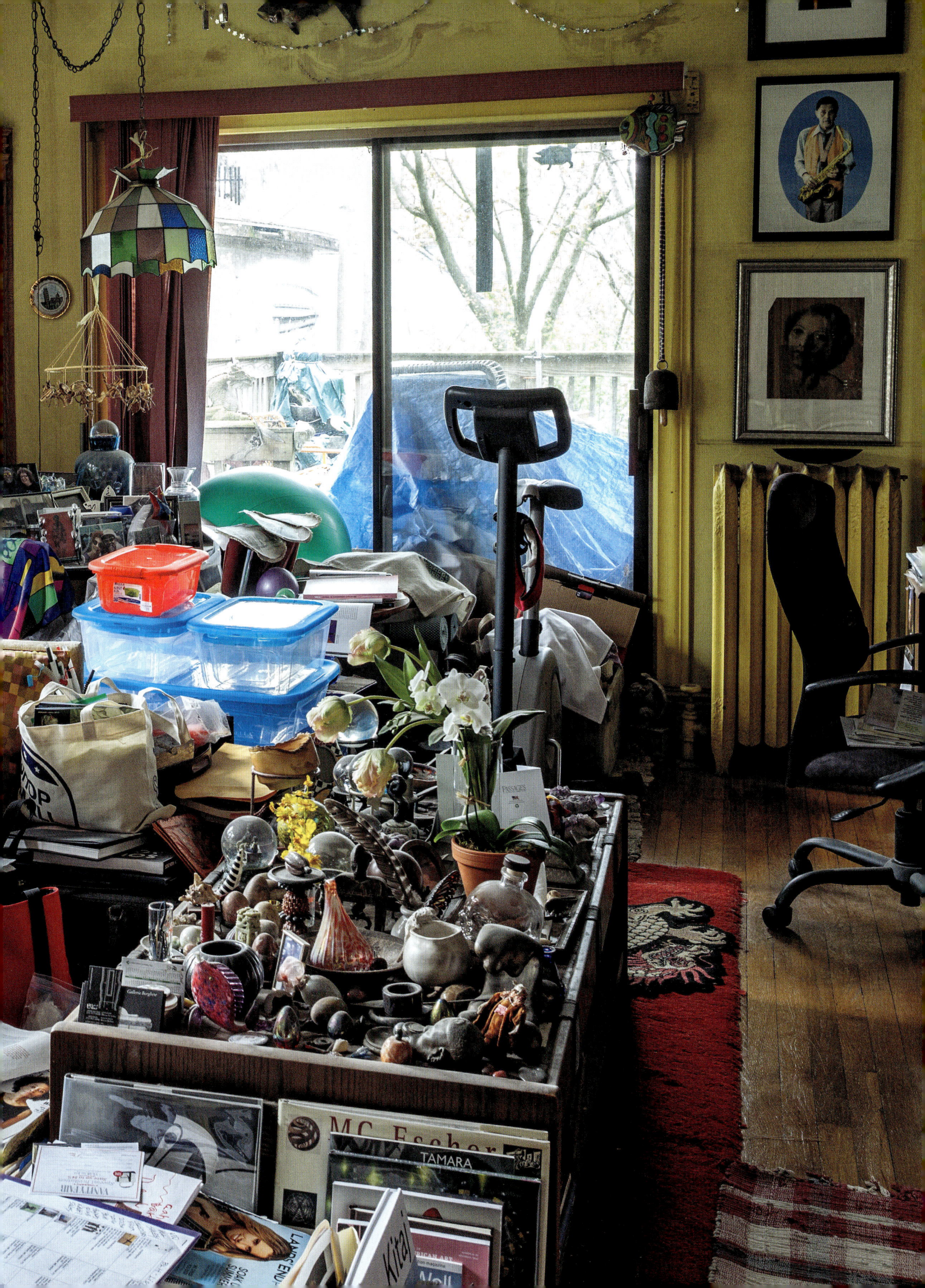
MC Escher
TAMARA
Kitaj

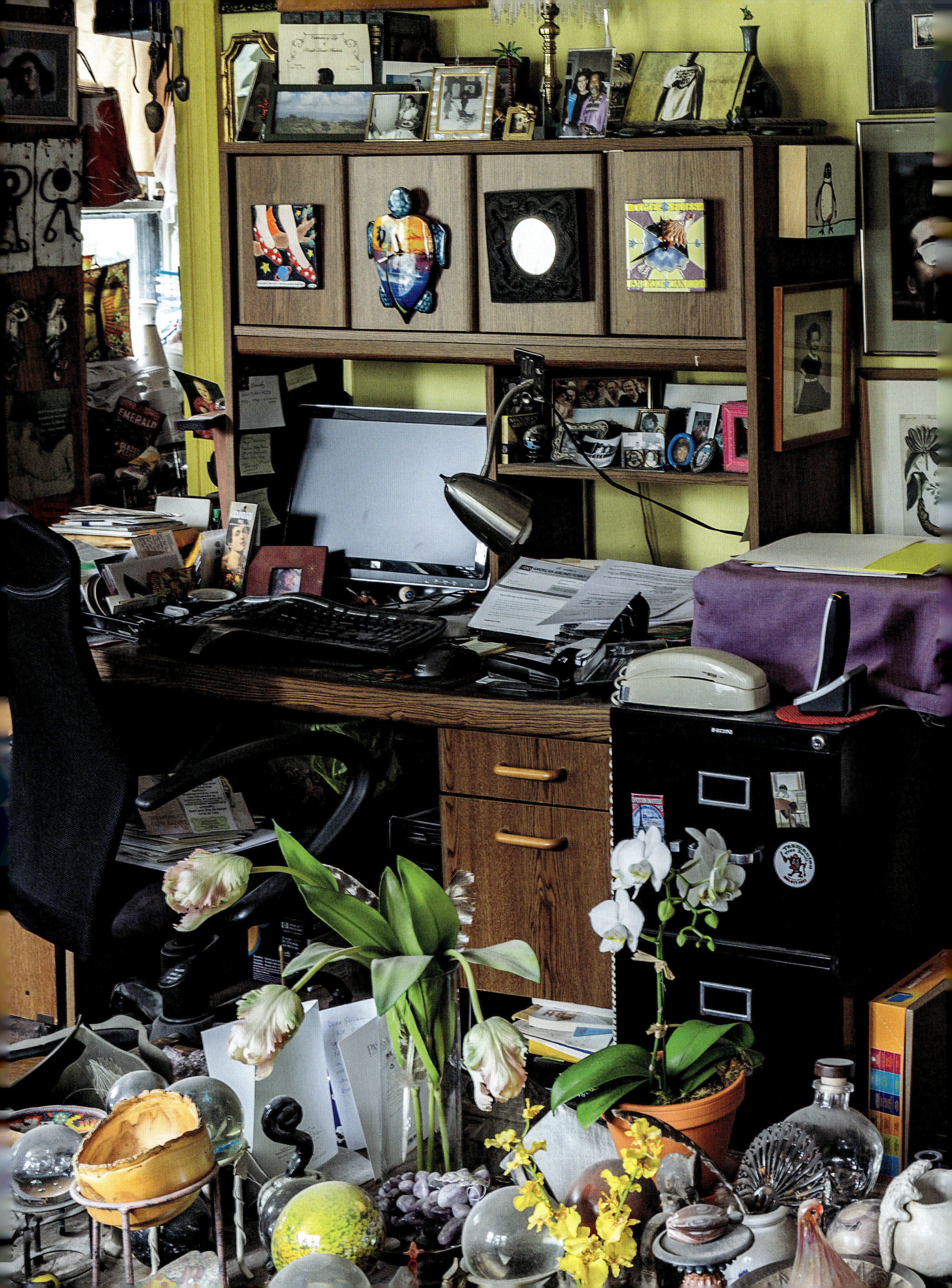
EMERALD

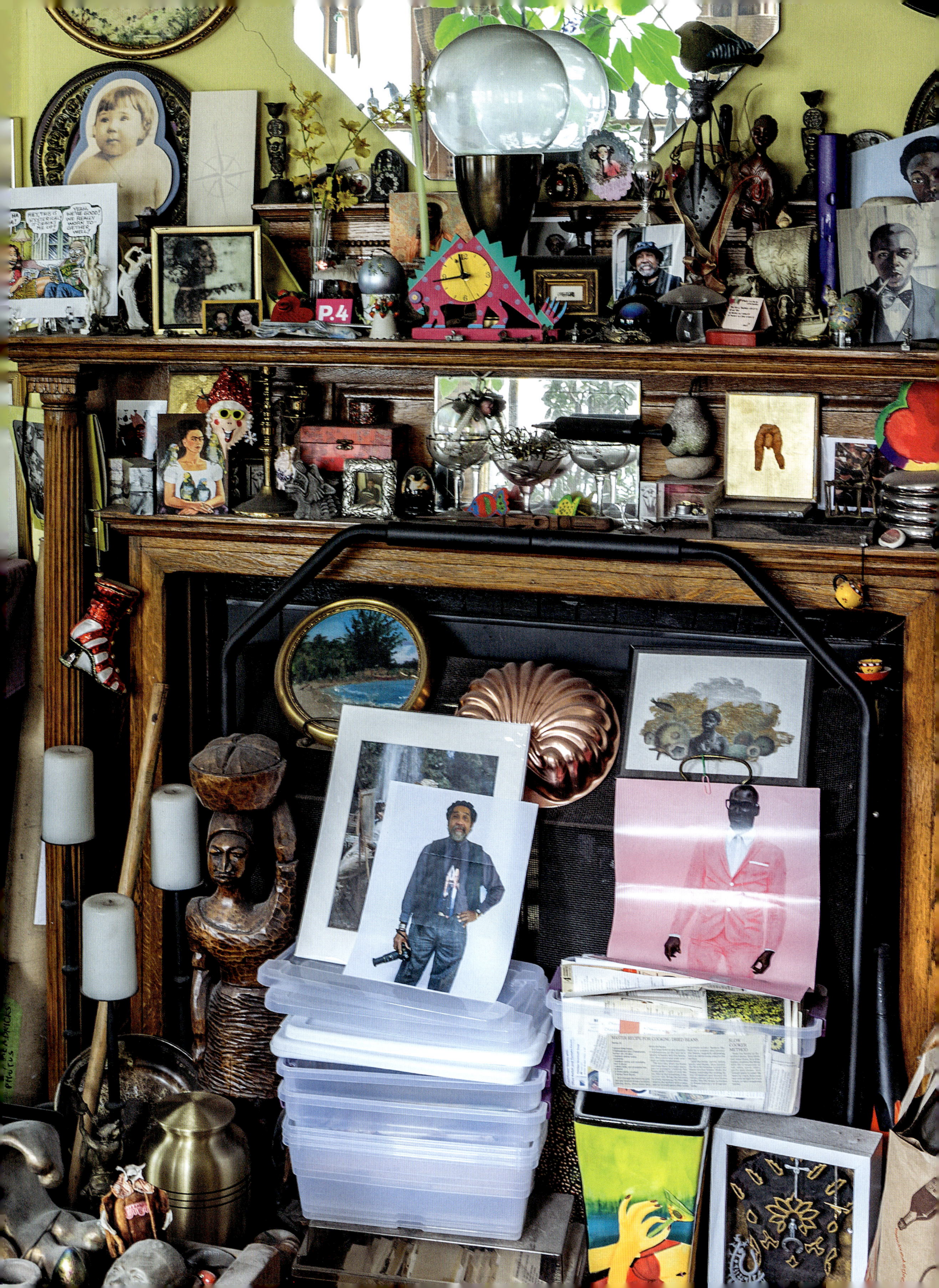
HEY, THIS IS HYSTERICAL! IT CRACKS ME UP!
YEAH, WE'RE GOOD! WE REALLY WORK TOGETHER WELL!
P.4
MASTER RECIPE FOR COOKING DRIED BEANS
SLOW COOKER METHOD

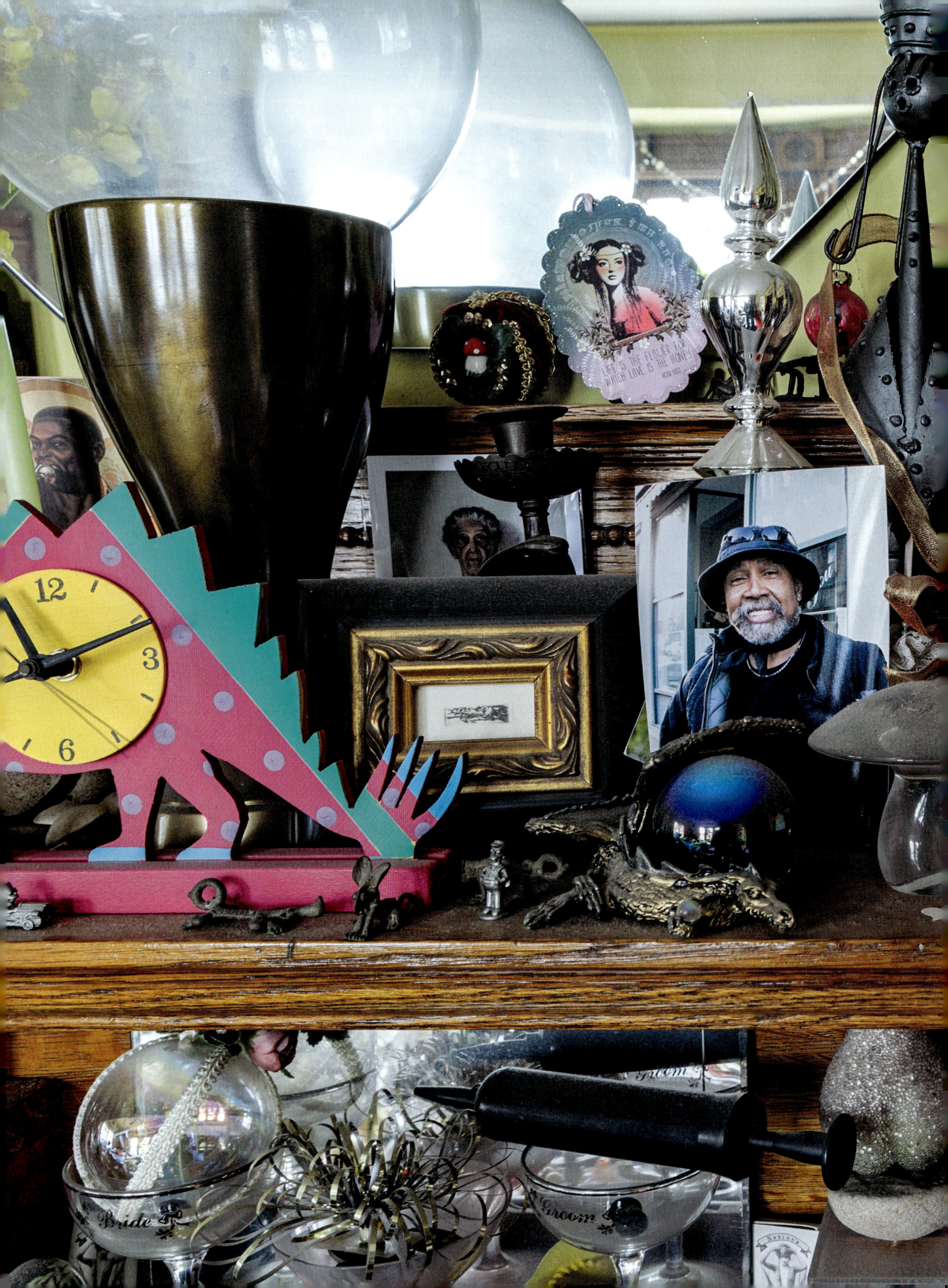
12
3
6
LIFE IS THE FLOWER FOR
WHICH LOVE IS THE HONEY
Bride
Groom

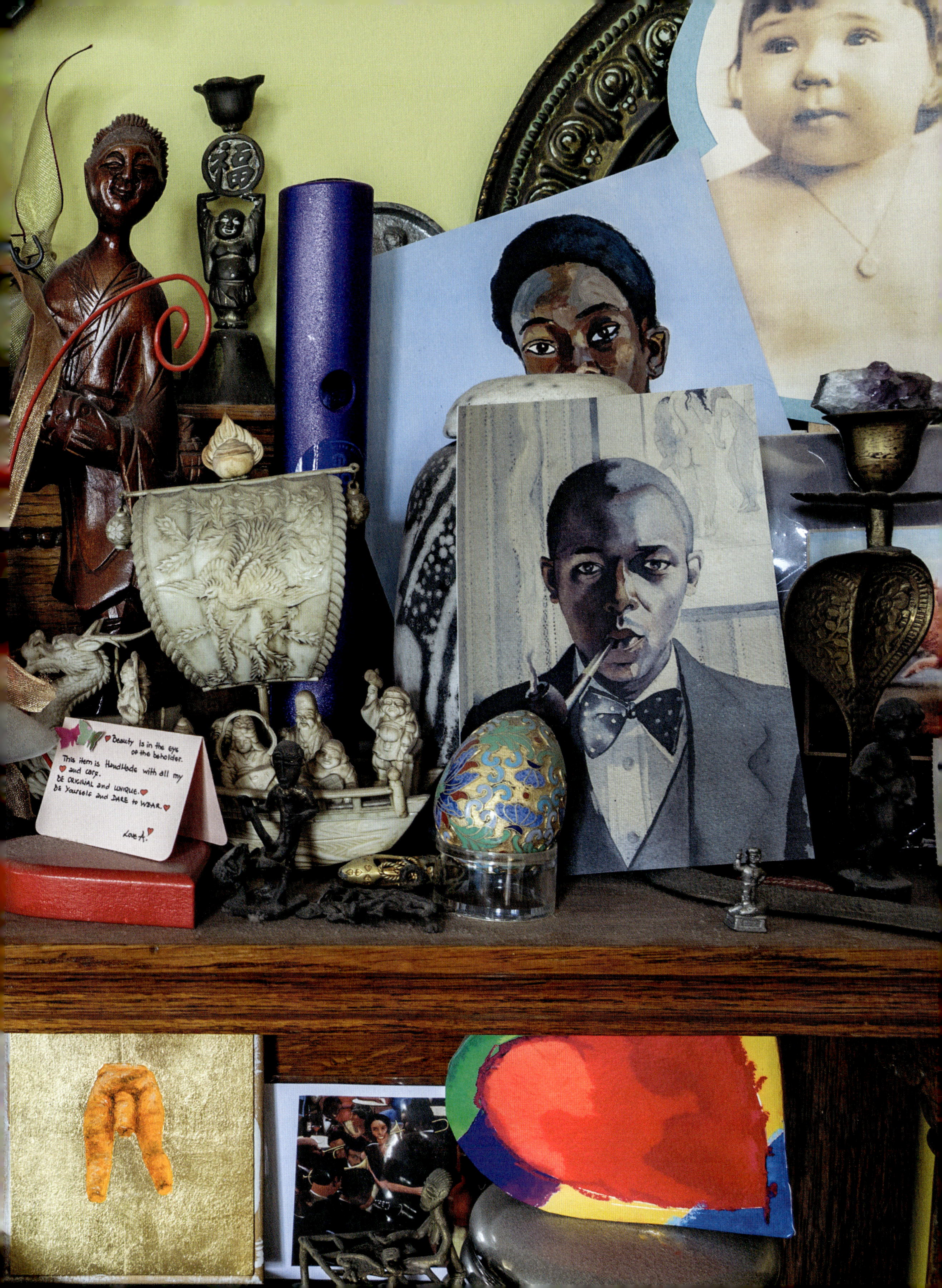
Beauty is in the eye of the beholder.
This item is HandMade with all my and care.
BE ORIGINAL and UNIQUE.
BE Yourself and DARE to WEAR.
Love A.

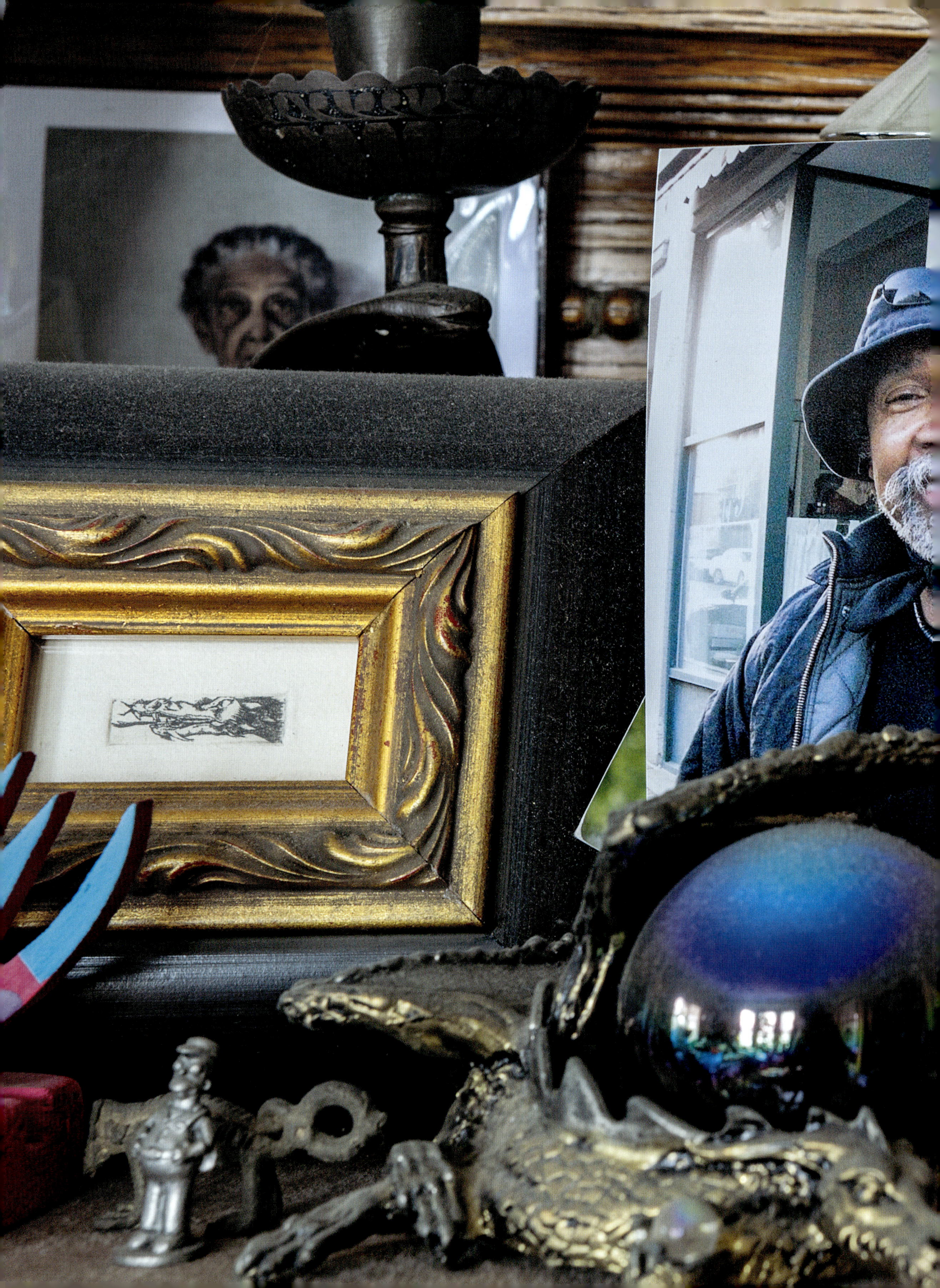

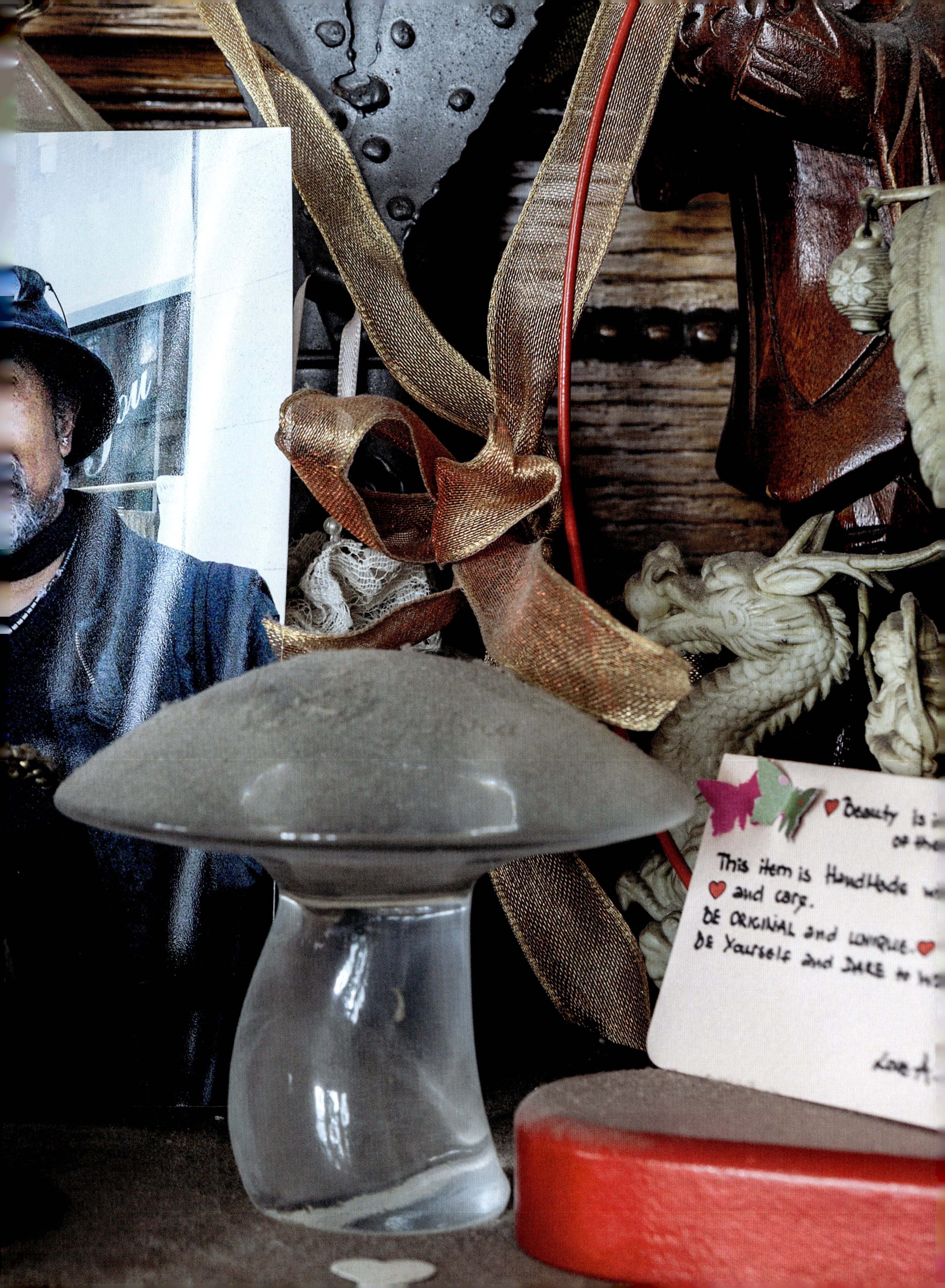

Beauty is
This item is HandMade
and care.
BE ORIGINAL and UNIQUE.
BE Yourself and DARE

# “Honky Dory”

# In a conversation with my wife I said, in response to dialogue

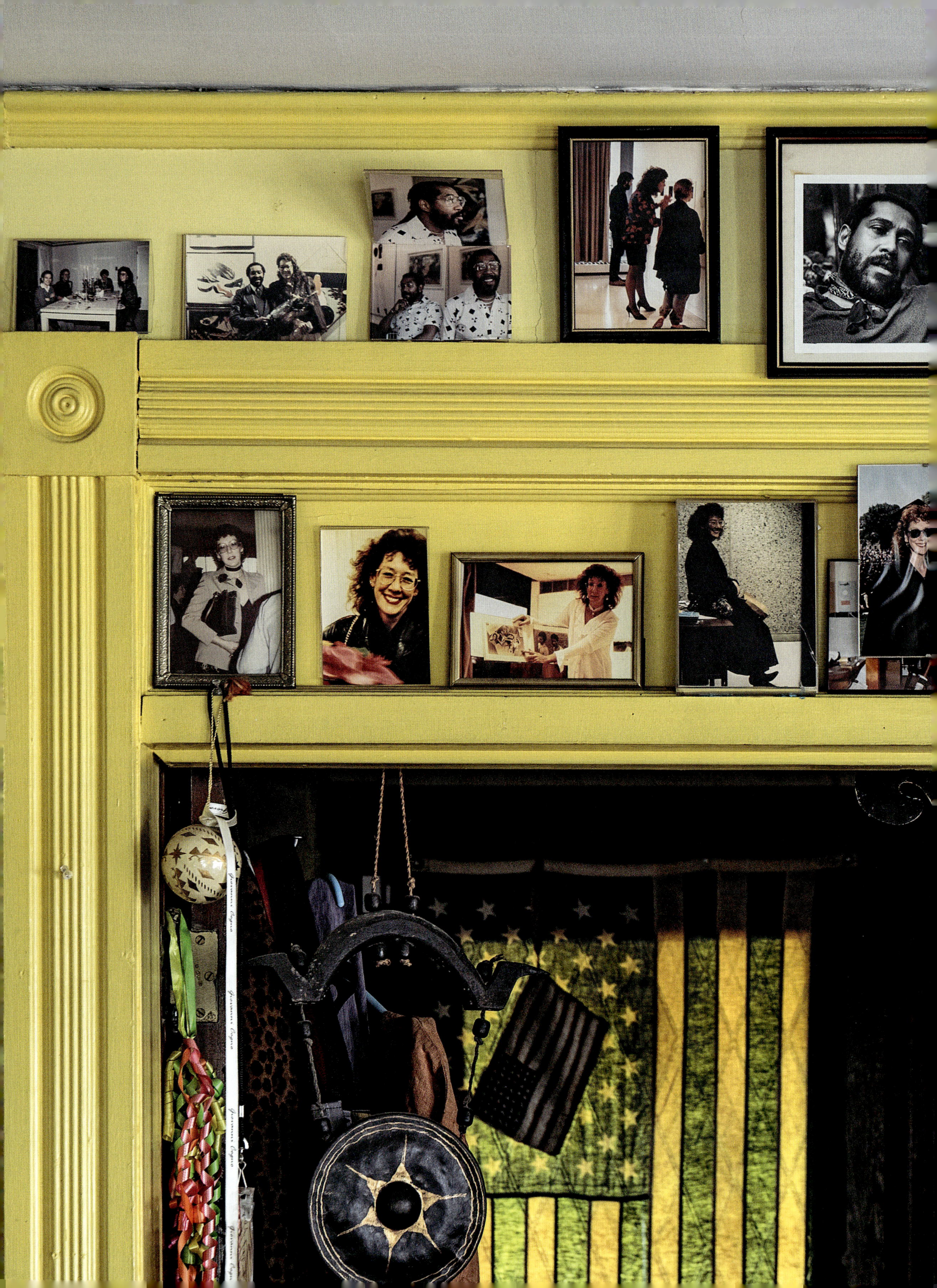

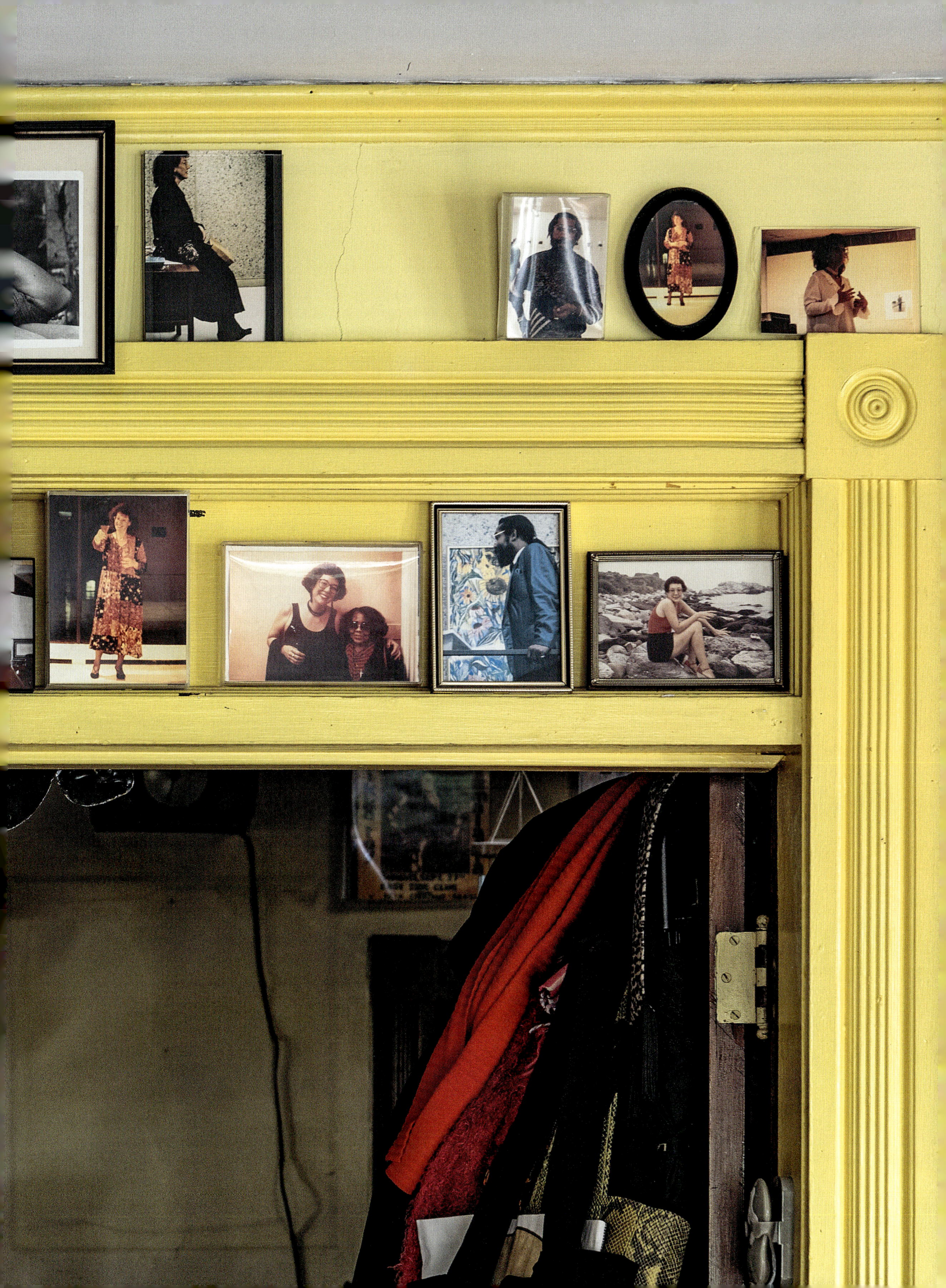

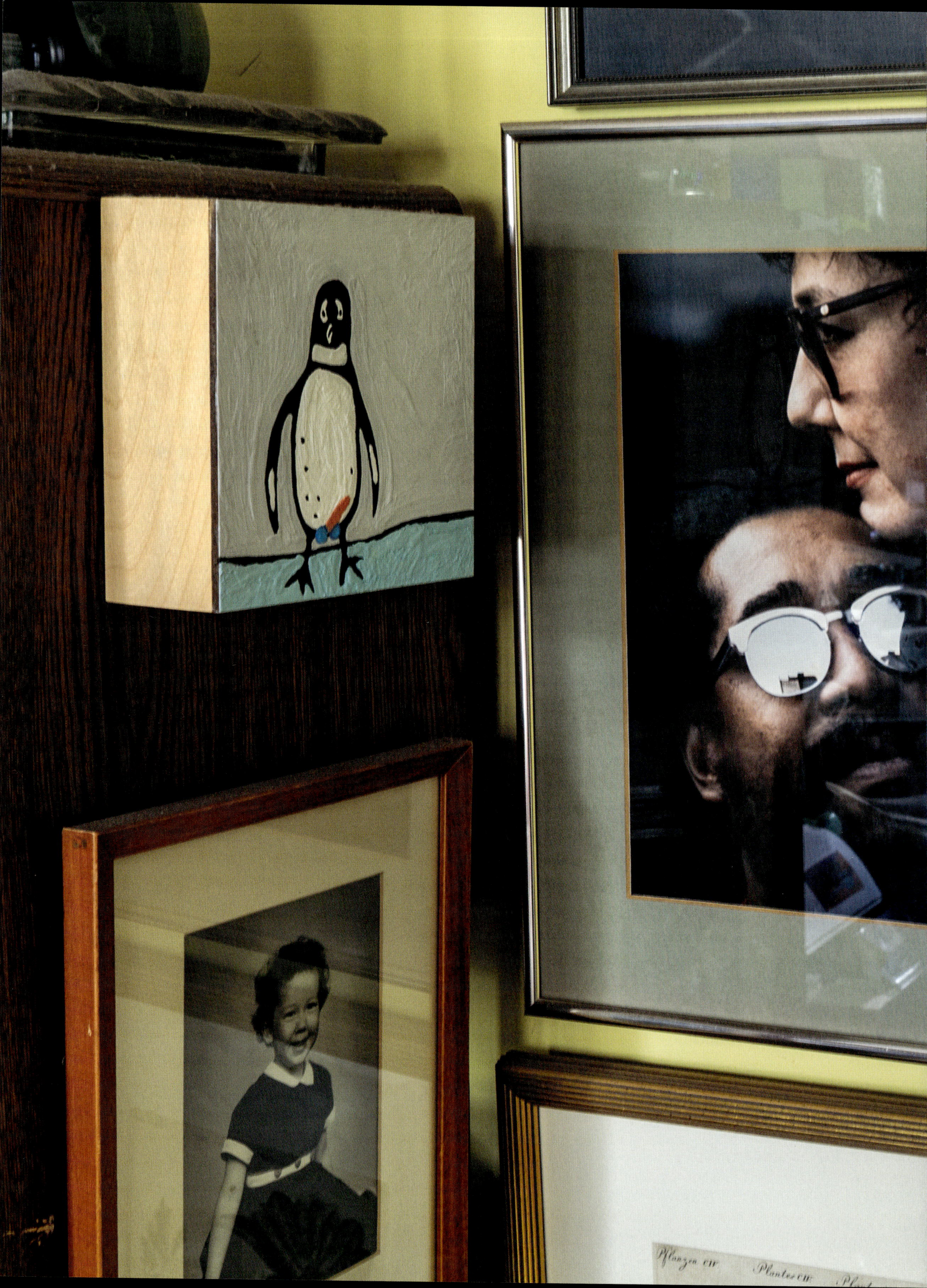
Pflanzen CII
Plantes CII

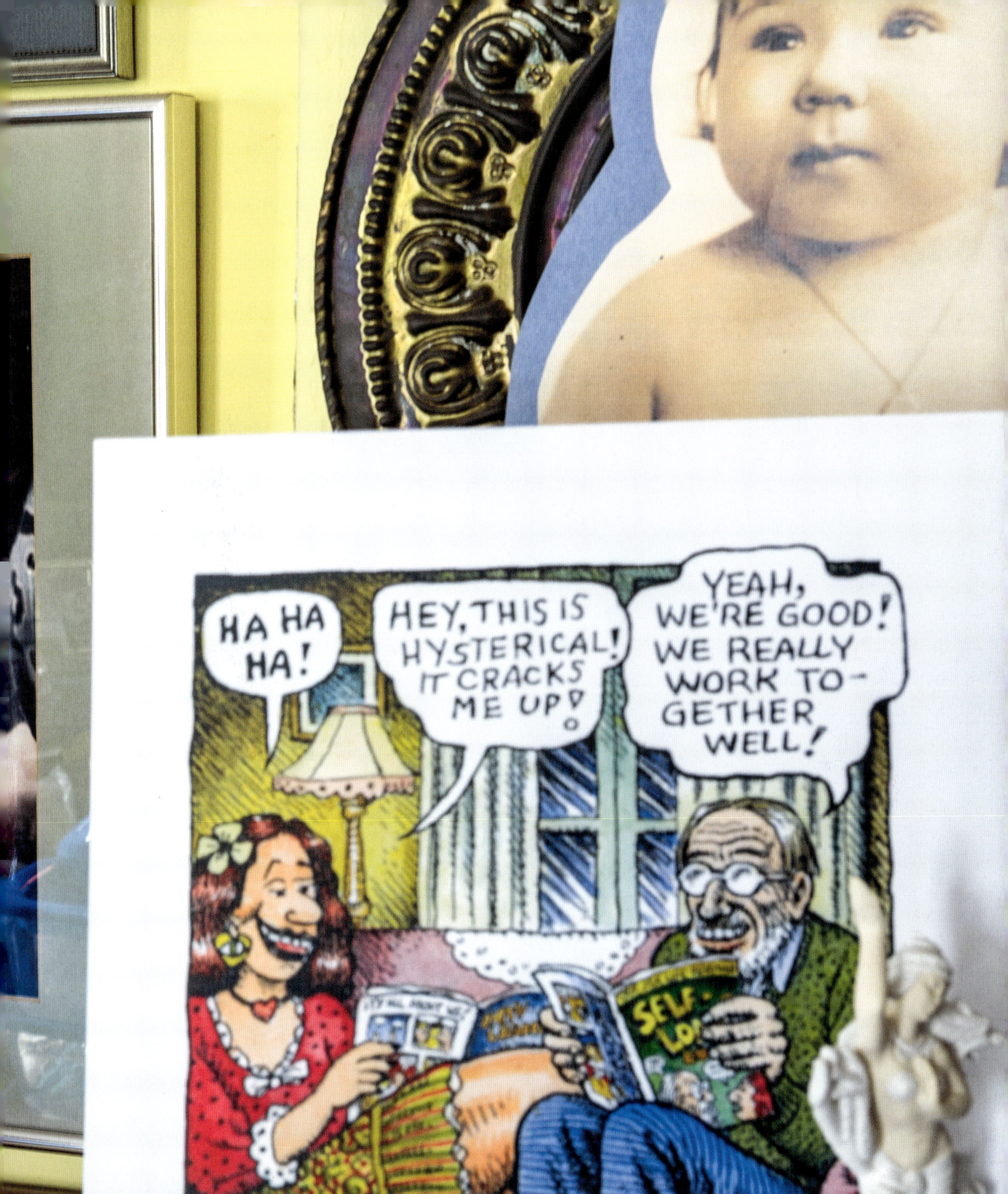

HA HA HA!
HEY, THIS IS HYSTERICAL! IT CRACKS ME UP!
YEAH, WE'RE GOOD! WE REALLY WORK TO-GETHER WELL!

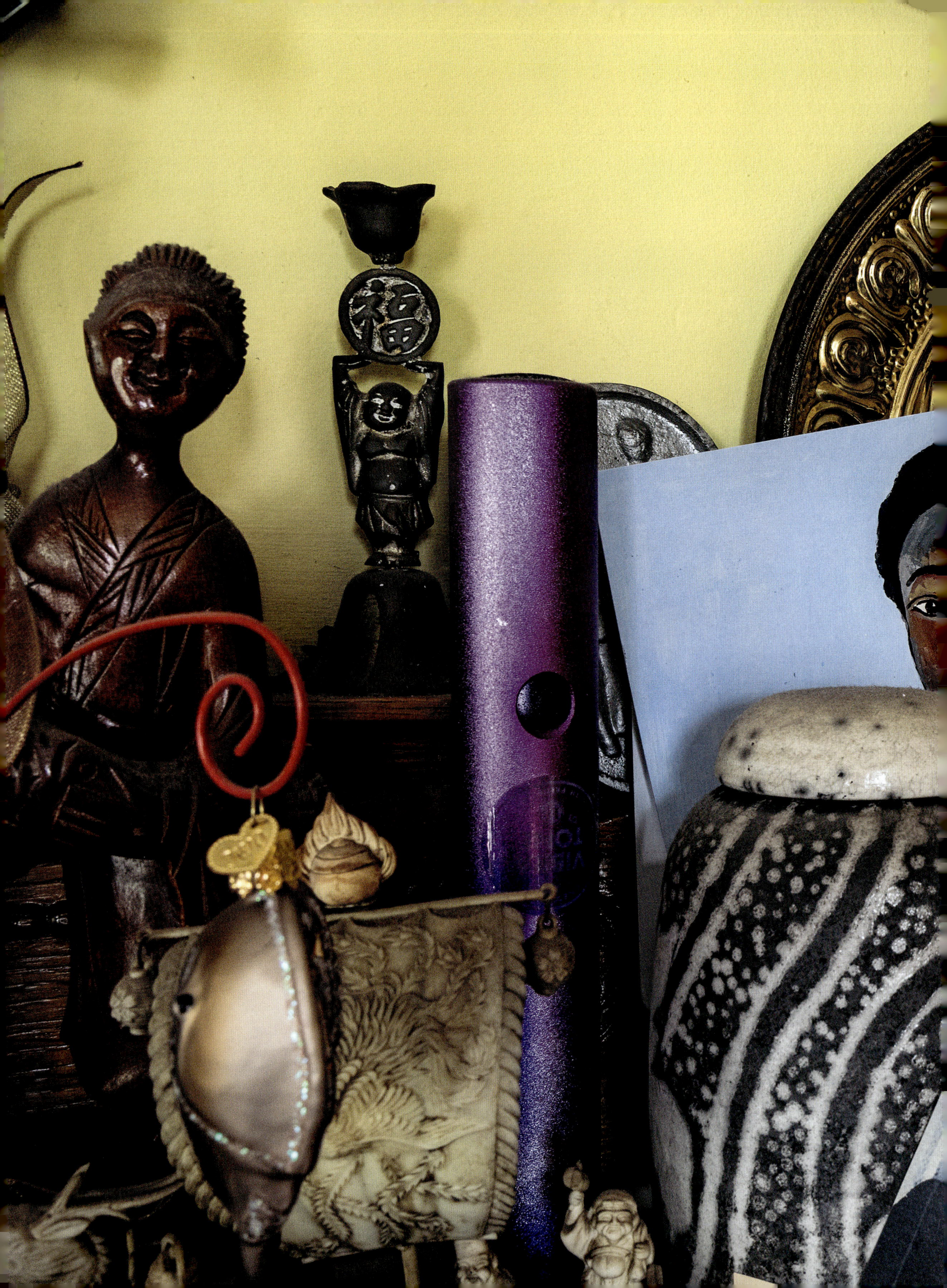
福

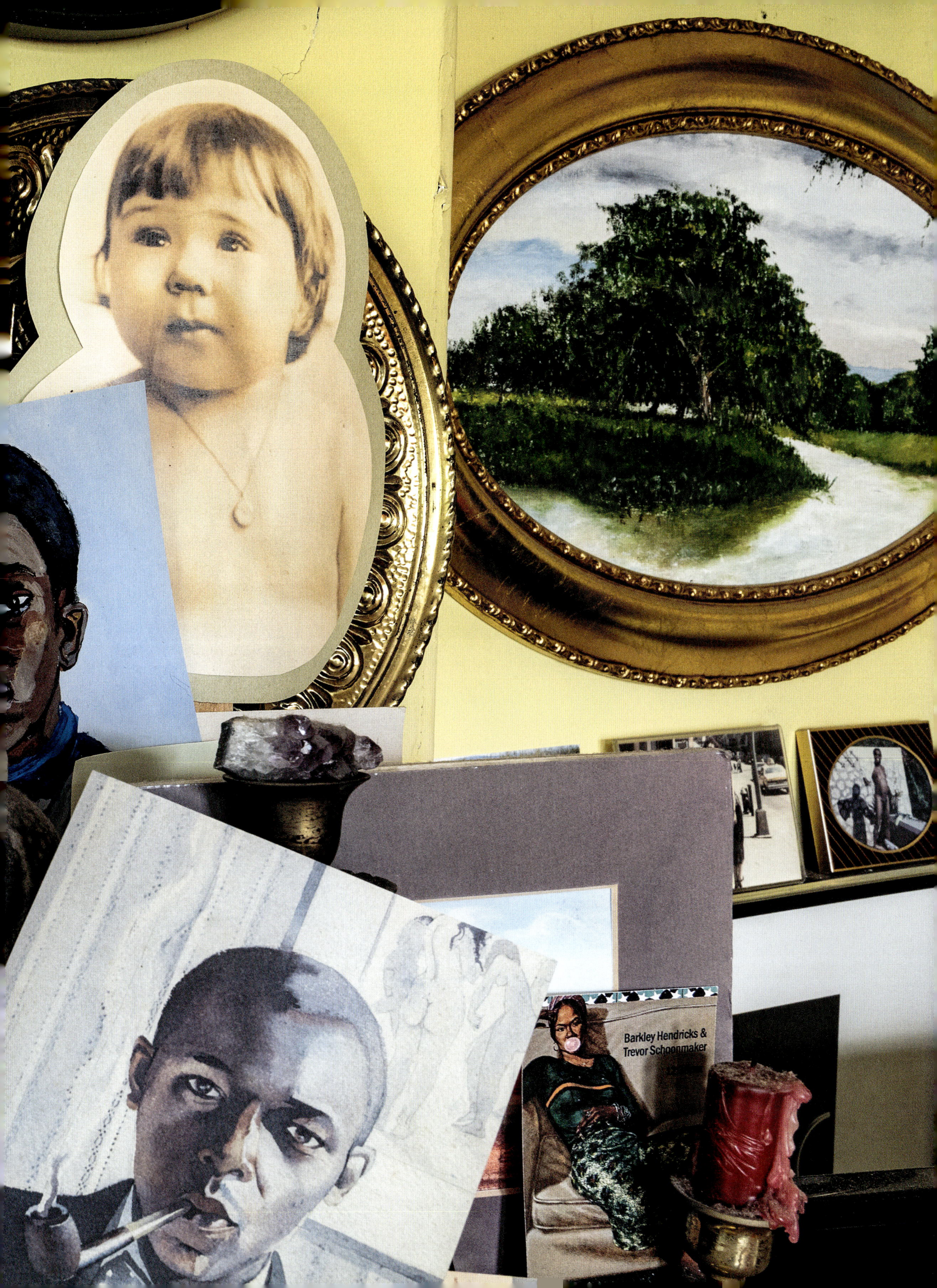
Barkley Hendricks &
Trevor Schoonmaker

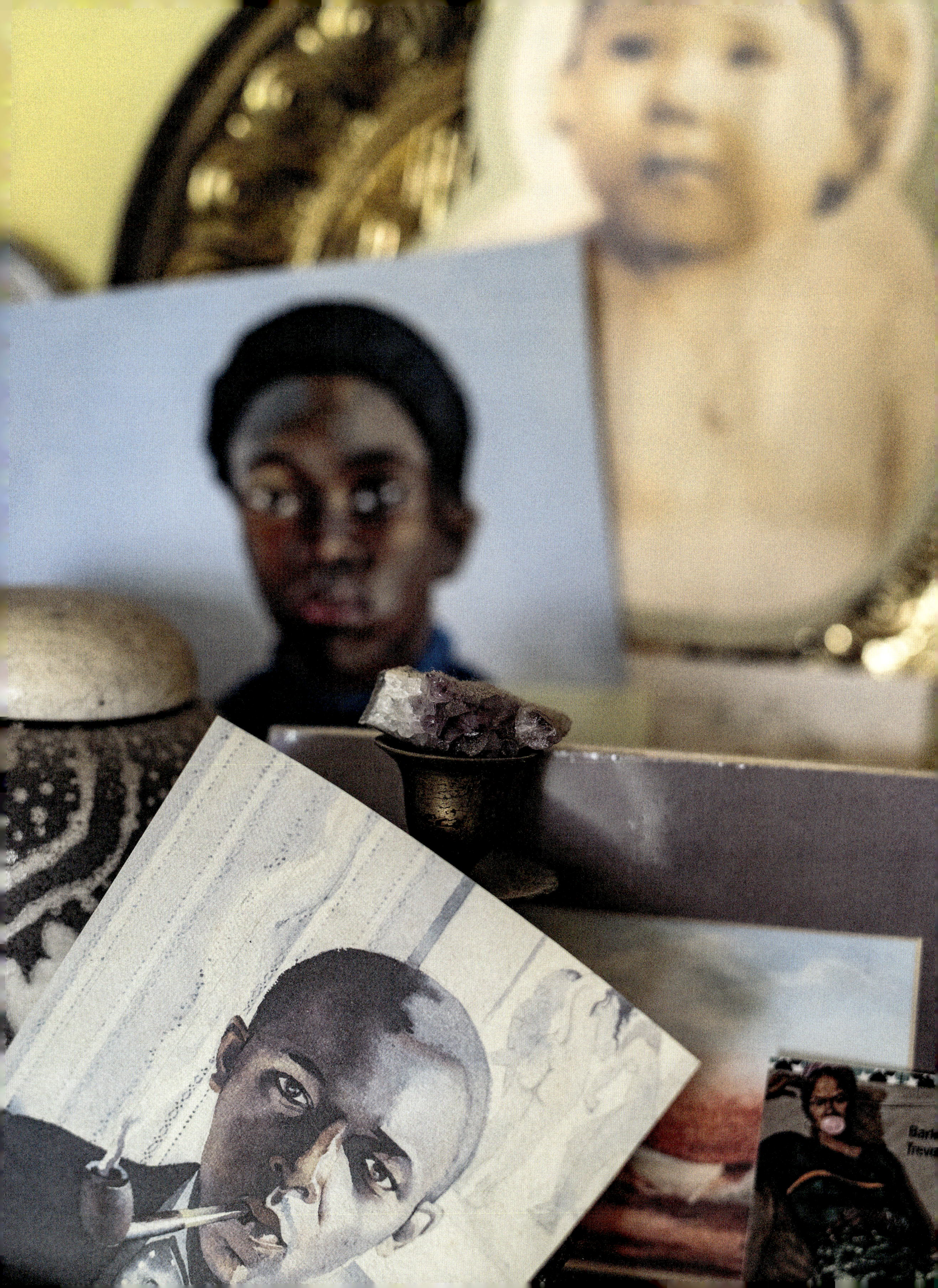

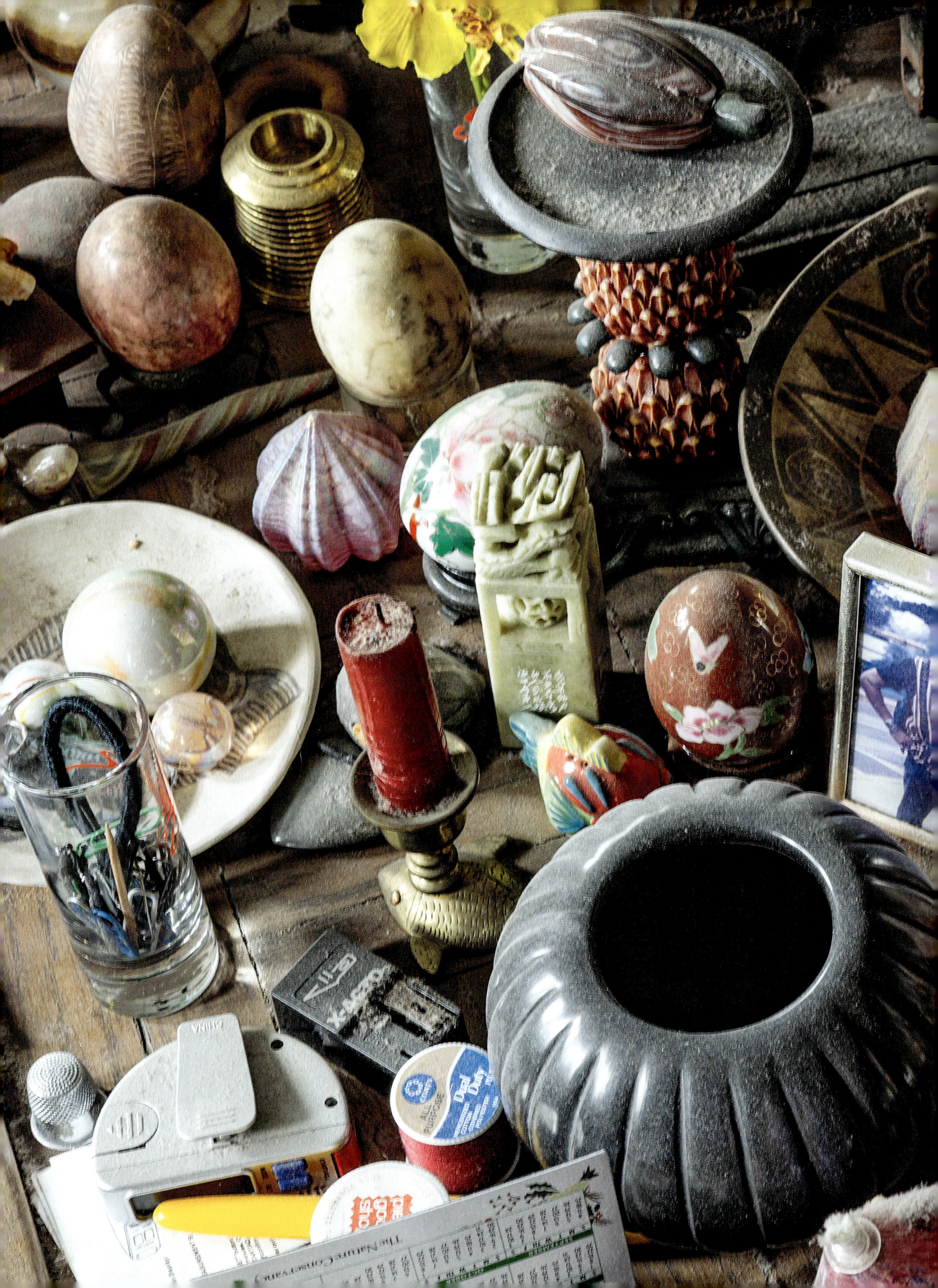
X-ACTO
Dual Duty
The Nature Conservancy

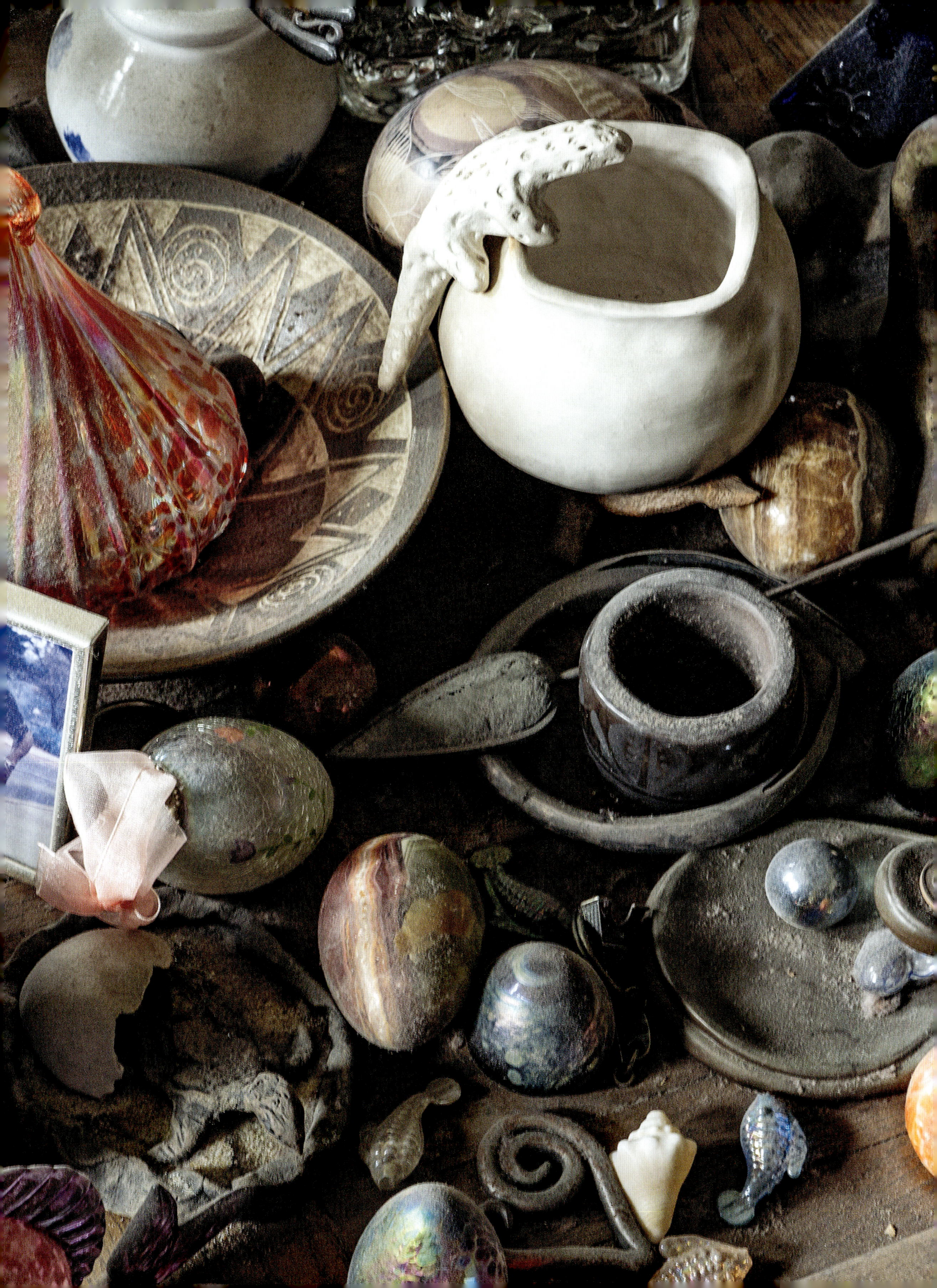

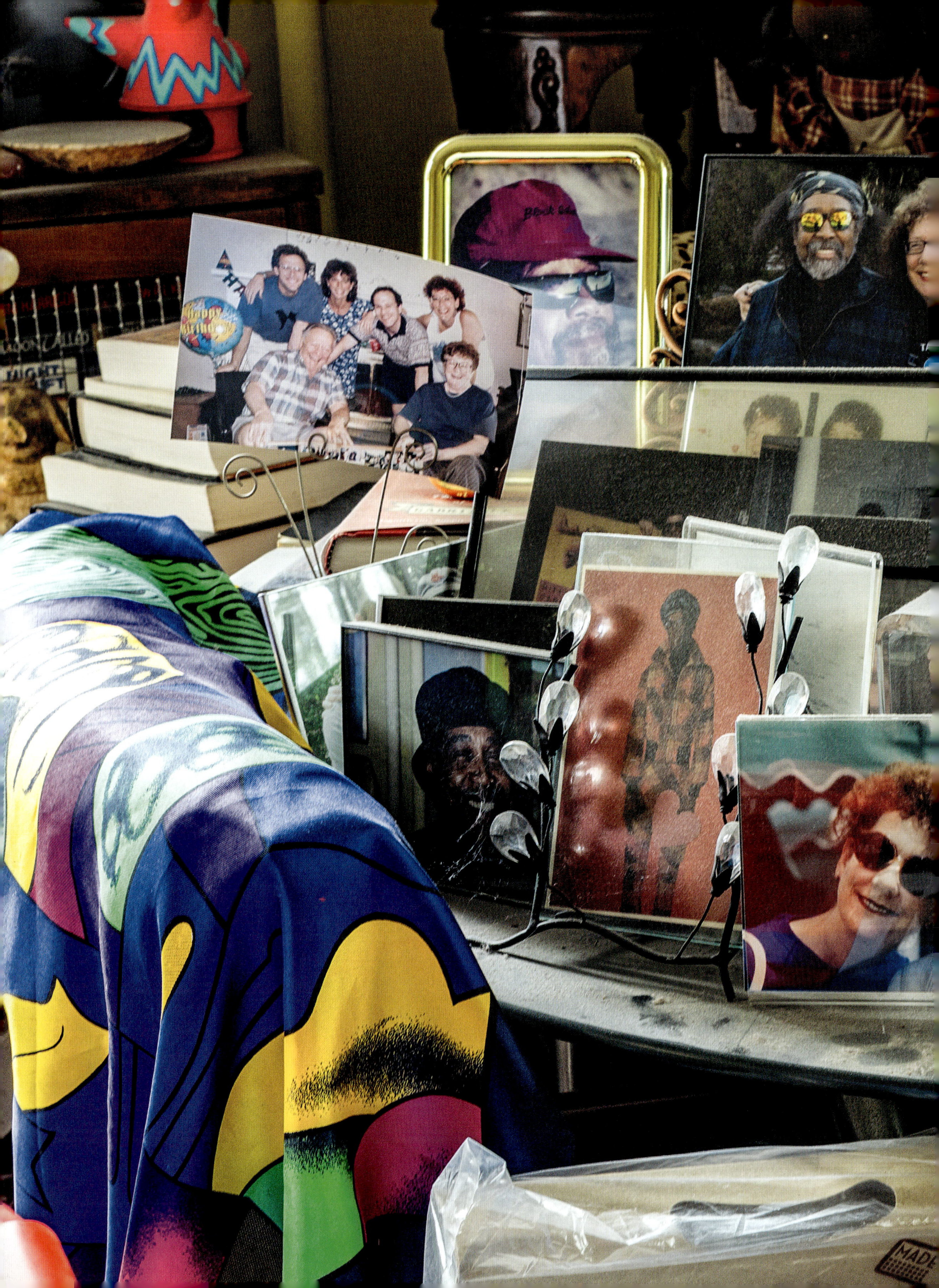

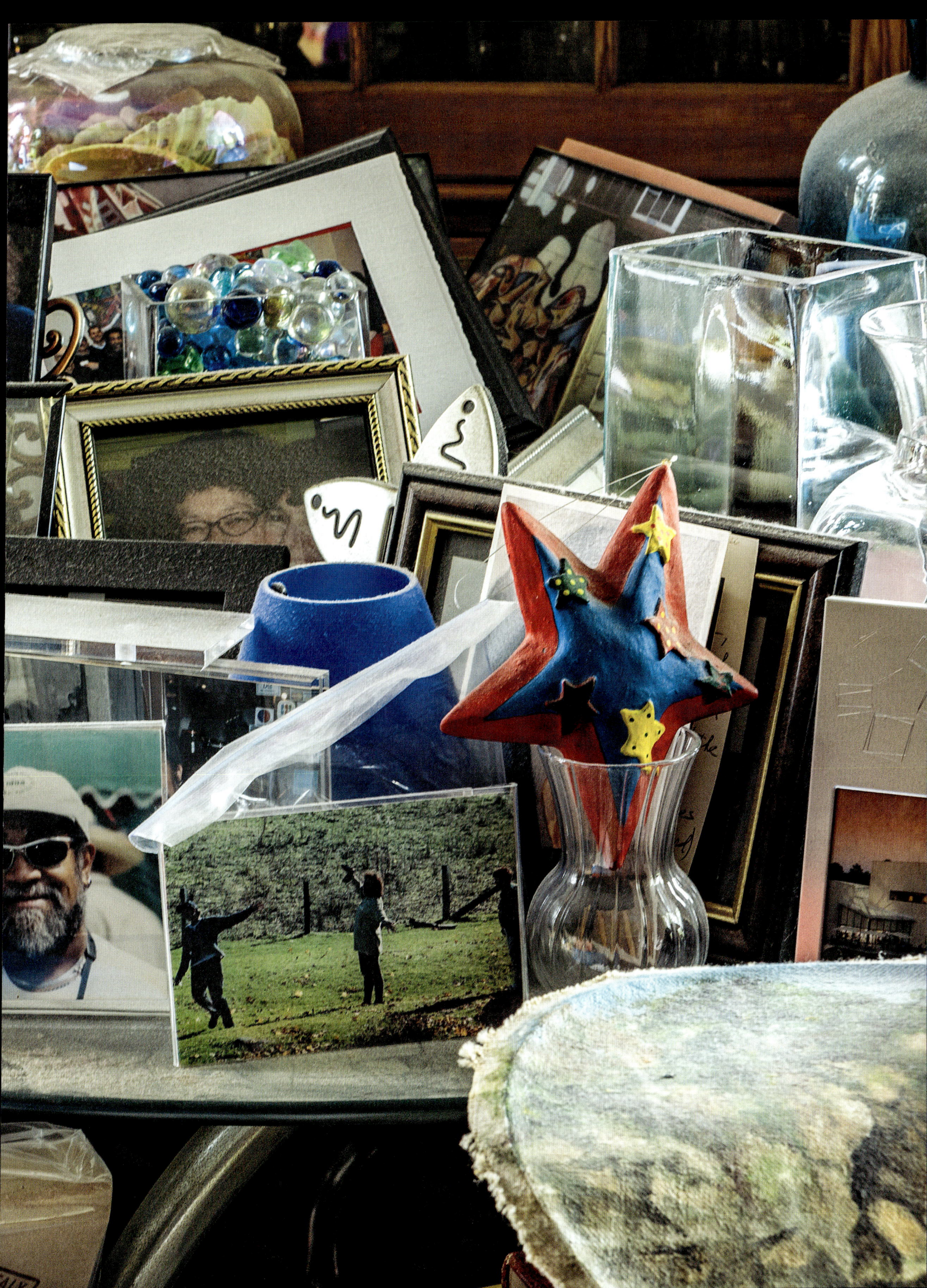

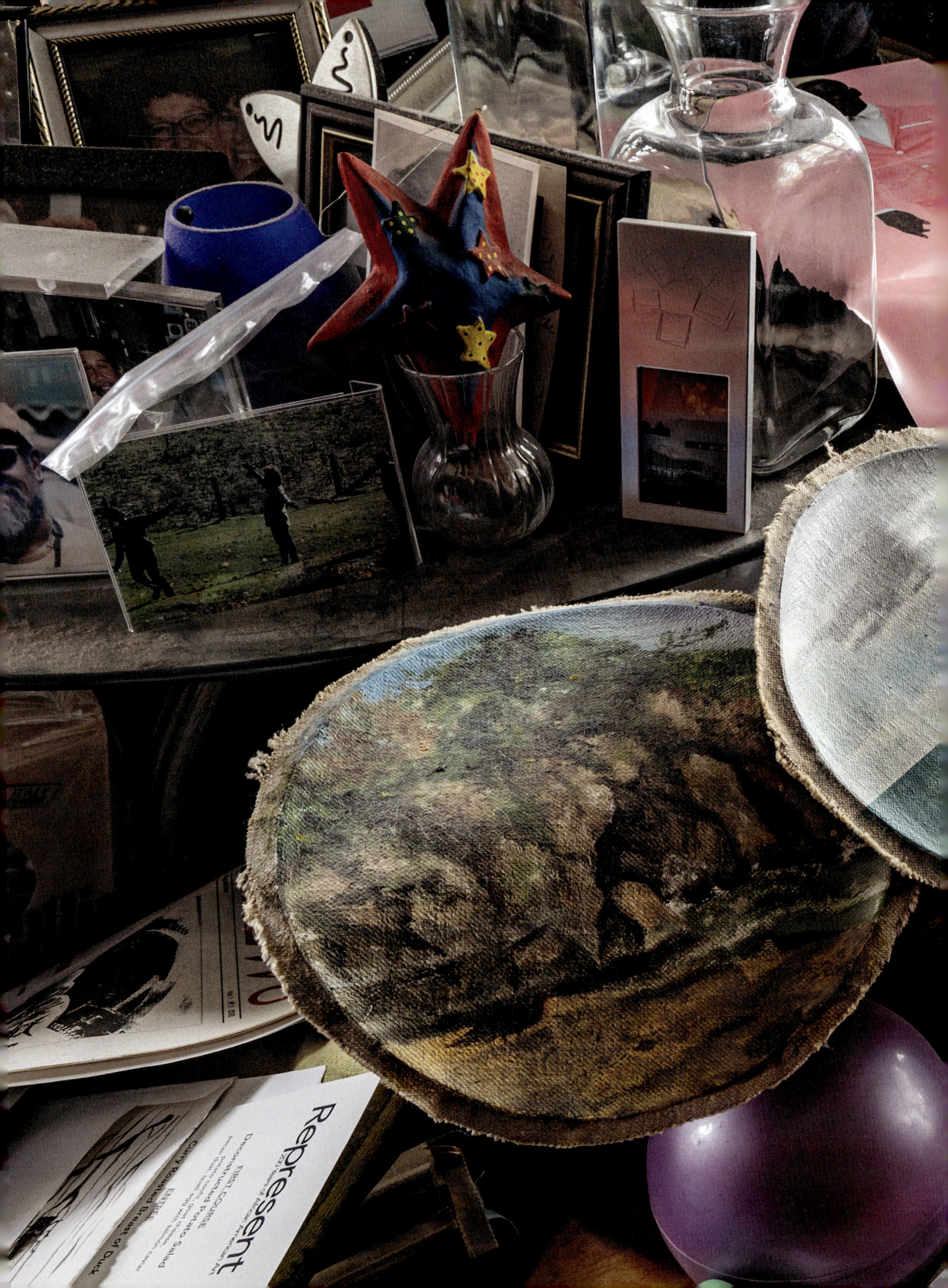
Represent
200 Years of African American Art
FIRST COURSE
Deconstructed Potato Salad
ENTRÉE
Curry Roasted Breast of Duck

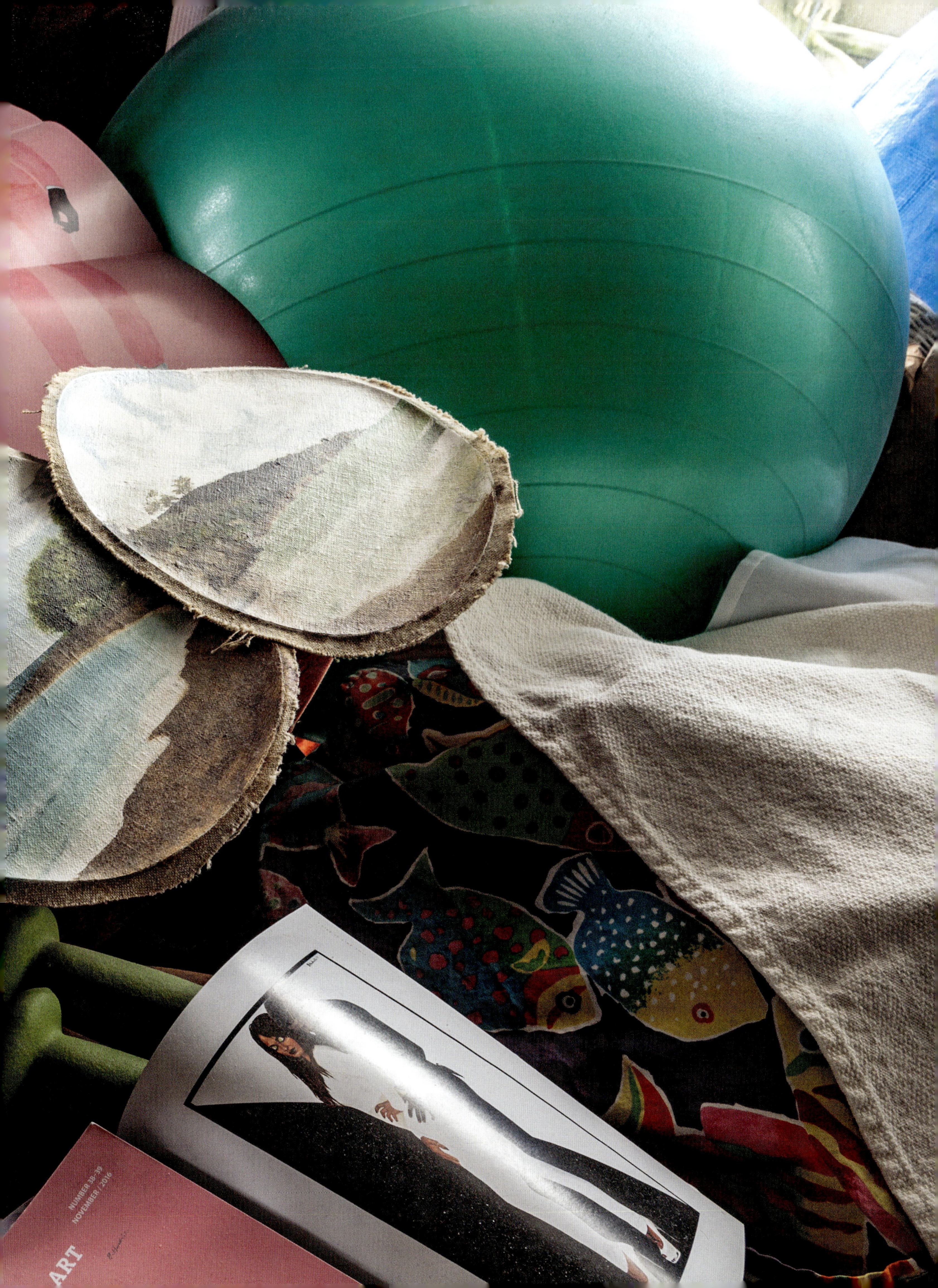
NUMBER 38–39
NOVEMBER / 2016
ART

# Hello Miles, hello "cannonball," hello Bill, hello John, hello Jimmy, hello Wynton and hello Paul. It's good to hear you again.

"HELLO MILES," September 6, 1976 (see p. 247)

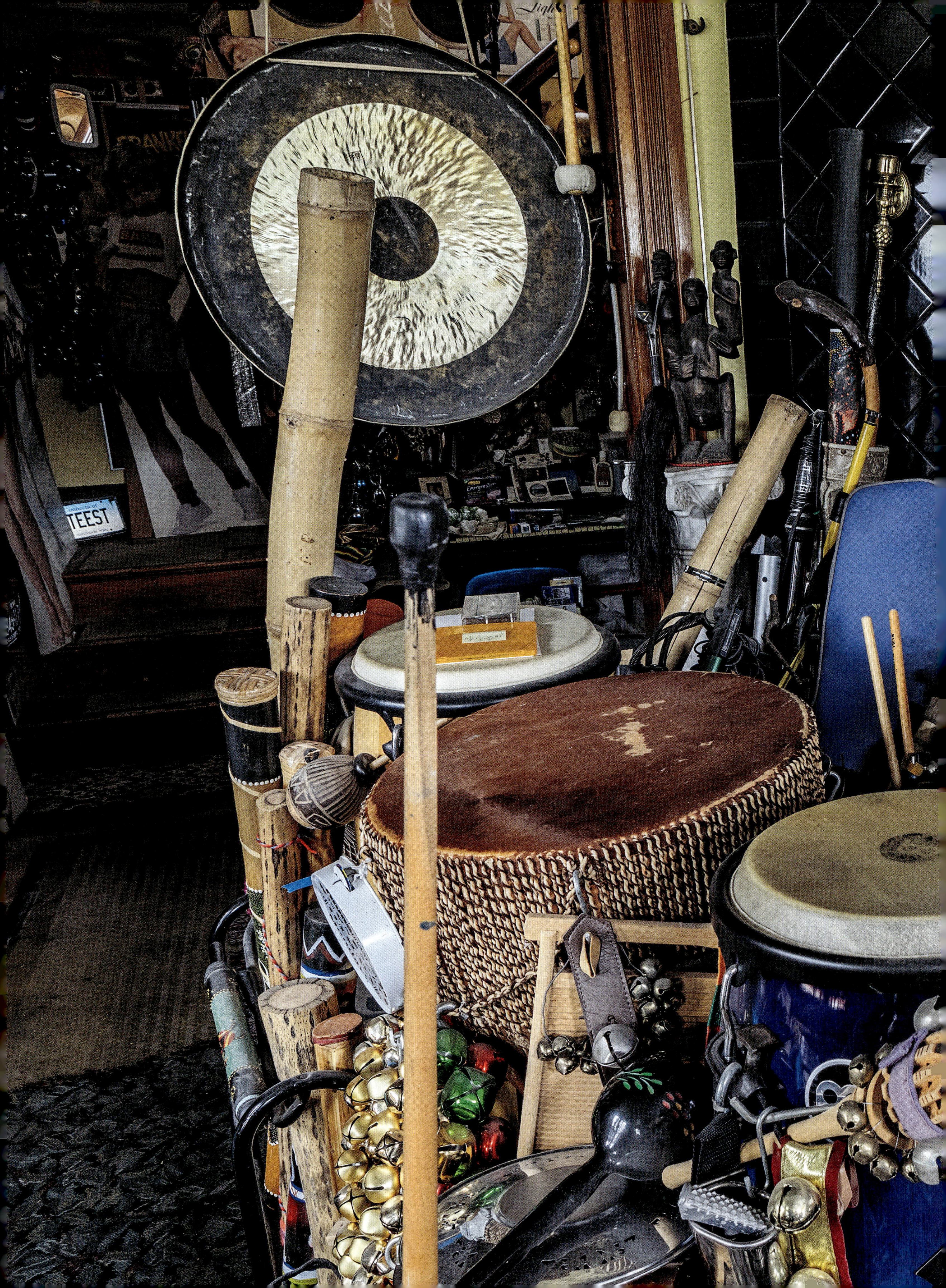
TEEST

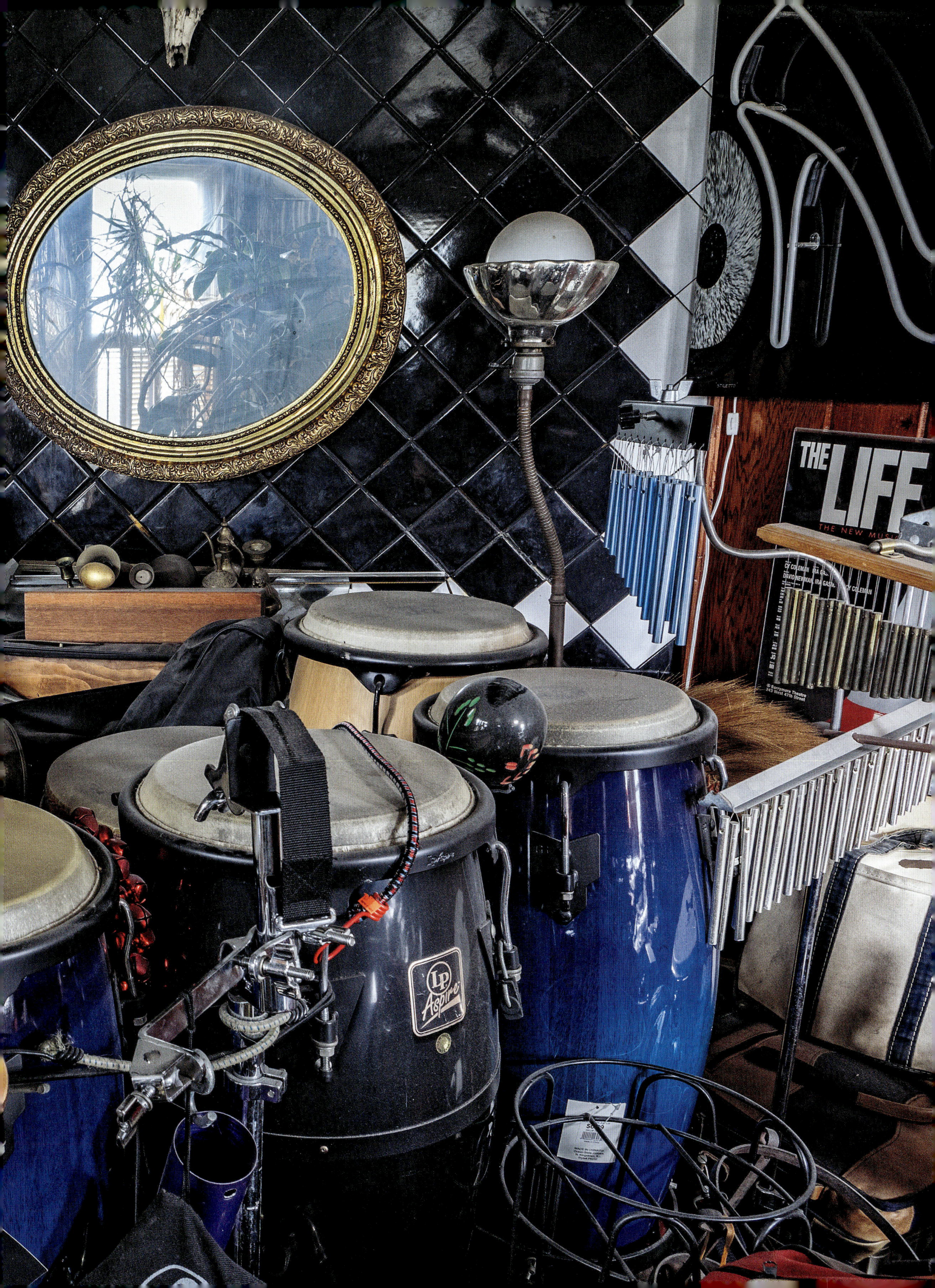
THE LIF
THE NEW MUS
CY COLEMAN
Barrymore Theatre
243 West 47th Street
LP
Aspire

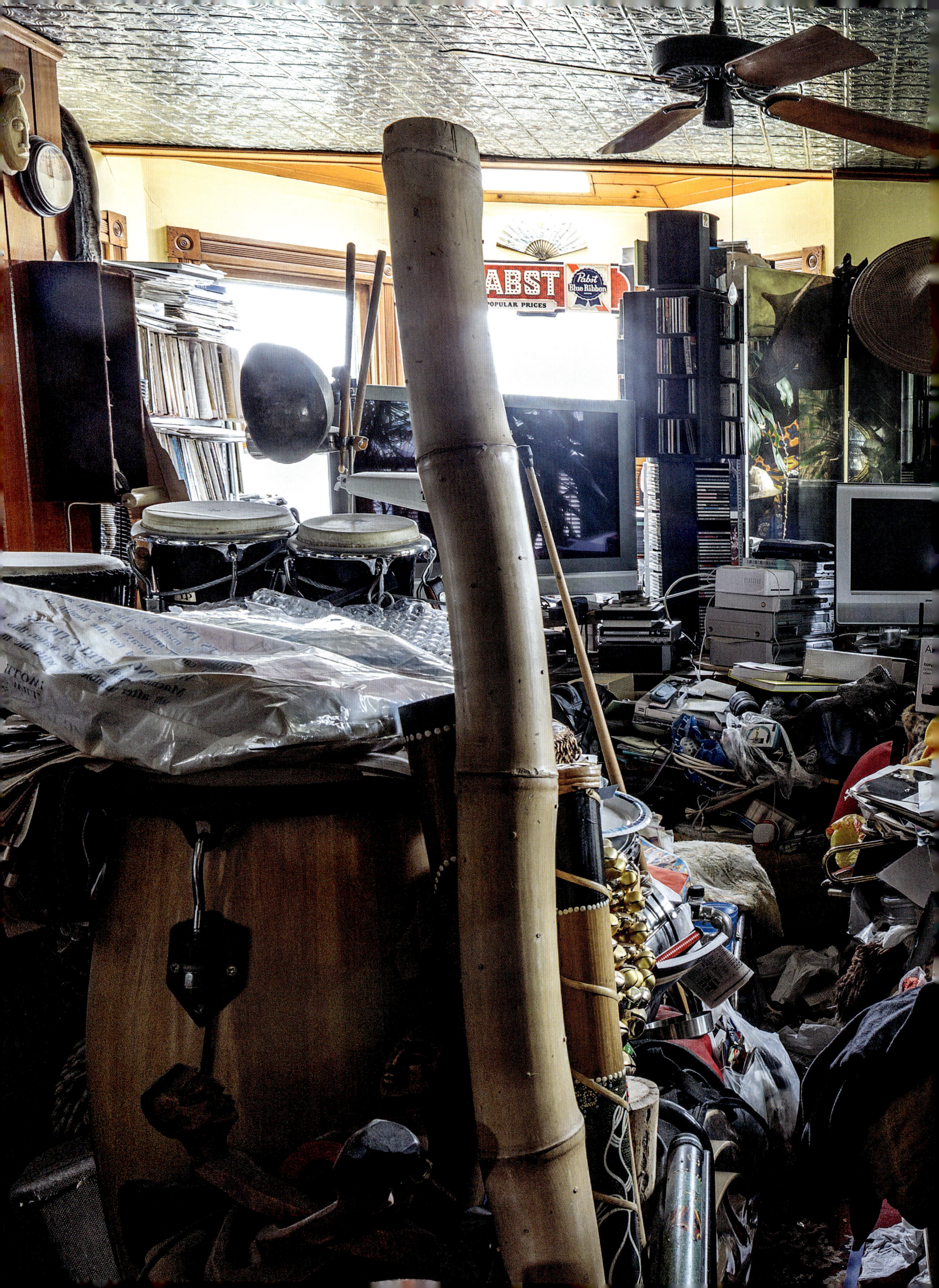
ABST
OPULAR PRICES
Pabst
Blue Ribbon

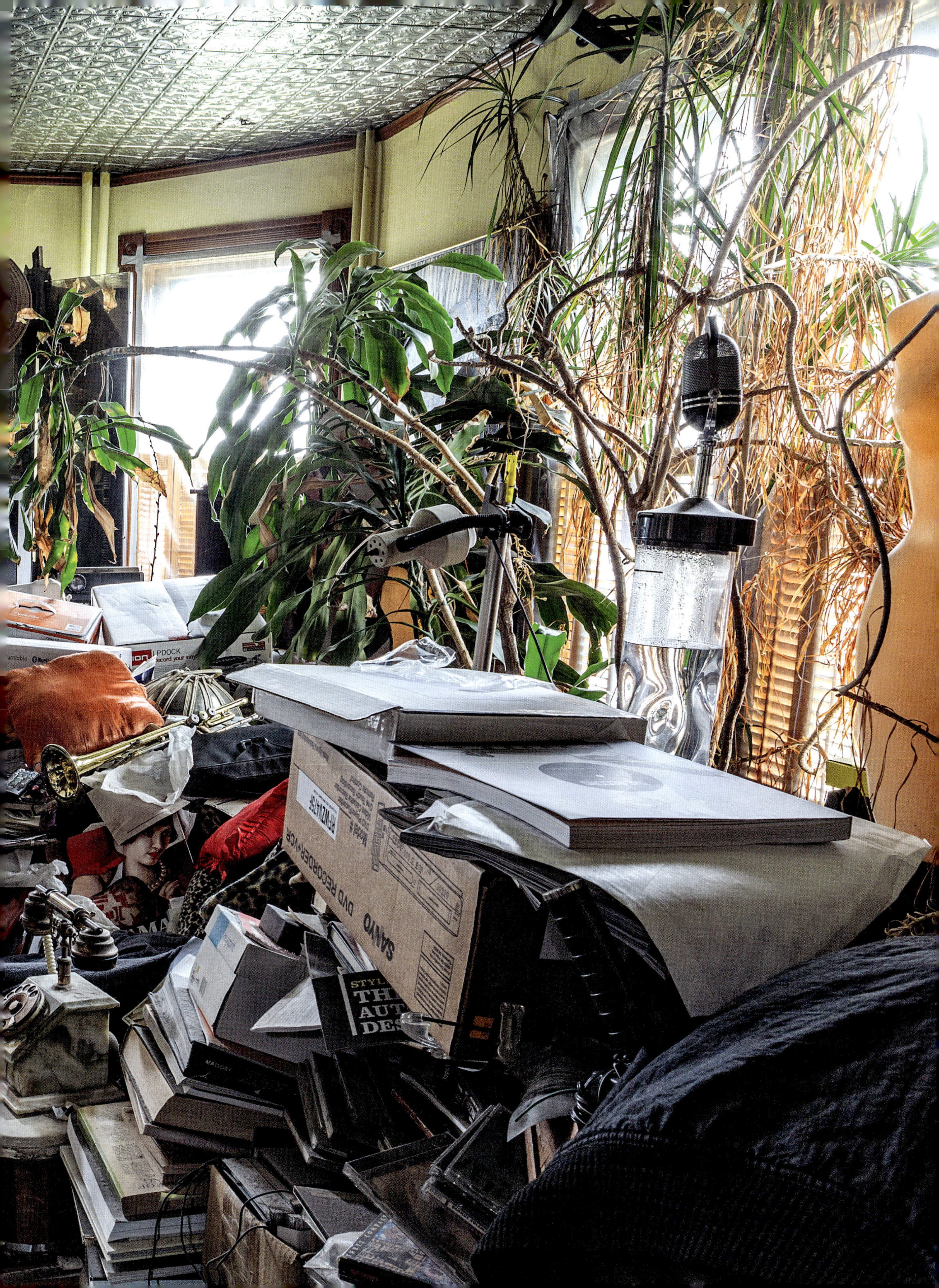
SANYO
DVD RECORDER/VCR

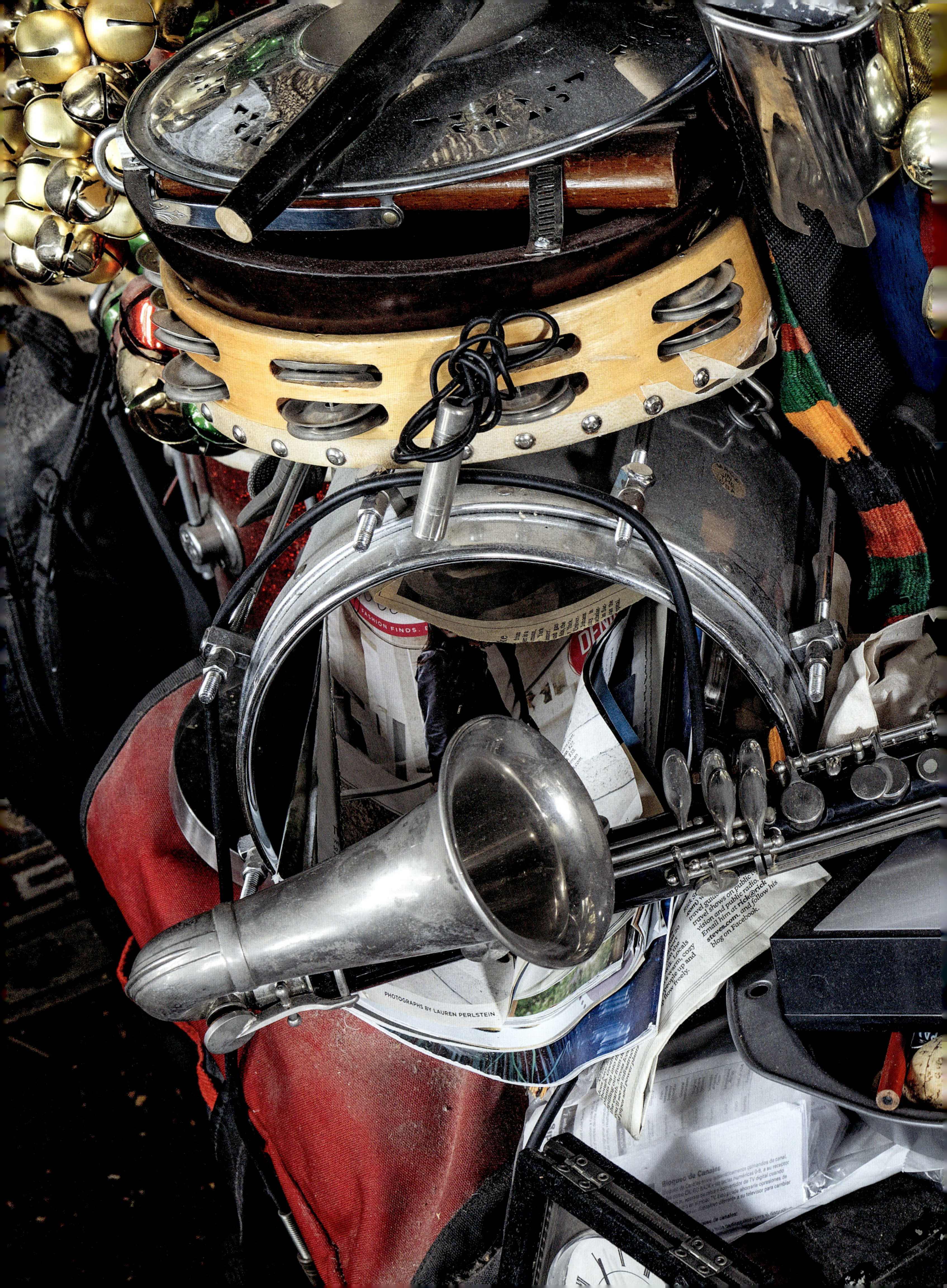
travel shows on public
vision and public radio.
Email him at rick@rick
steves.com, and follow his
blog on Facebook.
PHOTOGRAPHS BY LAUREN PERLSTEIN

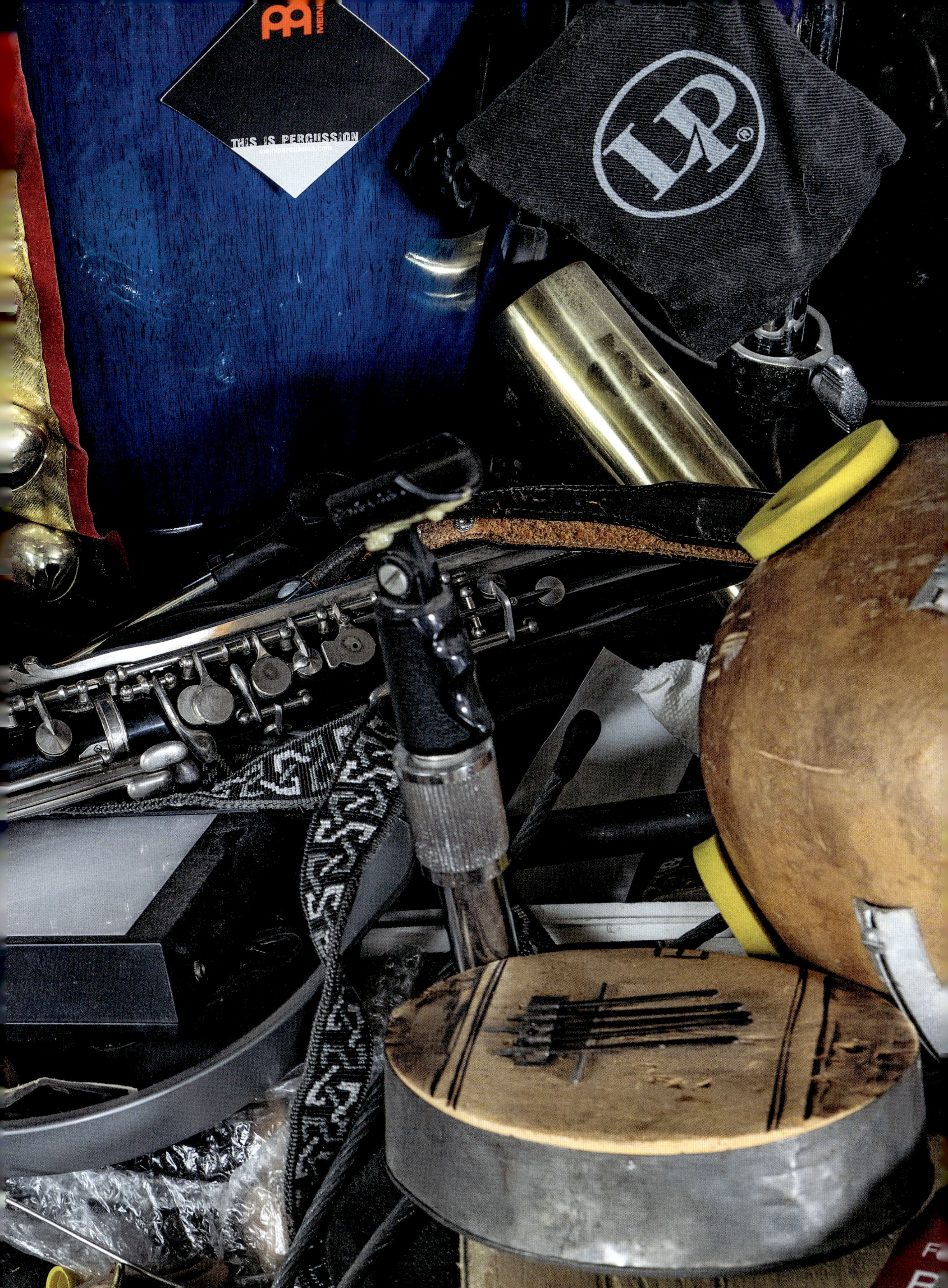
THIS IS PERCUSSION
meinlpercussion.com
LP

# I want to watch from the audience at the same time act in the drama

 

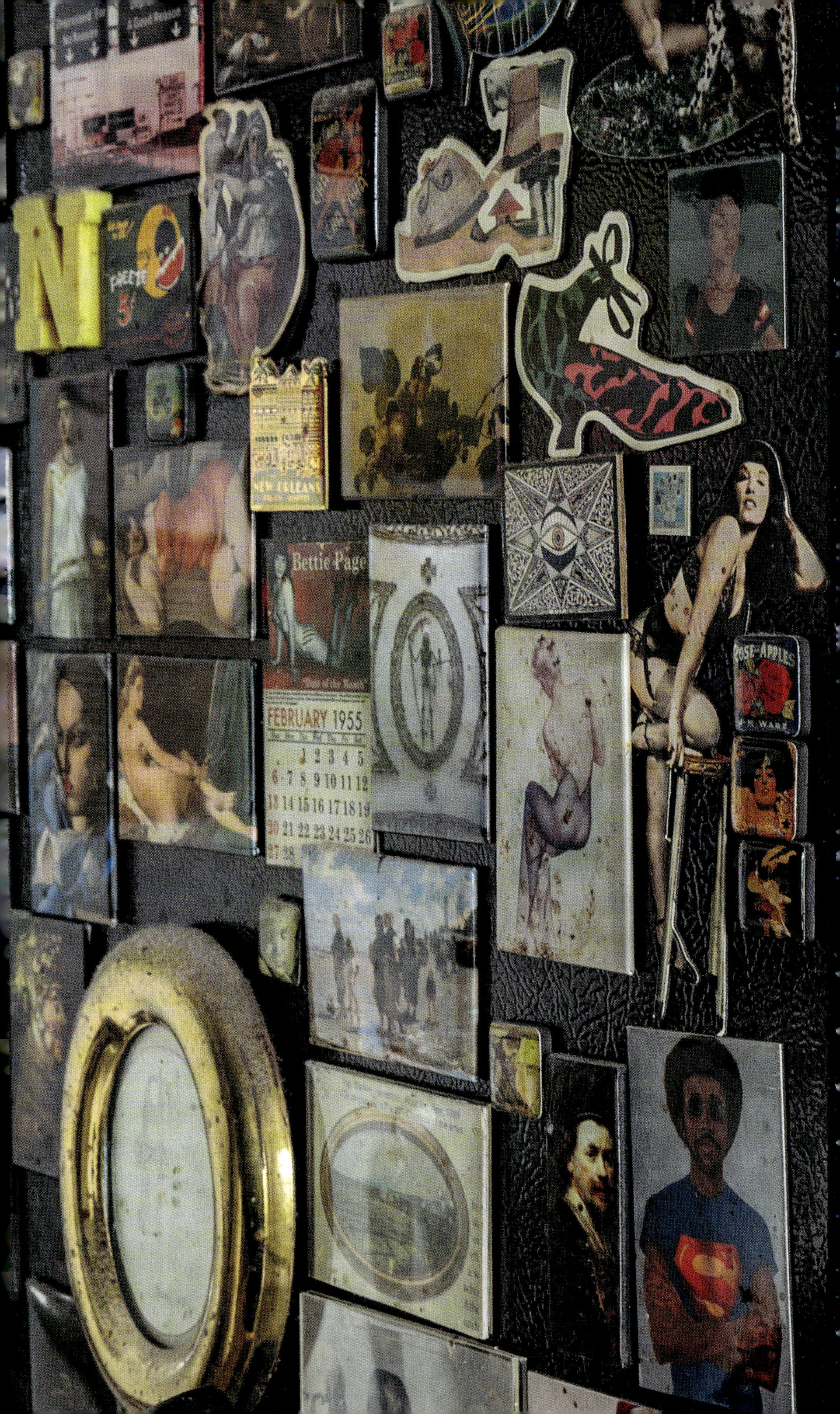

N
NEW ORLEANS
Bettie Page
"Date of the Month"
FEBRUARY 1955
1 2 3 4 5
6 7 8 9 10 11 12
13 14 15 16 17 18 19
20 21 22 23 24 25 26
ROSE APPLES

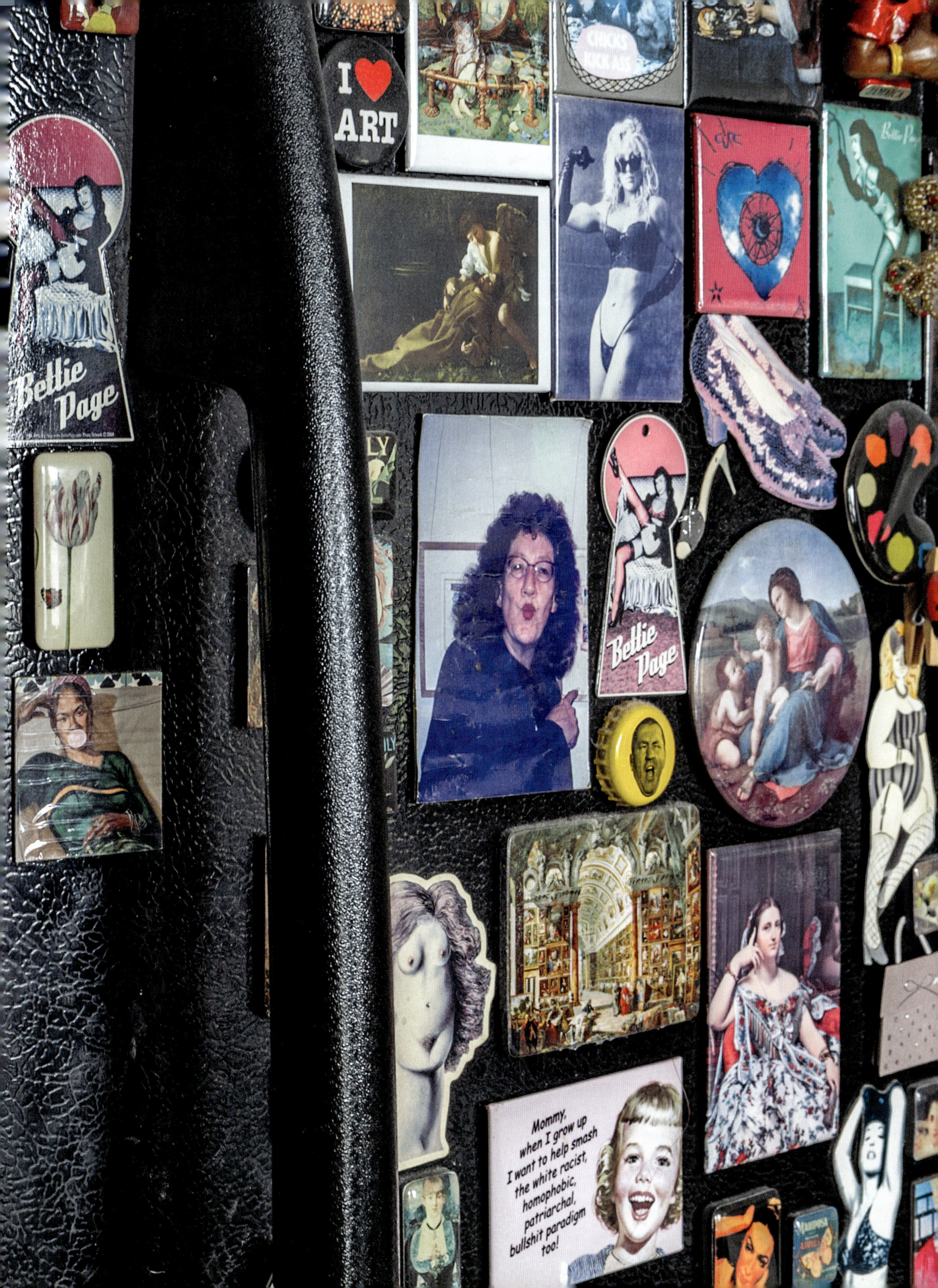

I ♥ ART
Bettie Page
Bettie Page
Mommy, when I grow up I want to help smash the white racist, homophobic, patriarchal, bullshit paradigm too!

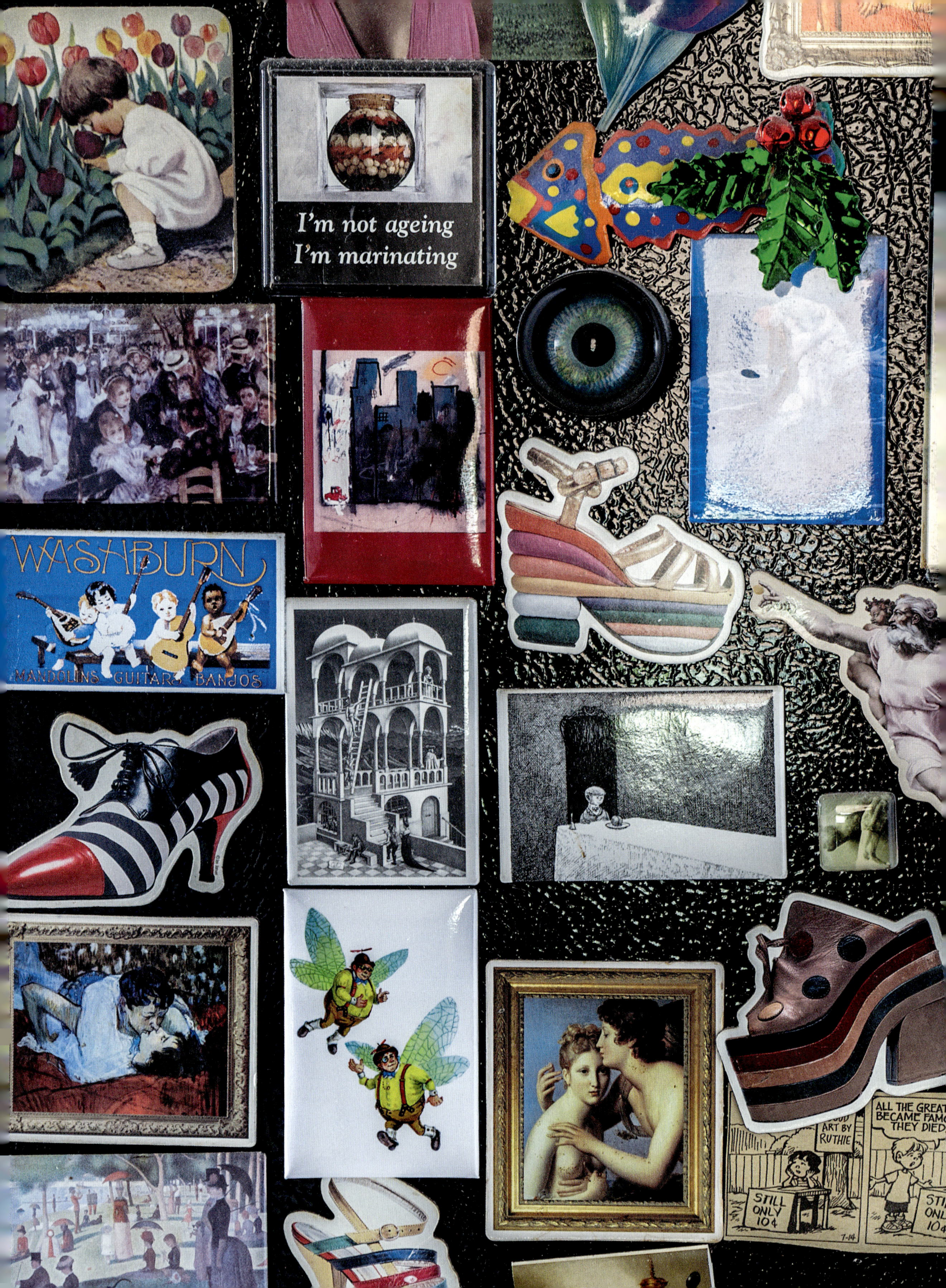
I'm not ageing
I'm marinating
WASHBURN
MANDOLINS GUITARS BANJOS
ART BY
RUTHIE
STILL
ONLY
10¢
ALL THE GREAT
BECAME FAMO
THEY DIED

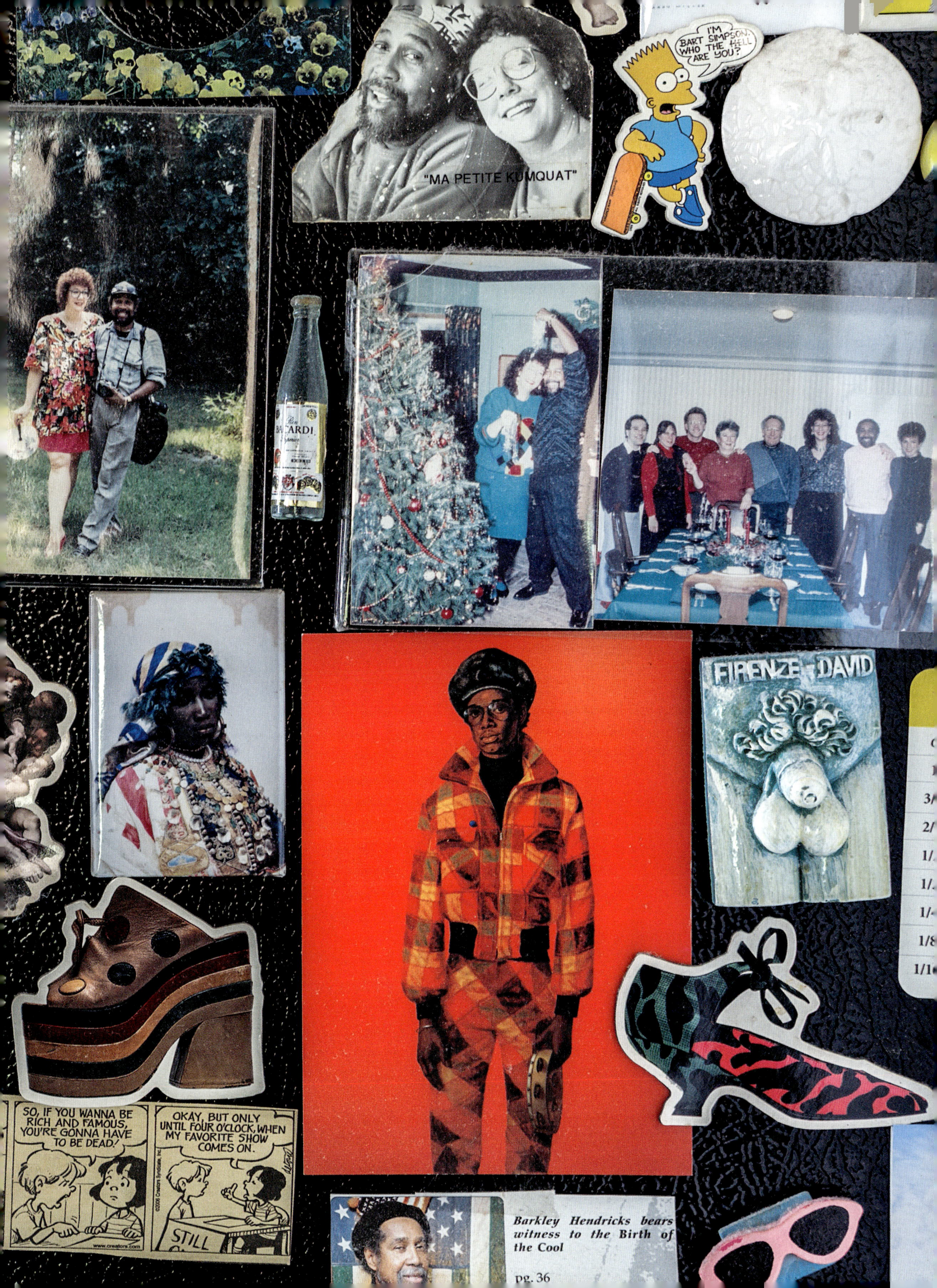
"MA PETITE KUMQUAT"
I'M BART SIMPSON. WHO THE HELL ARE YOU?
BACARDI
FIRENZE DAVID
SO, IF YOU WANNA BE RICH AND FAMOUS, YOU'RE GONNA HAVE TO BE DEAD!
OKAY, BUT ONLY UNTIL FOUR O'CLOCK, WHEN MY FAVORITE SHOW COMES ON.
STILL
Barkley Hendricks bears witness to the Birth of the Cool
pg. 36

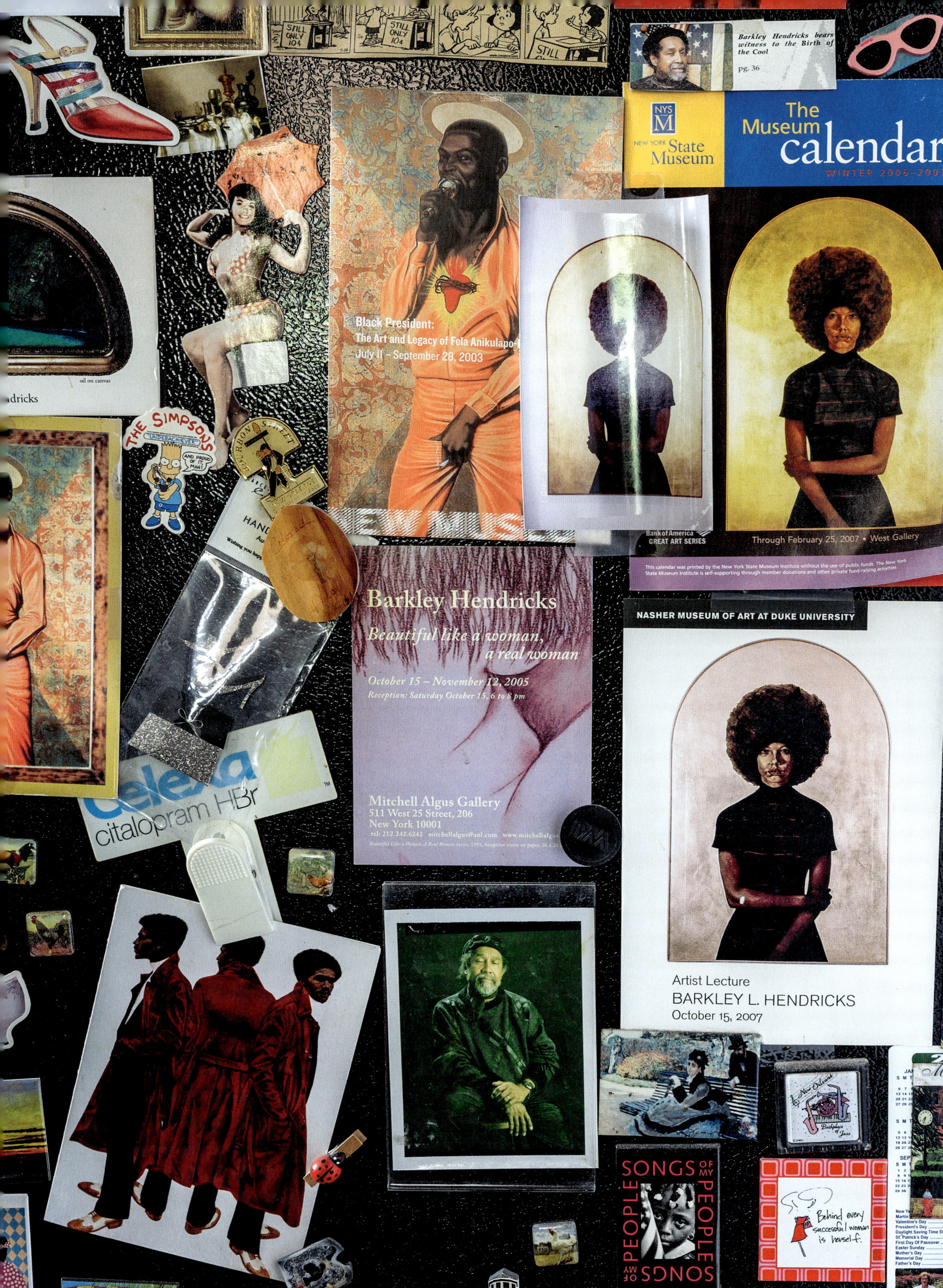

Barkley Hendricks bears witness to the Birth of the Cool
pg. 36
NYS M
NEW YORK State Museum
The Museum calendar
WINTER 2006–200
Black President:
The Art and Legacy of Fela Anikulapo-
July 11 – September 28, 2003
Bank of America GREAT ART SERIES
Through February 25, 2007 • West Gallery
This calendar was printed by the New York State Museum Institute without the use of public funds. The New York State Museum Institute is self-supporting through member donations and other private fund-raising activities.
oil on canvas
THE SIMPSONS
UNDERACHIEVER
AND PROUD OF IT MAN!
Barkley Hendricks
Beautiful like a woman, a real woman
October 15 – November 12, 2005
Reception: Saturday October 15, 6 to 8 pm
Mitchell Algus Gallery
511 West 25 Street, 206
New York 10001
NASHER MUSEUM OF ART AT DUKE UNIVERSITY
Artist Lecture
BARKLEY L. HENDRICKS
October 15, 2007
citalopram HBr
SONGS OF MY PEOPLE
Behind every successful woman is herself.

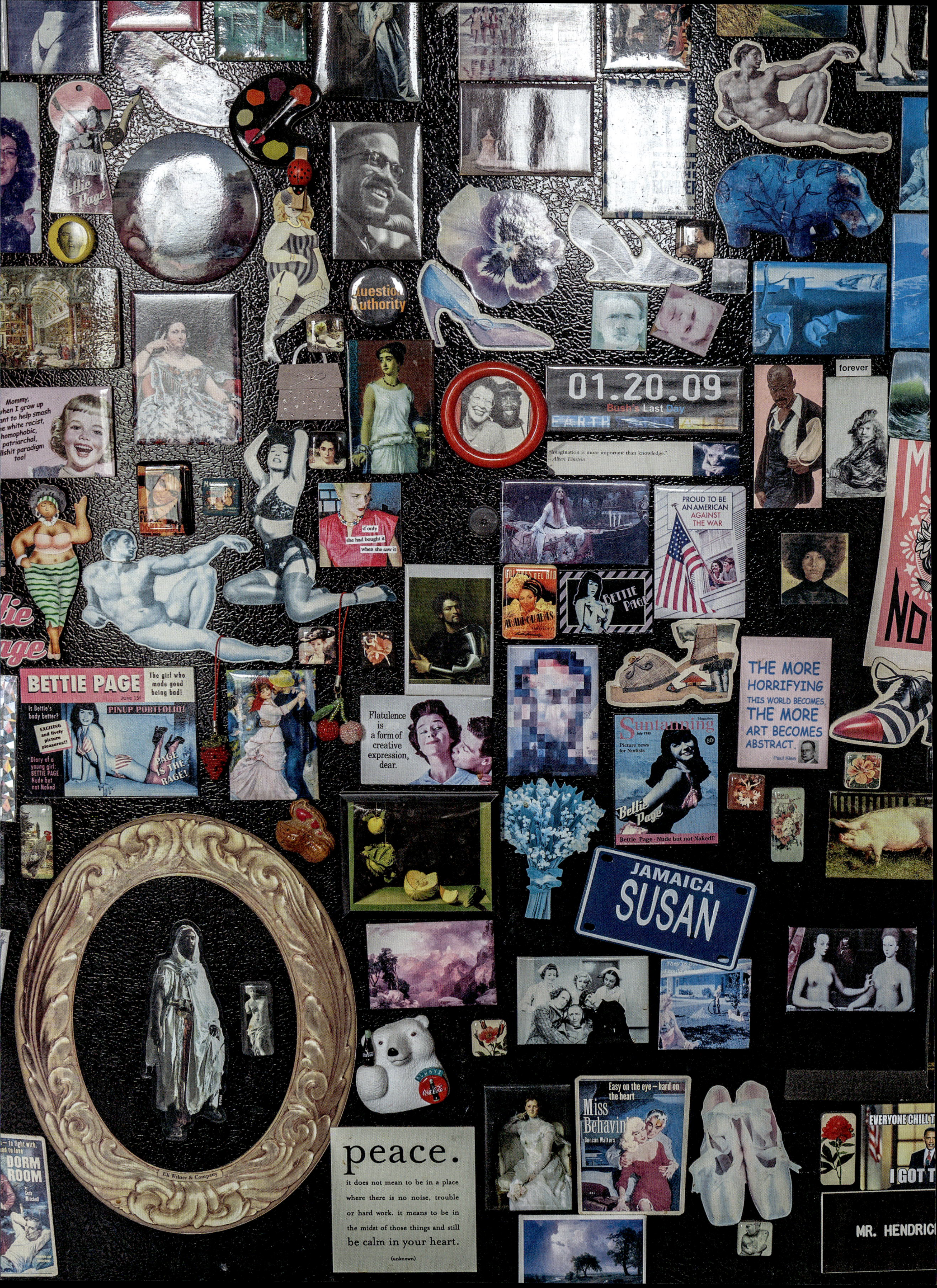

Bettie Page
Question Authority
01.20.09
Bush's Last Day
EARTH
forever
"Imagination is more important than knowledge."
Albert Einstein
PROUD TO BE AN AMERICAN AGAINST THE WAR
if only she had bought it when she saw it
BETTIE PAGE
BETTIE PAGE
The girl who made good being bad!
PINUP PORTFOLIO!
Is Bettie's body better?
EXCITING and lively picture pleasures!
Diary of a young girl. BETTIE PAGE Nude but not Naked
PAGE IS THE RAGE!
Flatulence is a form of creative expression, dear.
THE MORE HORRIFYING THIS WORLD BECOMES, THE MORE ART BECOMES ABSTRACT.
Paul Klee
Suntanning
Picture news for Nudists
Bettie Page
Bettie Page · Nude but not Naked!
JAMAICA
SUSAN
Eli Wilner & Company
peace.
it does not mean to be in a place where there is no noise, trouble or hard work. it means to be in the midst of those things and still be calm in your heart.
(unknown)
Easy on the eye – hard on the heart
Miss Behavin
Duncan Walters
DORM ROOM
EVERYONE CHILL

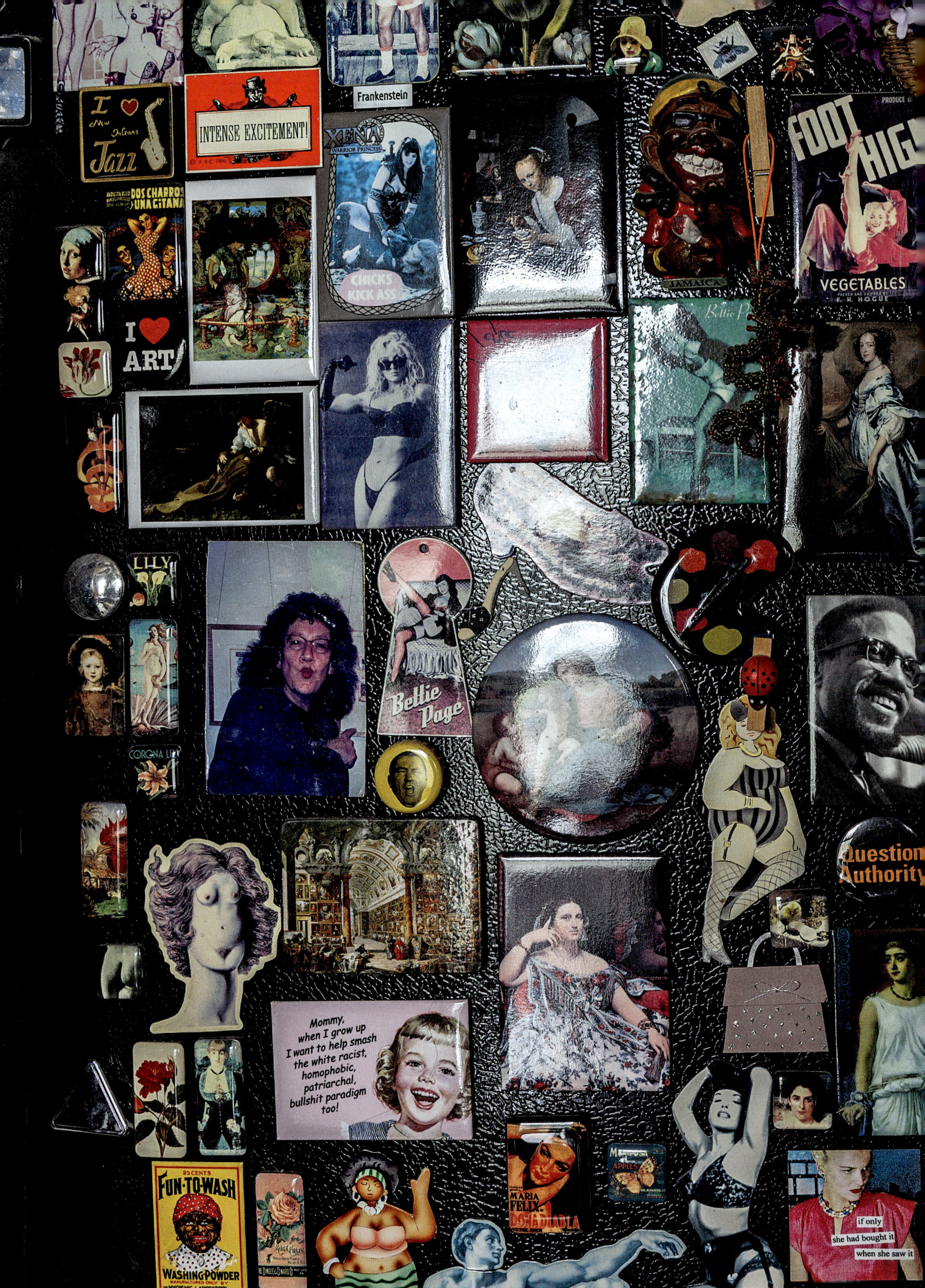

Frankenstein
INTENSE EXCITEMENT!
I ♥ New Orleans Jazz
DOS CHARROS Y UNA GITANA
XENA
WARRIOR PRINCESS
CHICKS KICK ASS
FOOT HIGH
VEGETABLES
JAMAICA
I ♥ ART
LILY
Bettie Page
Question Authority
Mommy, when I grow up I want to help smash the white racist, homophobic, patriarchal, bullshit paradigm too!
25 CENTS
FUN-TO-WASH
WASHING POWDER
MARIA FELIX
DOÑA DIABLA
if only she had bought it when she saw it

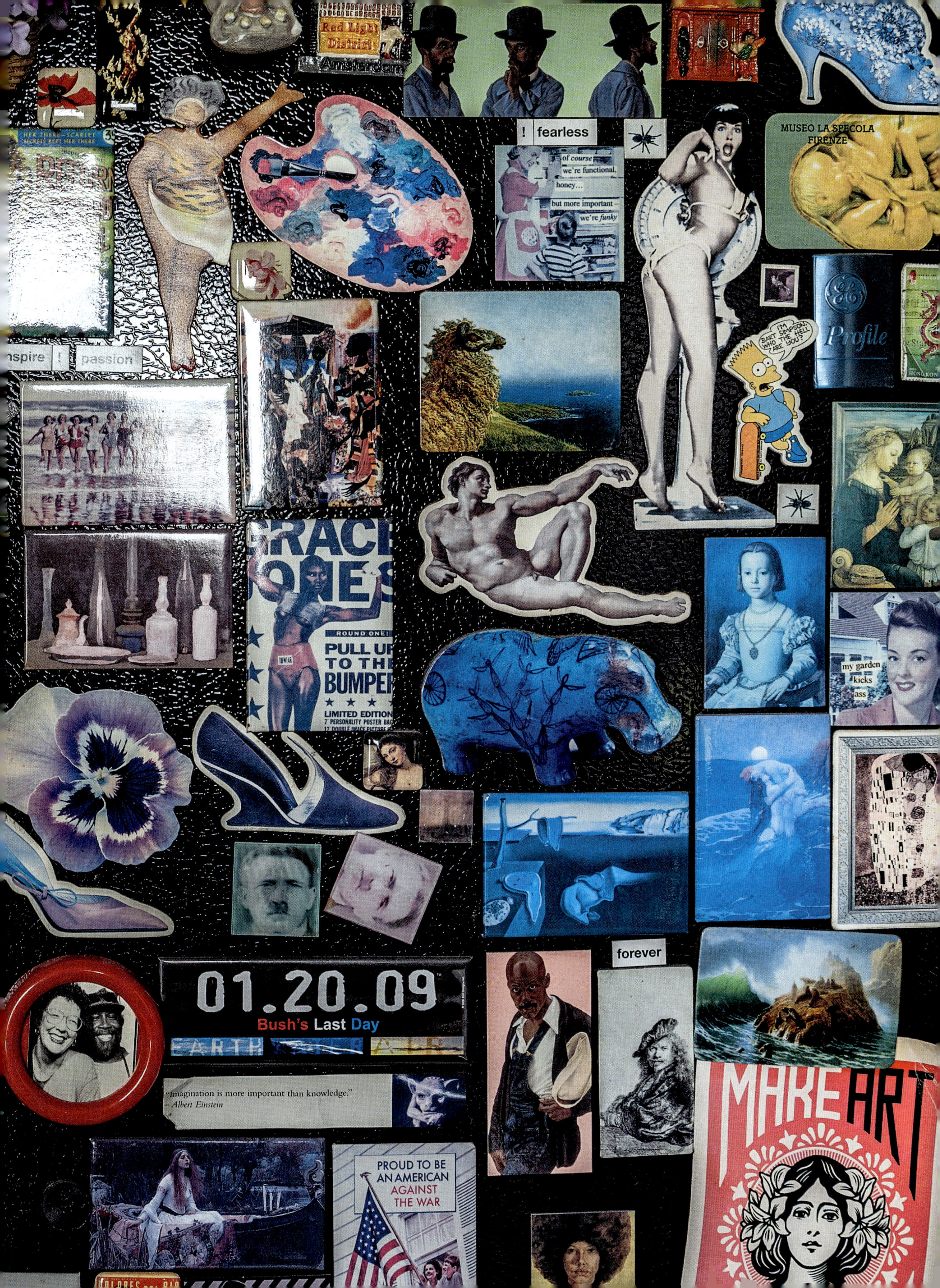

Red Light District
Amsterdam
! fearless
of course we're functional, honey... but more important we're funky
MUSEO LA SPECOLA FIRENZE
Profile
I'M BART SIMPSON. WHO THE HELL ARE YOU?
! passion
ROUND ONE
PULL UP TO THE BUMPER
LIMITED EDITION
my garden kicks ass
forever
01.20.09
Bush's Last Day
"Imagination is more important than knowledge."
– Albert Einstein
PROUD TO BE AN AMERICAN AGAINST THE WAR
MAKE ART

# 2nd Floor

# Hallway, Studio, Bedroom, Office

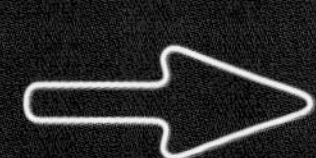

# The old days in my other studios were happy ones too. So nice is this feeling it is almost like I have been transported back.

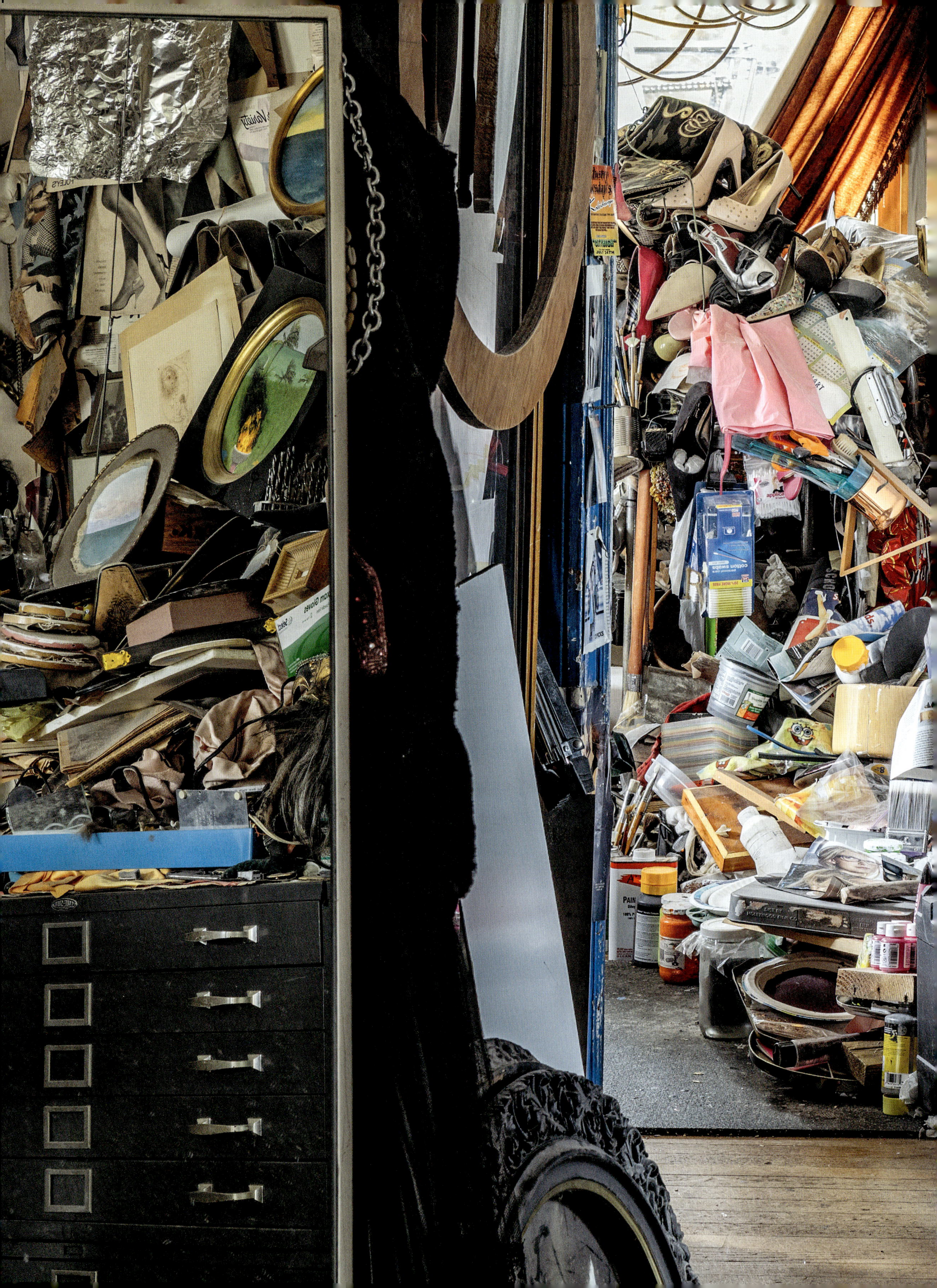

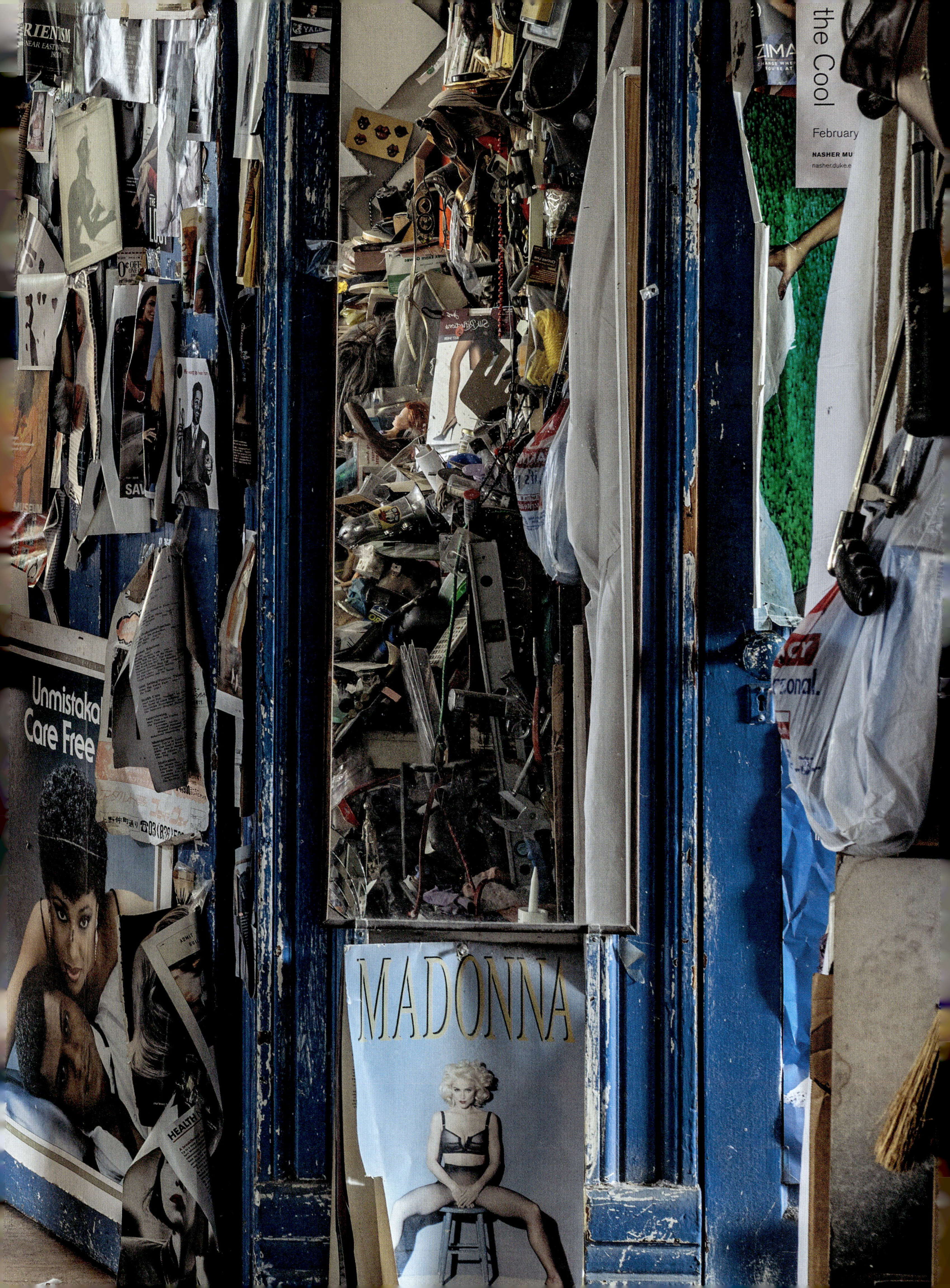

the Cool
February
NASHER MU
Unmistaka
Care Free
MADONNA

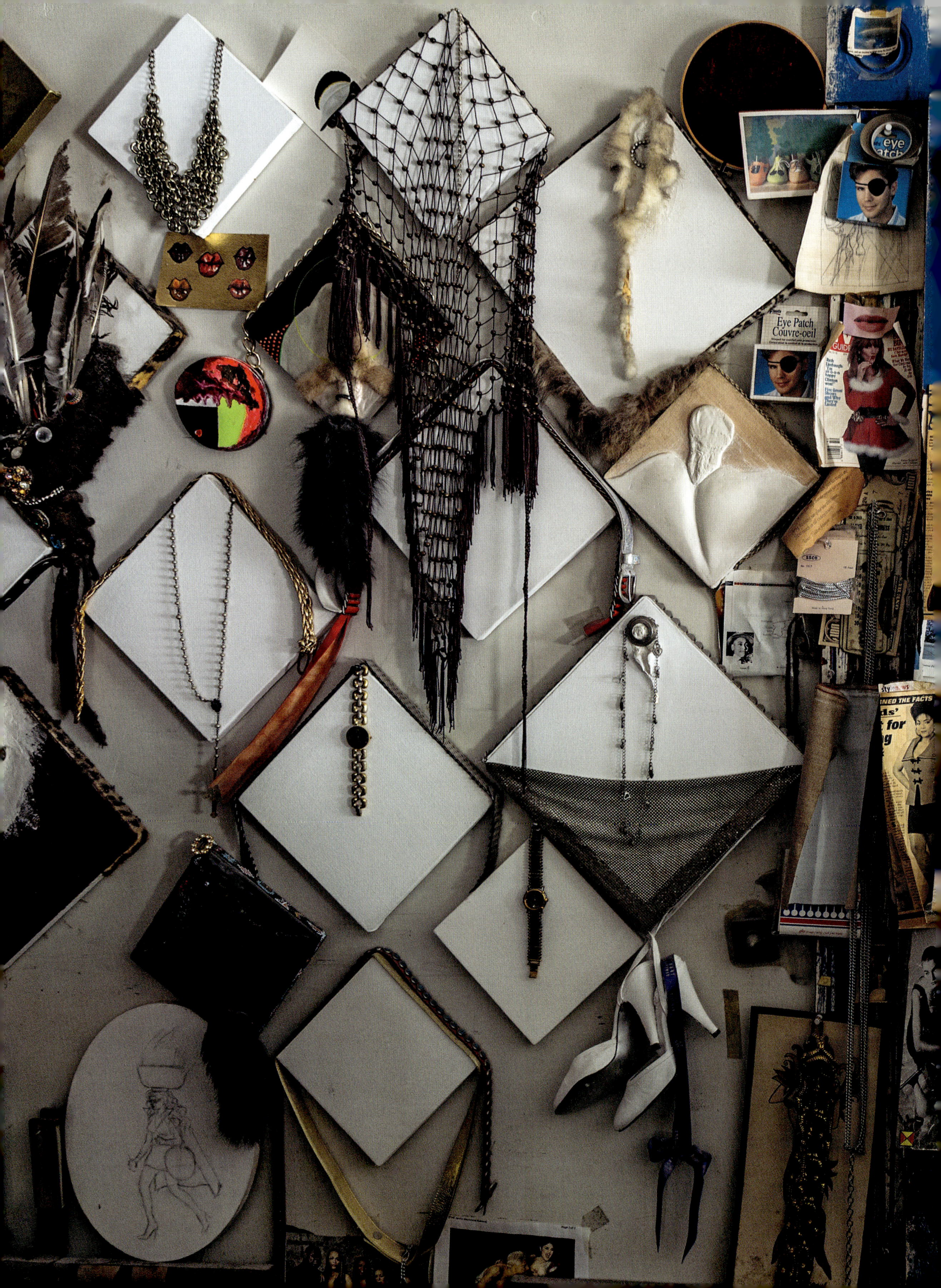
Eye Patch
Couvre-oeil

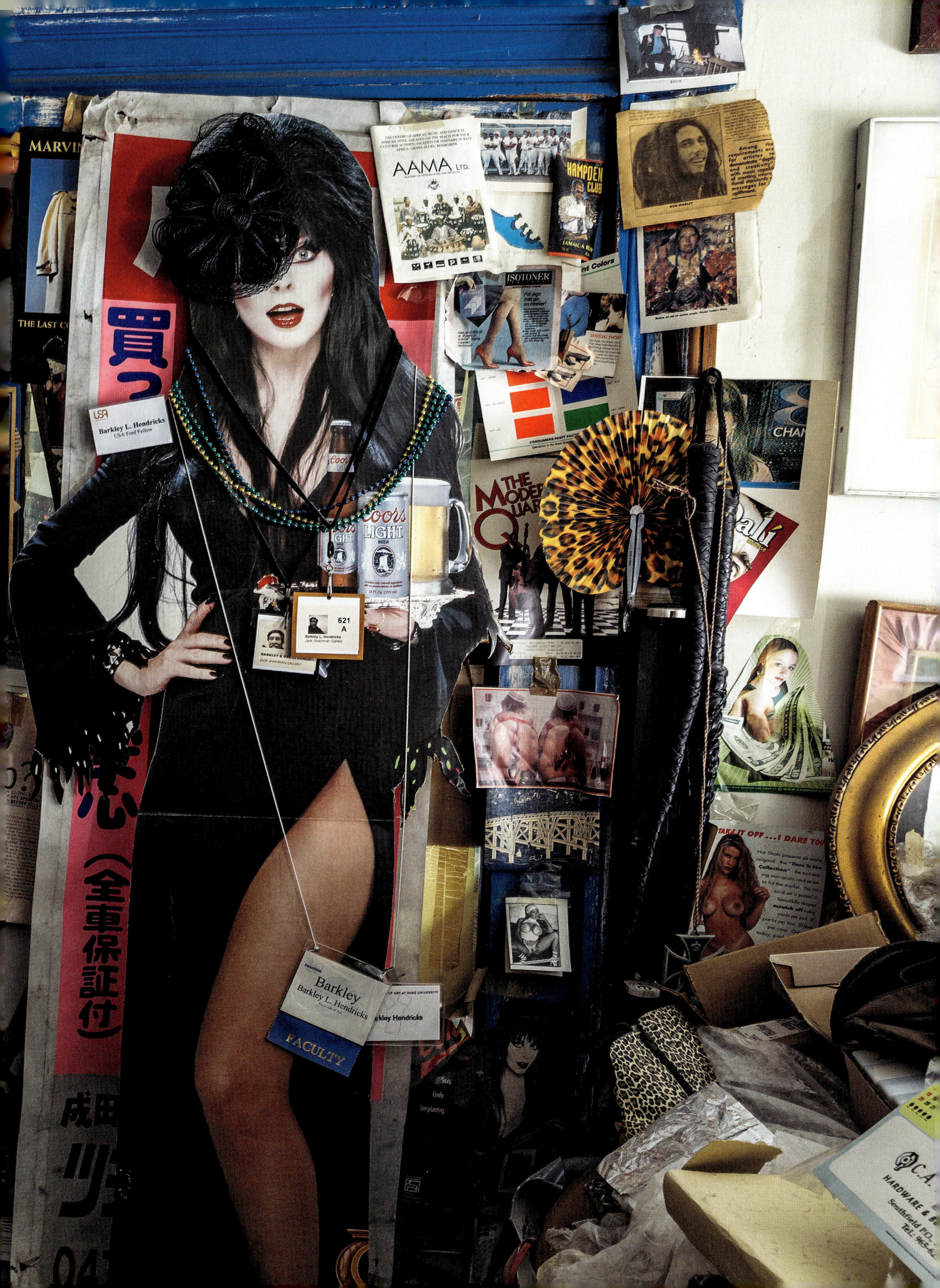

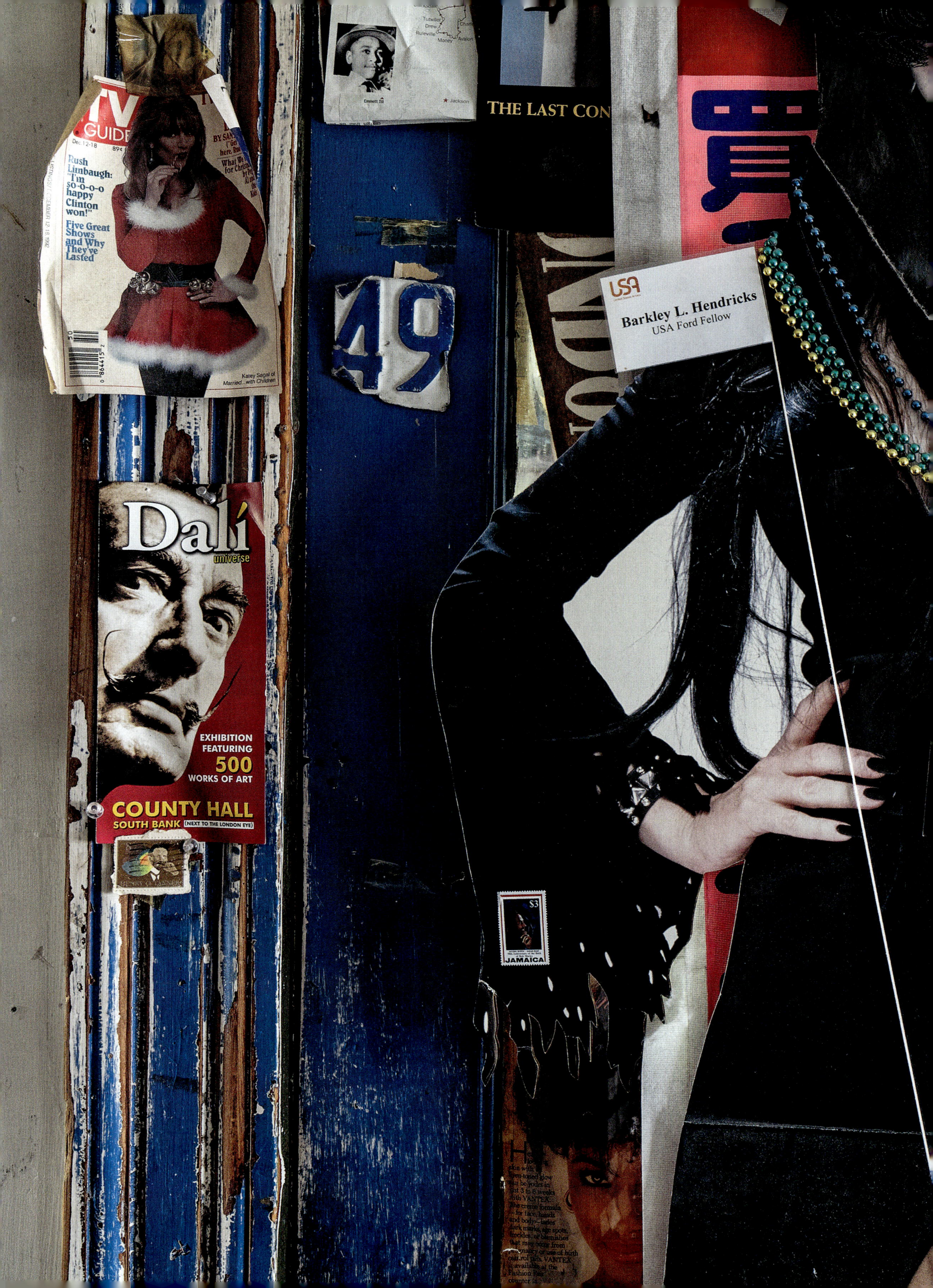

TV GUIDE
Dec 12-18
Rush Limbaugh: "I'm so-o-o-o happy Clinton won!"
Five Great Shows and Why They've Lasted
Katey Segal of Married...with Children
Emmett Till
THE LAST CON
49
USA
Barkley L. Hendricks
USA Ford Fellow
Dalí
universe
EXHIBITION FEATURING
500
WORKS OF ART
COUNTY HALL
SOUTH BANK
(NEXT TO THE LONDON EYE)
$3
JAMAICA

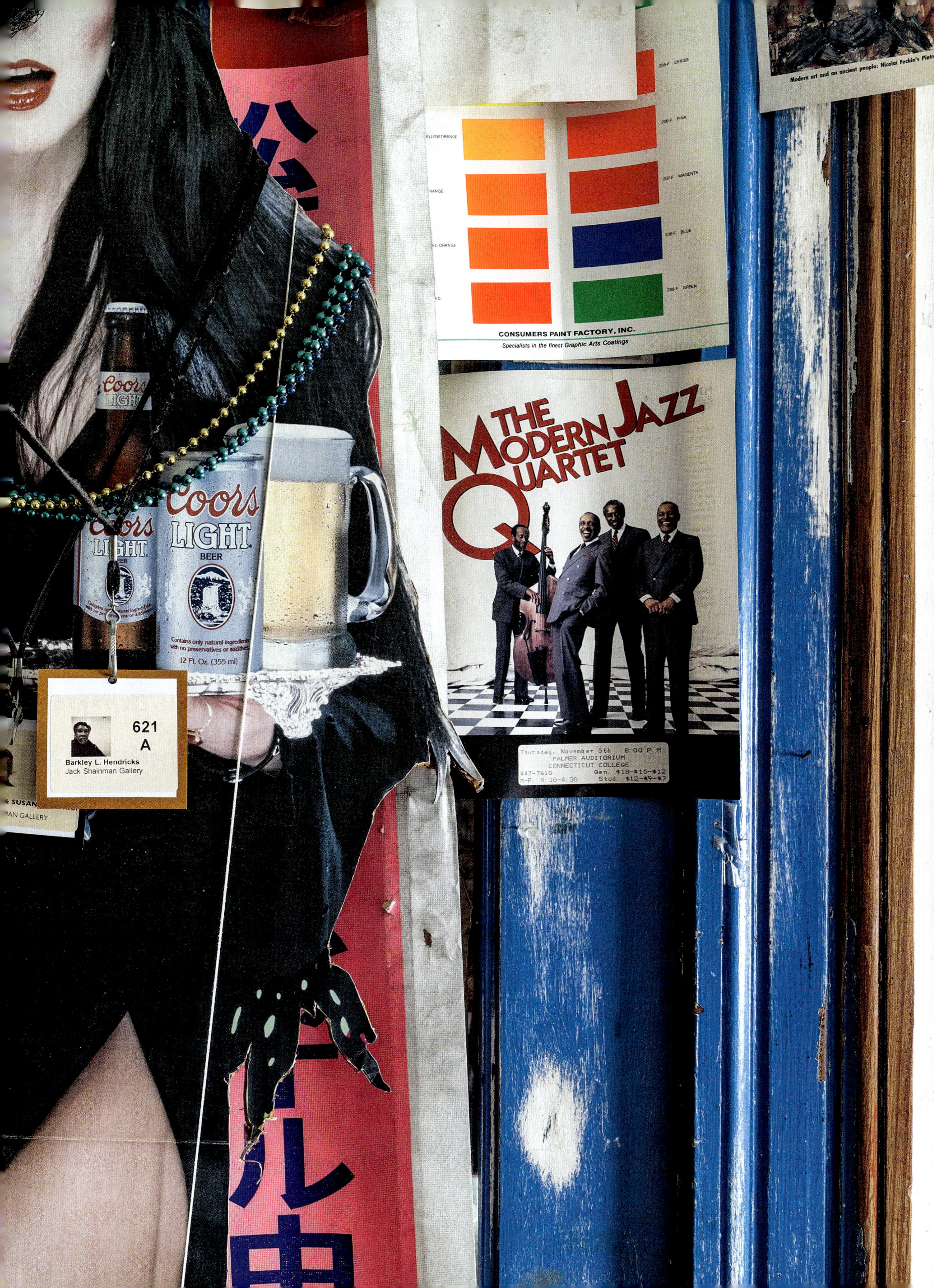
Modern art and an ancient people: Nicolai Fechin's Pietro
205-F CERISE
206-F PINK
207-F MAGENTA
208-F BLUE
209-F GREEN
CONSUMERS PAINT FACTORY, INC.
Specialists in the finest Graphic Arts Coatings
THE MODERN JAZZ QUARTET
Thursday, November 5th 8:00 P.M.
PALMER AUDITORIUM
CONNECTICUT COLLEGE
447-7610 Gen. $18-$15-$12
M-F, 9:30-4:30 Stud. $12-$9-$7
Coors LIGHT BEER
12 Fl. Oz. (355 ml)
621
A
Barkley L. Hendricks
Jack Shainman Gallery

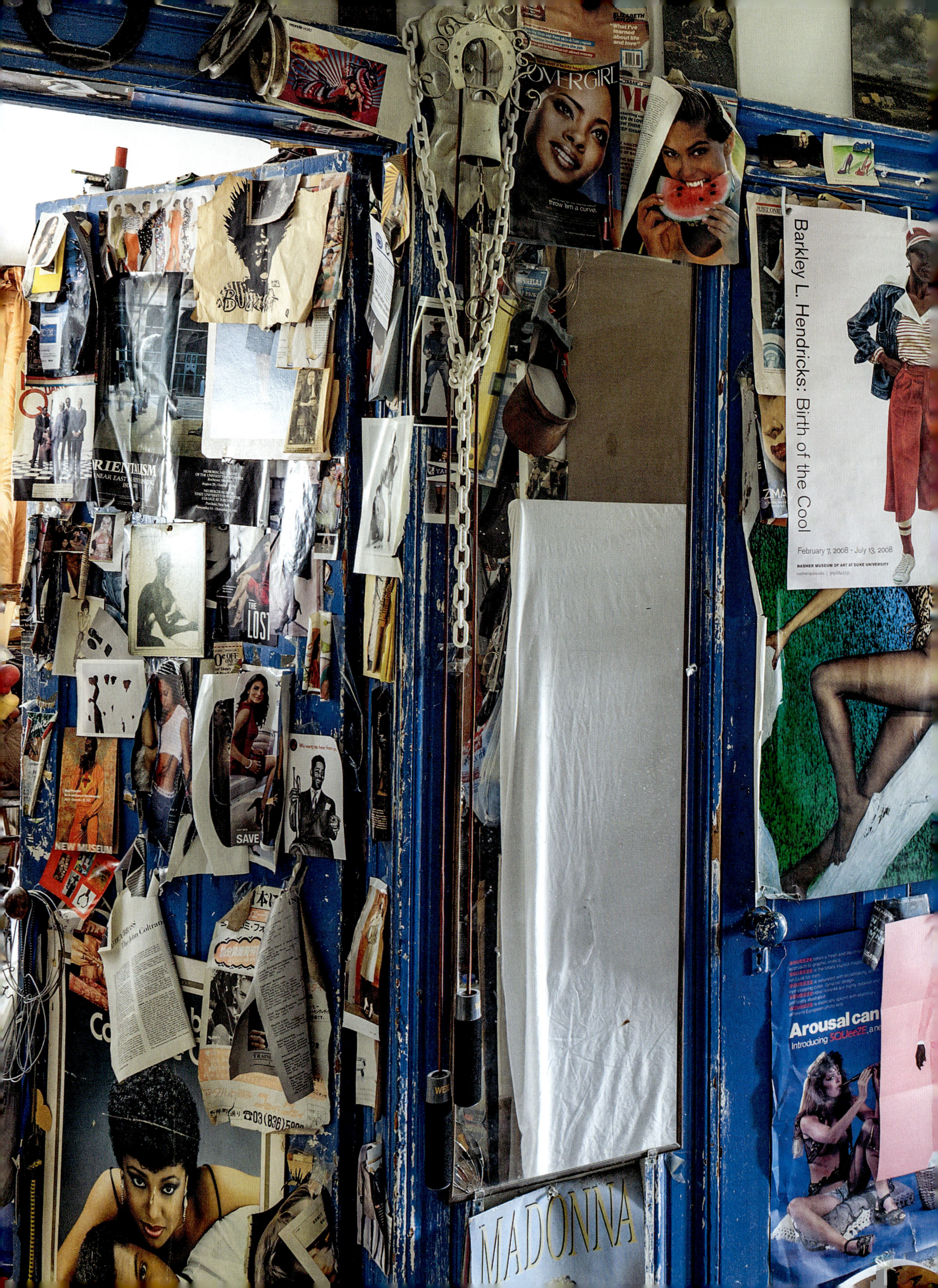

OVERGIRL
throw 'em a curve.
Barkley L. Hendricks: Birth of the Cool
February 7, 2008 - July 13, 2008
NASHER MUSEUM OF ART AT DUKE UNIVERSITY
RIENTALISM
NEAR EAST
LOST
SAVE
NEW MUSEUM
Arousal can
MADONNA

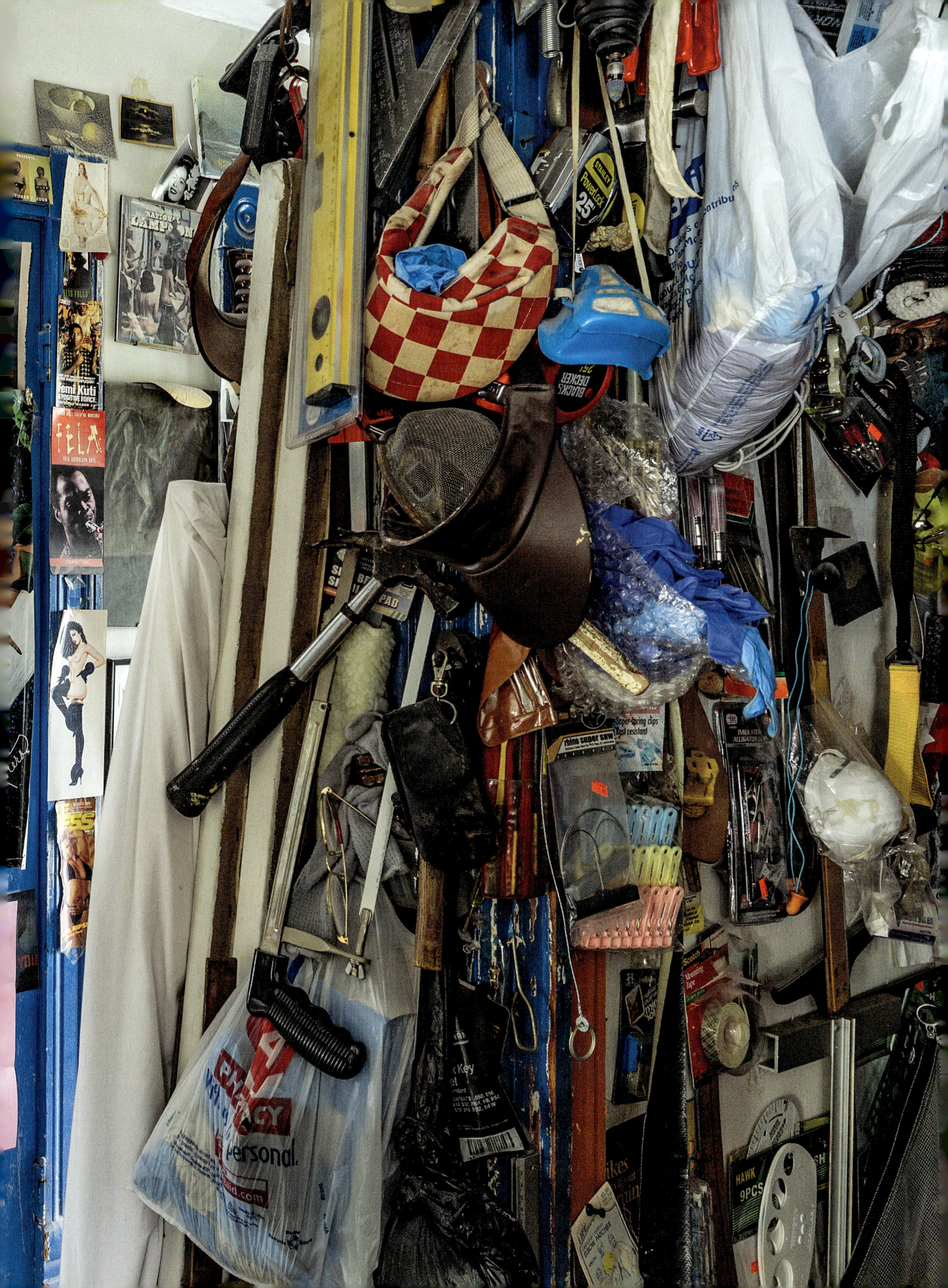
STANLEY
PowerLock
25'
Femi Kuti
& POSITIVE FORCE
FELA
HAWK
9PCS
personal.

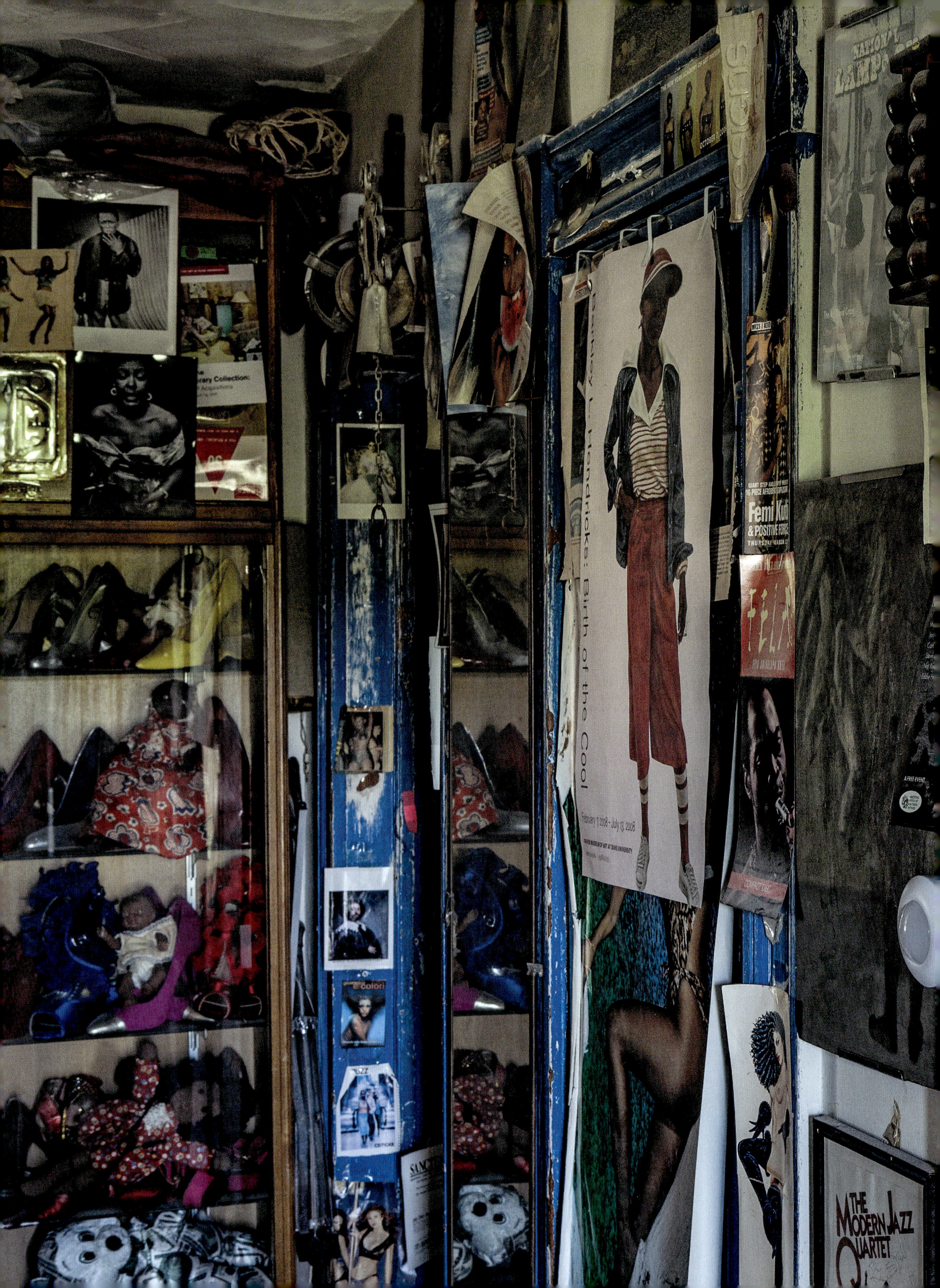

Hendricks: Birth of the Cool
July 13, 2008
Femi Kuti
& POSITIVE FORCE
THE MODERN JAZZ QUARTET

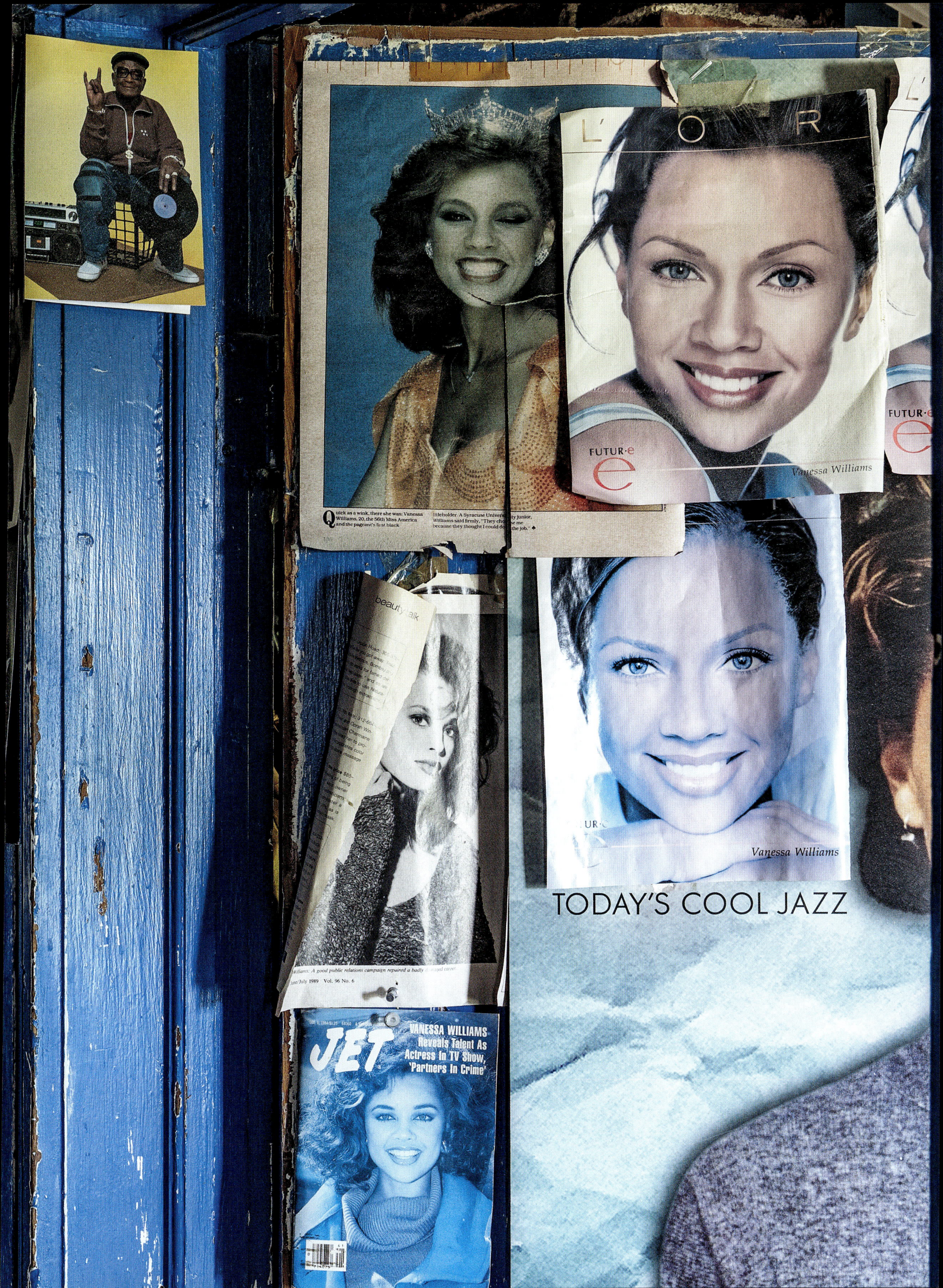
L' O R
FUTUR·e
e
Vanessa Williams
TODAY'S COOL JAZZ
JET
VANESSA WILLIAMS
Reveals Talent As
Actress In TV Show,
'Partners In Crime'

# Don’t play with grandmas guns

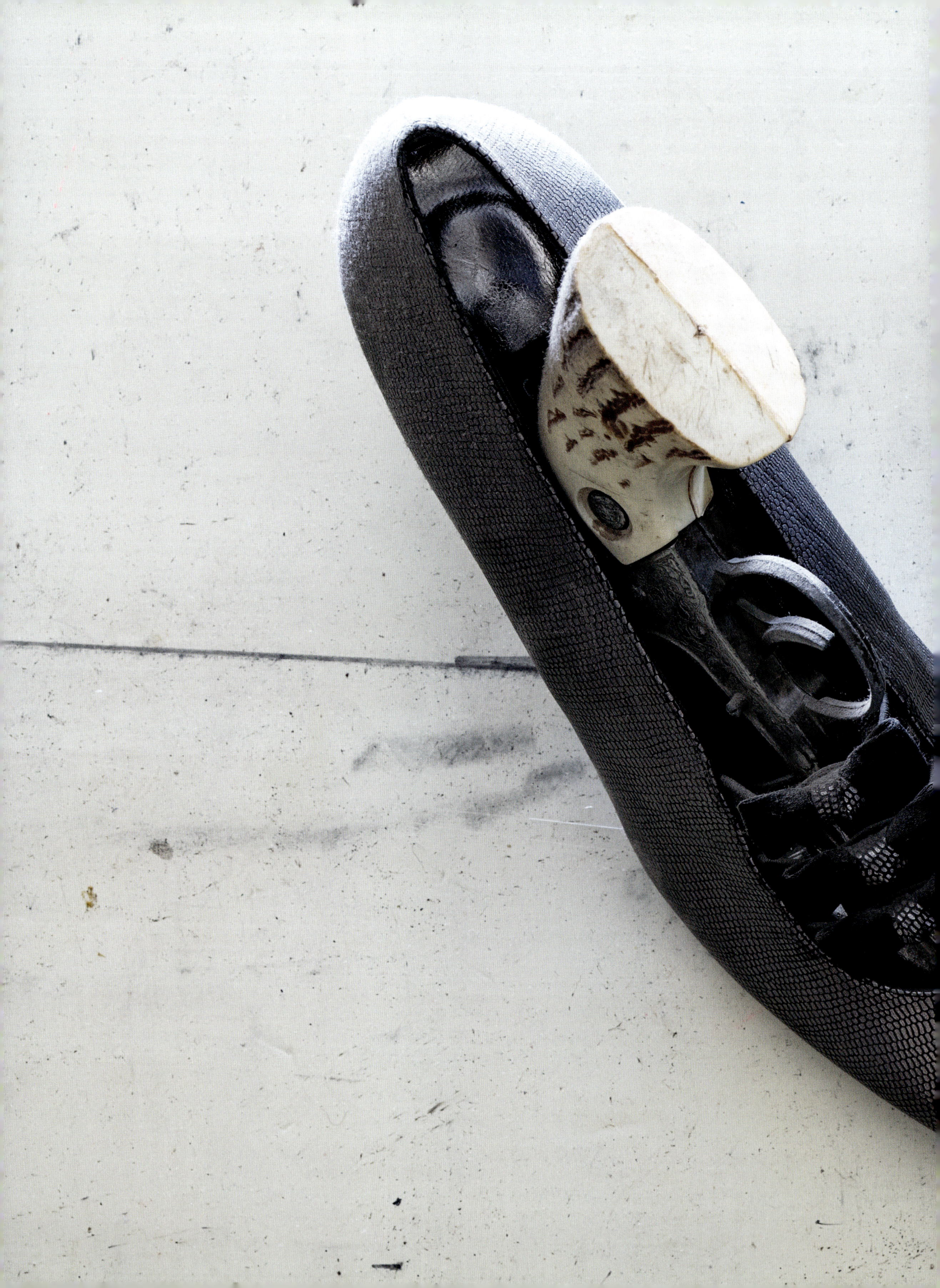

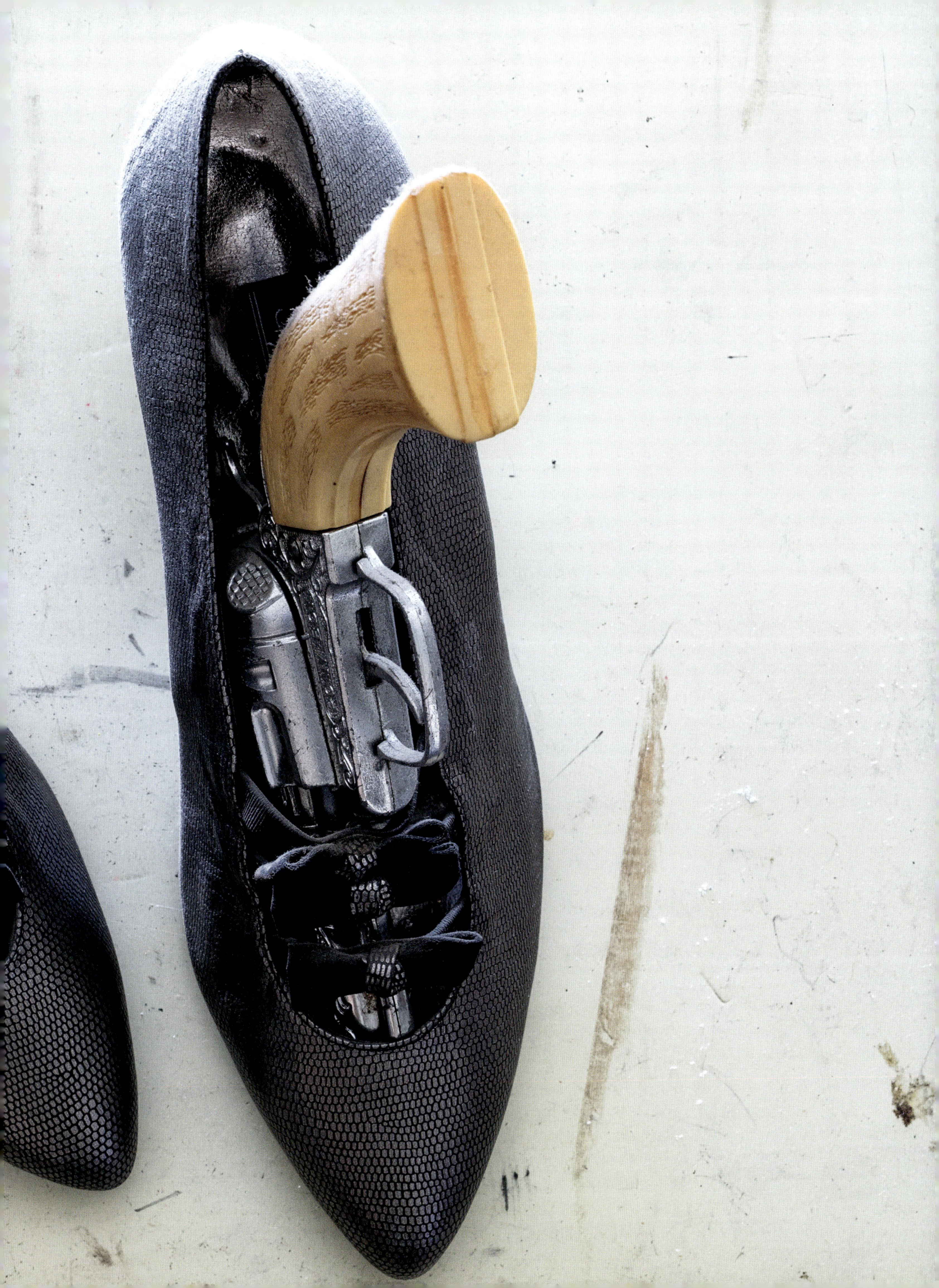

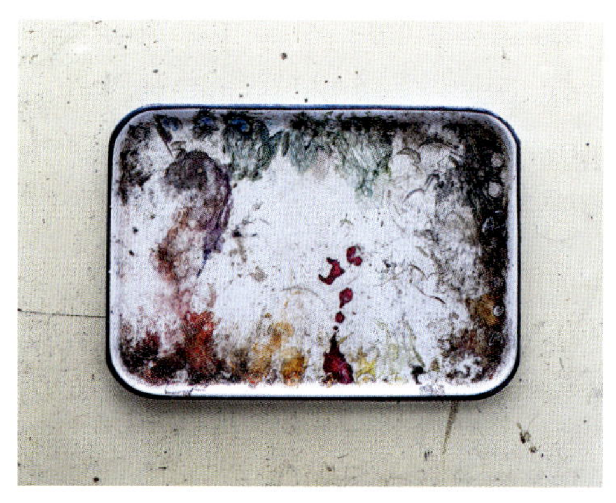

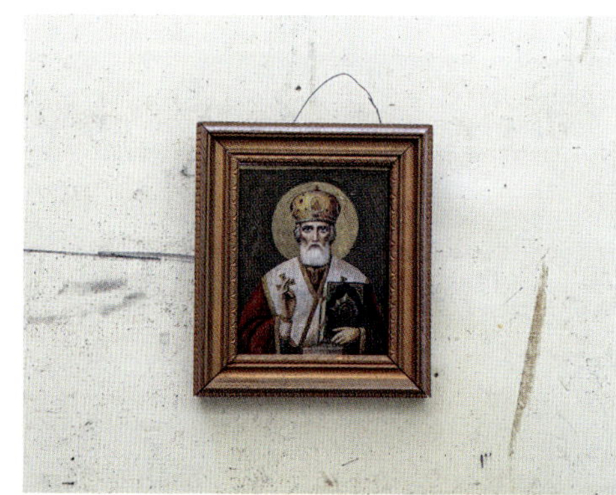

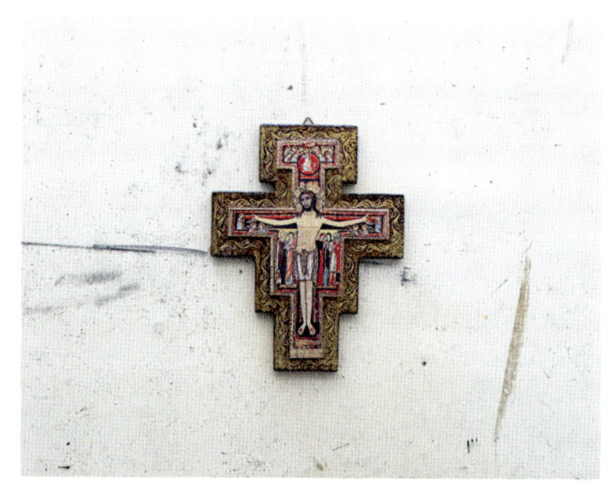

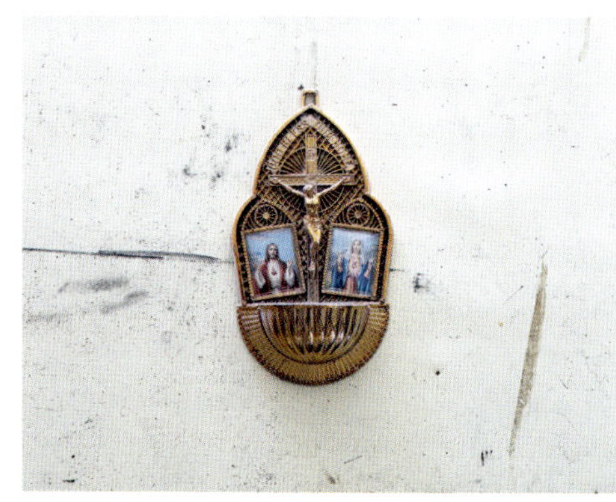

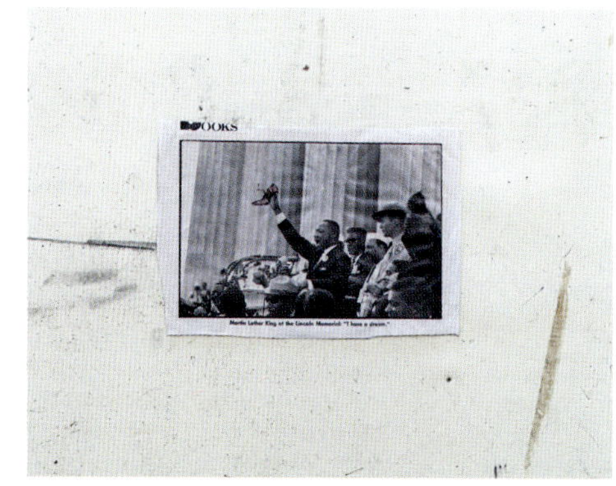

OOKS
Martin Luther King at the Lincoln Memorial: "I have a dream."

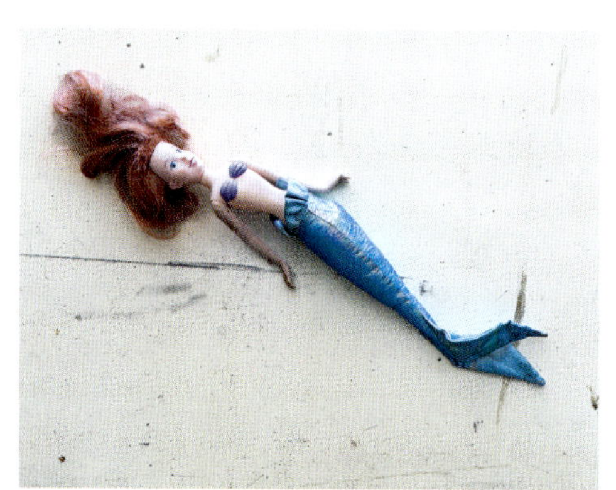

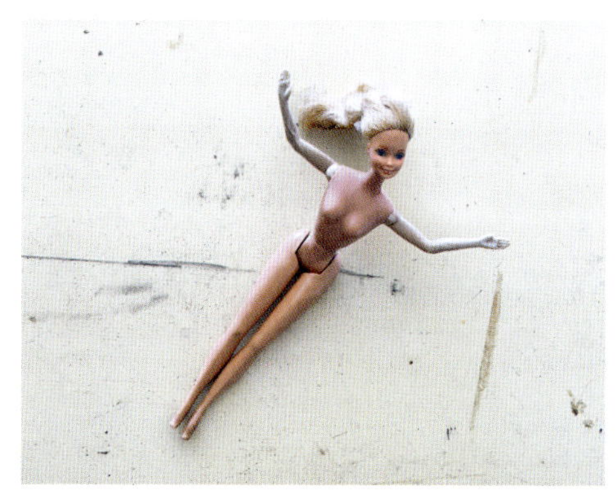

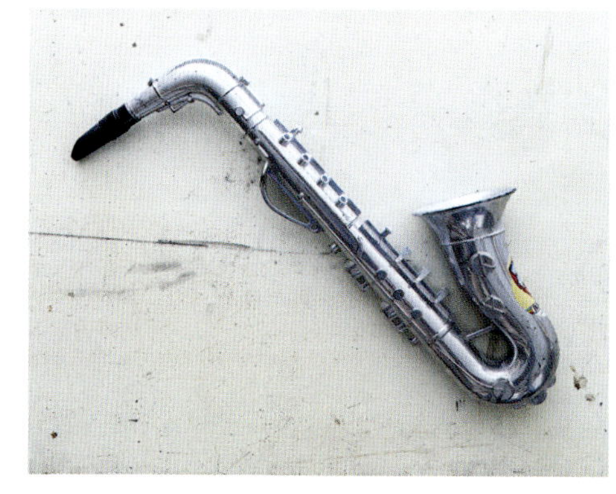

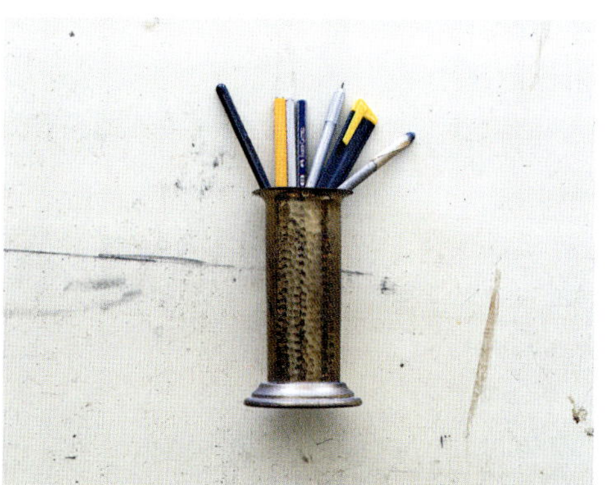

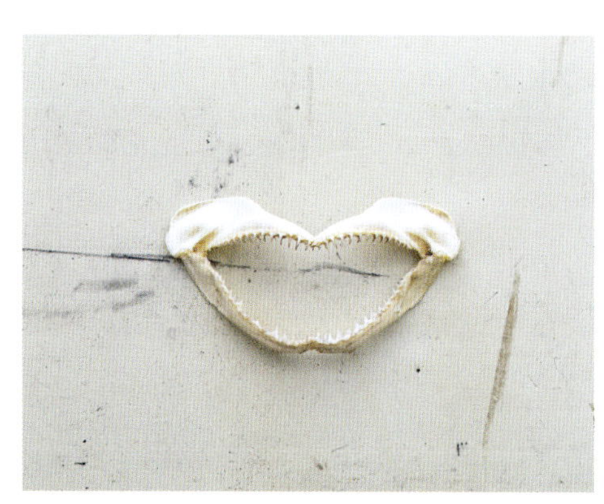

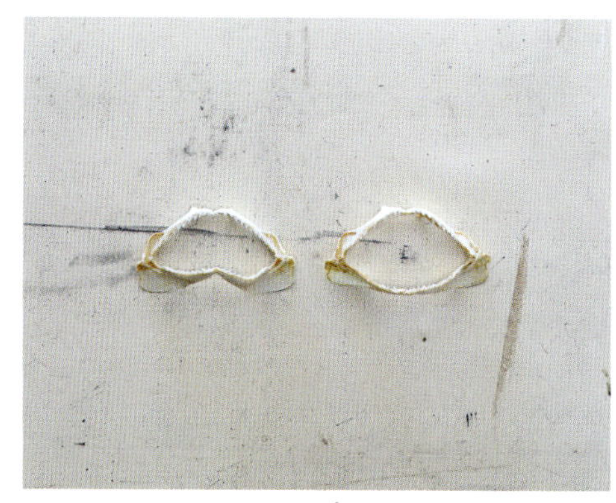

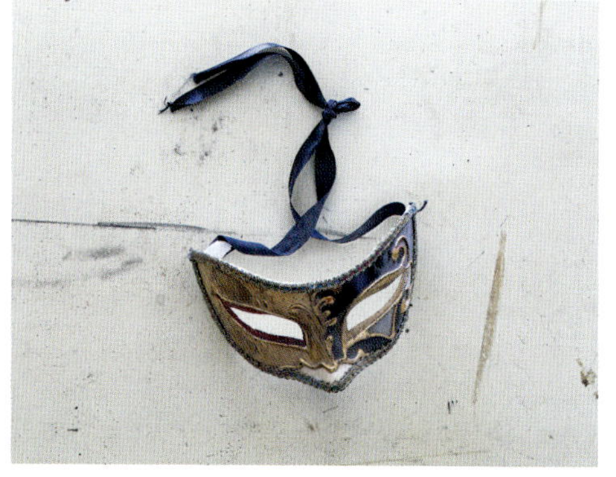

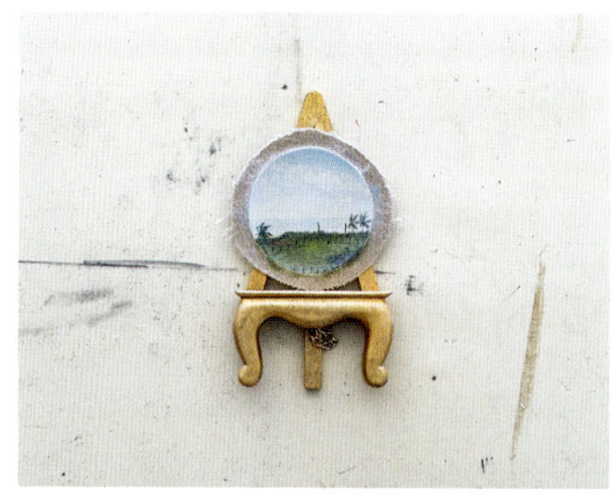

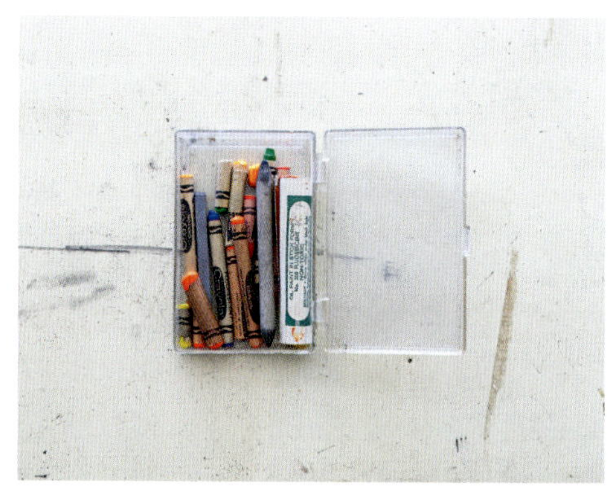

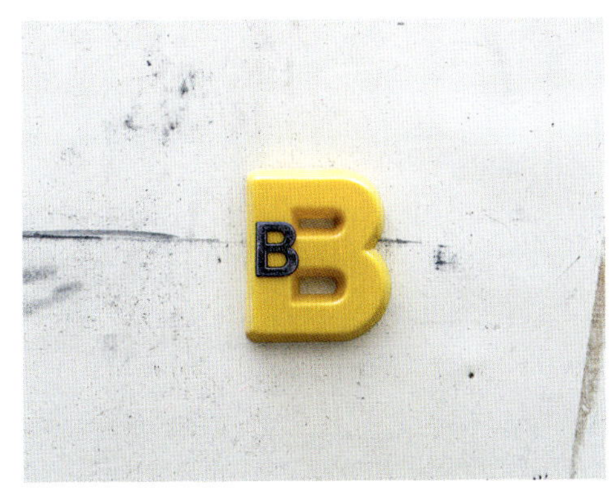
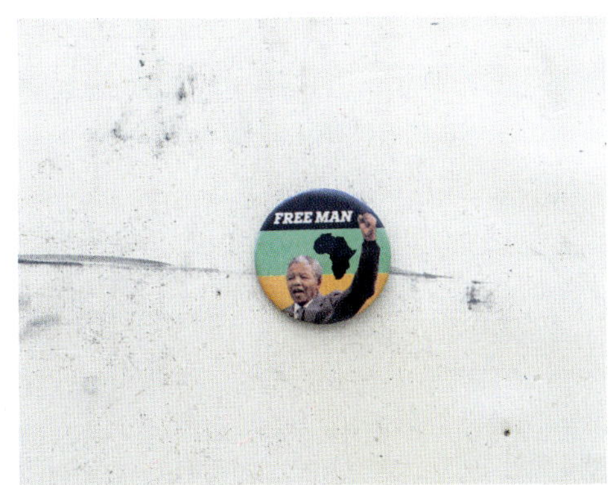
FREE MAN
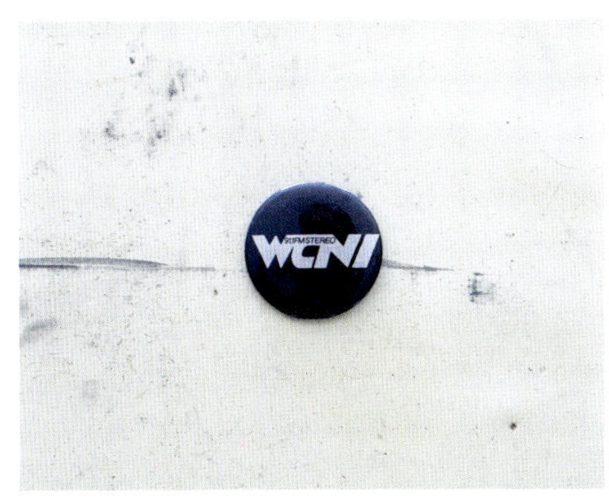
WCNI
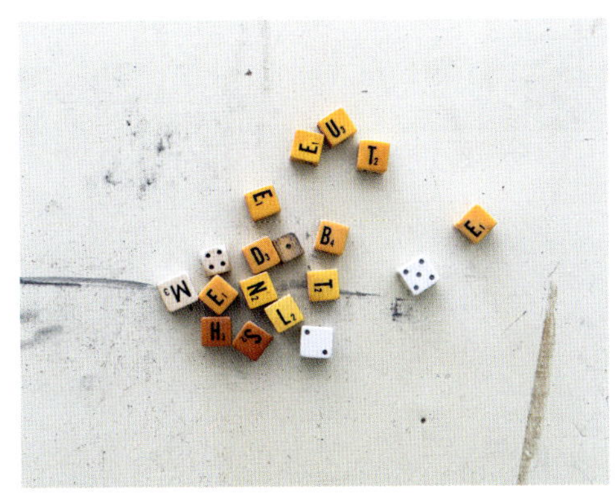
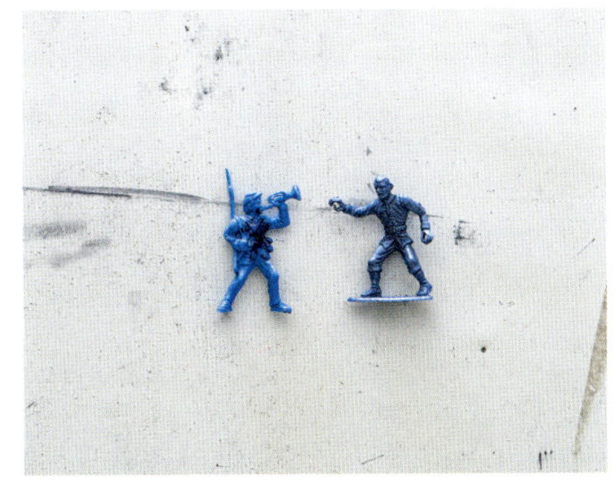
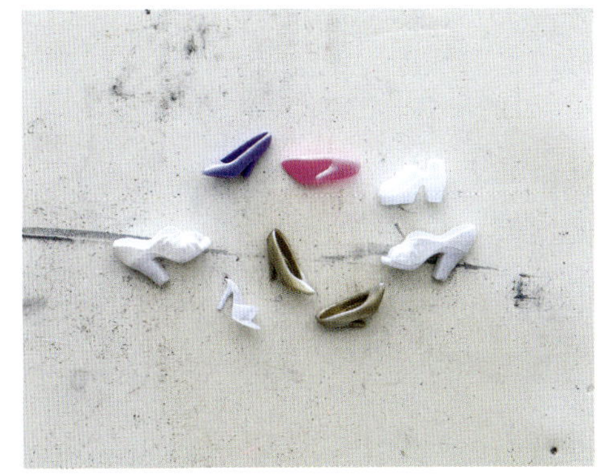
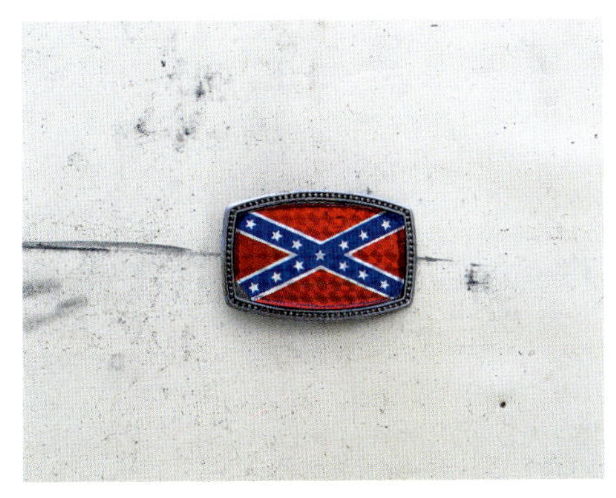
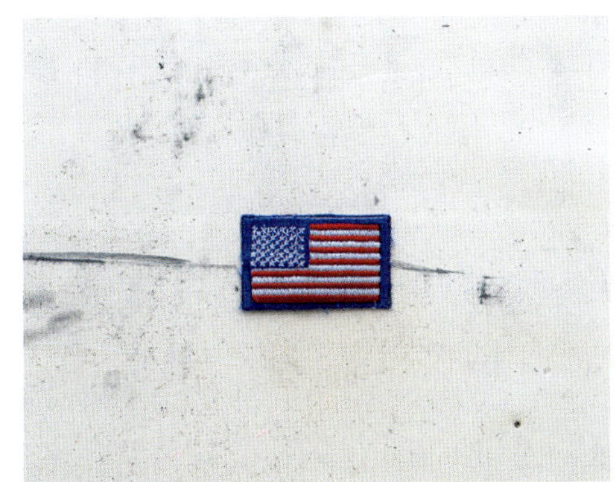
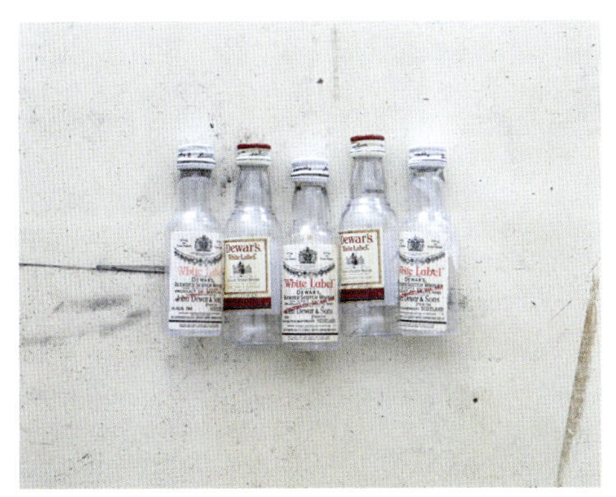
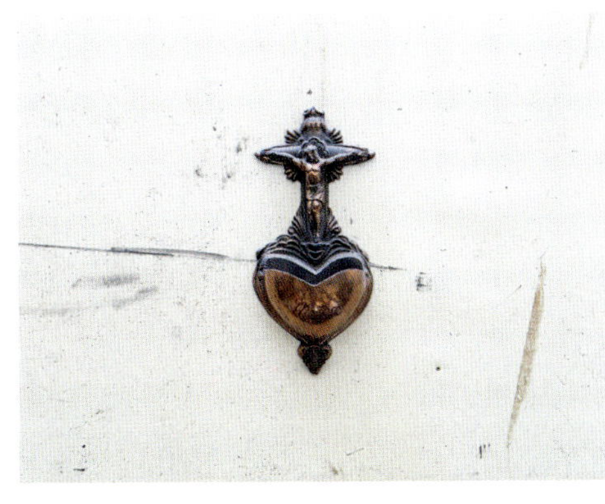
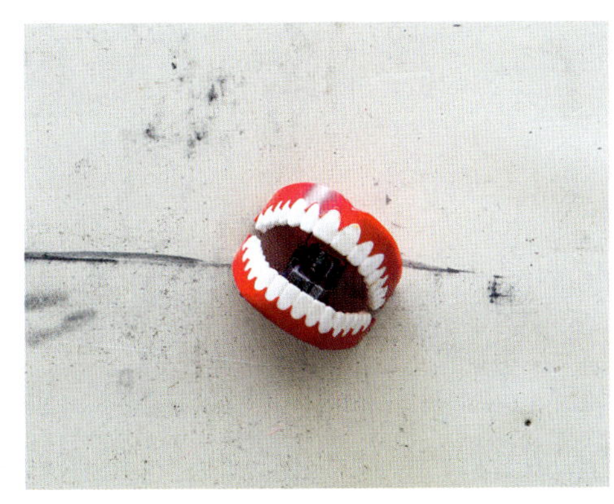
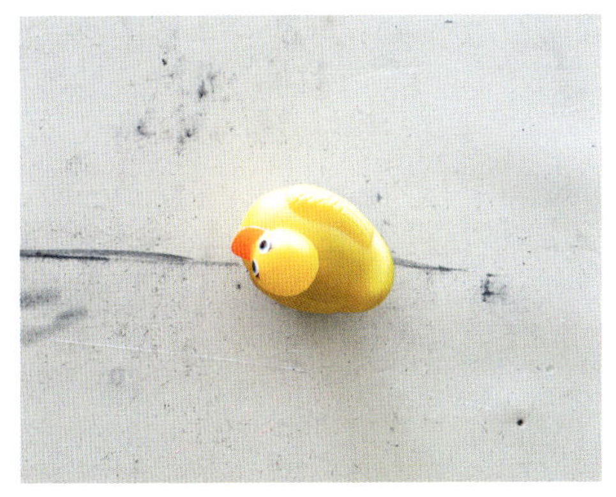
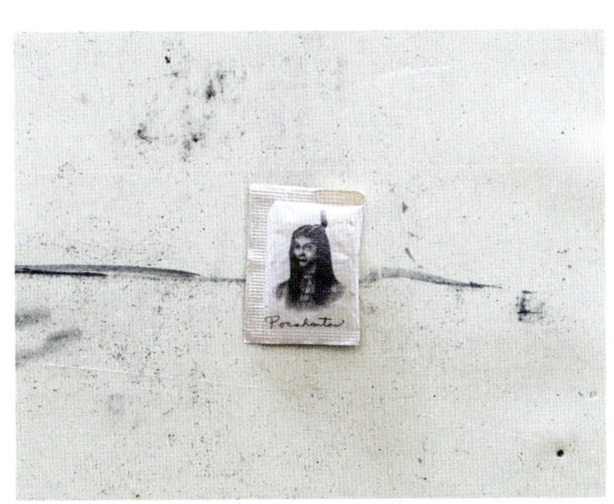

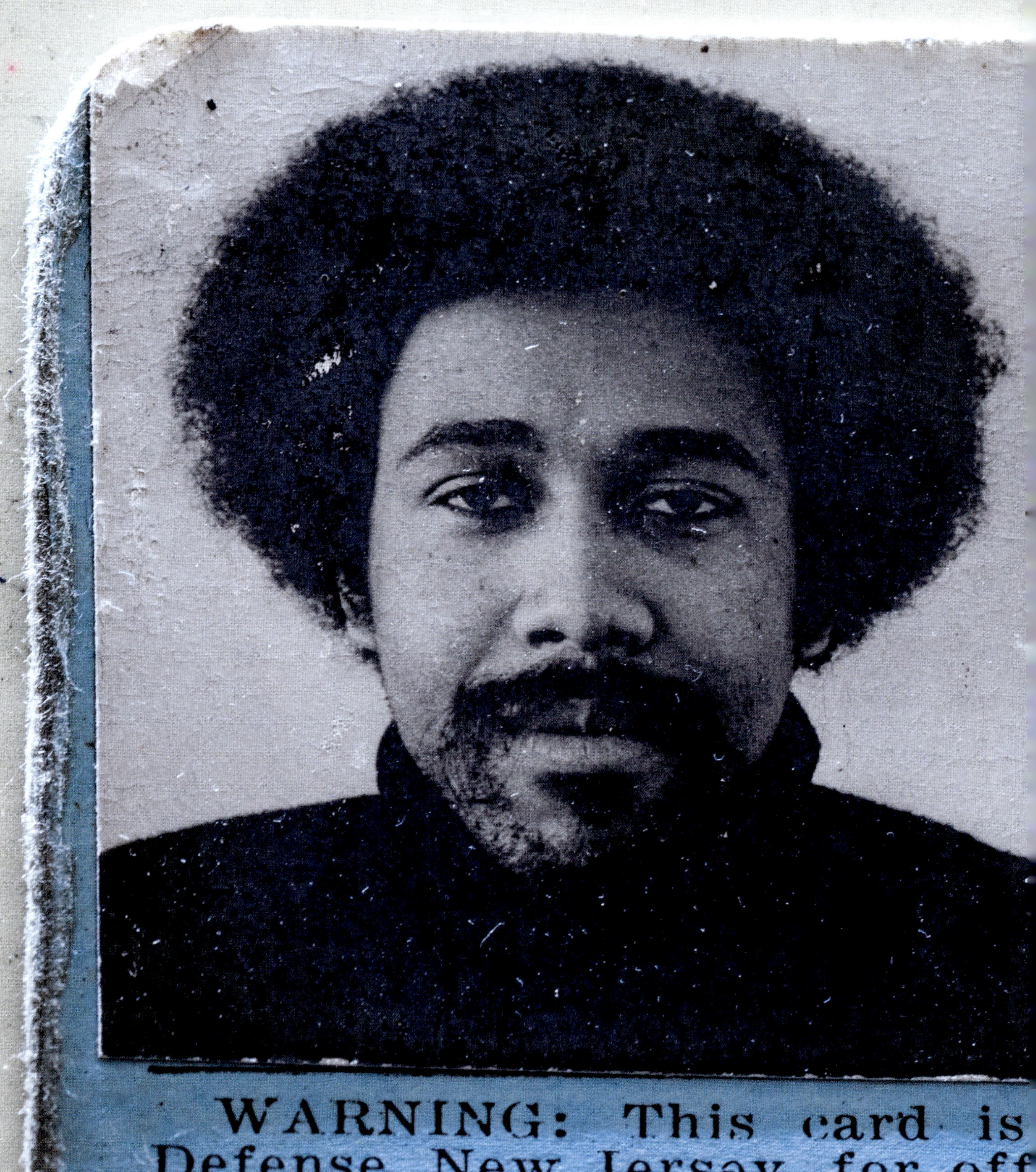
WARNING: This card is
Defense, New Jersey, for off
issued. Its use by any othe
finder will return promptly
ment of Defense, Armory,

## IDENTIFYING DATA

Height 68"

Weight 166

Hair Black

Eyes Brown

Date of Birth 16Apr45

ssued by the Department of
al use of the person to whom
person is unlawful. If found,
› The Chief of Staff, Depart-
mory Drive, Trenton, N. J.

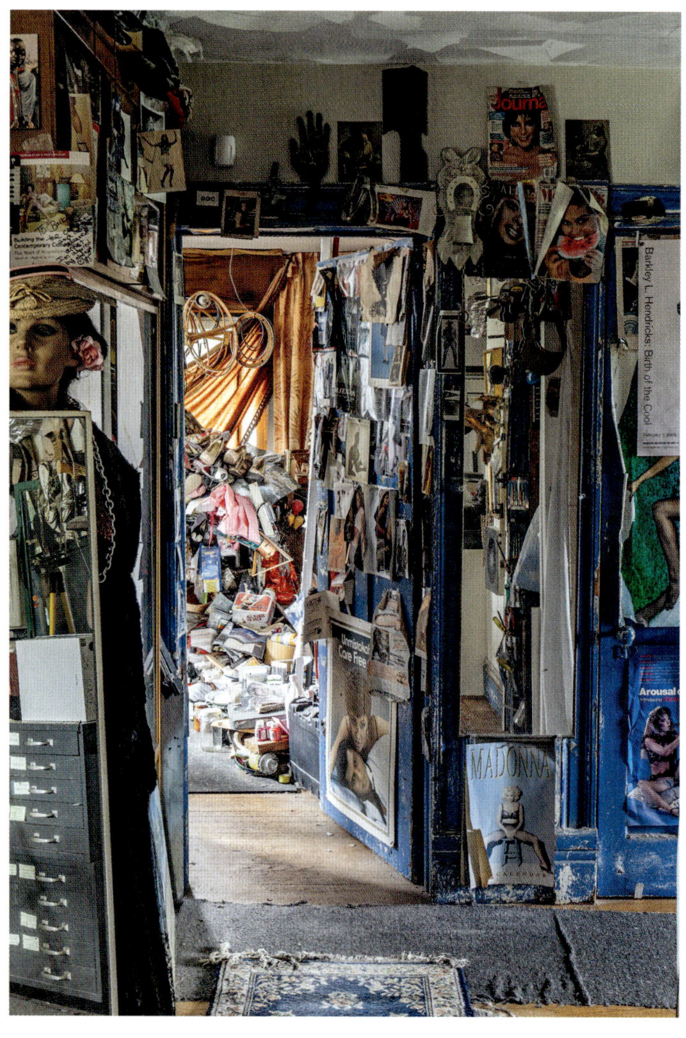
Barkley L. Hendricks: Birth of the Cool
MADONNA

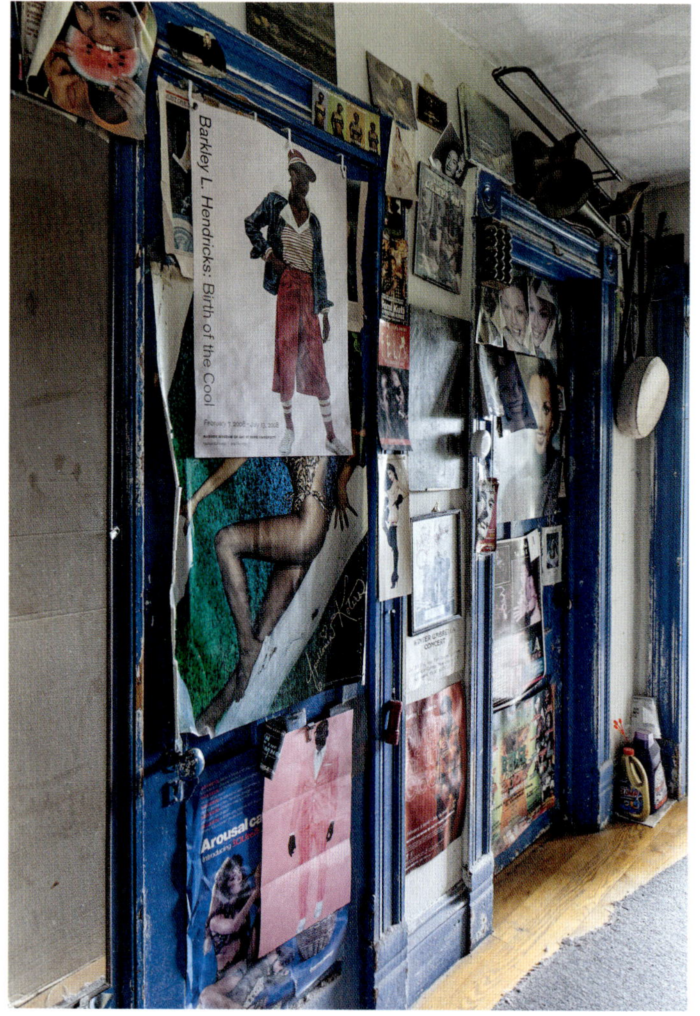
Barkley L. Hendricks: Birth of the Cool

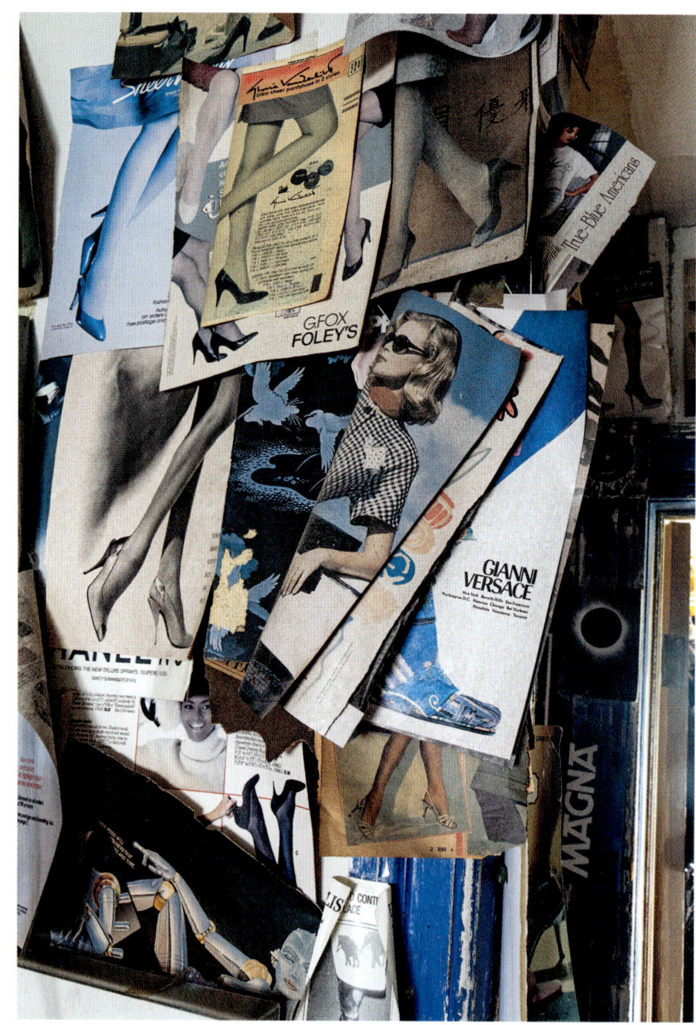
G.FOX
FOLEY'S
GIANNI
VERSACE
MAGNA

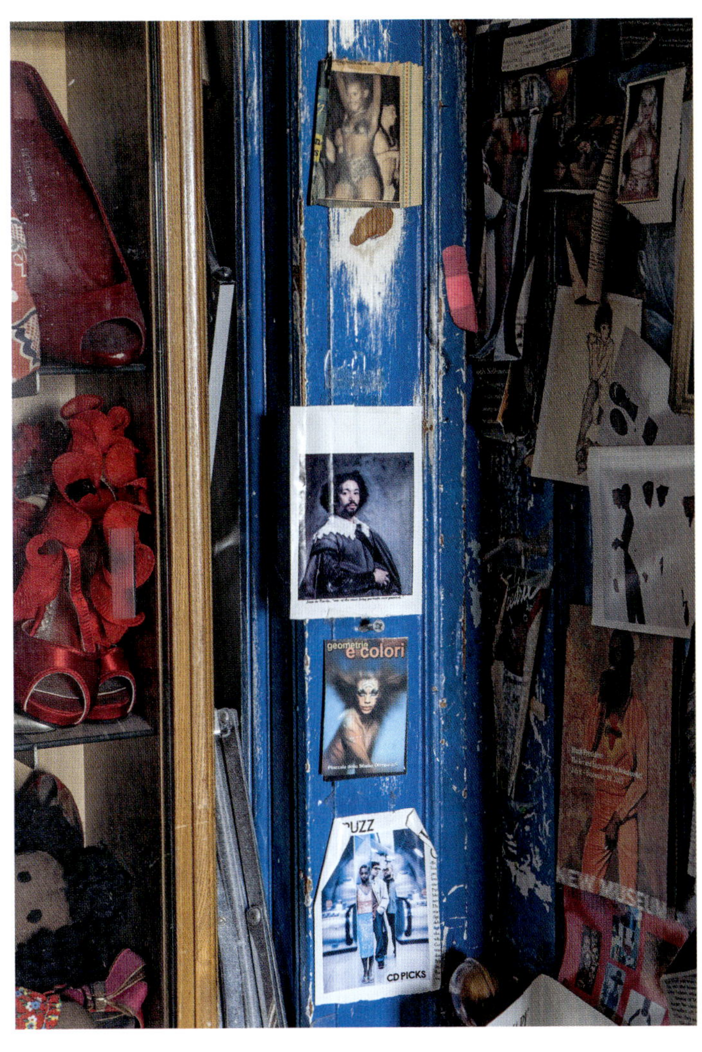
geometrie e colori
PUZZ
CD PICKS
NEW MUSEUM

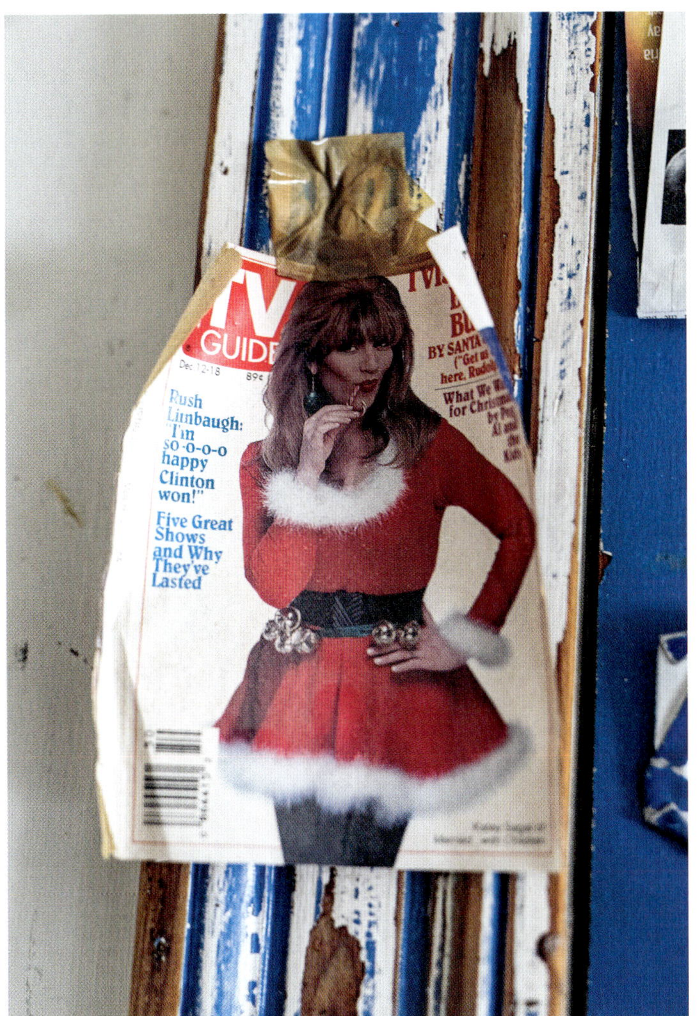
TV GUIDE
Dec 12-18
89¢
BY SANTA
Rush Limbaugh: "I'm so-o-o-o happy Clinton won!"
Five Great Shows and Why They've Lasted

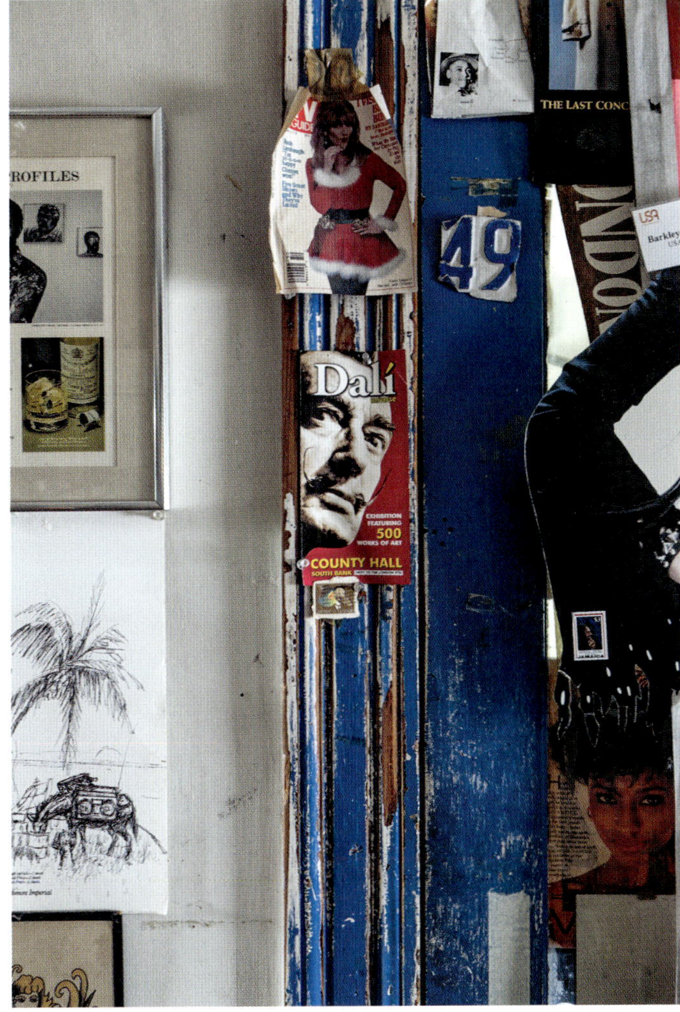
49
Dalí
EXHIBITION FEATURING
500
WORKS OF ART
COUNTY HALL
SOUTH BANK

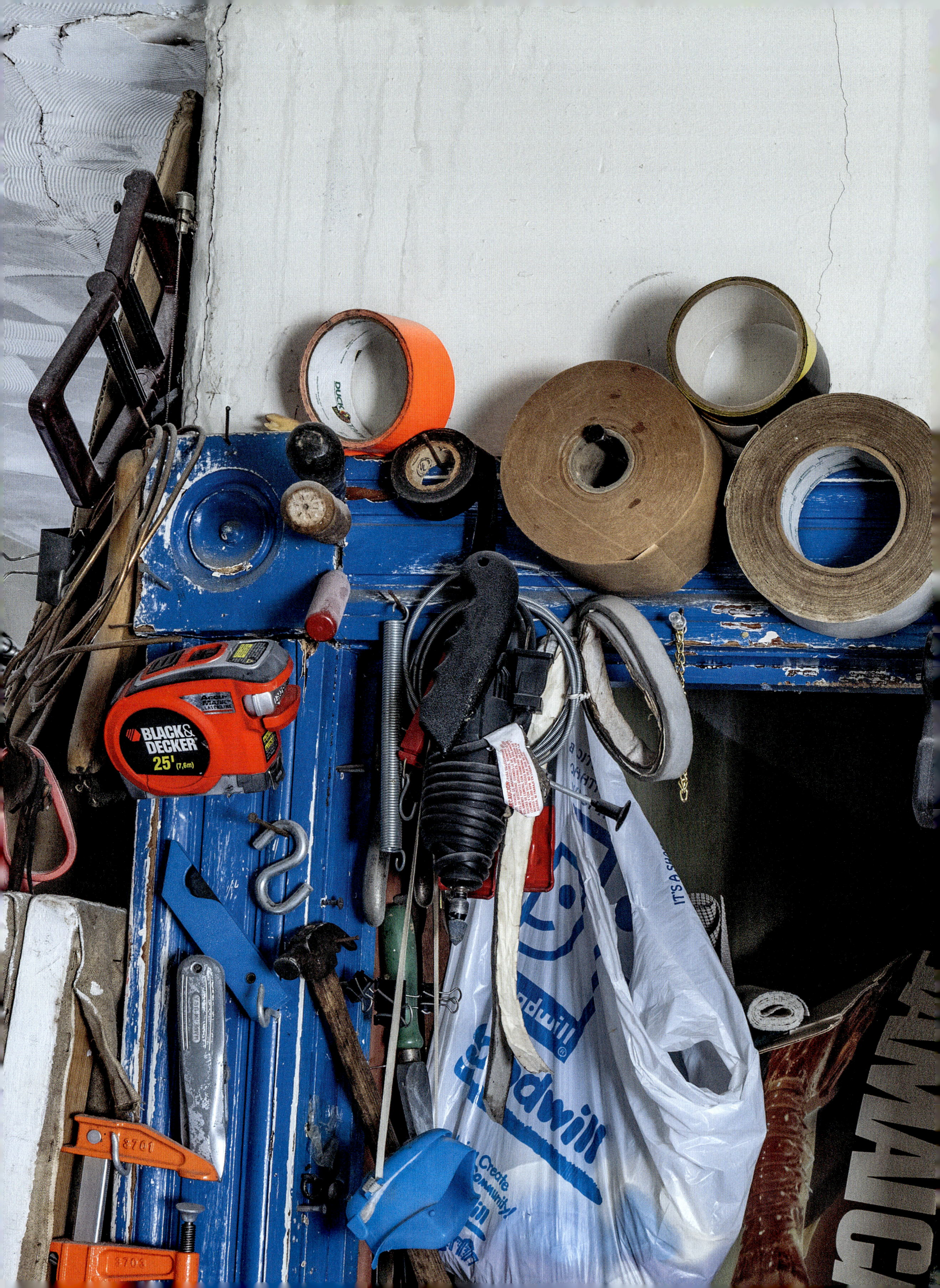

BLACK&DECKER
25' (7,6m)

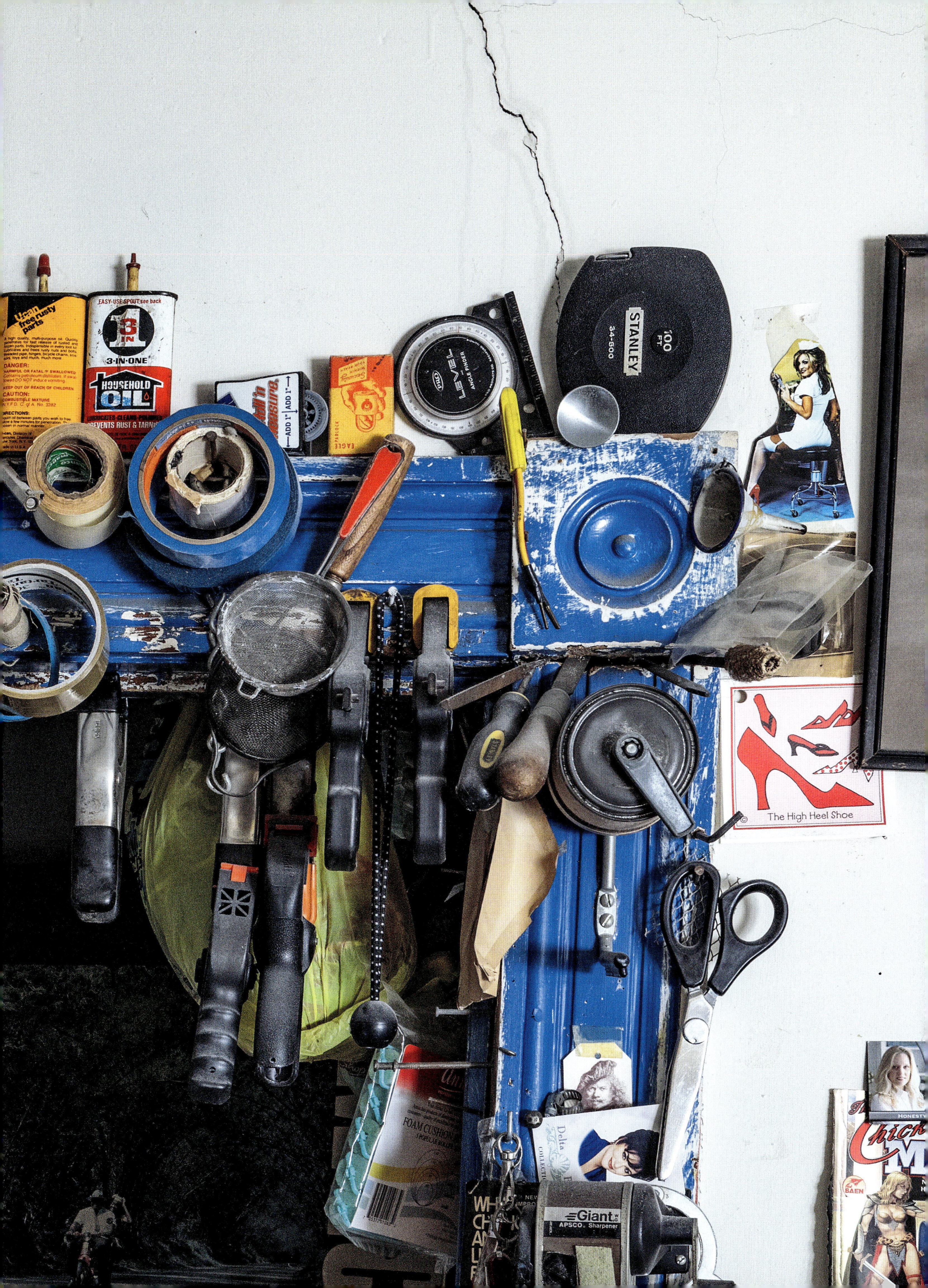
Ucan free rusty parts
EASY-USE SPOUT see back
3-IN-ONE
HOUSEHOLD OIL
LEVEL
ANGLE FINDER
STANLEY
100 FT
34-600
EAGLE
The High Heel Shoe
FOAM CUSHION
Giant
APSCO. Sharpener
BAEN
HONESTY

**In many circles Helmut and I are considered pornographers. Not to mention sexists. In my own defense I wish only to record the moments I love.**

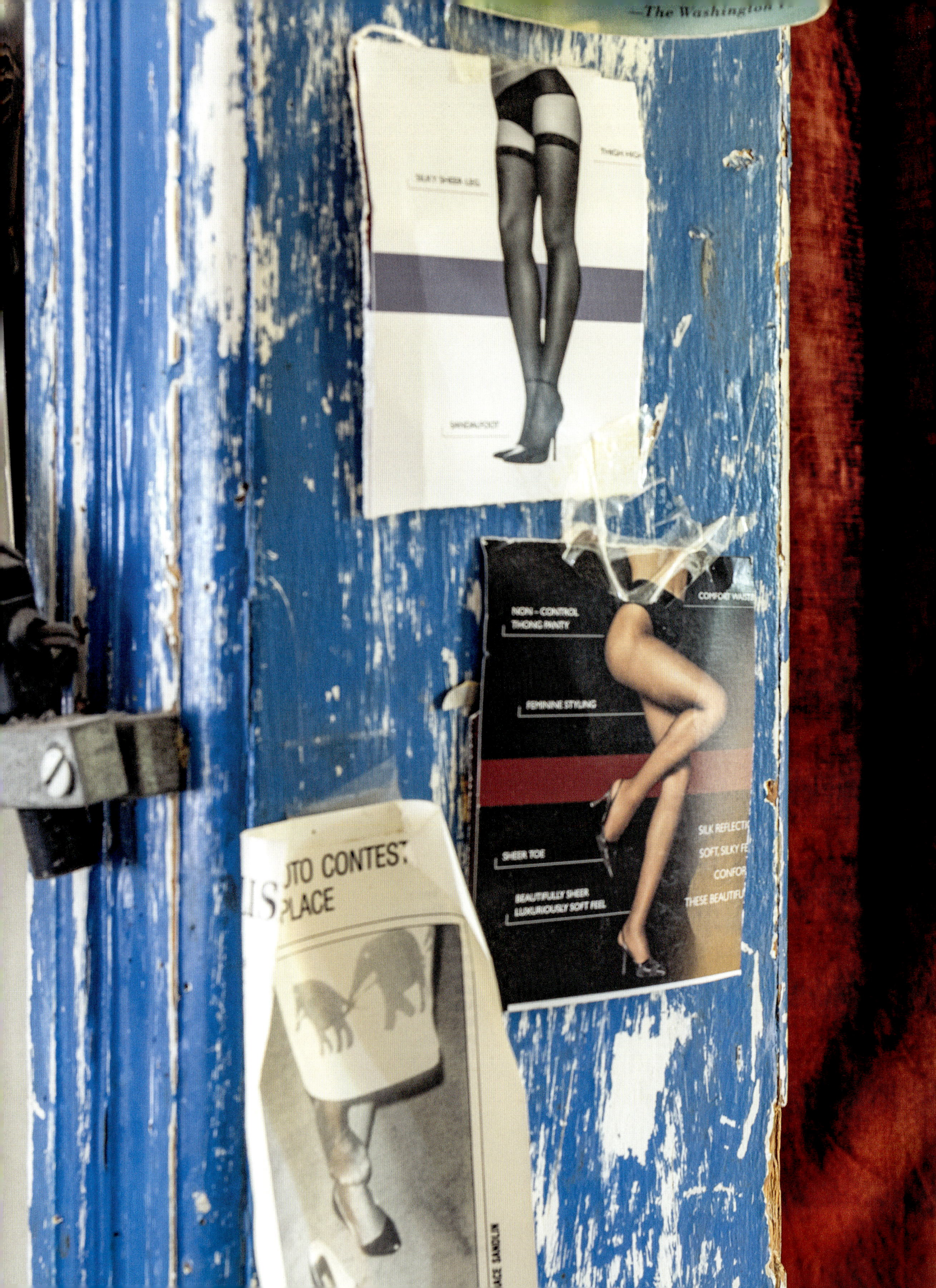

—The Washington
SILKY SHEER LEG
SANDALFOOT
NON-CONTROL
THONG PANTY
FEMININE STYLING
SHEER TOE
BEAUTIFULLY SHEER
LUXURIOUSLY SOFT FEEL
PLACE

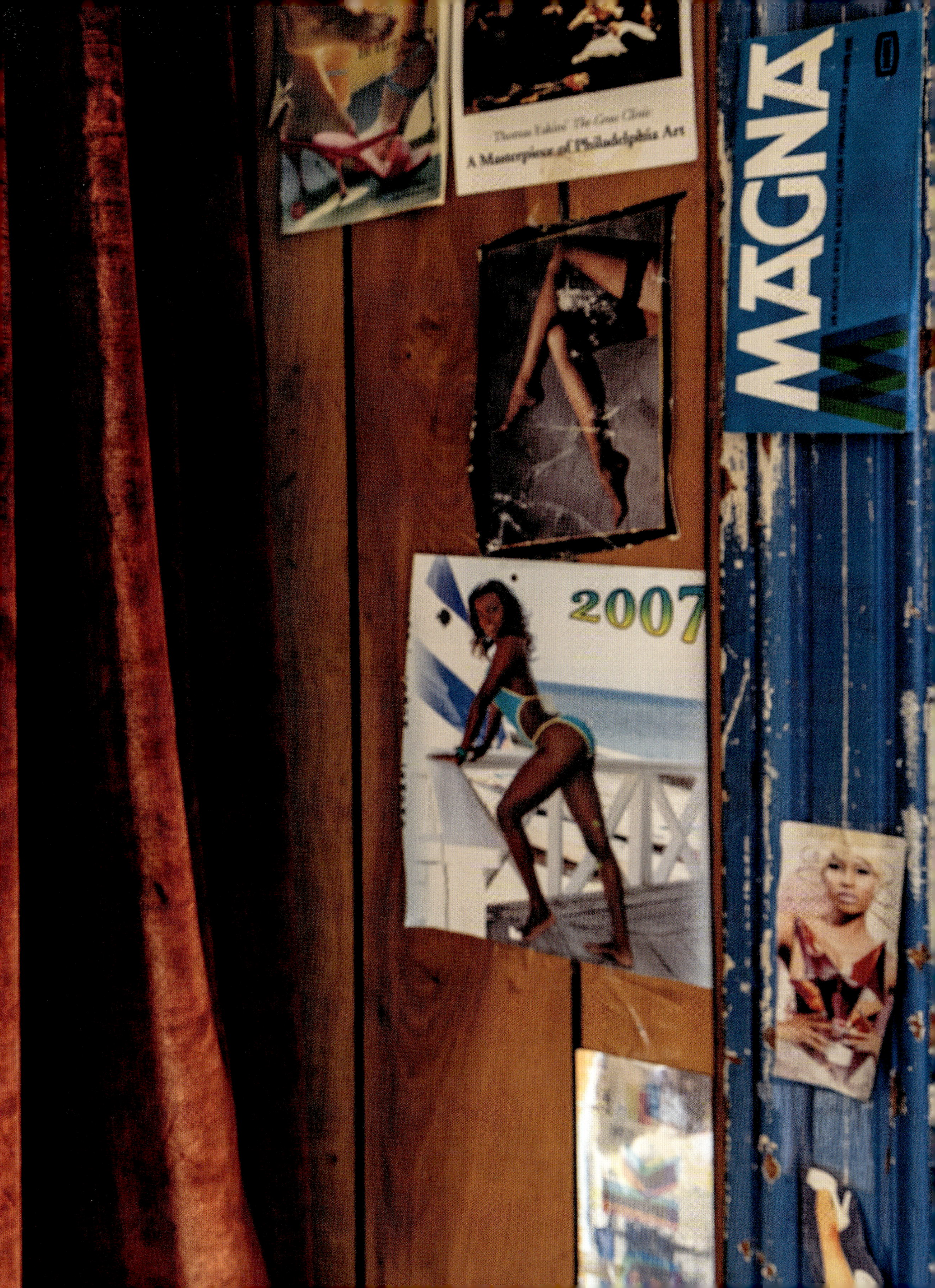
Thomas Eakins' The Gross Clinic
A Masterpiece of Philadelphia Art
2007
MAGNA

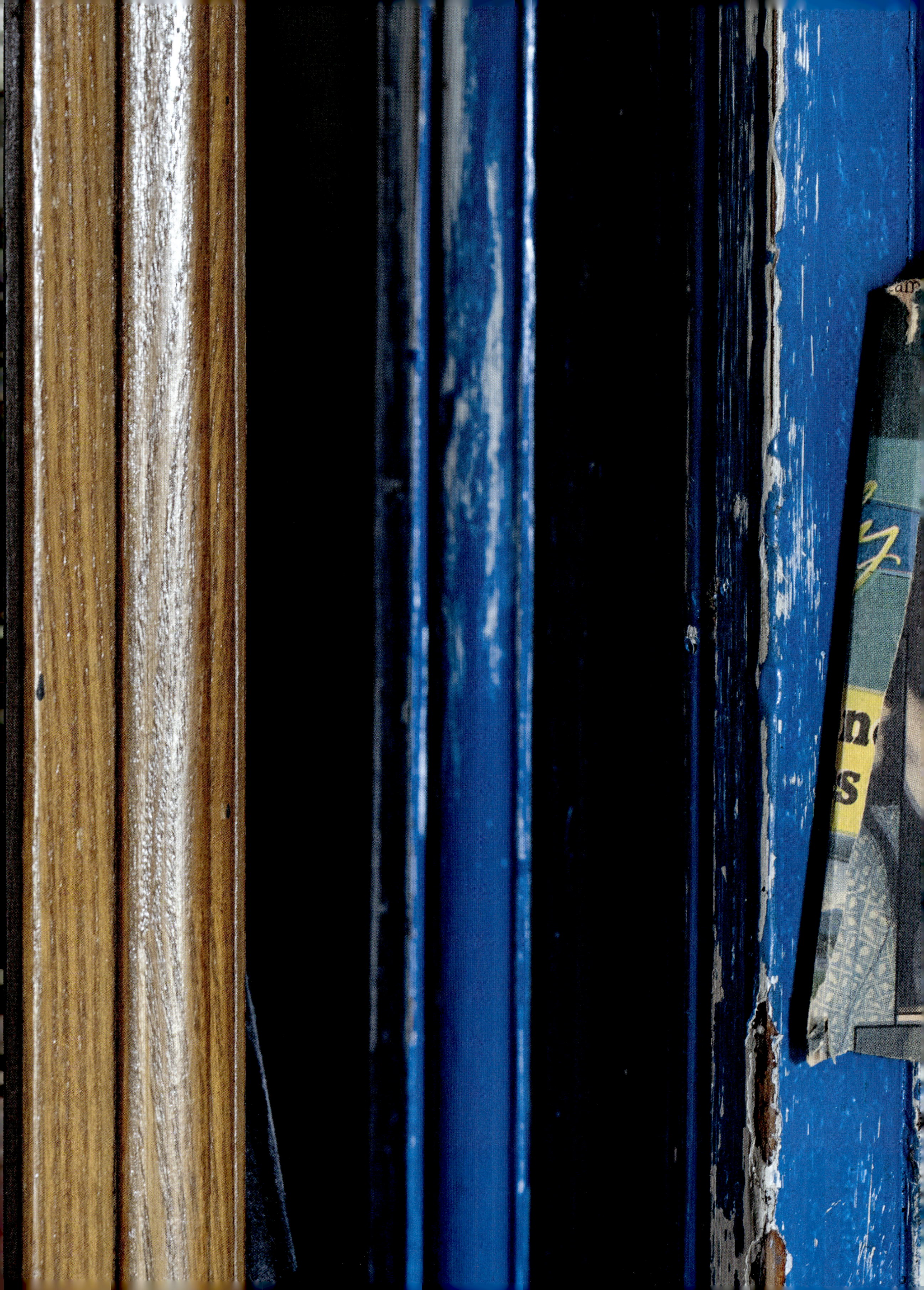

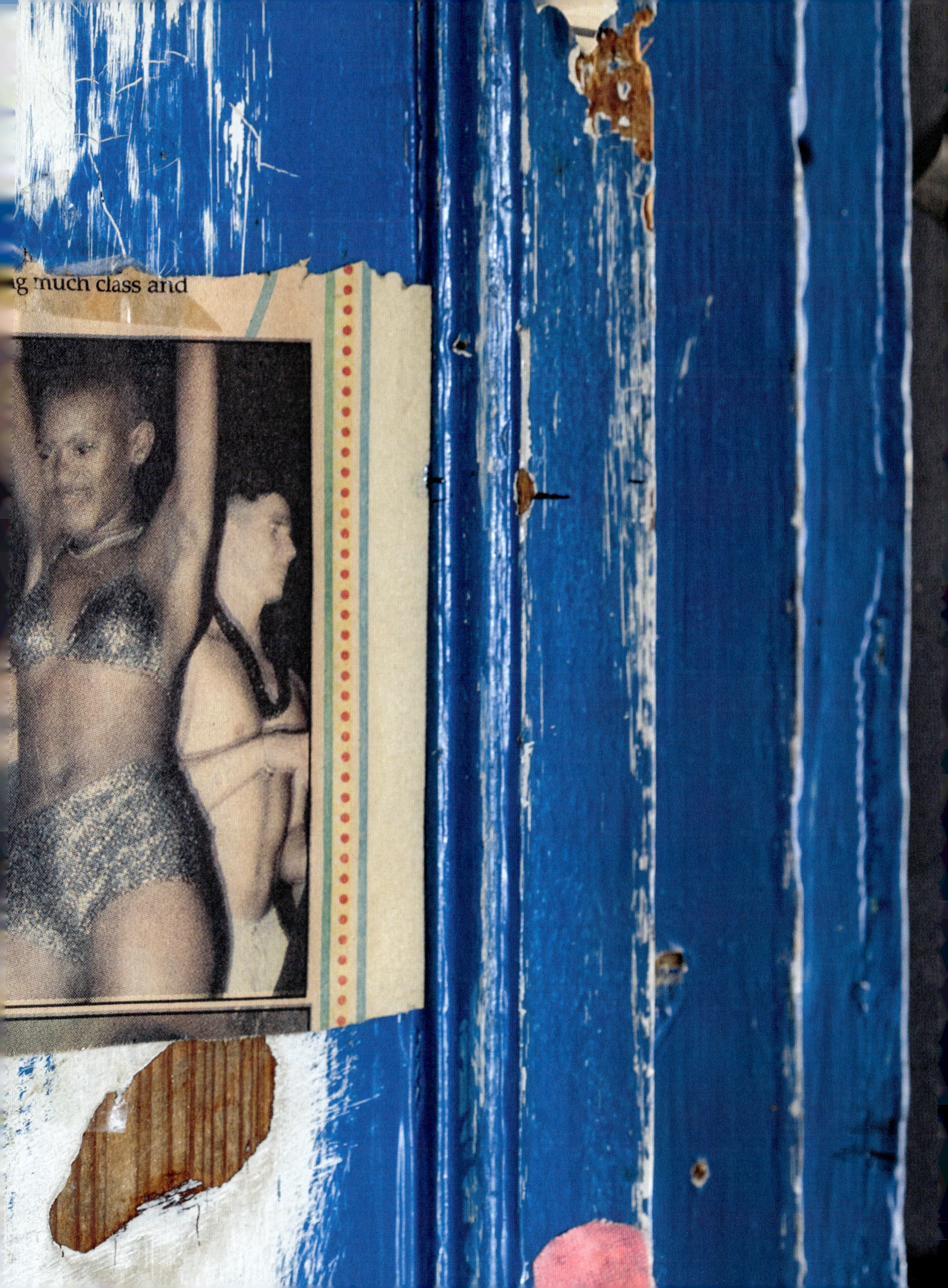
g much class and

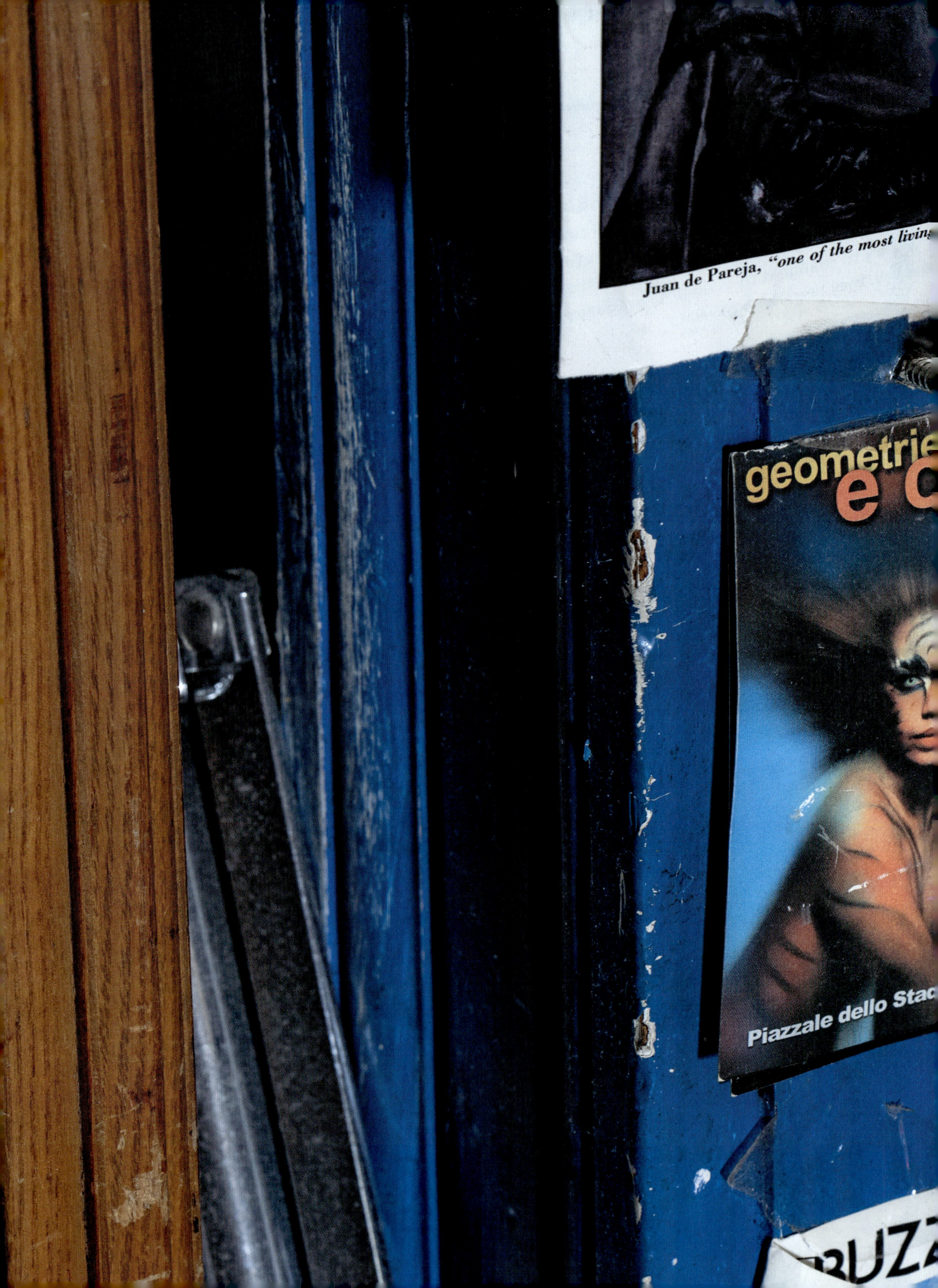

Juan de Pareja, "one of the most living
geometrie
e c
Piazzale dello Stac
BUZZ

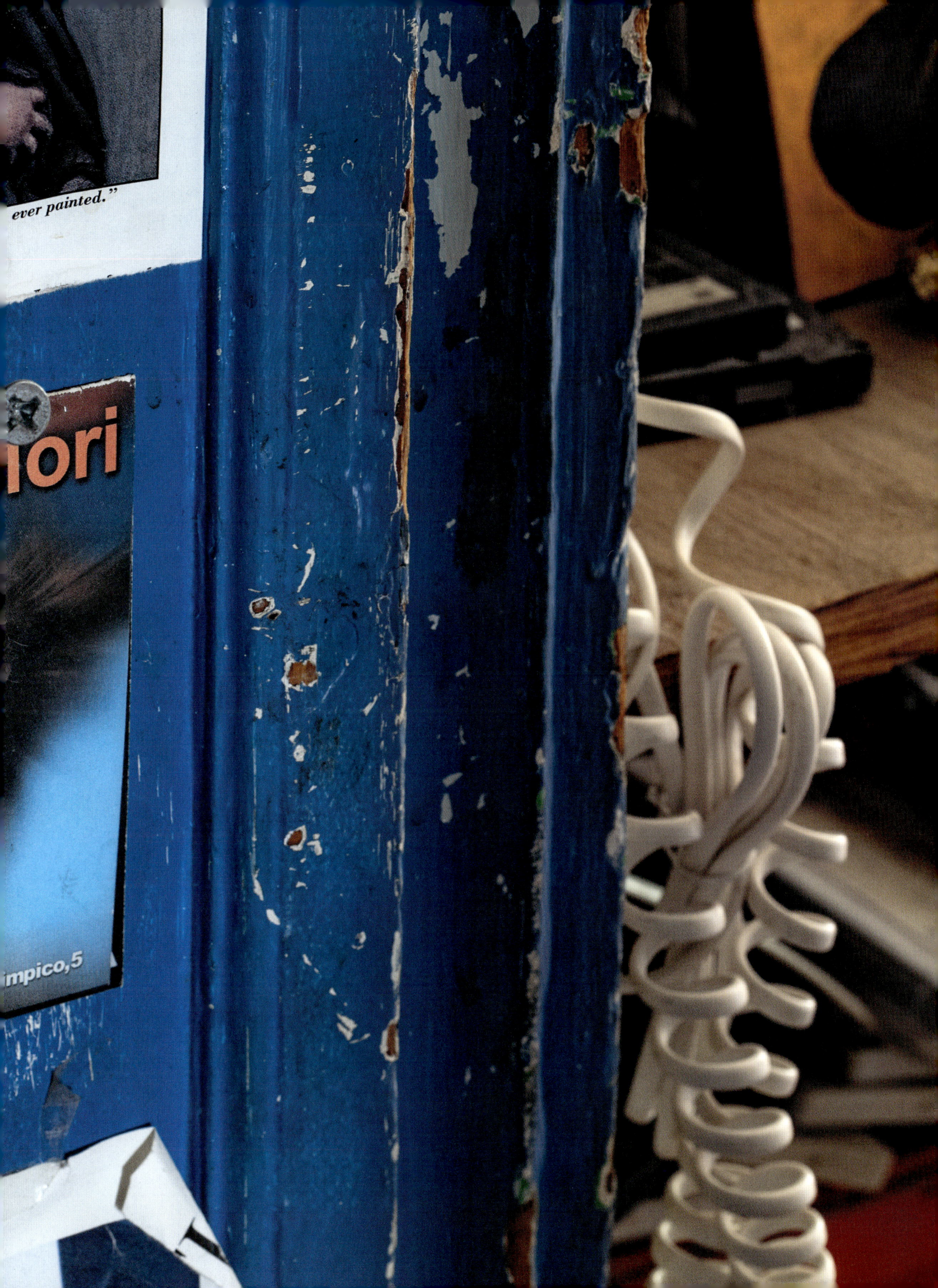
ever painted.”
iori
impico,5

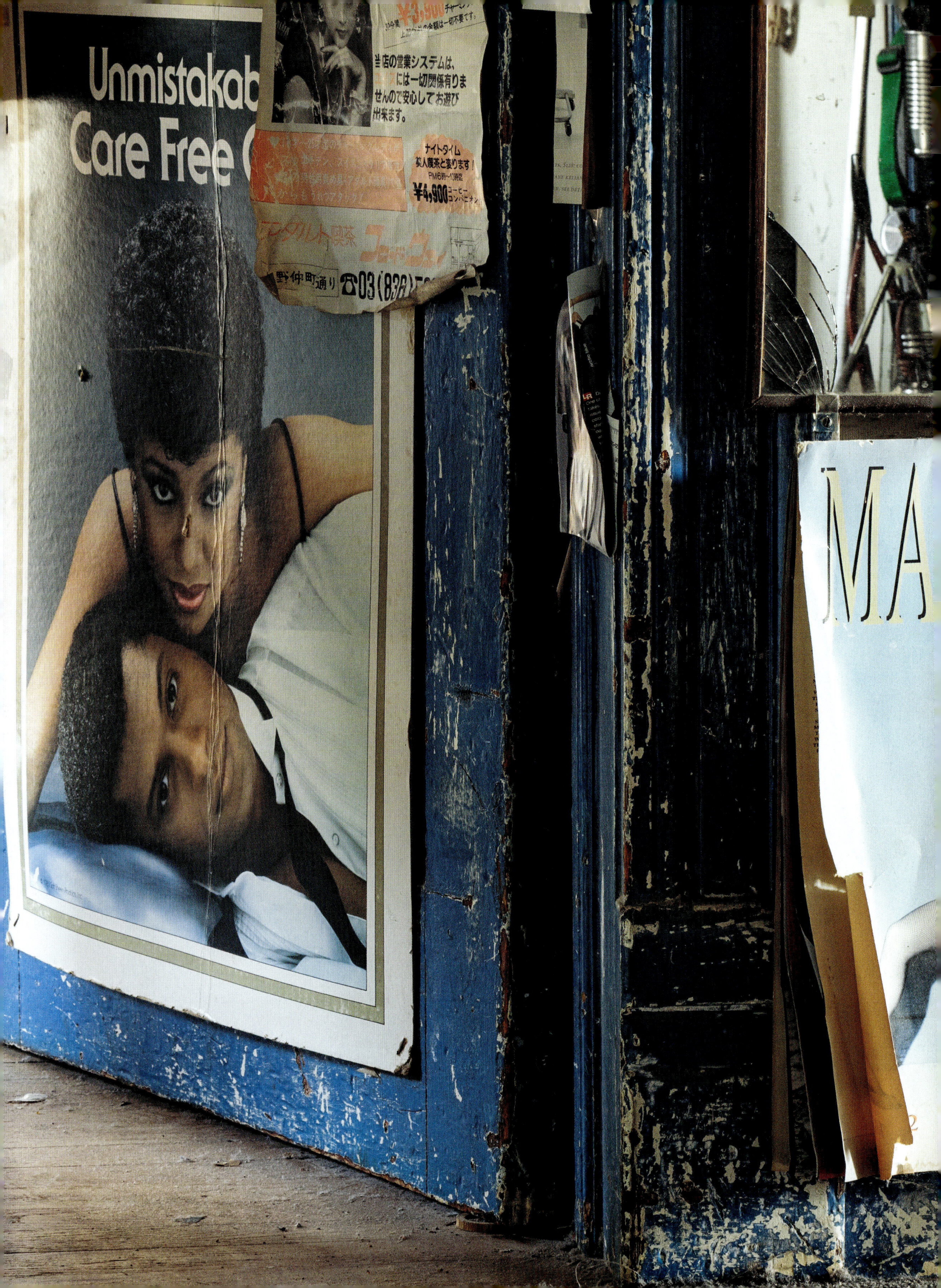

Unmistakab
Care Free
¥3,900
当店の営業システムは、
には一切関係有りま
せんので安心してお遊び
出来ます。
ナイトタイム
美人喫茶と変ります！
PM6時～12時迄
¥4,900
コーヒー
コンパニオン
野仲町通り
03(83
MA

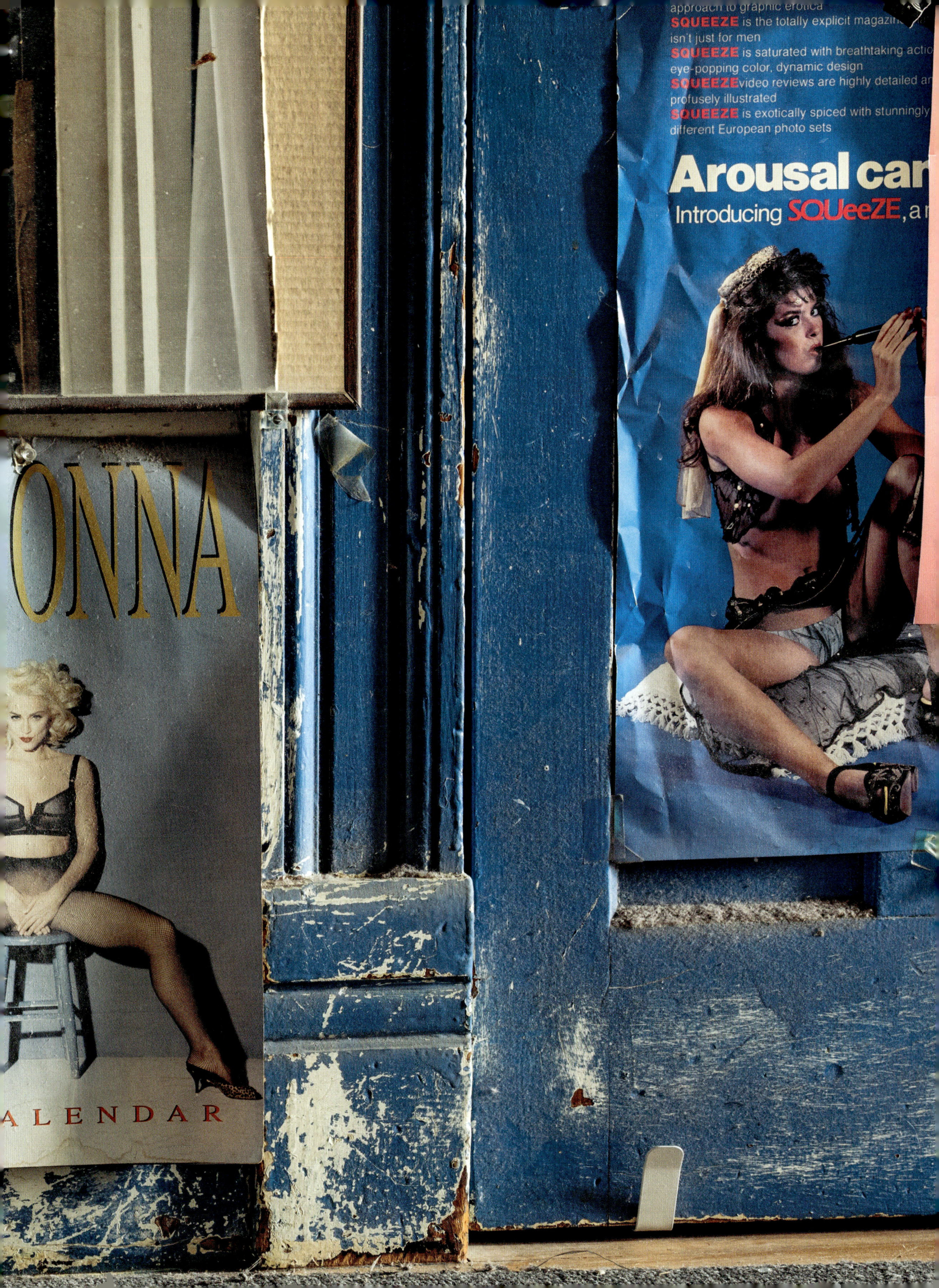
approach to graphic erotica
SQUEEZE is the totally explicit magazi
isn't just for men
SQUEEZE is saturated with breathtaking actio
eye-popping color, dynamic design
SQUEEZE video reviews are highly detailed ar
profusely illustrated
SQUEEZE is exotically spiced with stunningly
different European photo sets
Arousal car
Introducing SQUeeZE, a
ONNA
ALENDAR

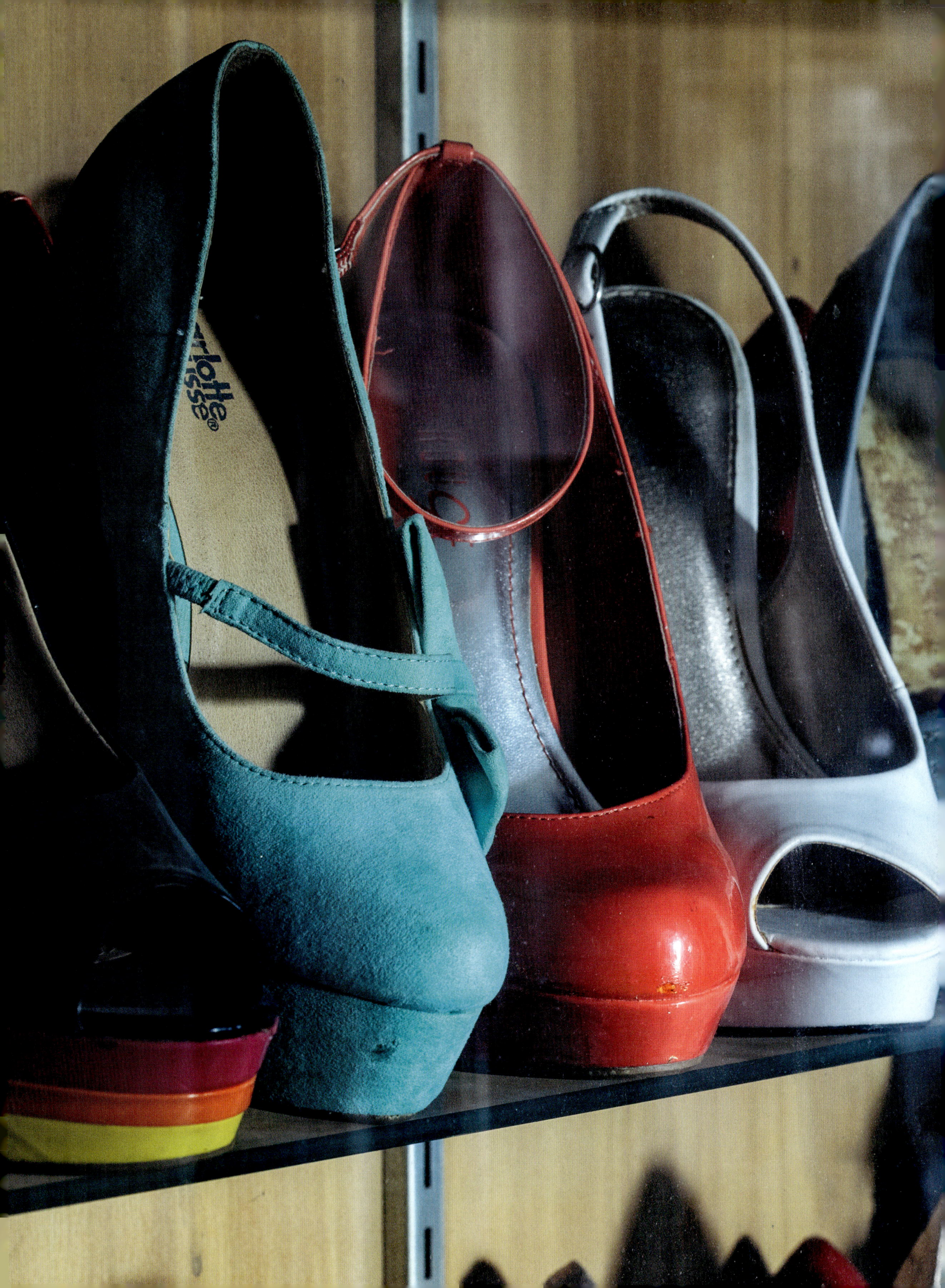

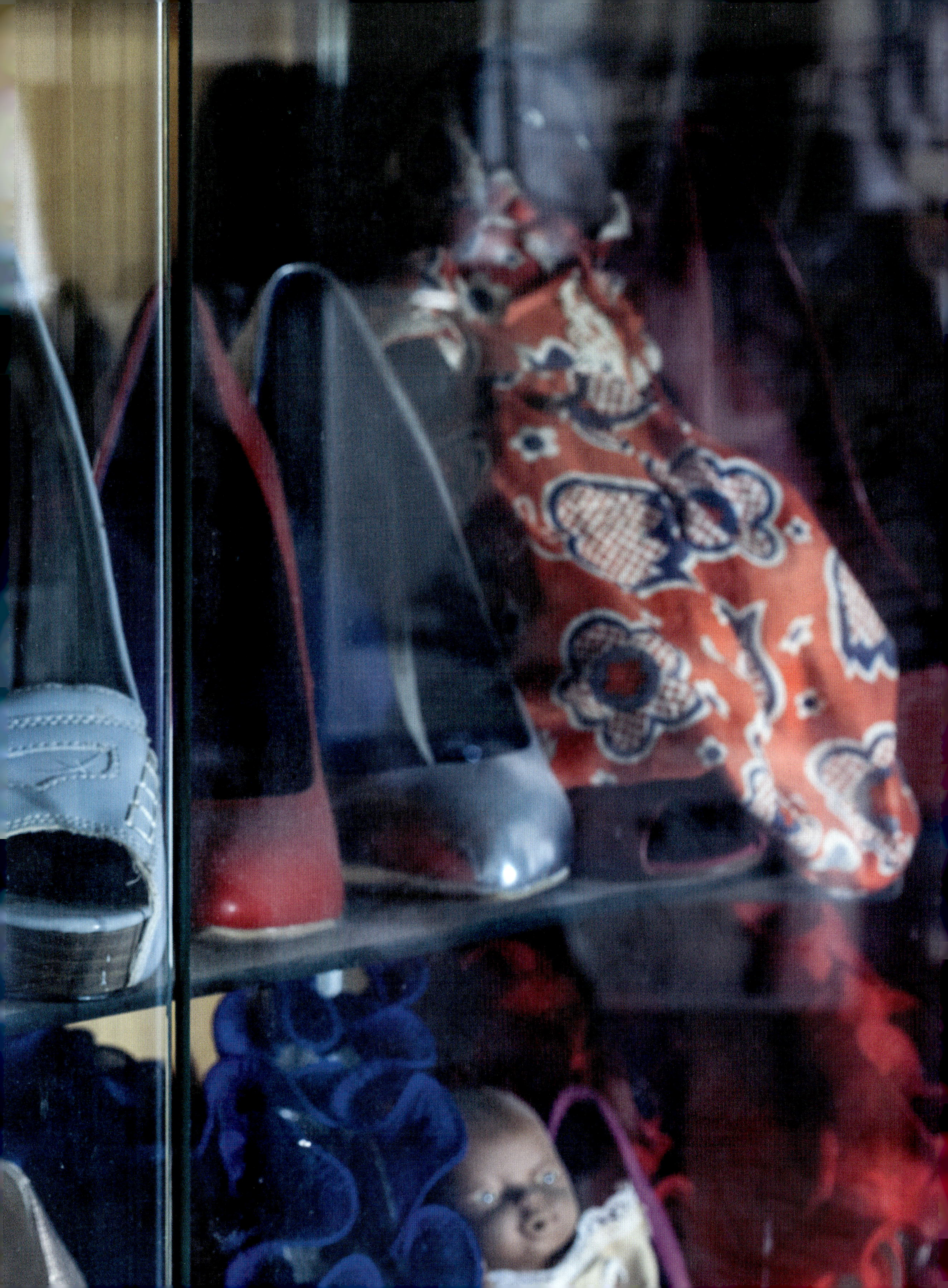

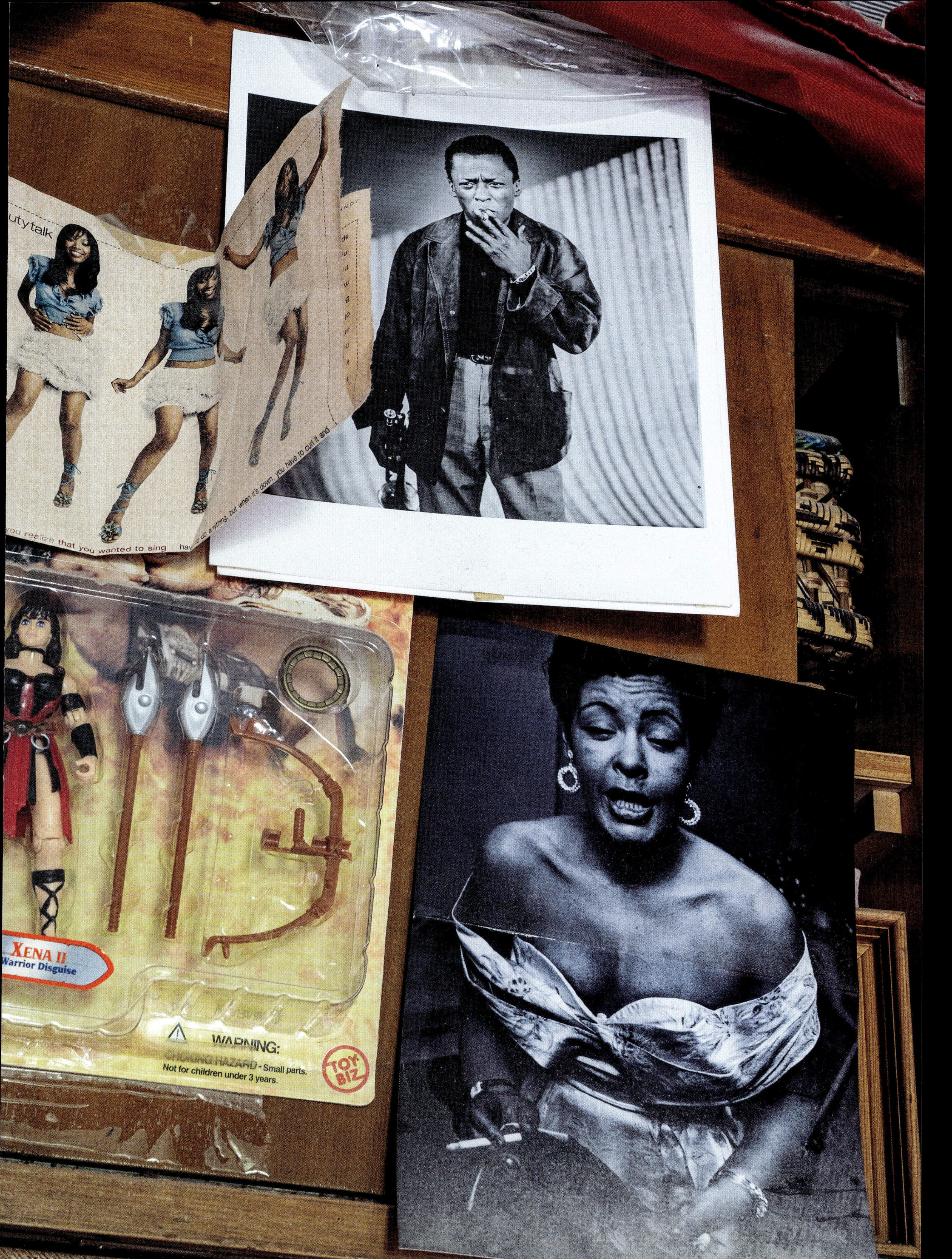
you realize that you wanted to sing
XENA II
Warrior Disguise
WARNING:
CHOKING HAZARD - Small parts.
Not for children under 3 years.
TOY BIZ

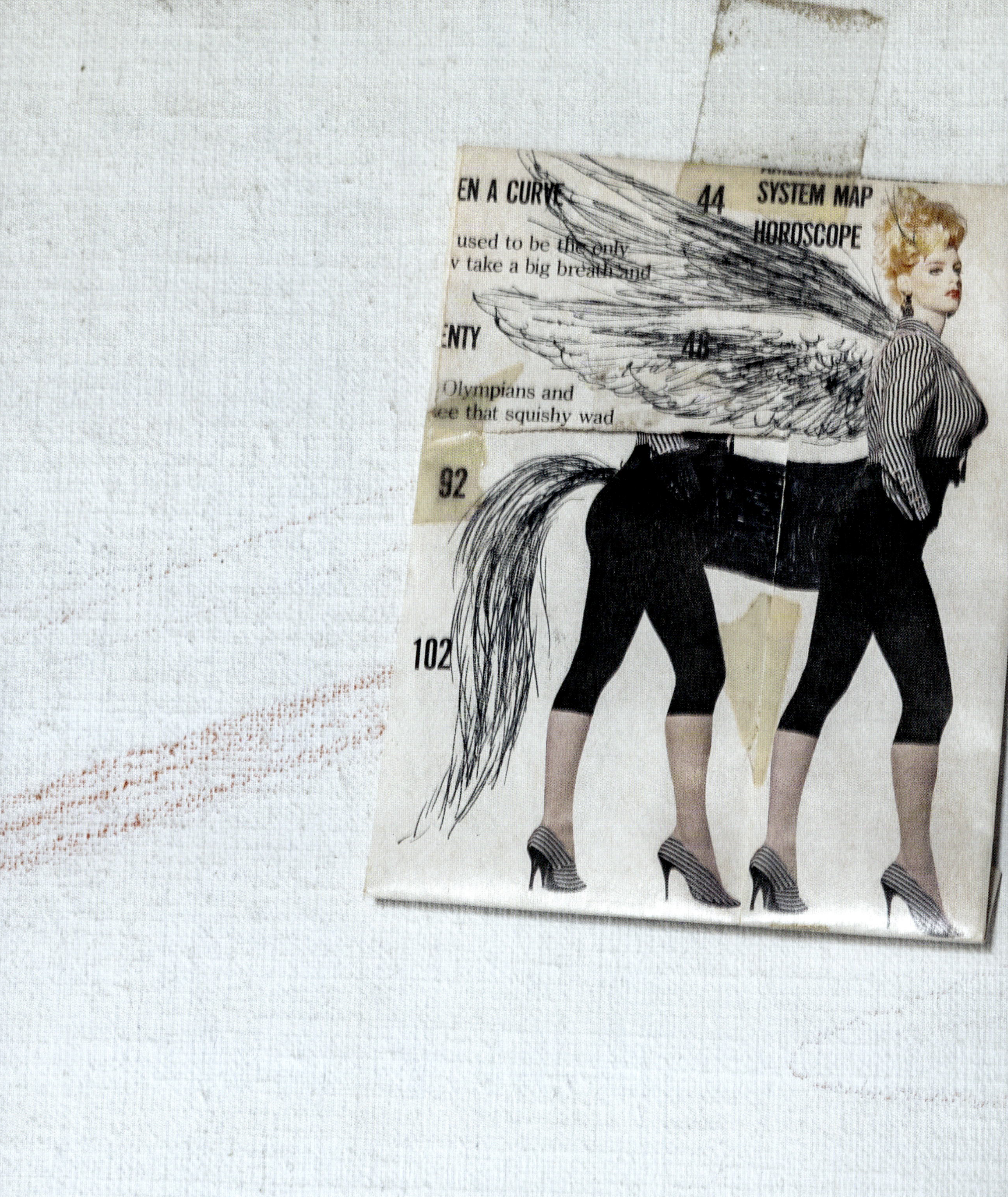
EN A CURVE
44
SYSTEM MAP
HOROSCOPE
used to be the only
v take a big breath and
ENTY
48
Olympians and
ee that squishy wad
92
102

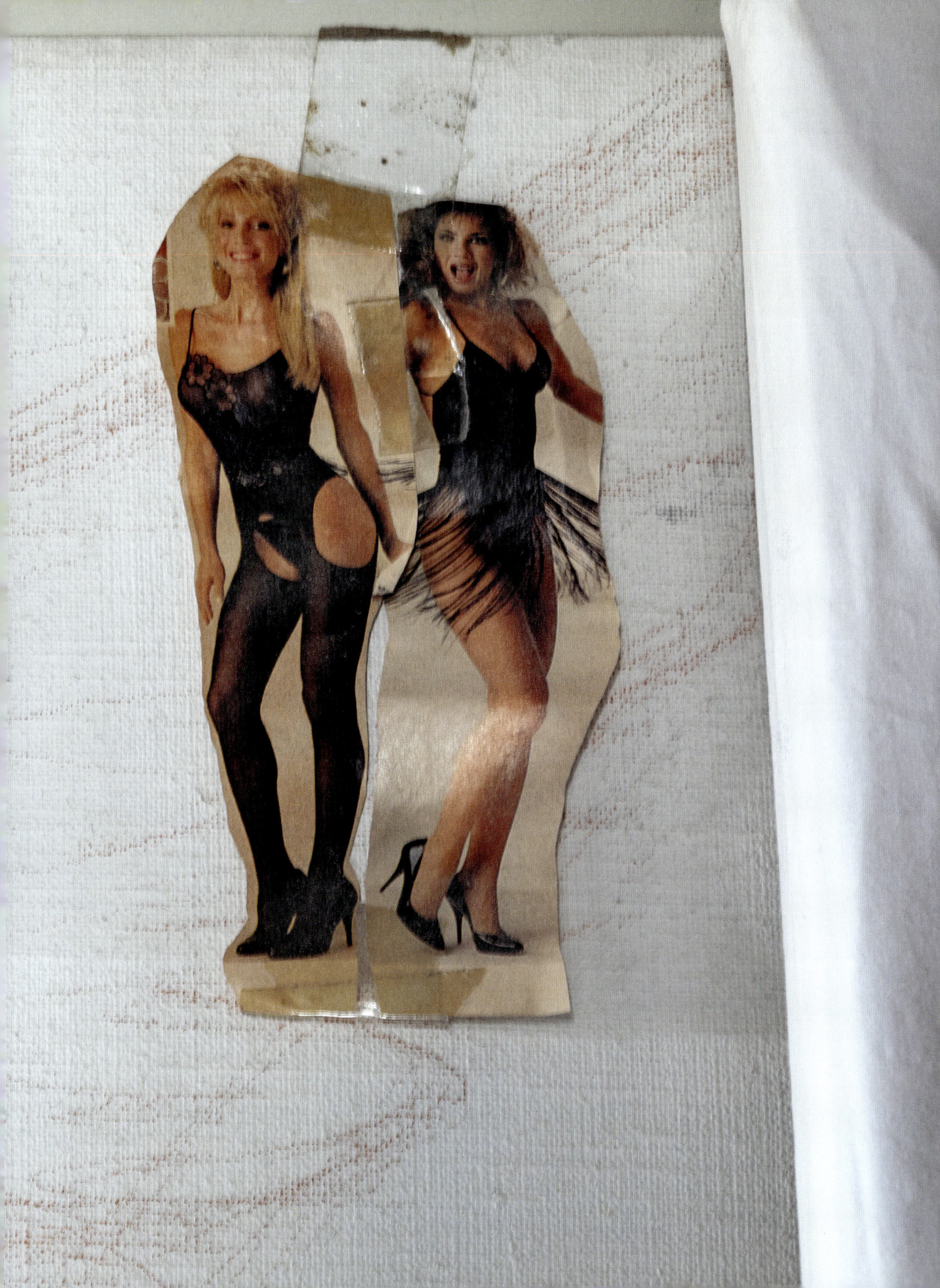

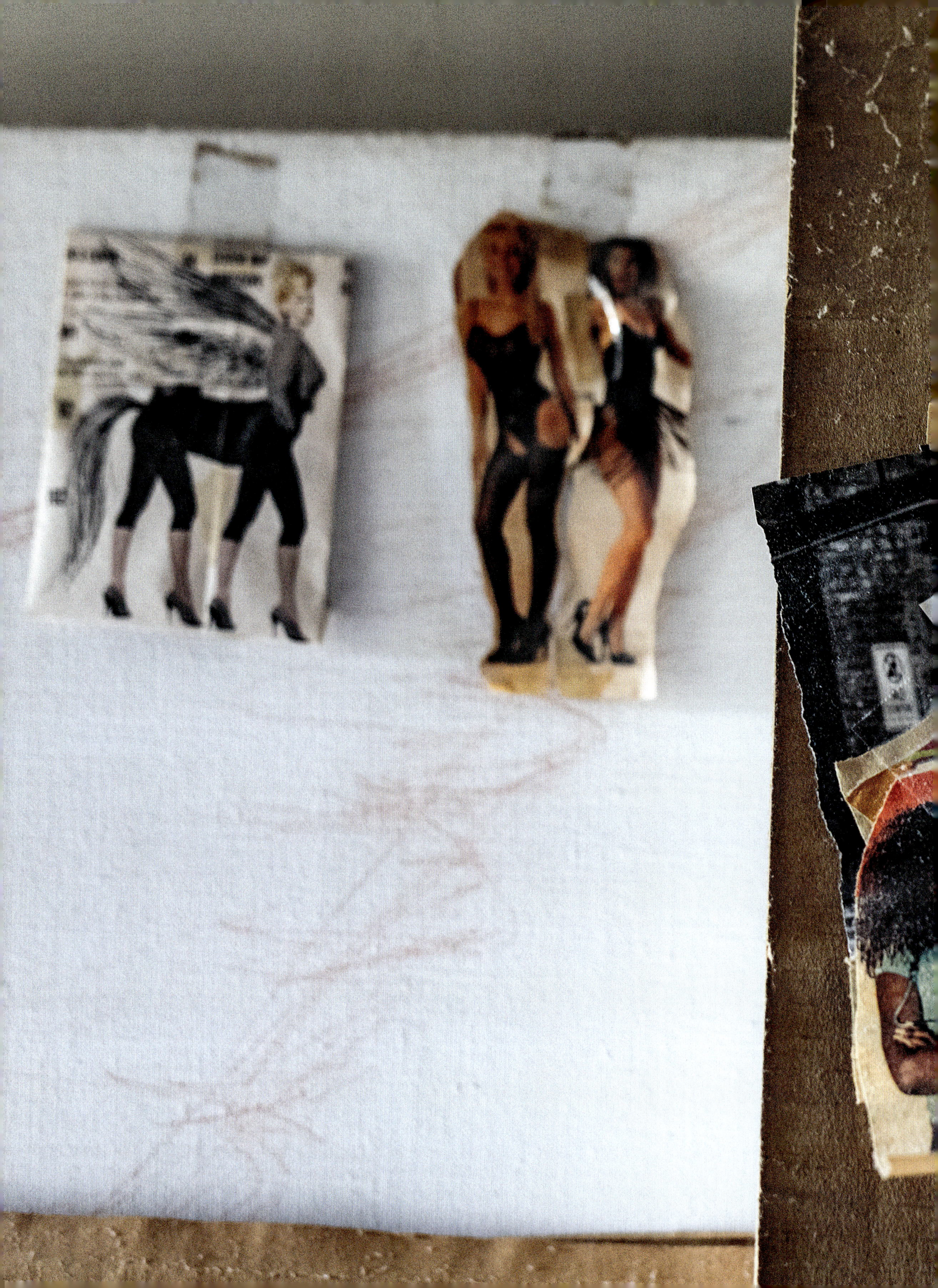

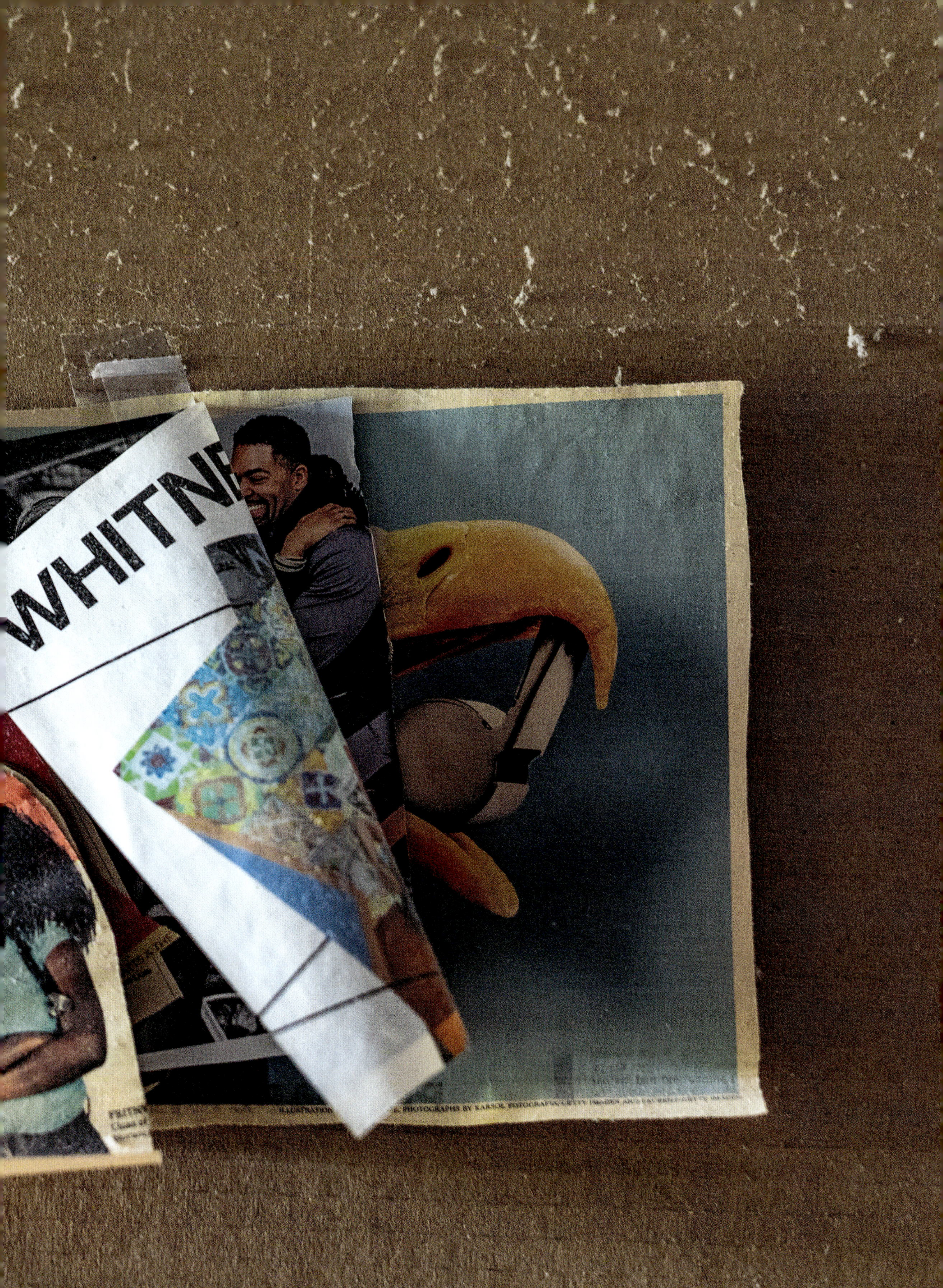
WHITNE
PHOTOGRAPHS BY KARSOL FOTOGRAFIA/GETTY IMAGES

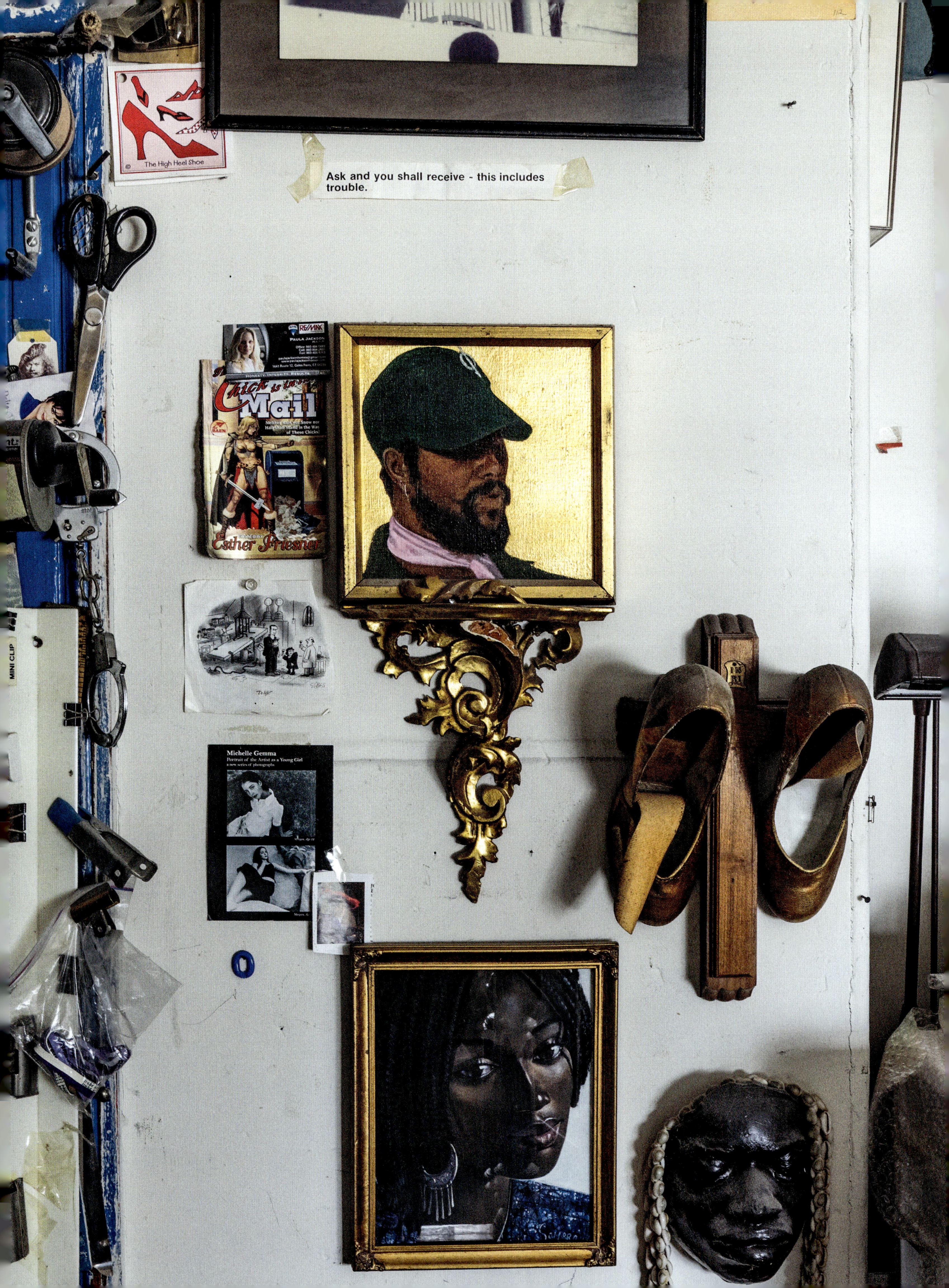
The High Heel Shoe
Ask and you shall receive - this includes trouble.
Esther Friesner
Michelle Gemma
Portrait of the Artist as a Young Girl
MINI CLIP

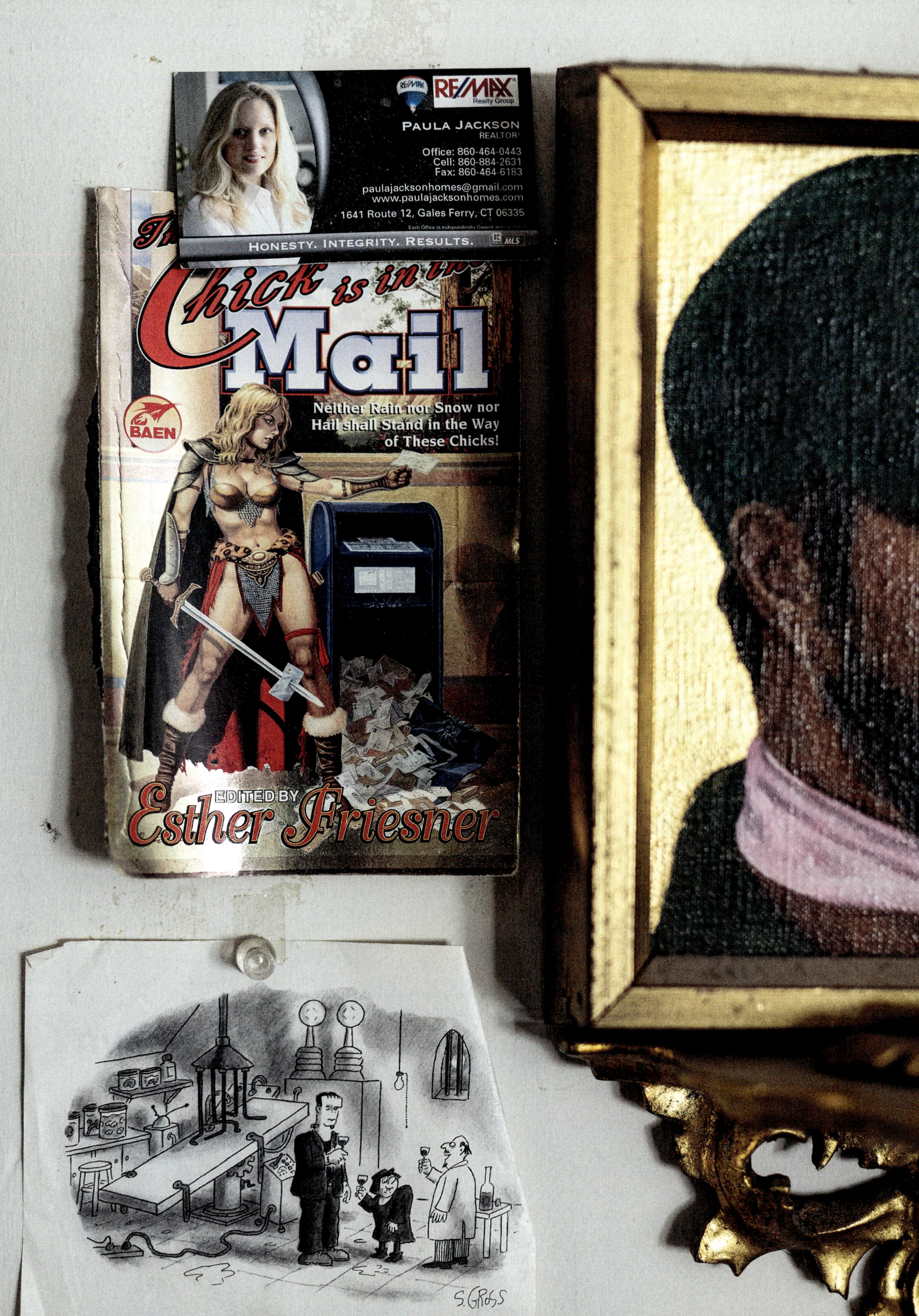
RE/MAX
RE/MAX Realty Group
PAULA JACKSON
REALTOR®
Office: 860-464-0443
Cell: 860-884-2631
Fax: 860-464-6183
paulajacksonhomes@gmail.com
www.paulajacksonhomes.com
1641 Route 12, Gales Ferry, CT 06335
HONESTY. INTEGRITY. RESULTS.
MLS
Chick is in
Mail
BAEN
Neither Rain nor Snow nor Hail shall Stand in the Way of These Chicks!
EDITED BY
Esther Friesner
S.GROSS

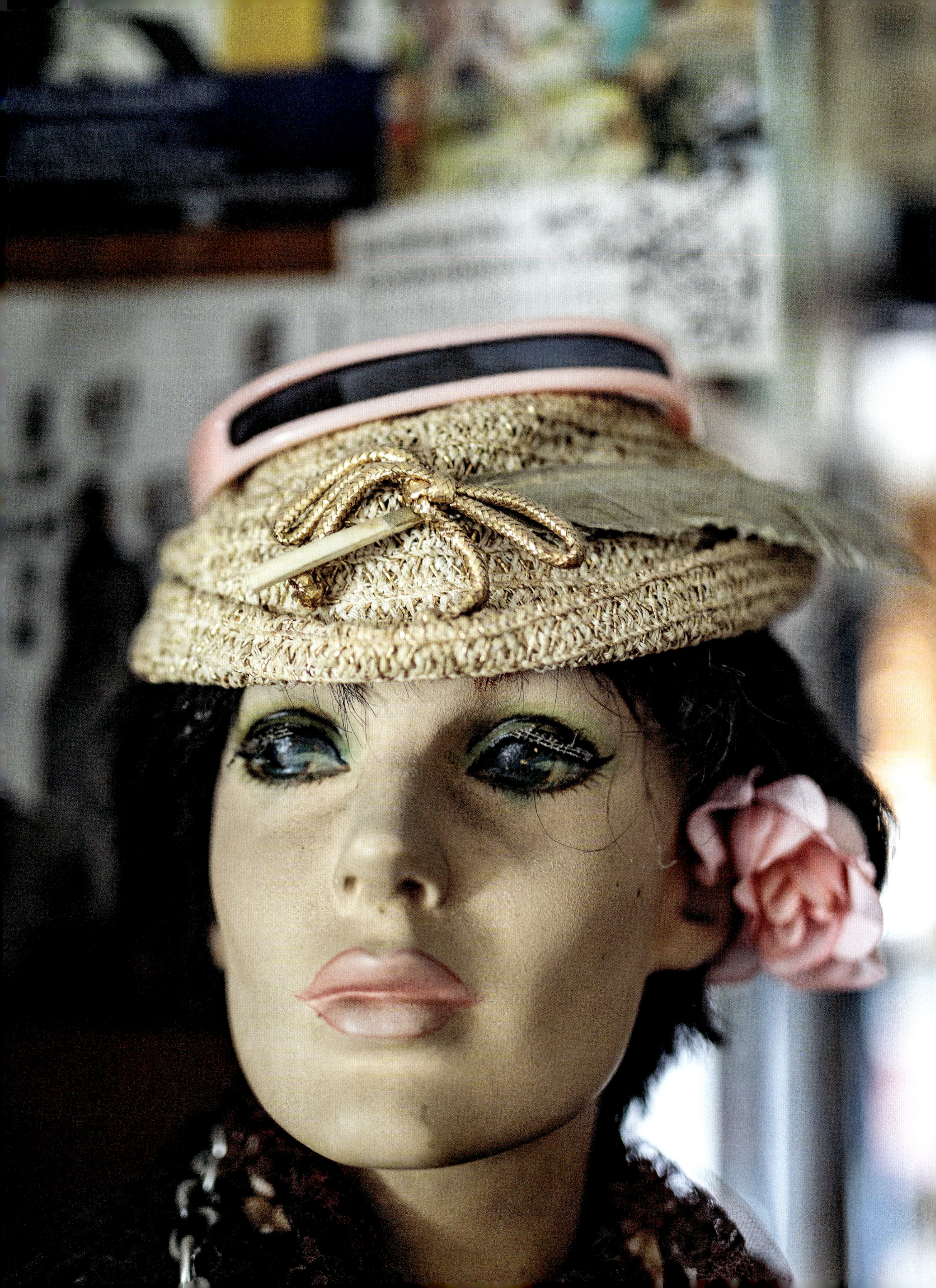

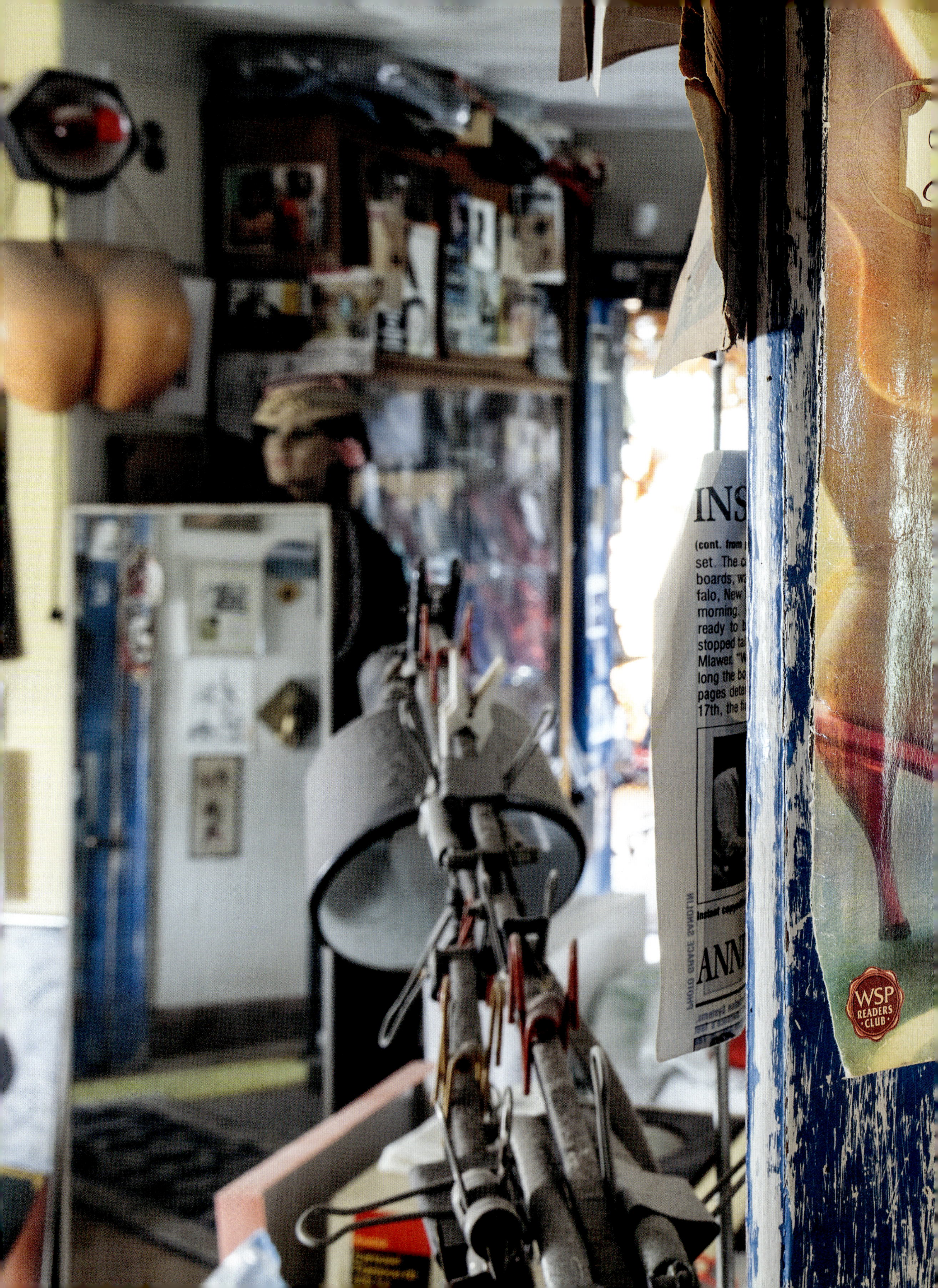

INS
(cont. from
set. The c
boards, wa
falo, New
morning.
ready to b
stopped ta
Mlawer. "W
long the bo
pages deter
17th, the fi
ANN
WSP
READERS
CLUB

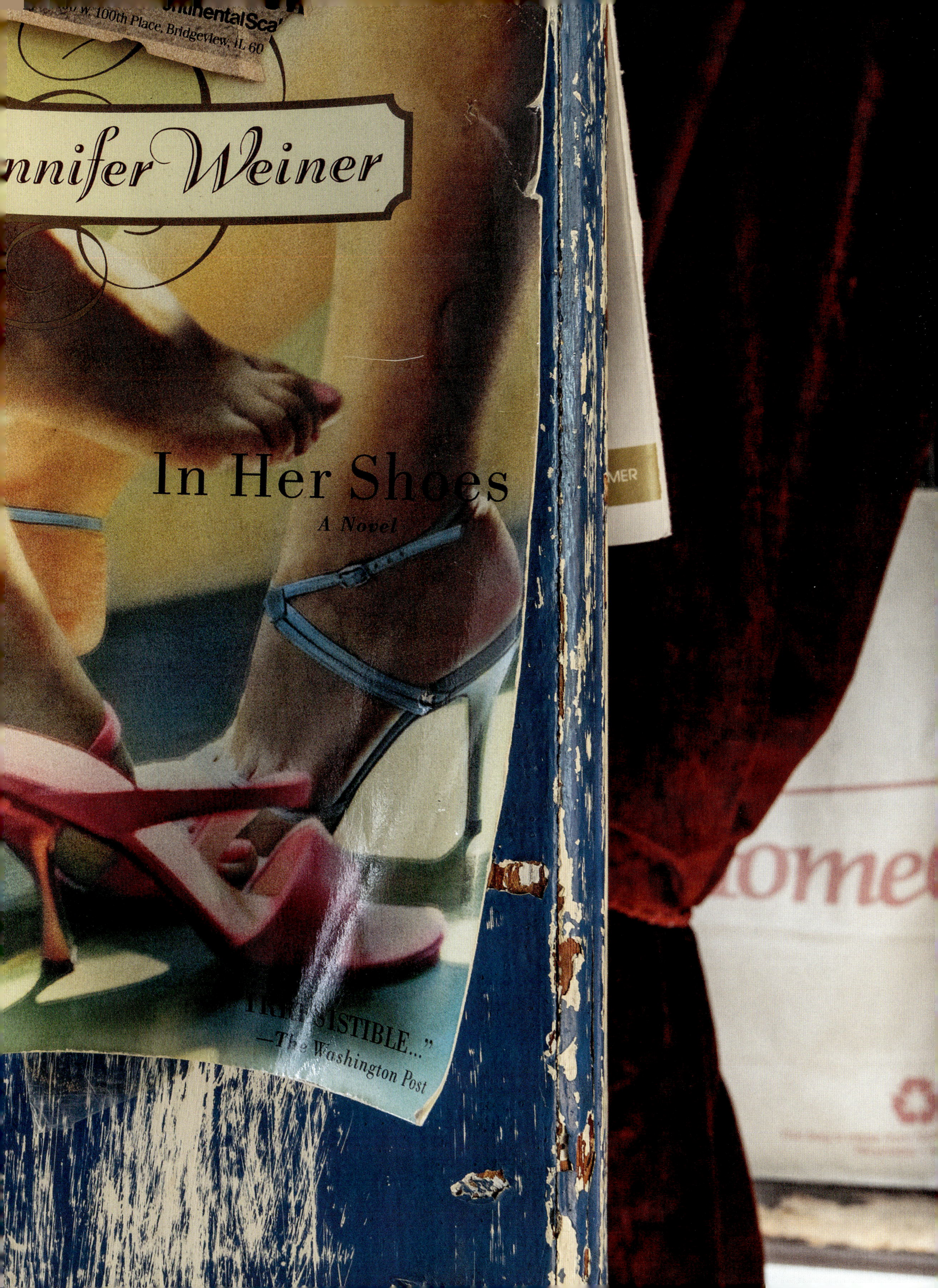

ntinentalSca
W. 100th Place, Bridgeview, IL 60
nnifer Weiner
In Her Shoes
A Novel
ISTIBLE..."
—The Washington Post

# Tonight as I paint it feels like old times in my studio. I have been in a post-bop mood. My studio has been filled with sounds of Horace Silver and Art Blakey.

“OLD TIMES - PRE BOP,” January 20, 1976 (see p. 247)

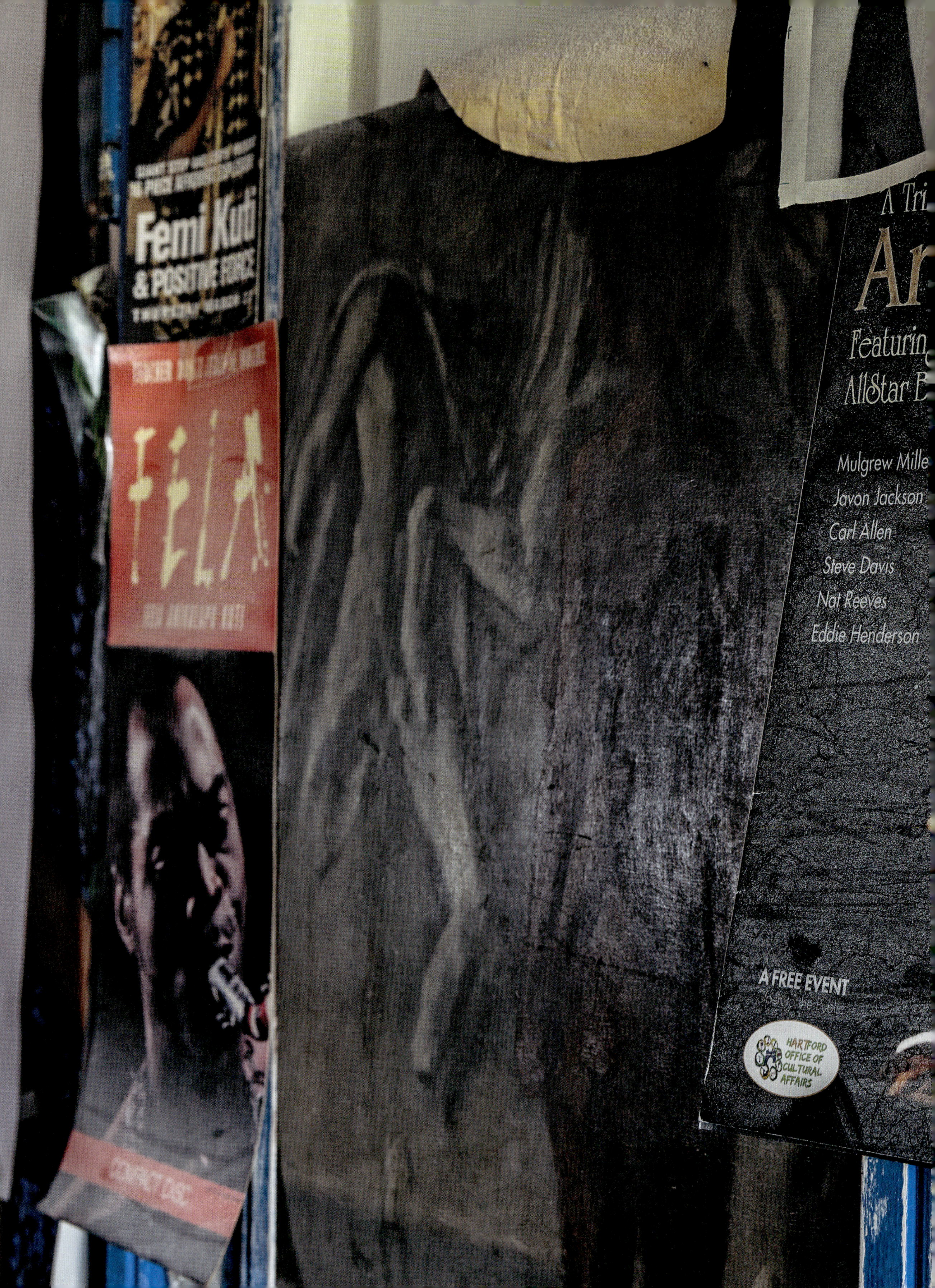
Femi Kuti
& POSITIVE FORCE
FELA
Javon Jackson
Carl Allen
Steve Davis
Nat Reeves
Eddie Henderson
A FREE EVENT
HARTFORD OFFICE OF CULTURAL AFFAIRS
COMPACT DISC

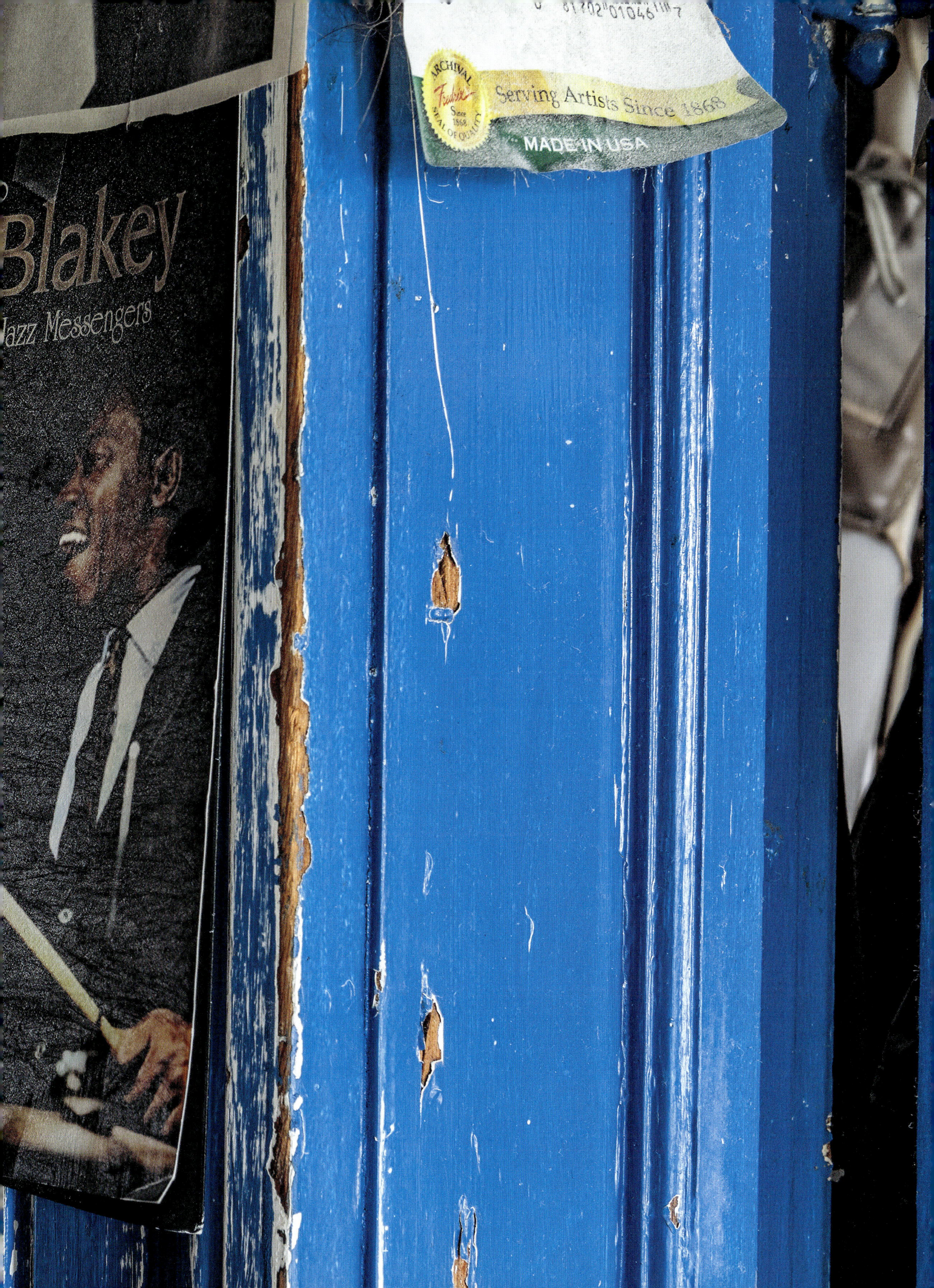
Blakey
Jazz Messengers
Serving Artists Since 1868
MADE IN USA

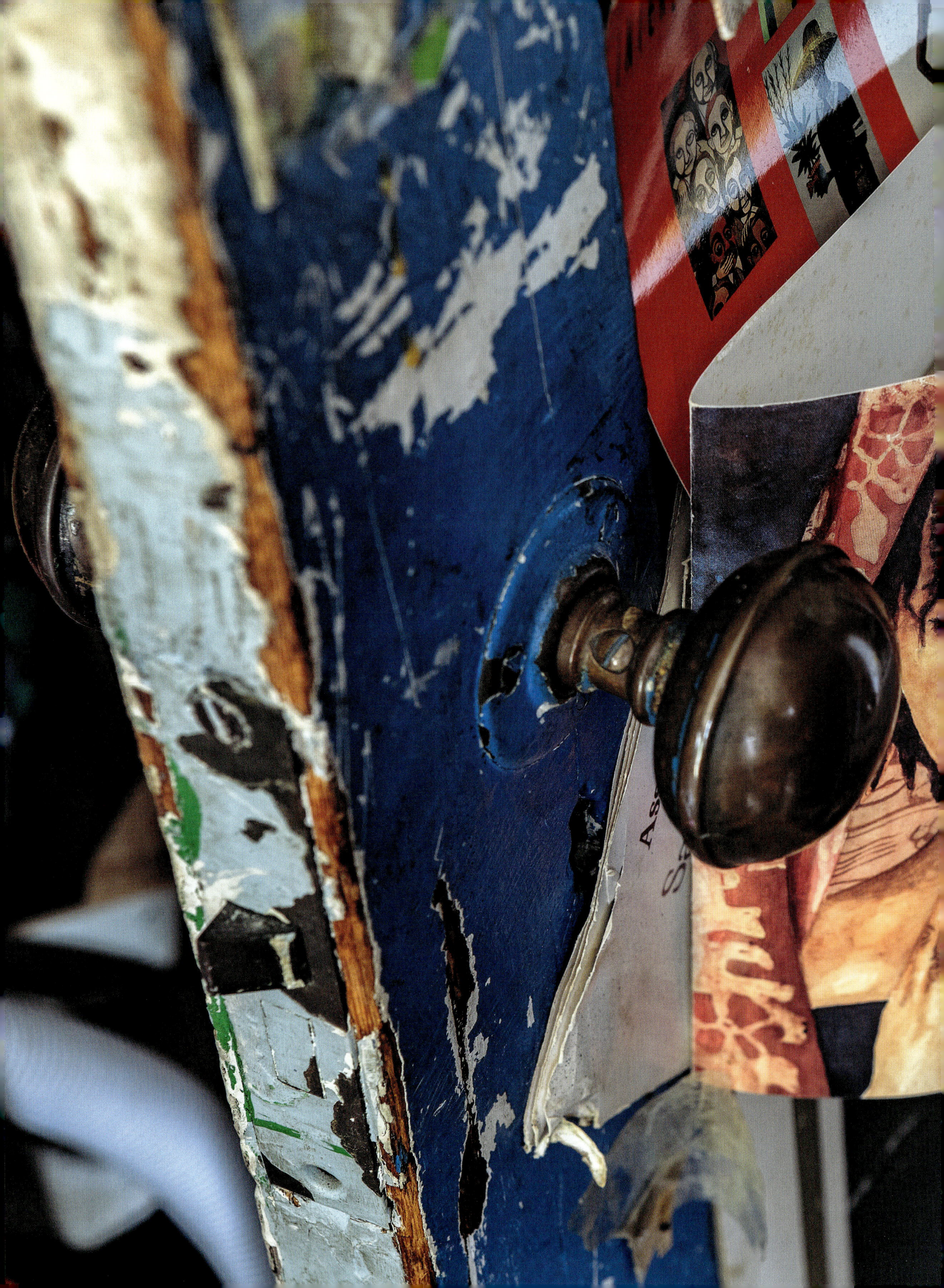

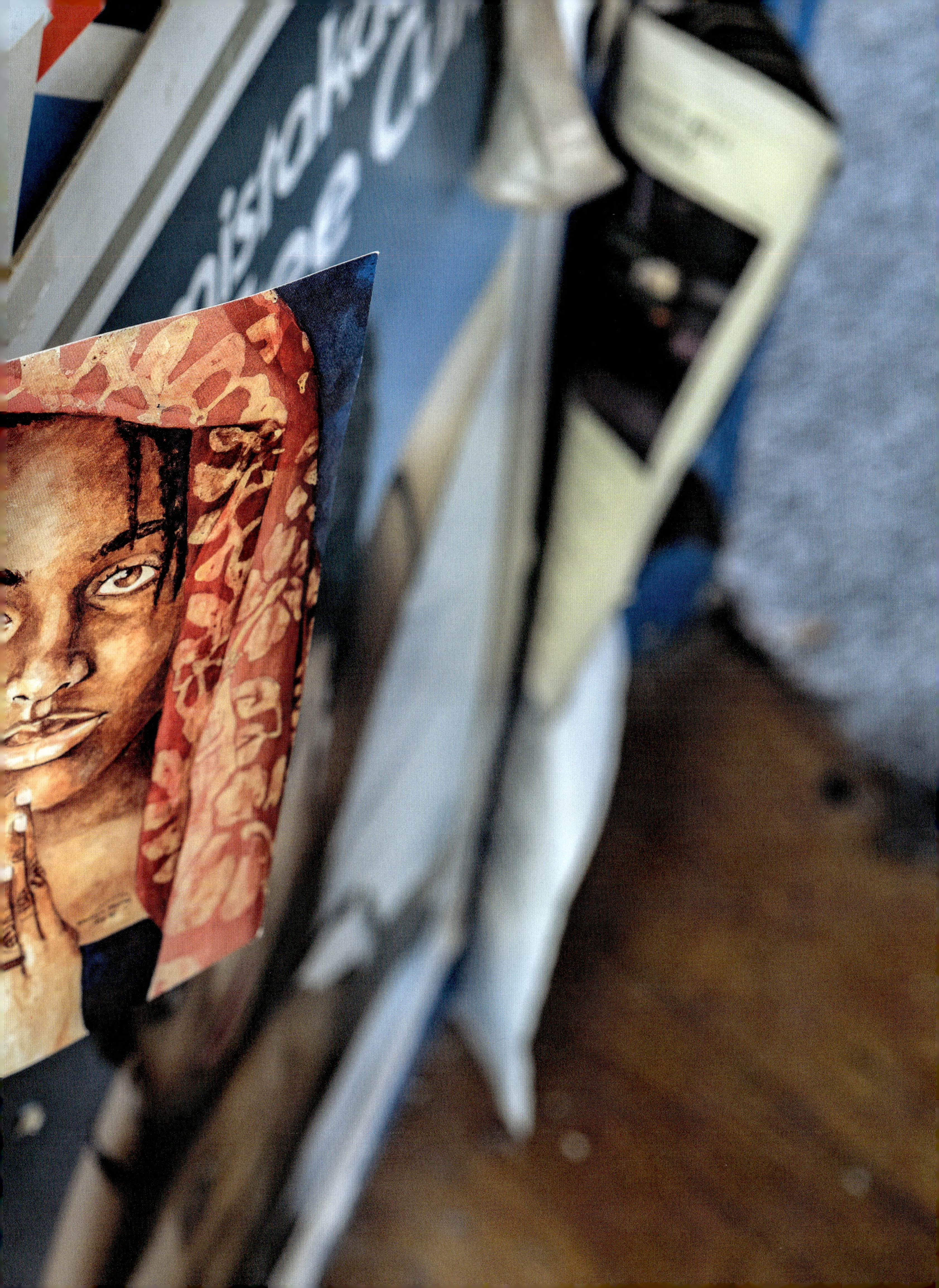

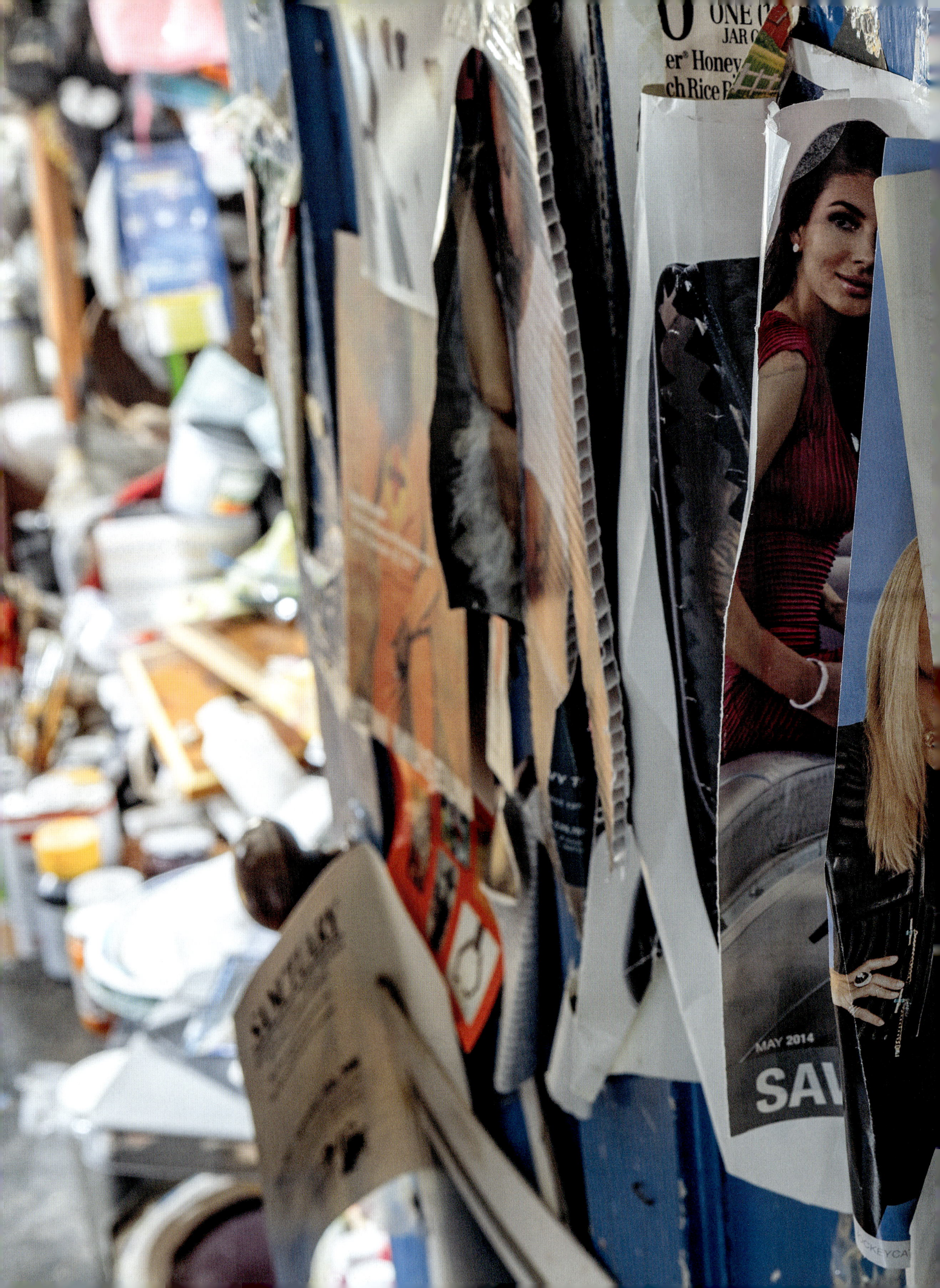
MAY 2014
SAV

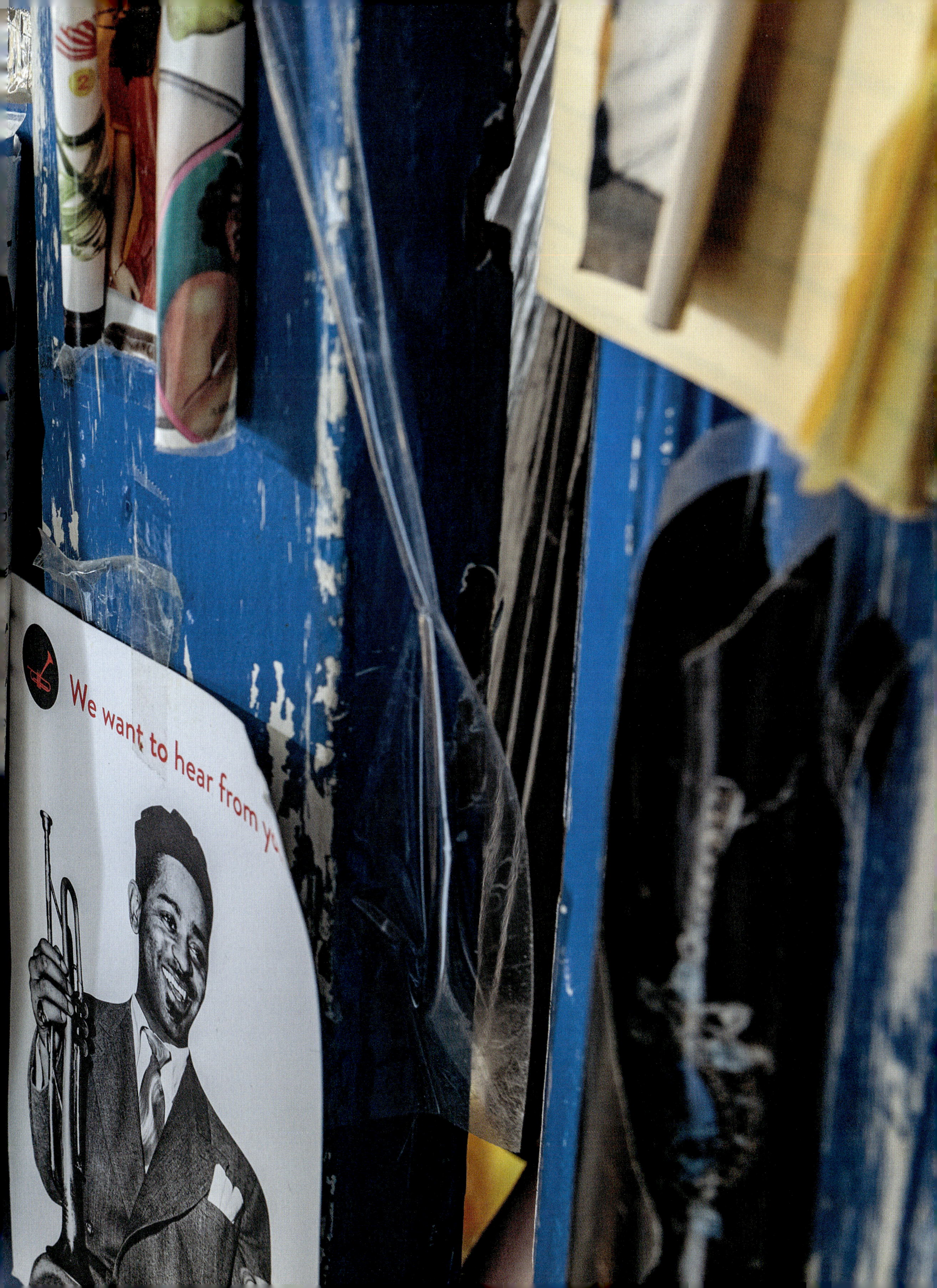
We want to hear from yo

**This morning I rose to the sound of Fela. My visuals was supplied by Atget.**

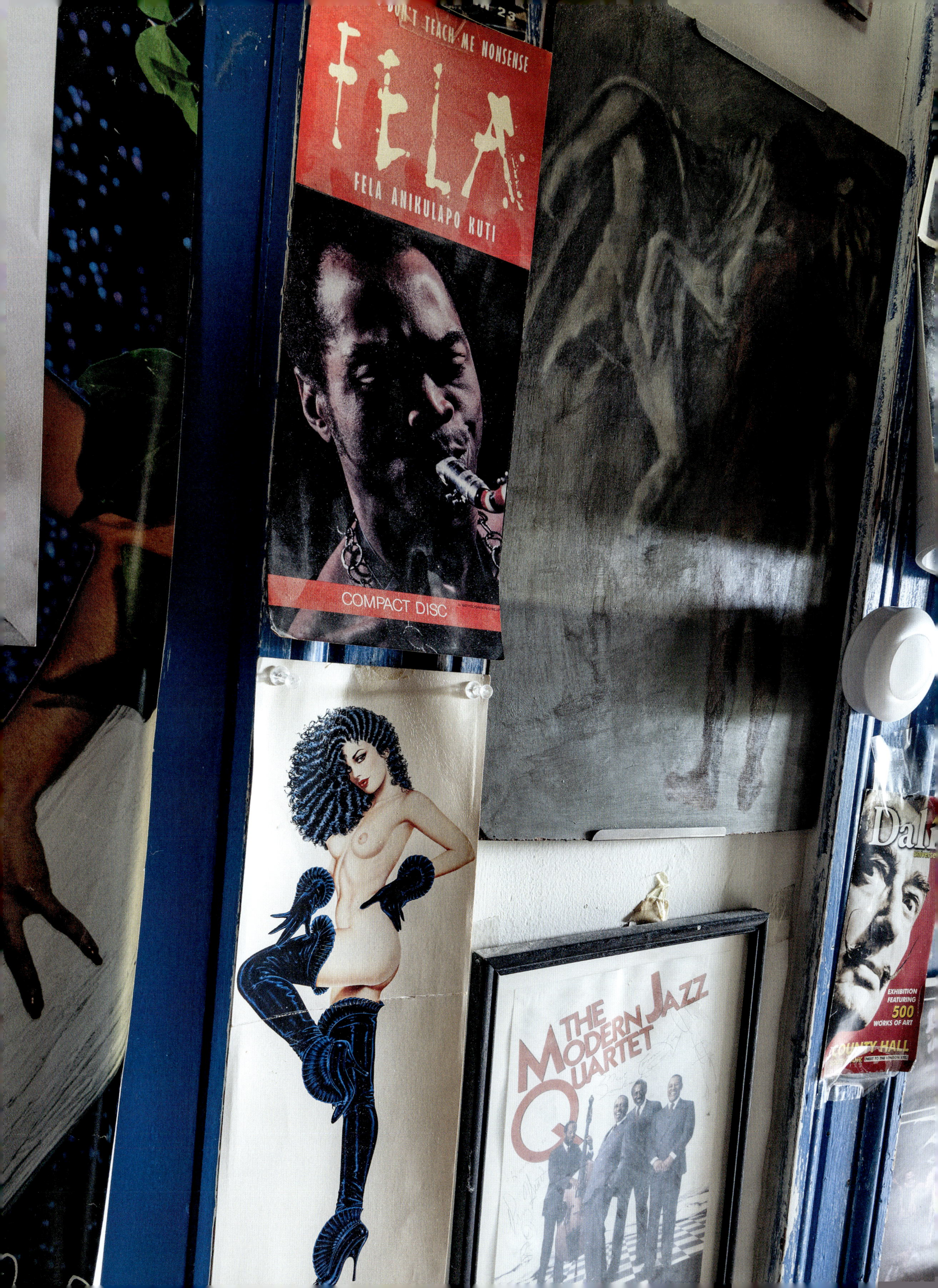

ON'T TEACH ME NONSENSE
FELA
FELA ANIKULAPO KUTI
COMPACT DISC
THE MODERN JAZZ QUARTET
EXHIBITION FEATURING
500
WORKS OF ART
COUNTY HALL

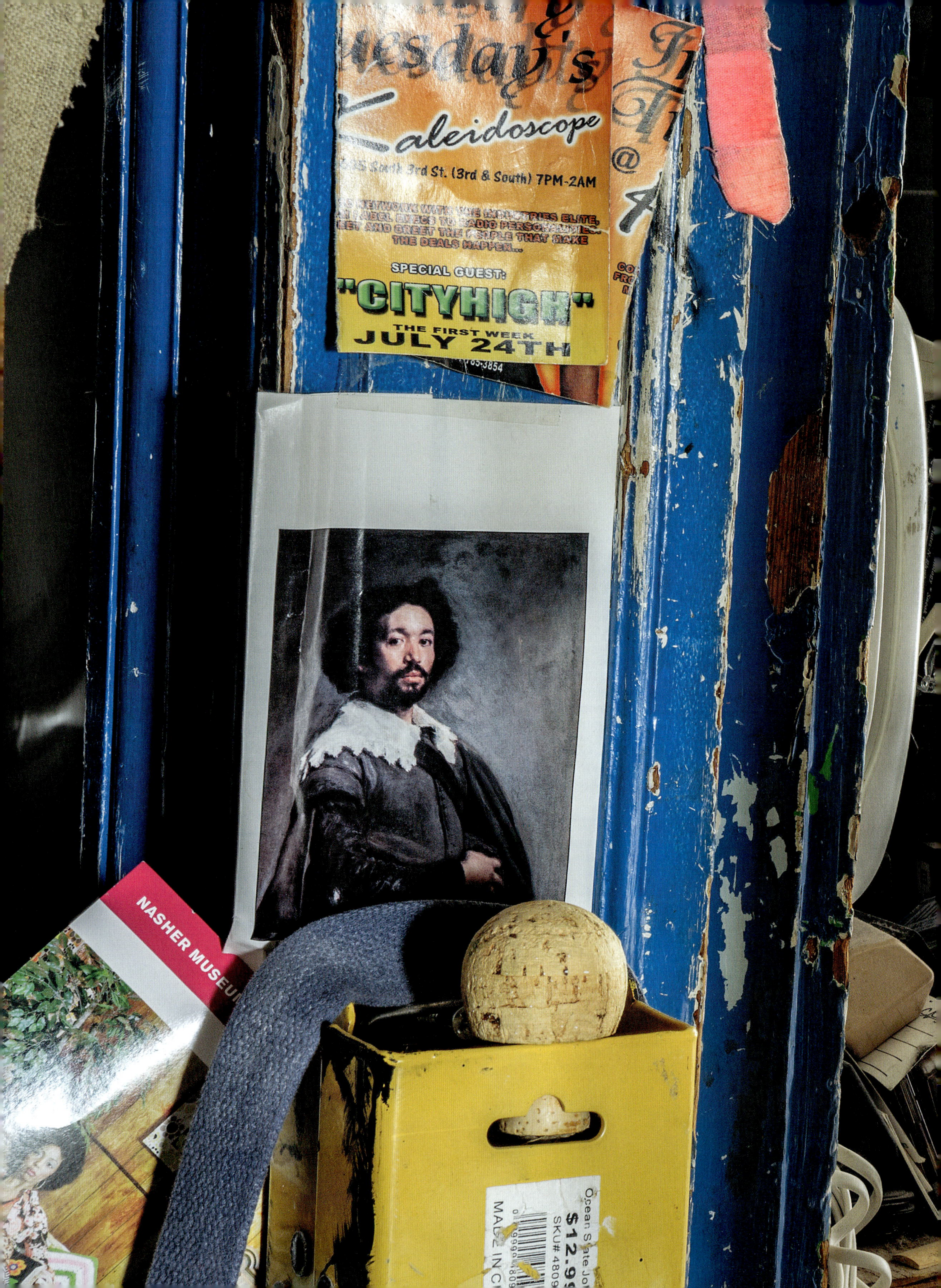

Kaleidoscope
(3rd & South) 7PM-2AM
SPECIAL GUEST:
"CITYHIGH"
THE FIRST WEEK
JULY 24TH
NASHER MUSEU

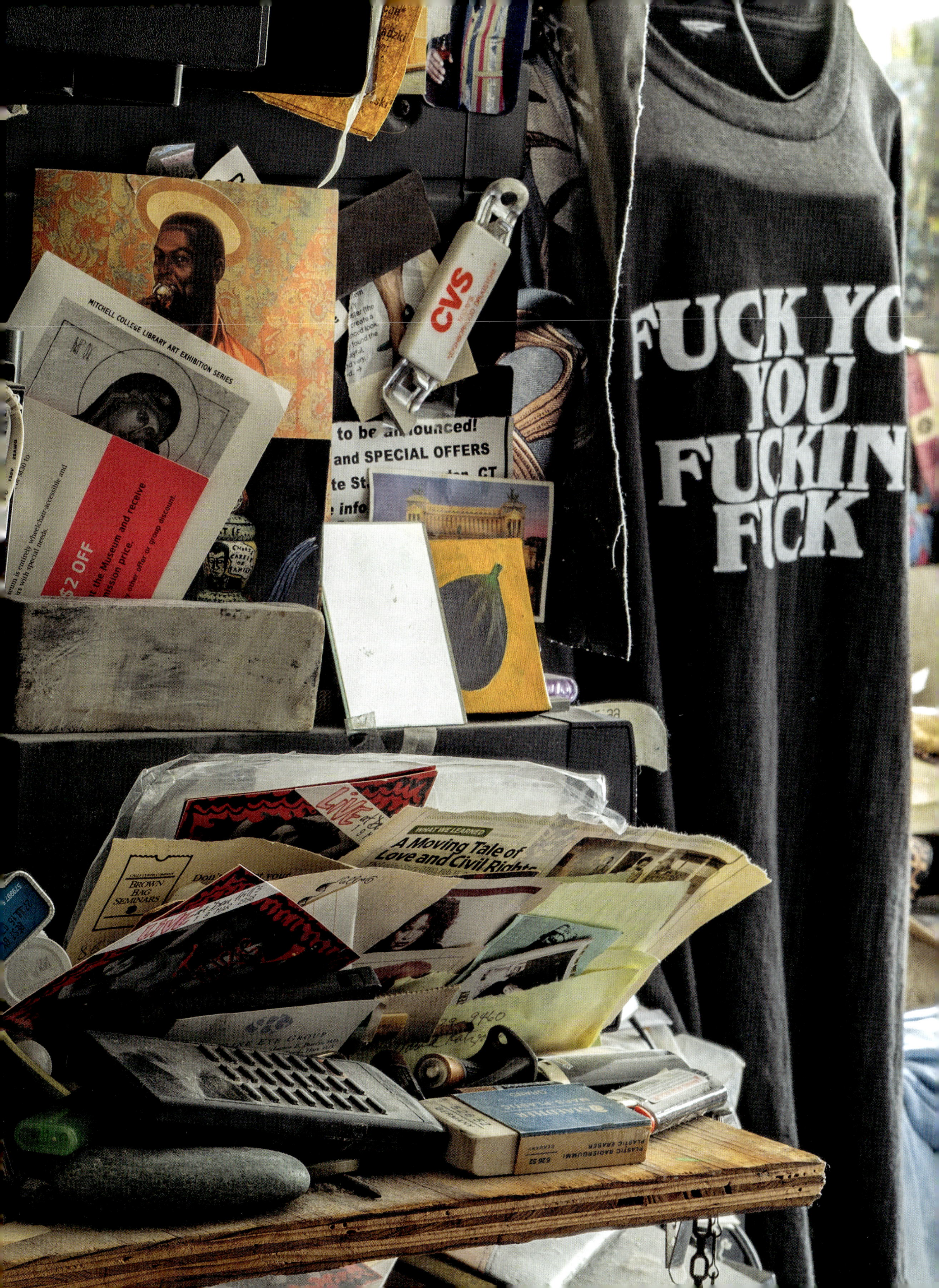

MITCHELL COLLEGE LIBRARY ART EXHIBITION SERIES
CVS
to be announced!
and SPECIAL OFFERS
$2 OFF
WHAT WE LEARNED
A Moving Tale of Love and Civil Rights
BROWN BAG SEMINARS
PLASTIC RADIERGUMMI
PLASTIC ERASER
FUCK YO
YOU
FUCKIN
FICK

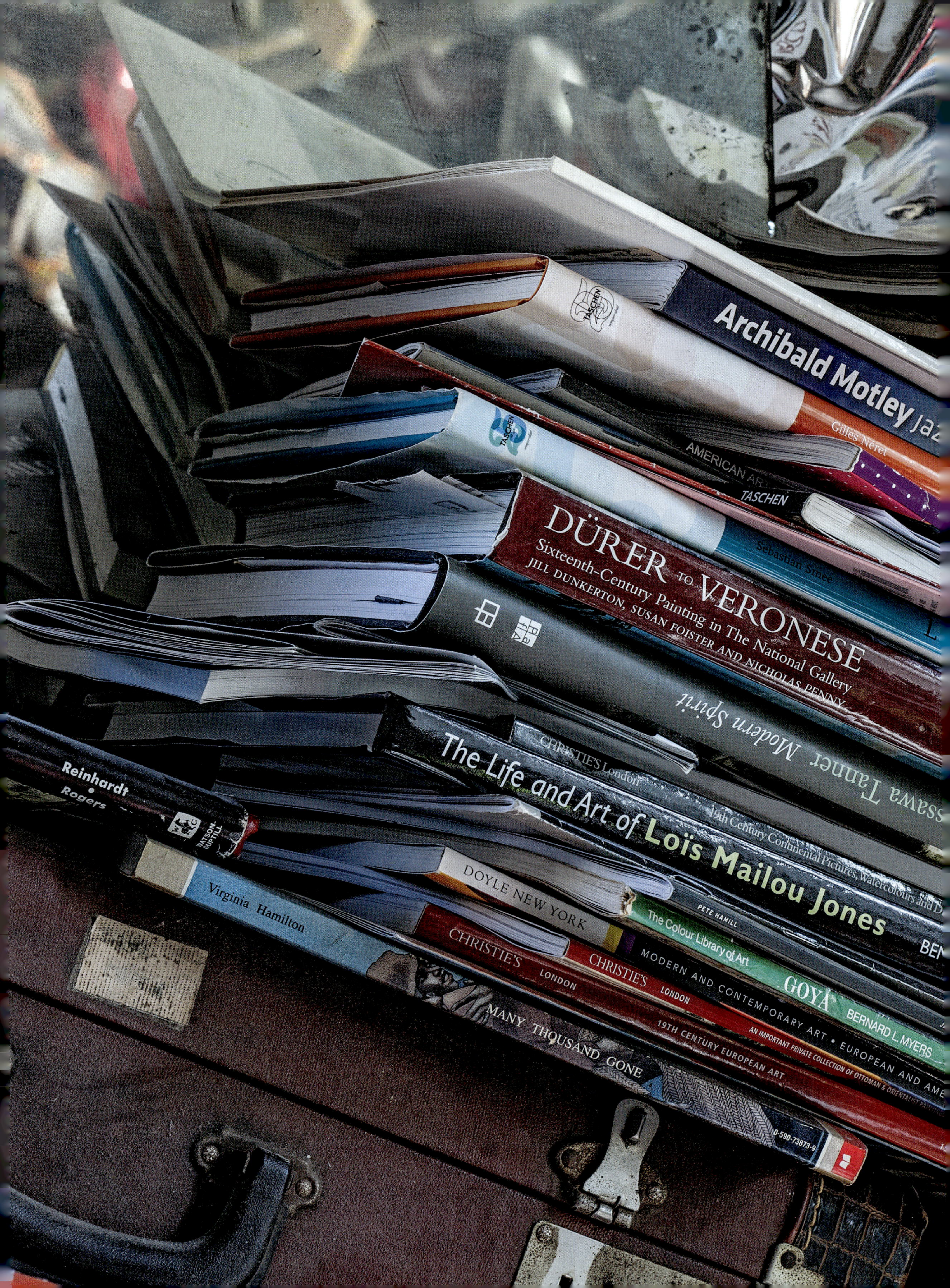

Archibald Motley
Gilles Néret
TASCHEN
TASCHEN
TASCHEN
Sebastian Smee
DÜRER TO VERONESE
Sixteenth-Century Painting in The National Gallery
JILL DUNKERTON, SUSAN FOISTER AND NICHOLAS PENNY
Tanner Modern Spirit
CHRISTIE'S London
19th Century Continental Pictures, watercolours and
The Life and Art of Loïs Mailou Jones
Reinhardt
Rogers
DOYLE NEW YORK
PETE HAMILL
The Colour Library of Art
GOYA
BERNARD L. MYERS
Virginia Hamilton
CHRISTIE'S
LONDON
CHRISTIE'S
LONDON
MODERN AND CONTEMPORARY ART • EUROPEAN AND
19TH CENTURY EUROPEAN ART
AN IMPORTANT PRIVATE COLLECTION OF OTTOMAN & ORIENTALIST
MANY THOUSAND GONE

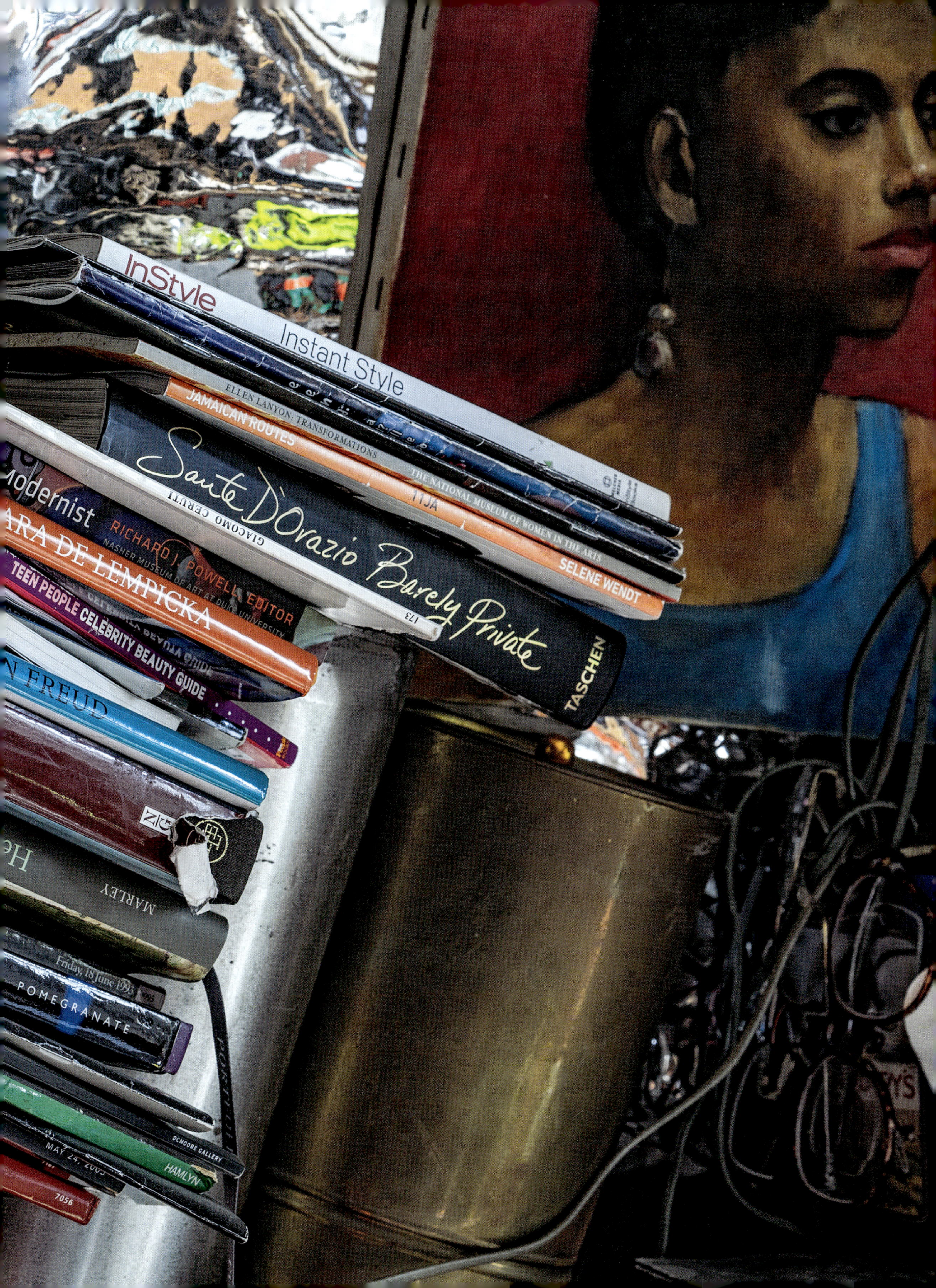
InStyle
Instant Style
ELLEN LANYON: TRANSFORMATIONS
JAMAICAN ROUTES
THE NATIONAL MUSEUM OF WOMEN IN THE ARTS
SELENE WENDT
Sante D'Orazio Barely Private
TASCHEN
GIACOMO CERUTI
RICHARD J. POWELL, EDITOR
TEEN PEOPLE CELEBRITY BEAUTY GUIDE
MARLEY
Friday, 18 June 1993
POMEGRANATE
DCMOORE GALLERY
HAMLYN

**If I stopped painting today what difference would it make. As I gaze out at my paintings sitting on the floor, what am I doing.**

“ ,” April 23, 1978 (see p. 236)

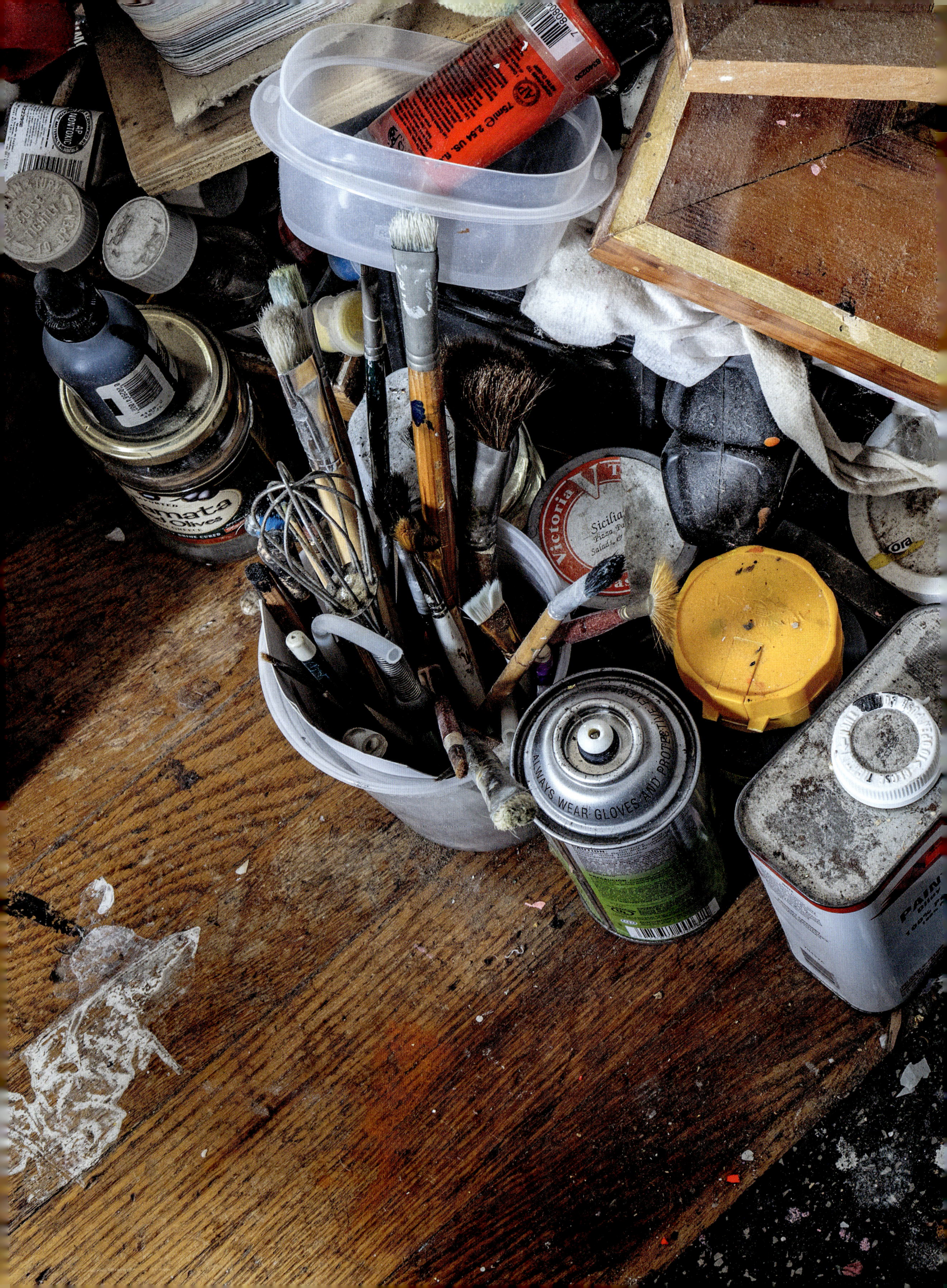

ALWAYS WEAR GLOVES AND PROTECTIVE
Victoria

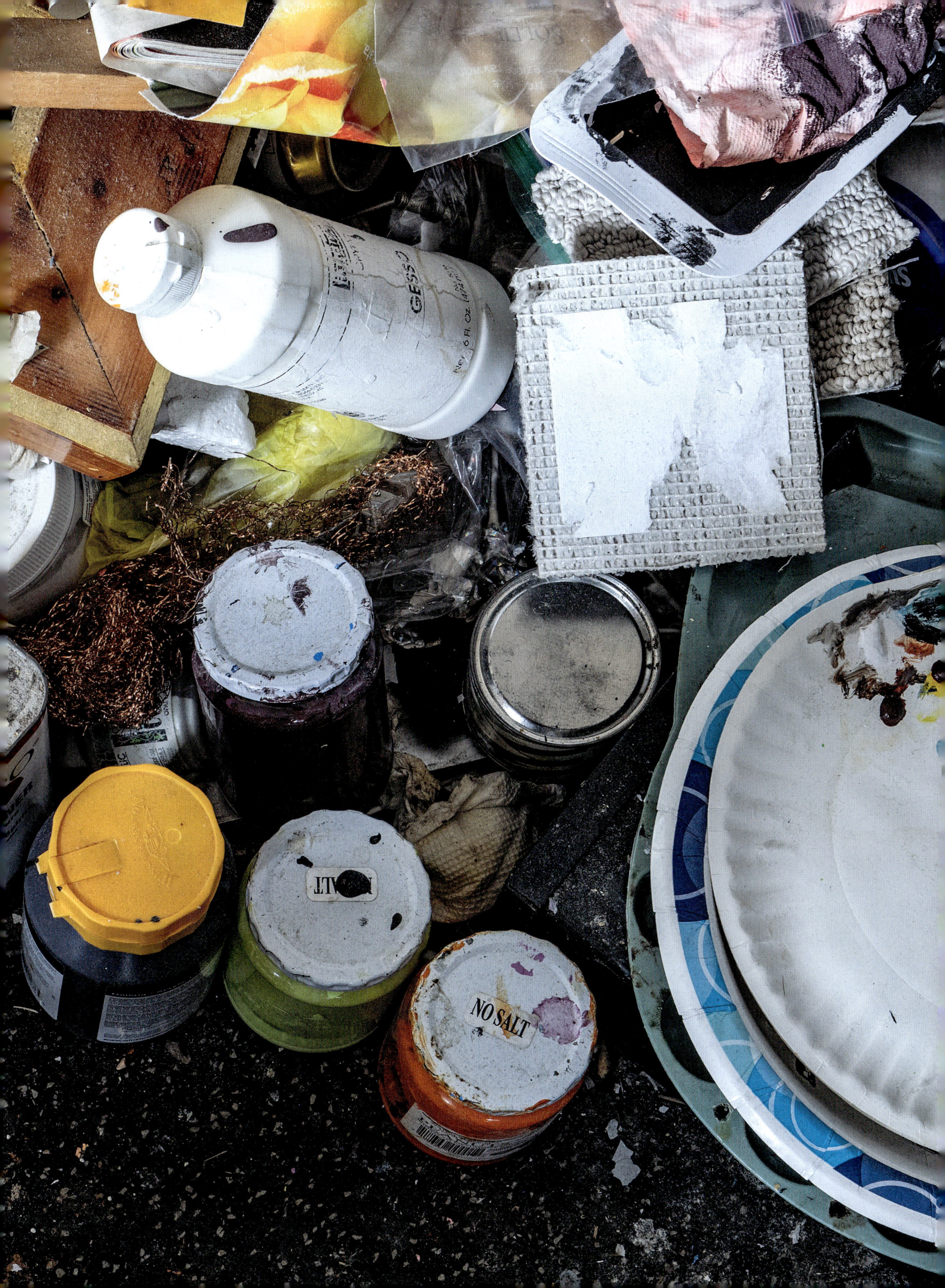

GESSO
NO SALT

**I'm pondering the prices.**

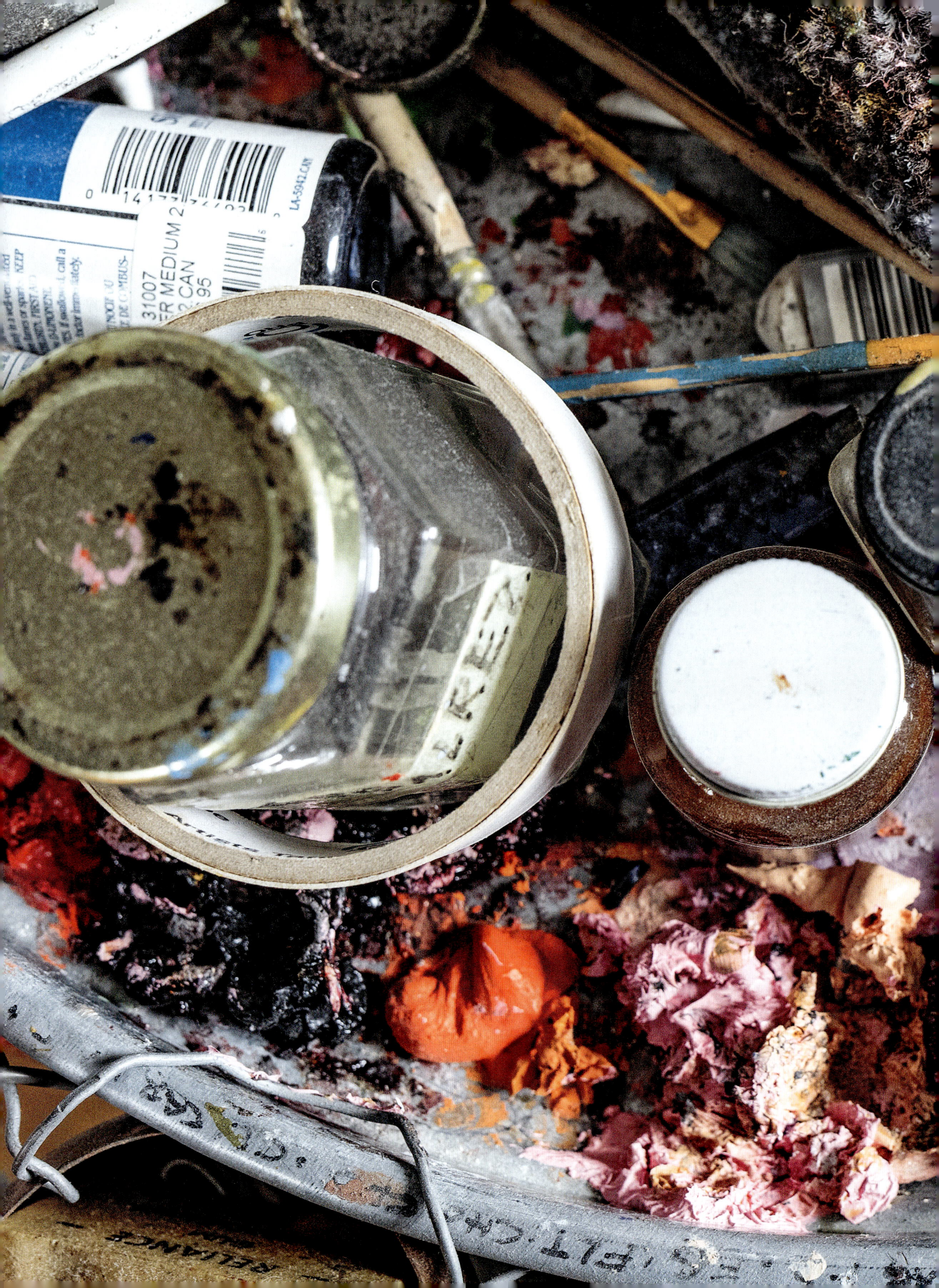

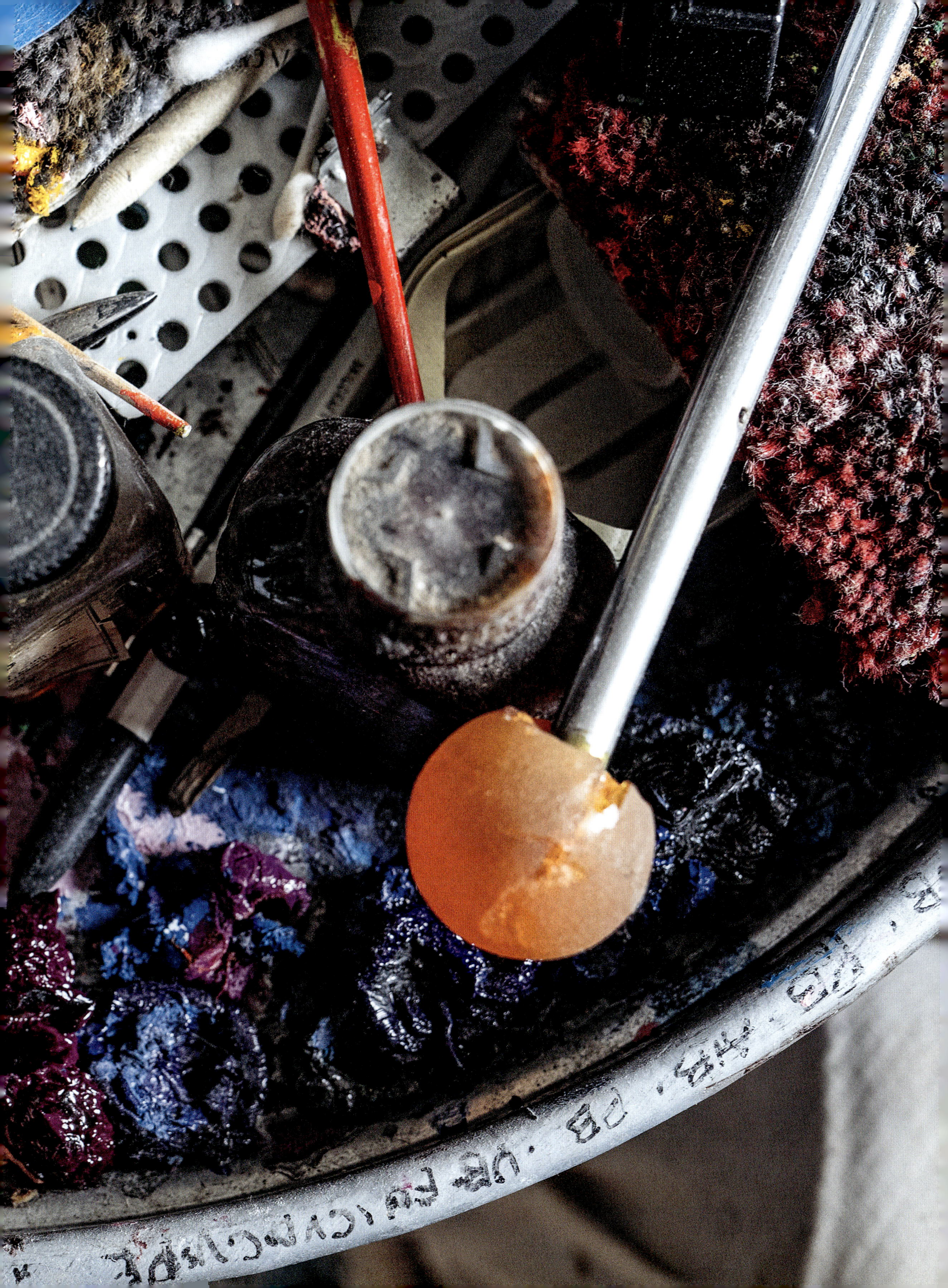

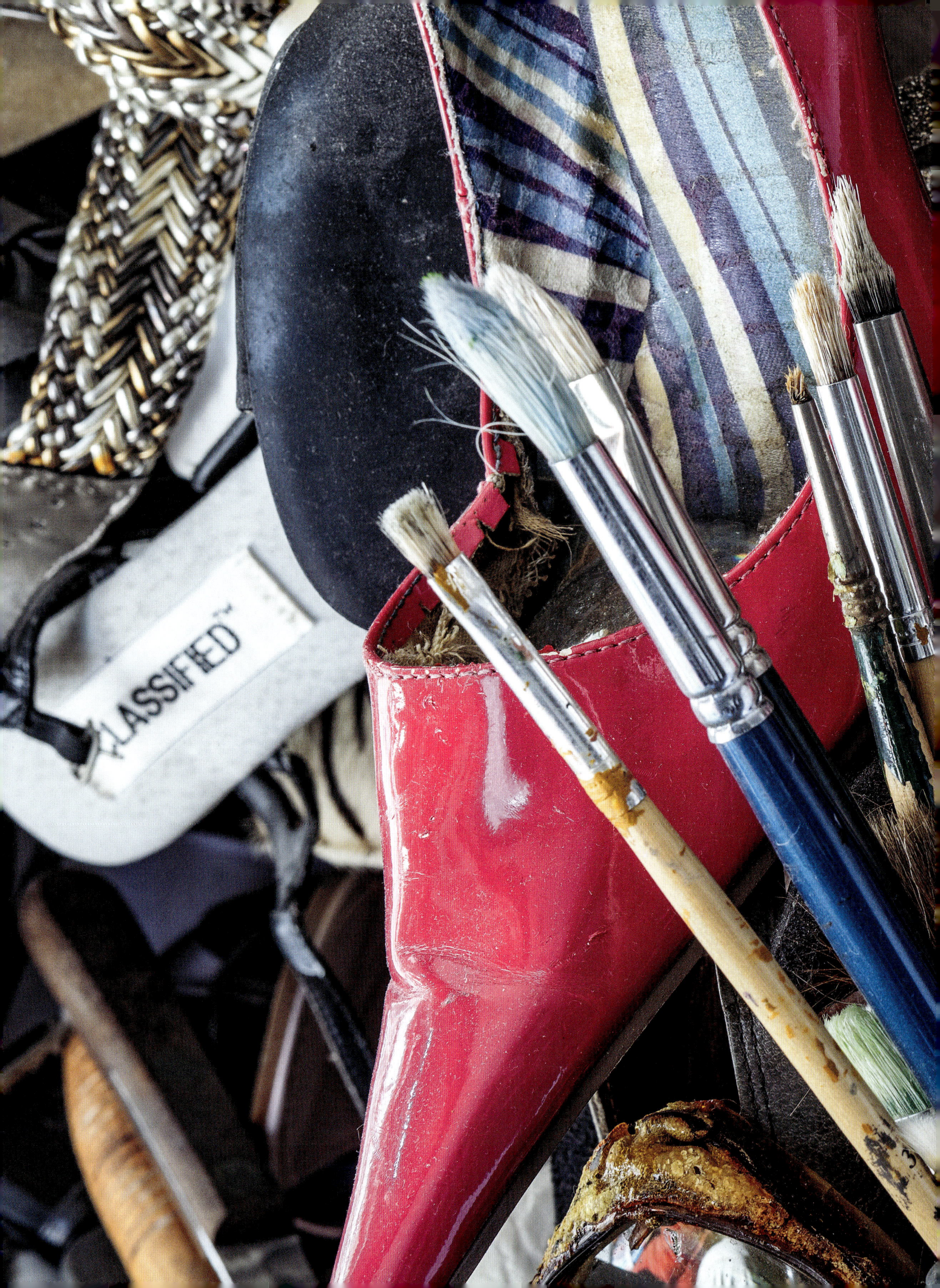
CLASSIFIED™

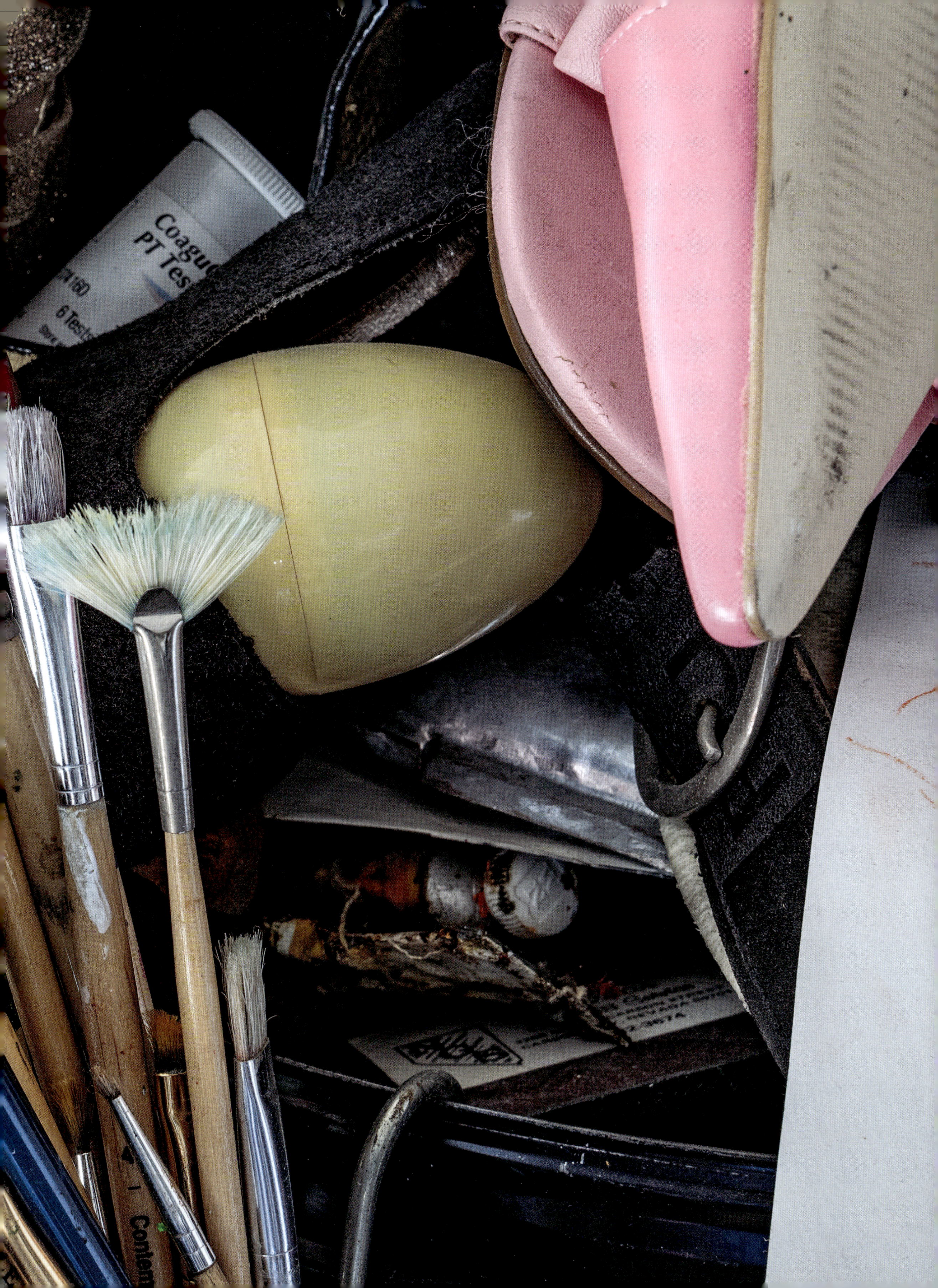

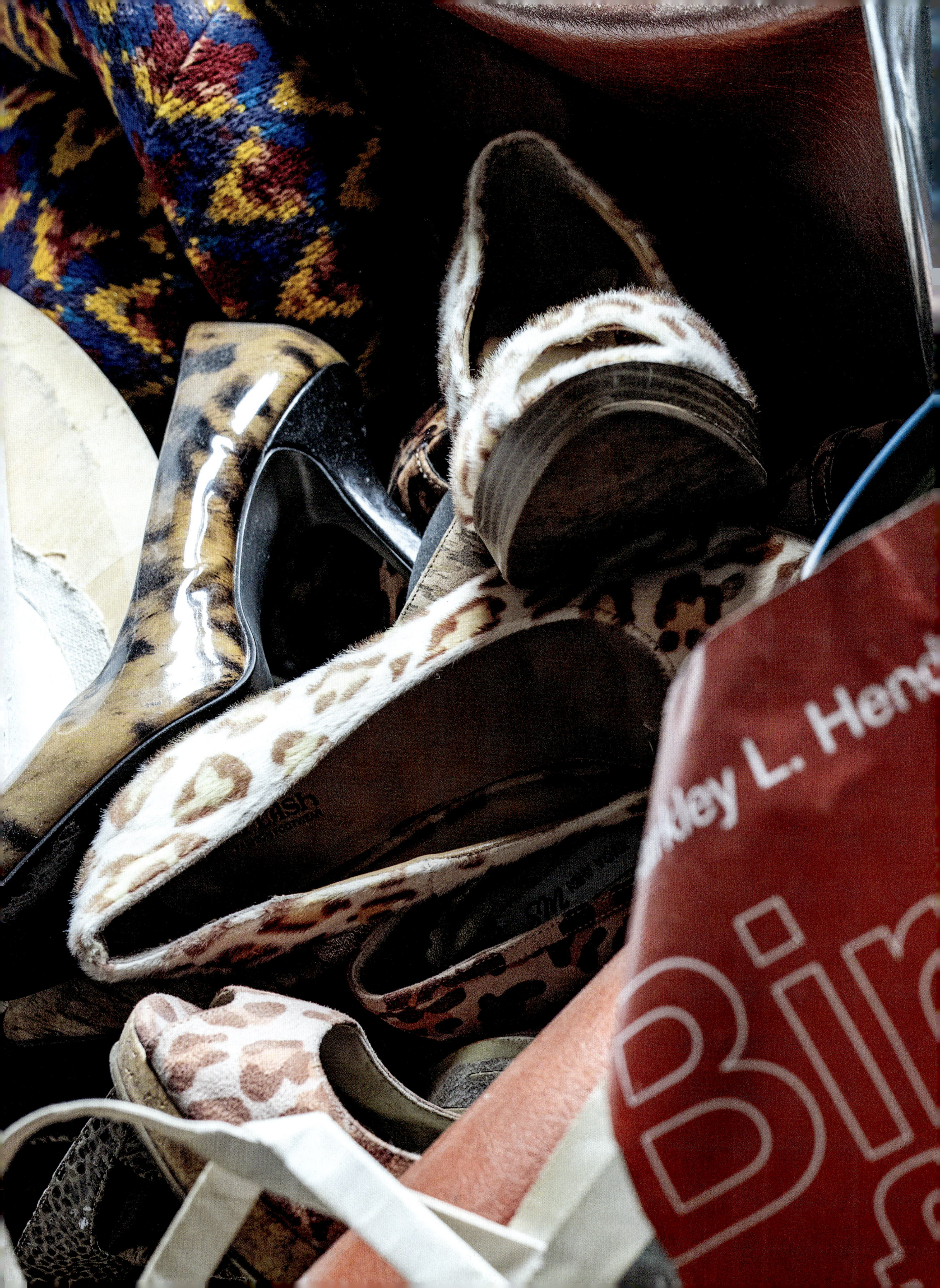

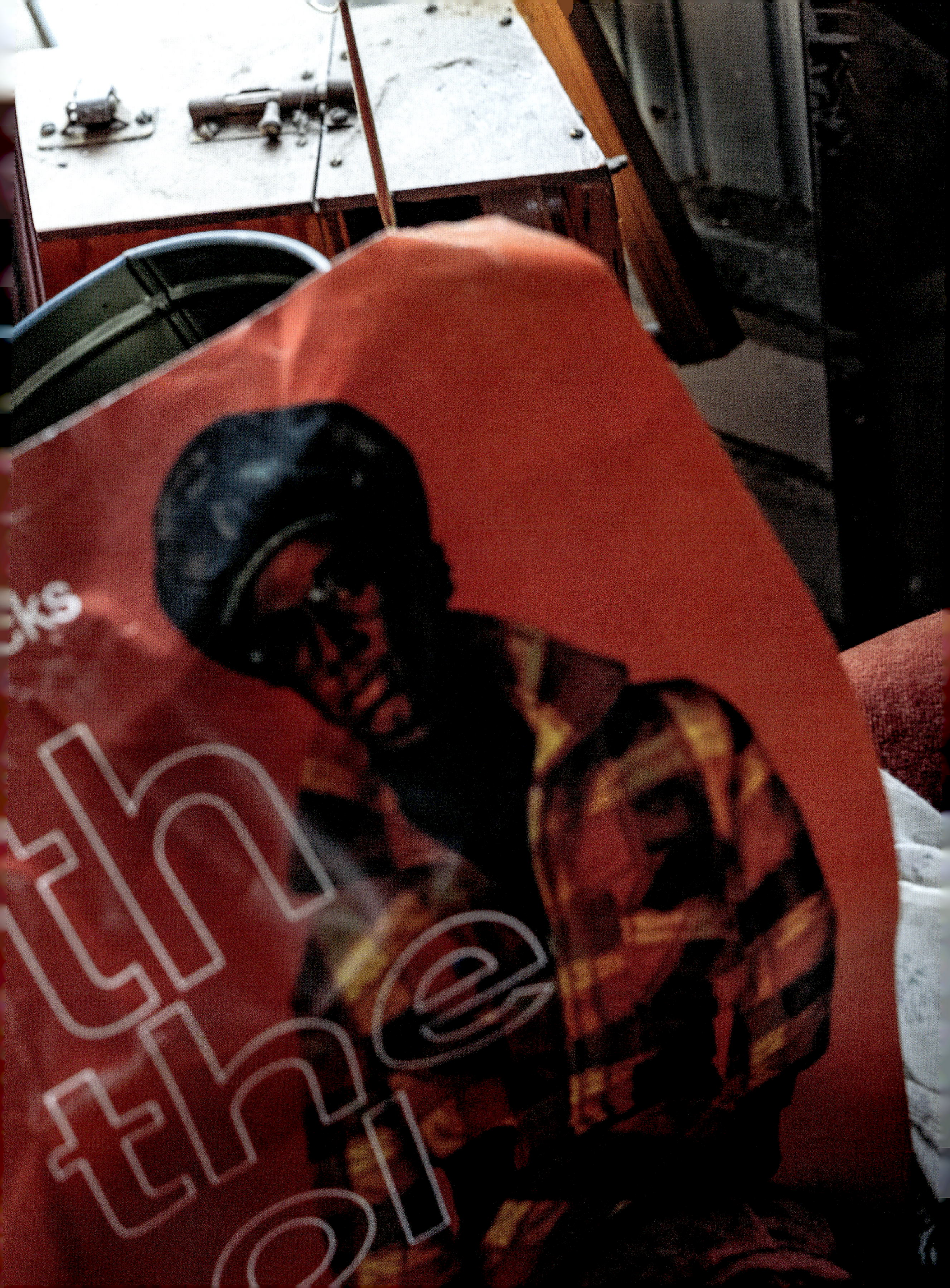

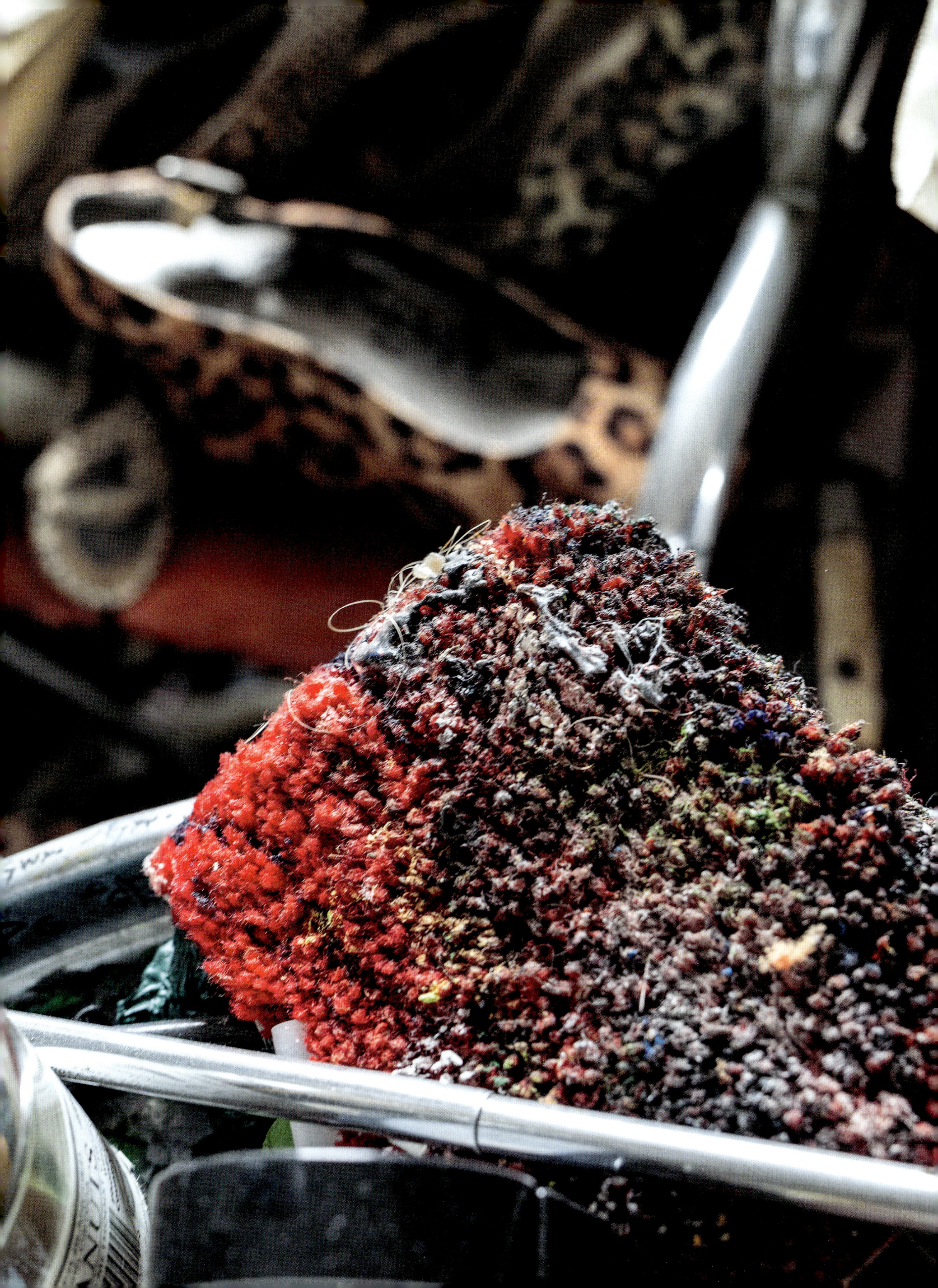

**Fetch those Jimmy Choos from the closet and strap them on real tight.**

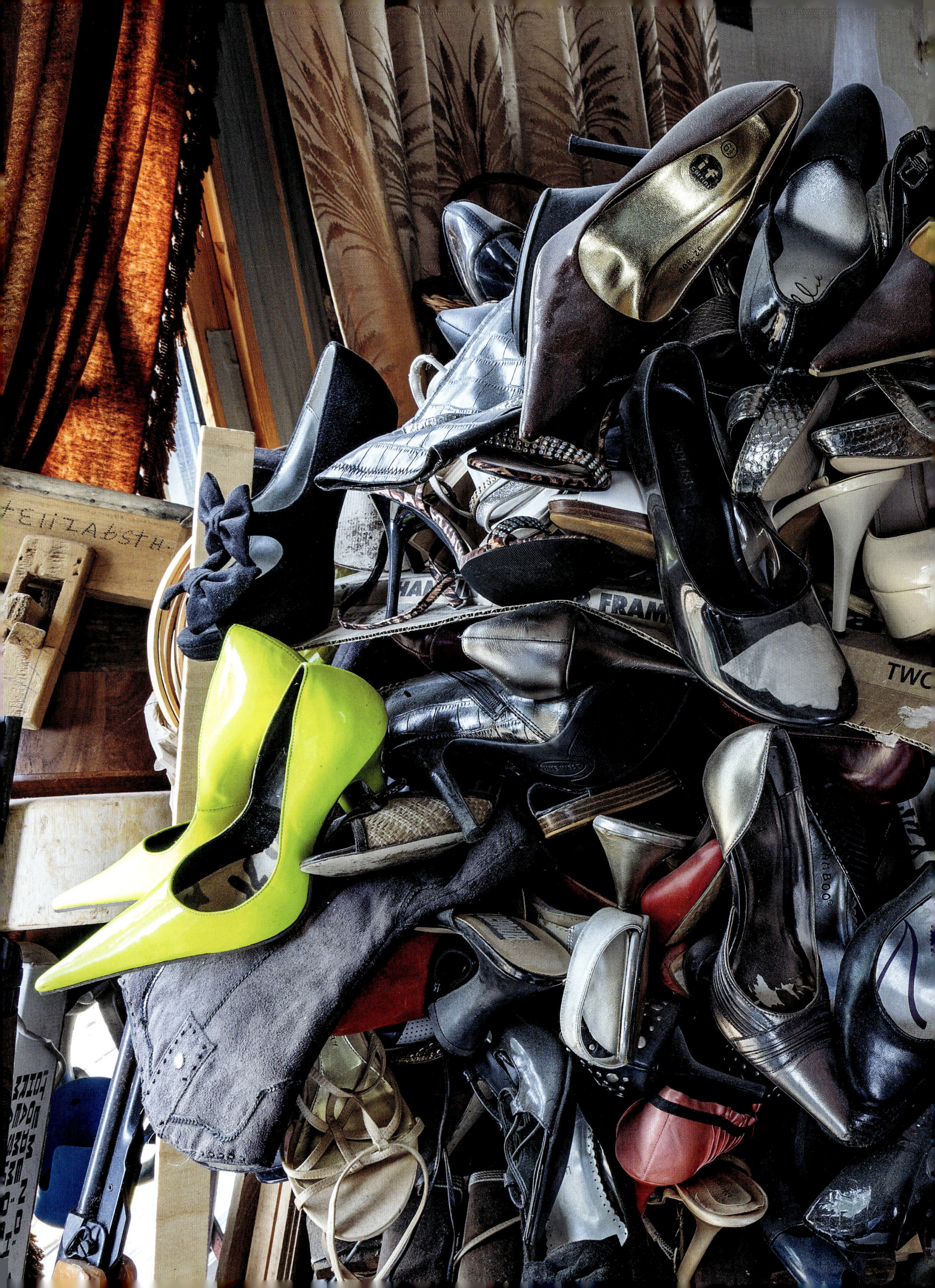

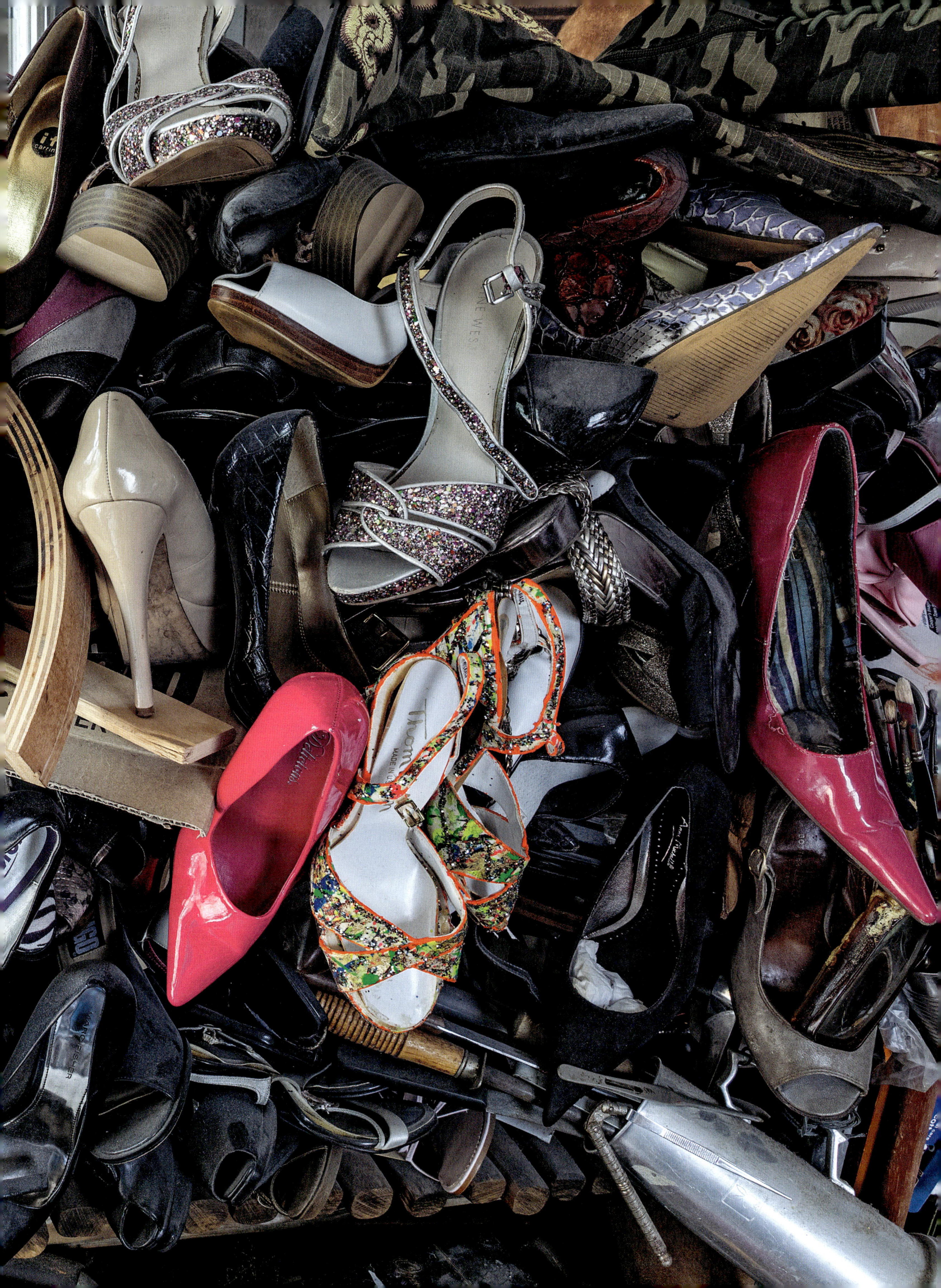

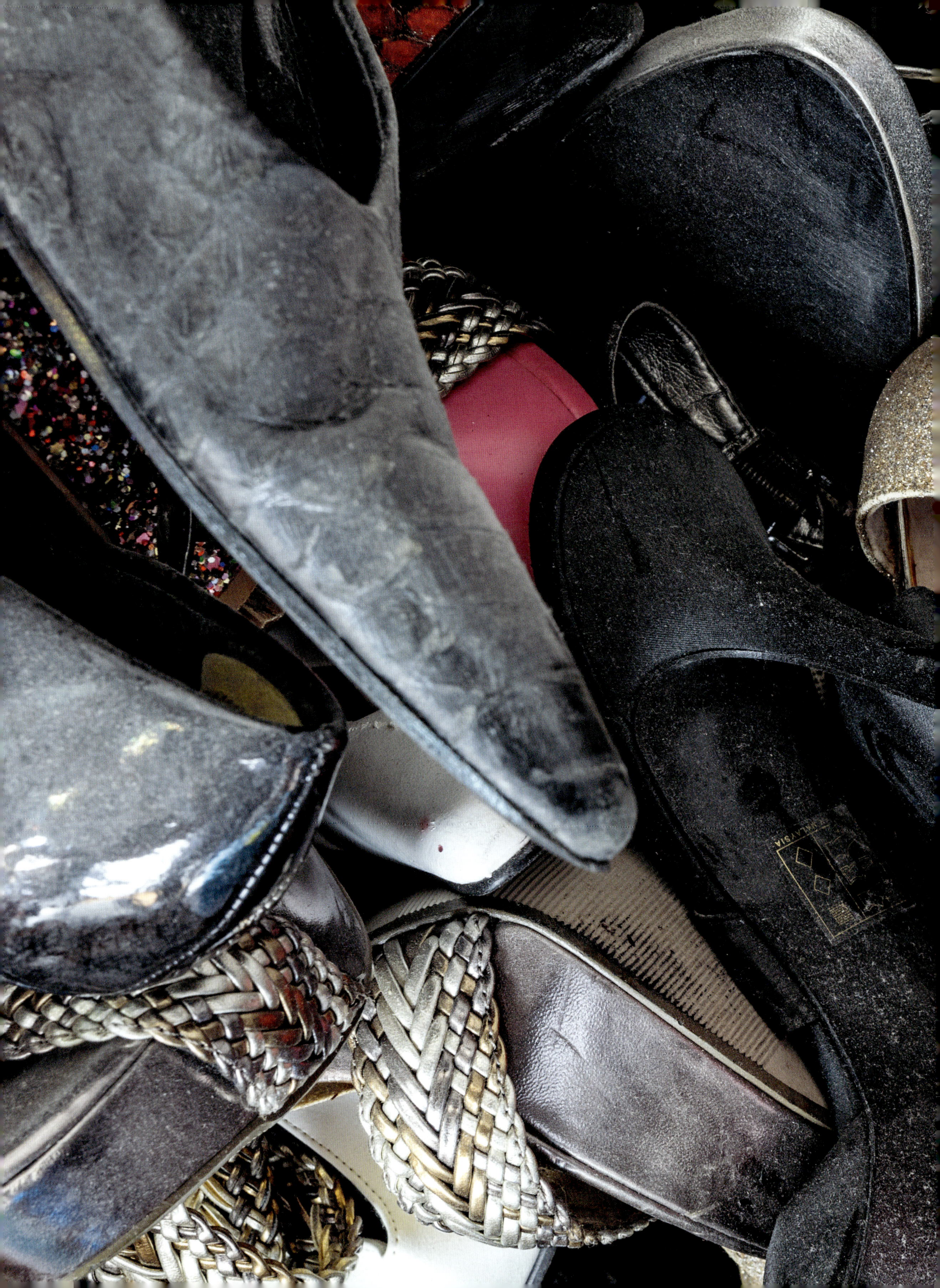

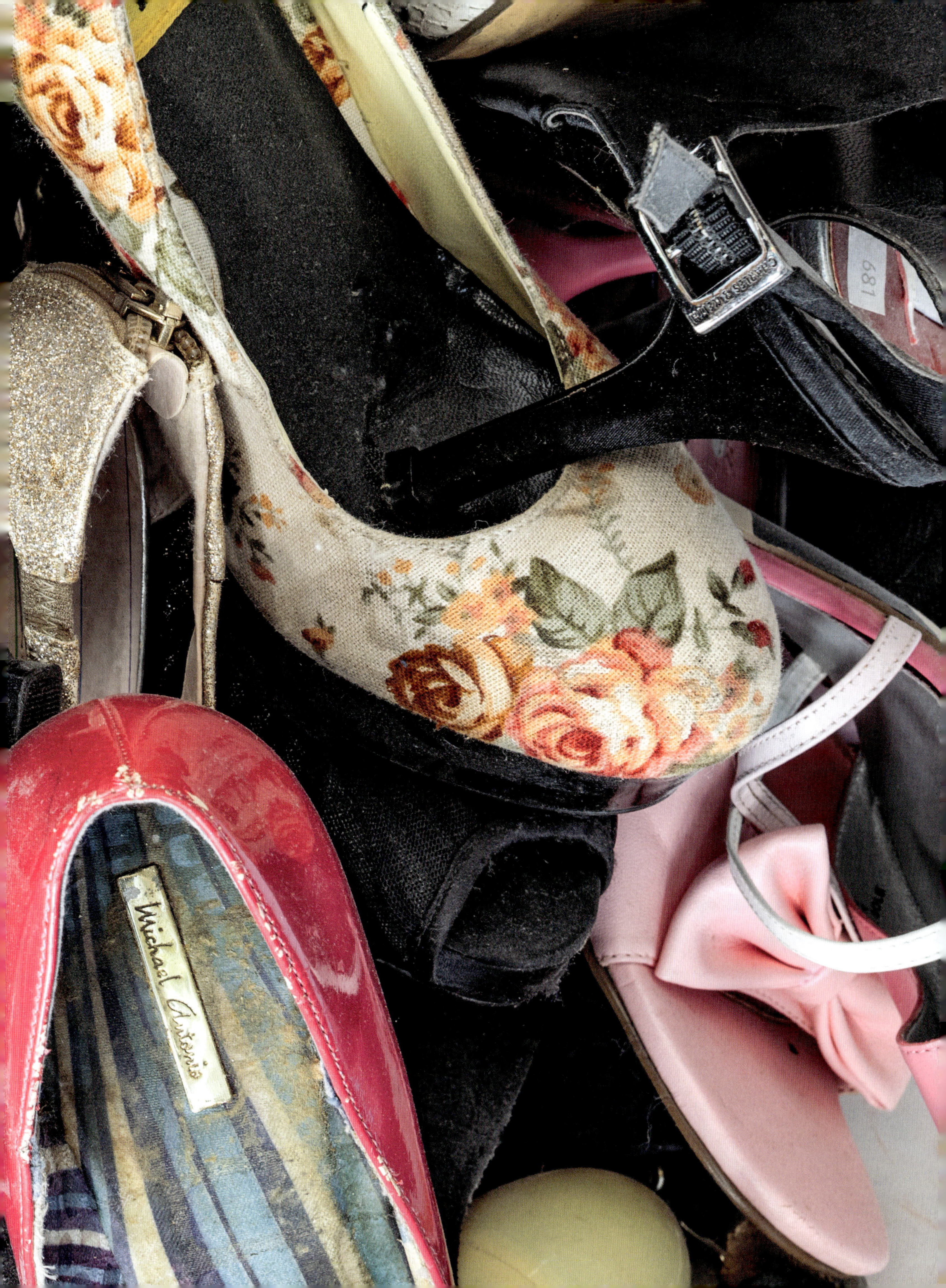
Michael Antonio

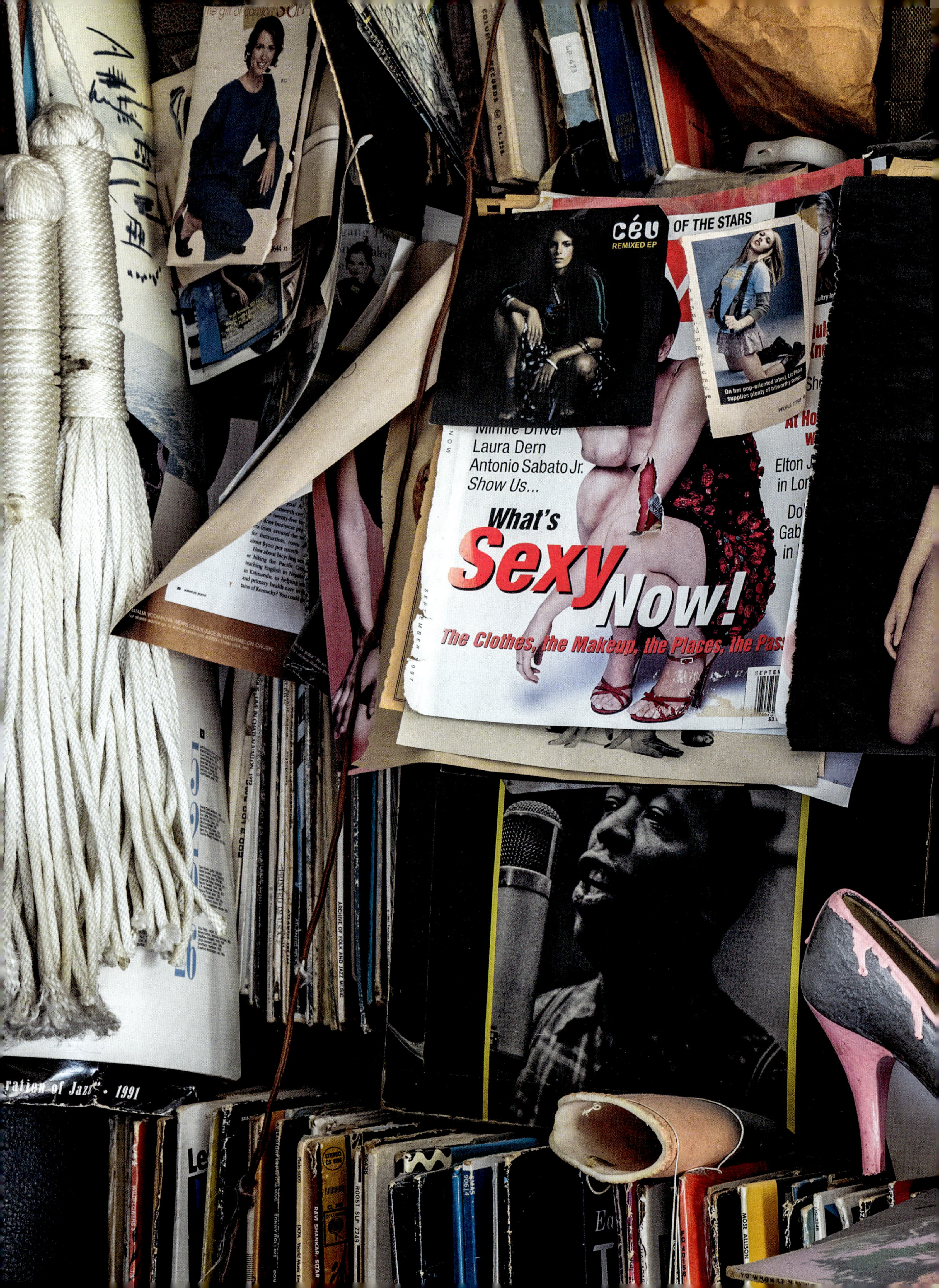
céu
REMIXED EP
OF THE STARS
Laura Dern
Antonio Sabato Jr.
Show Us...
What's
Sexy
Now!
The Clothes, the Makeup, the Places, the Pas
On her pop-oriented latest, Liz Phair supplies plenty of hitworthy songs
ARCHIVE OF FOLK AND JAZZ MUSIC
ROOST SLP 2249
RAVI SHANKAR, SITAR
MOSE ALLISON
ration of Jazz · 1991

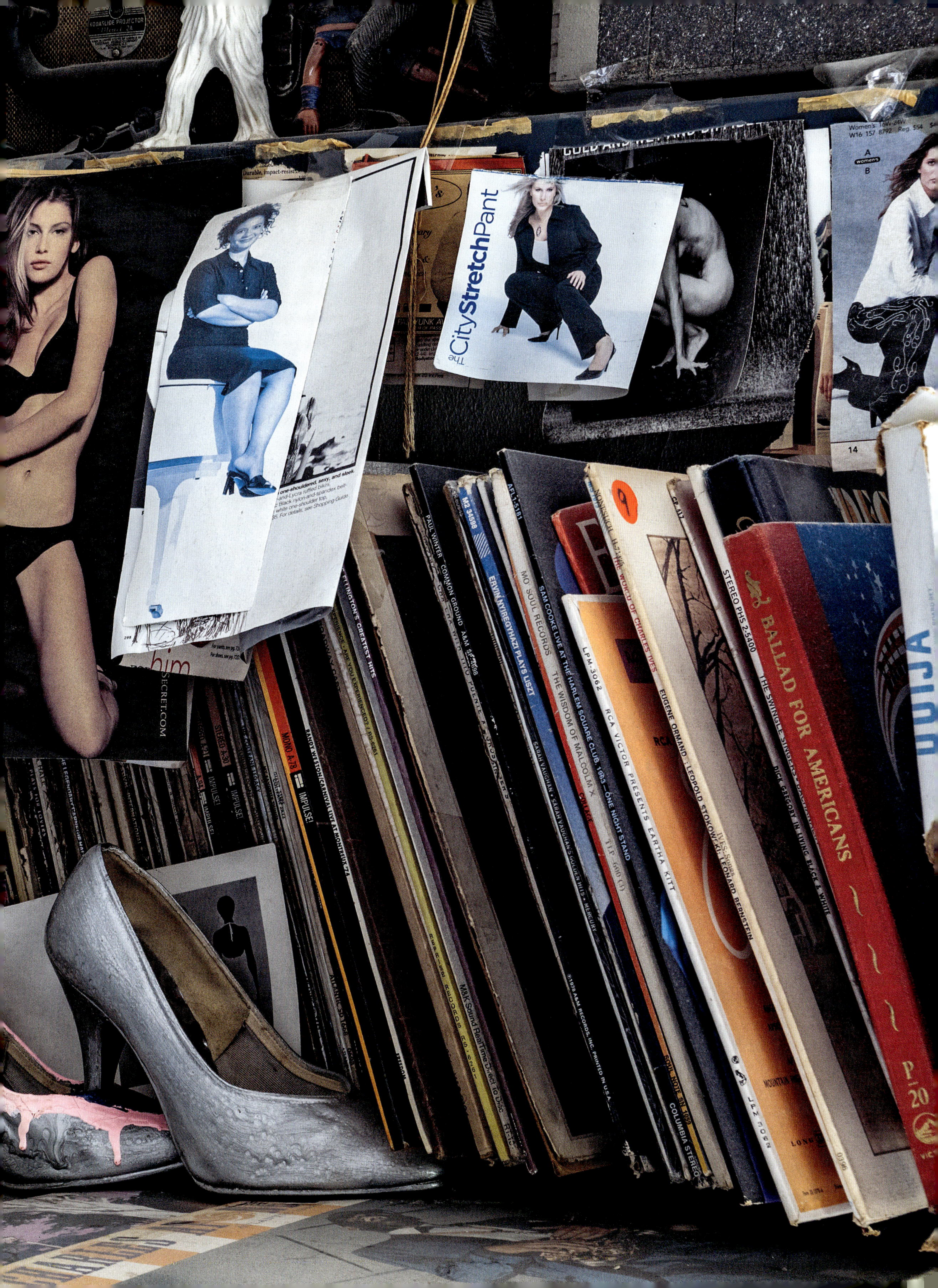

KODASLIDE PROJECTOR
The City Stretch Pant
PAUL WINTER COMMON GROUND A&M
ERVIN NYIREGYHAZI PLAYS LISZT
SAM COOKE LIVE AT THE HARLEM SQUARE CLUB, 1963—ONE NIGHT STAND
THE WISDOM OF MALCOLM X
LPM-3062 RCA VICTOR PRESENTS EARTHA KITT
EUGENE ORMANDY LEOPOLD STOKOWSKI LEONARD BERNSTEIN
STEREO PHS 2-5400 THE SWINGLE SINGERS
BALLAD FOR AMERICANS
MONO A-78 IMPULSE
COLUMBIA STEREO

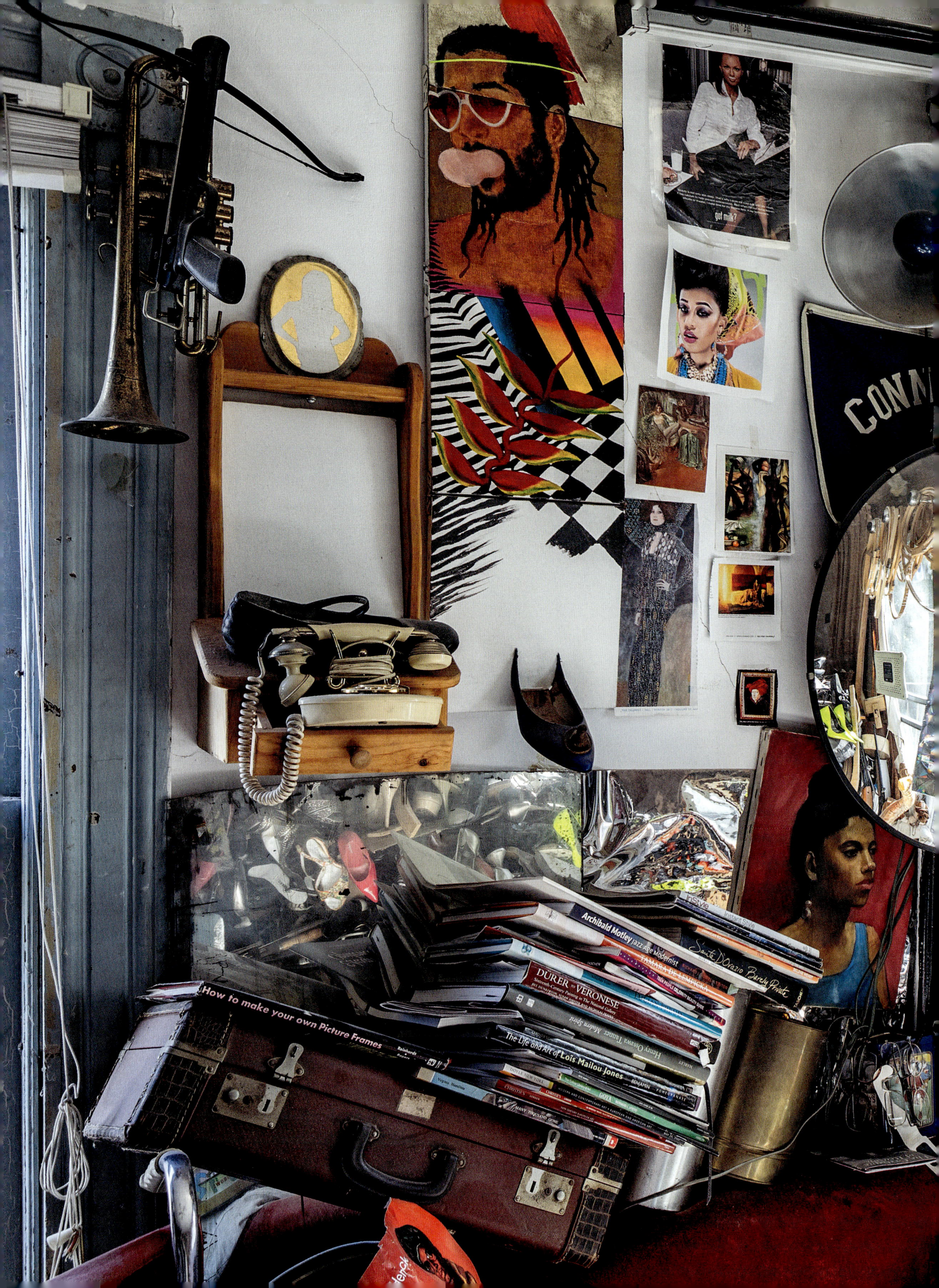
got milk?
CONN
InStyle
Instant Style
Archibald Motley Jazz Age Modernist
TASCHEN
TAMARA DE LEMPICKA
Sante D'Orazio Barely Private
DÜRER TO VERONESE
Sixteenth-Century Painting in The National Gallery
Henry Ossawa Tanner Modern Spirit
How to make your own Picture Frames
Reinhardt
The Life and Art of Loïs Mailou Jones
BENJAMIN
POMEGRANATE
DOYLE NEW YORK
GOYA
CHRISTIE'S
Virginia Hamilton
MANY THOUSAND GONE

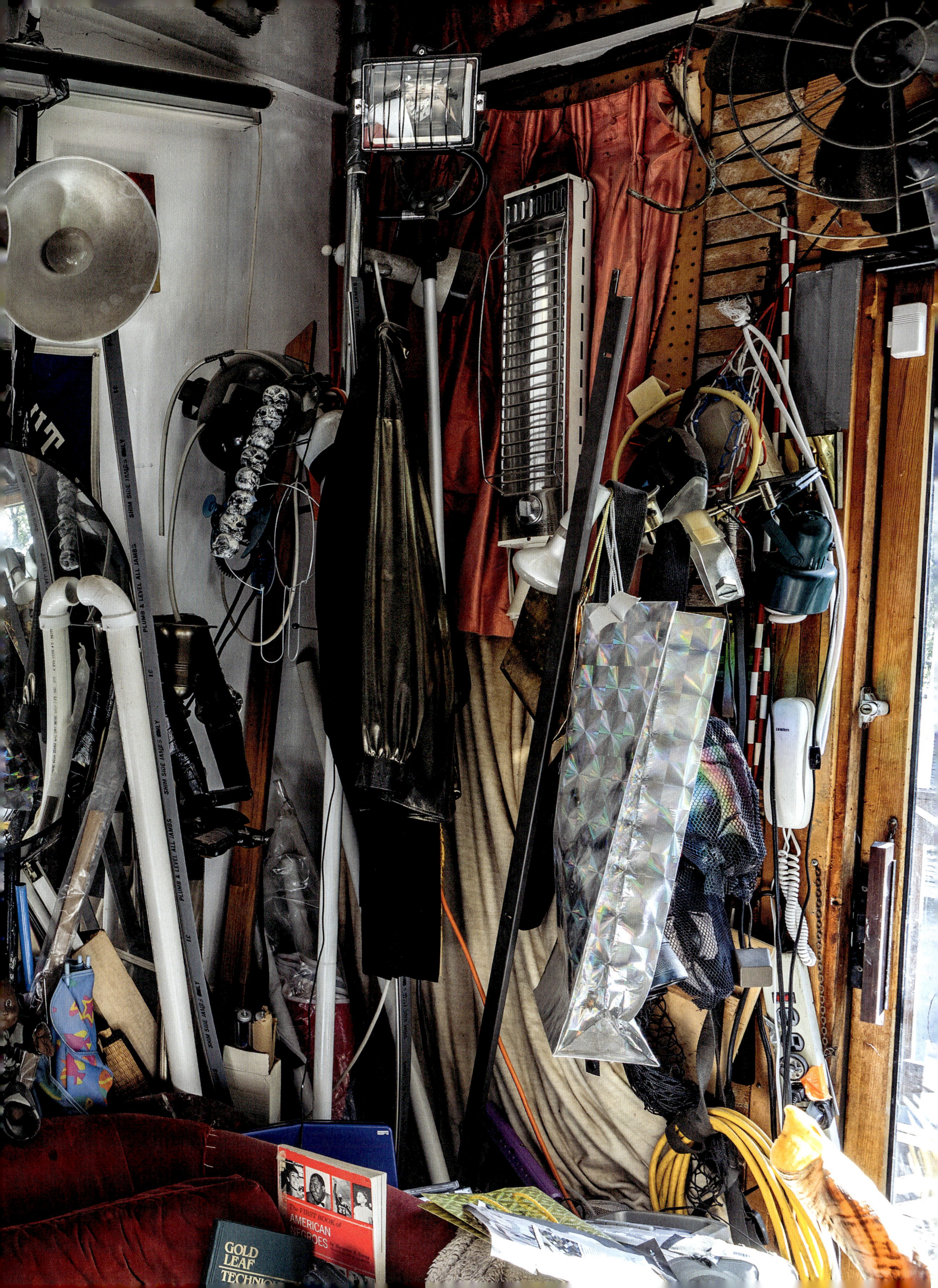
PLUMB & LEVEL ALL JAMBS
SHIM SIDE JAMBS
AMERICAN
NEGROES
GOLD
LEAF

**Is it possible to forcast ones own insanity? If so & if so? if so shit!**

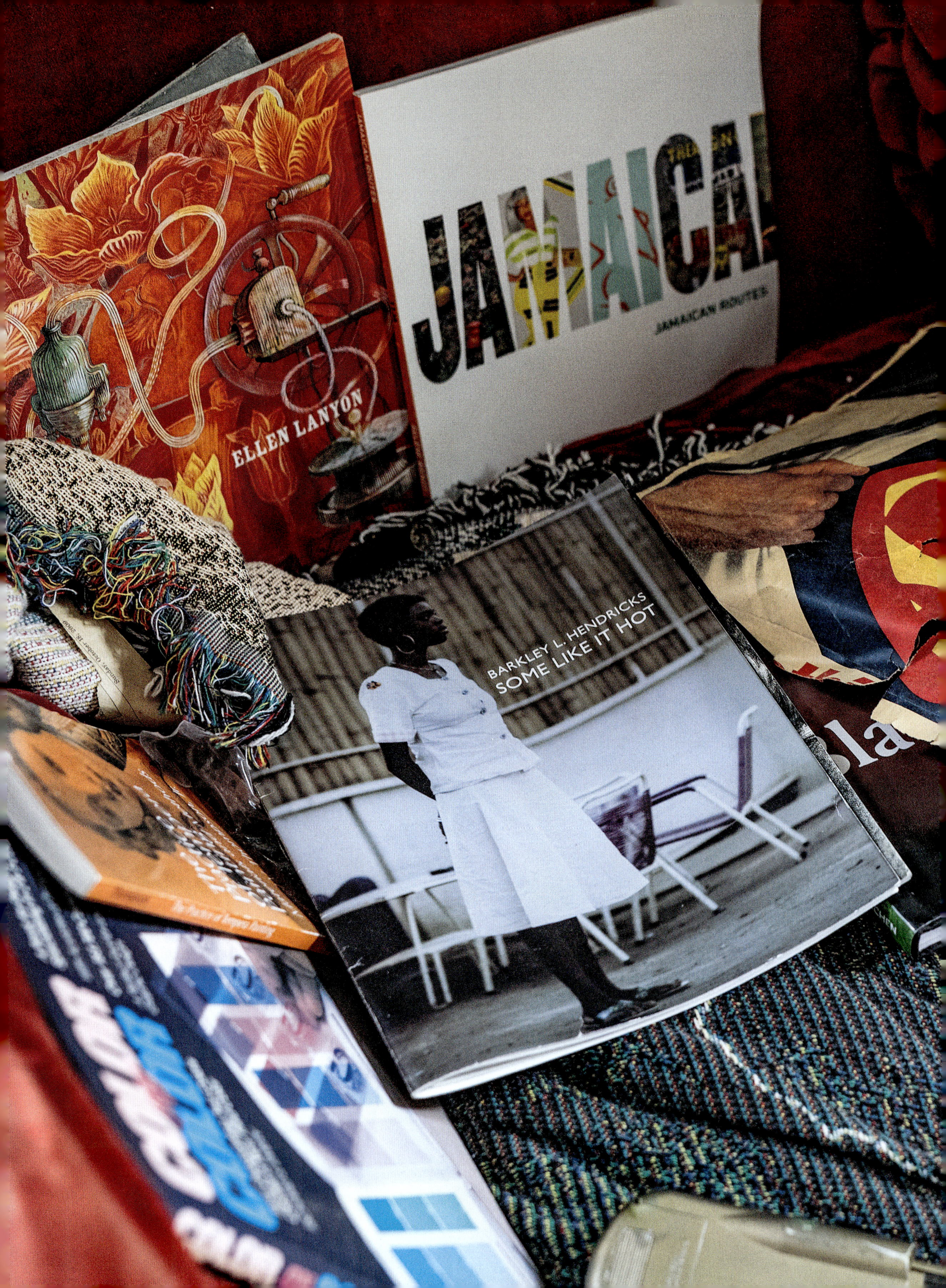
ELLEN LANYON
JAMAICA
JAMAICAN ROUTES
BARKLEY L. HENDRICKS
SOME LIKE IT HOT

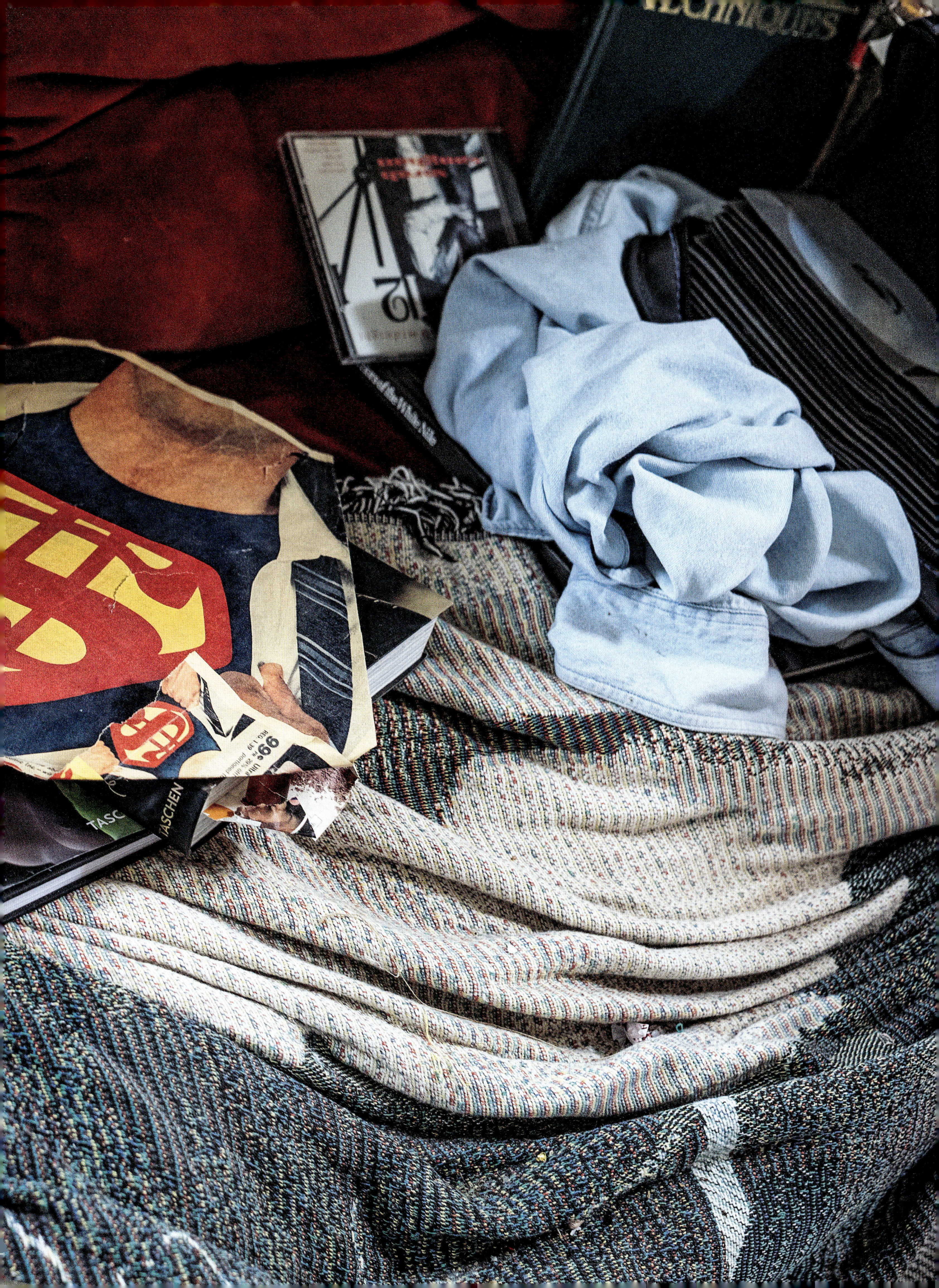

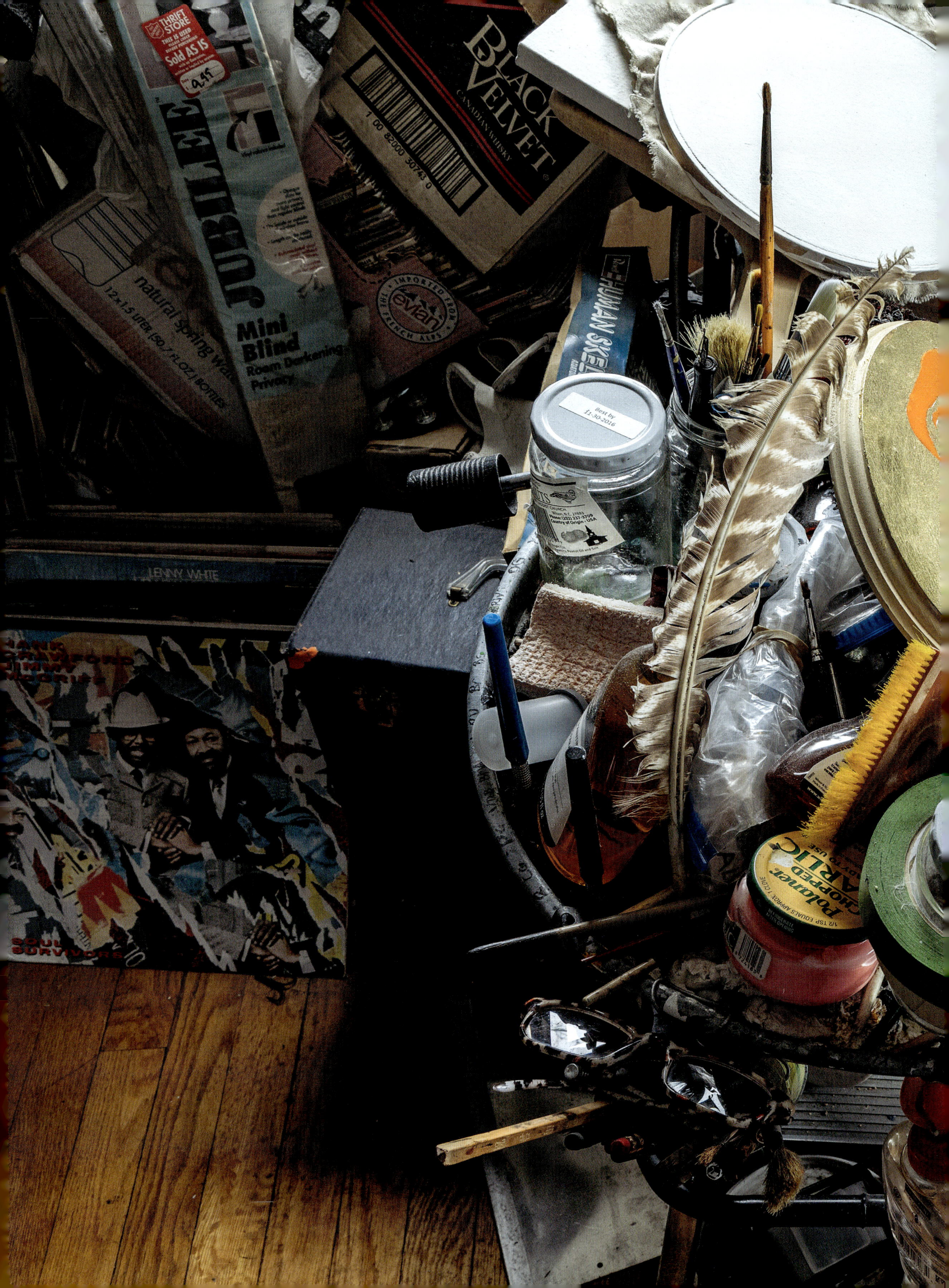
THRIFT STORE
Sold AS IS
JUBILEE
Mini Blind
Room Darkening
Privacy
BLACK VELVET
CANADIAN WHISKY
natural spring wa
12 x 1.5 LITER (50.7 FL OZ) BOTTLES
evian
IMPORTED FROM THE FRENCH ALPS
HUMAN SKE
LENNY WHITE
SOUL SURVIVORS

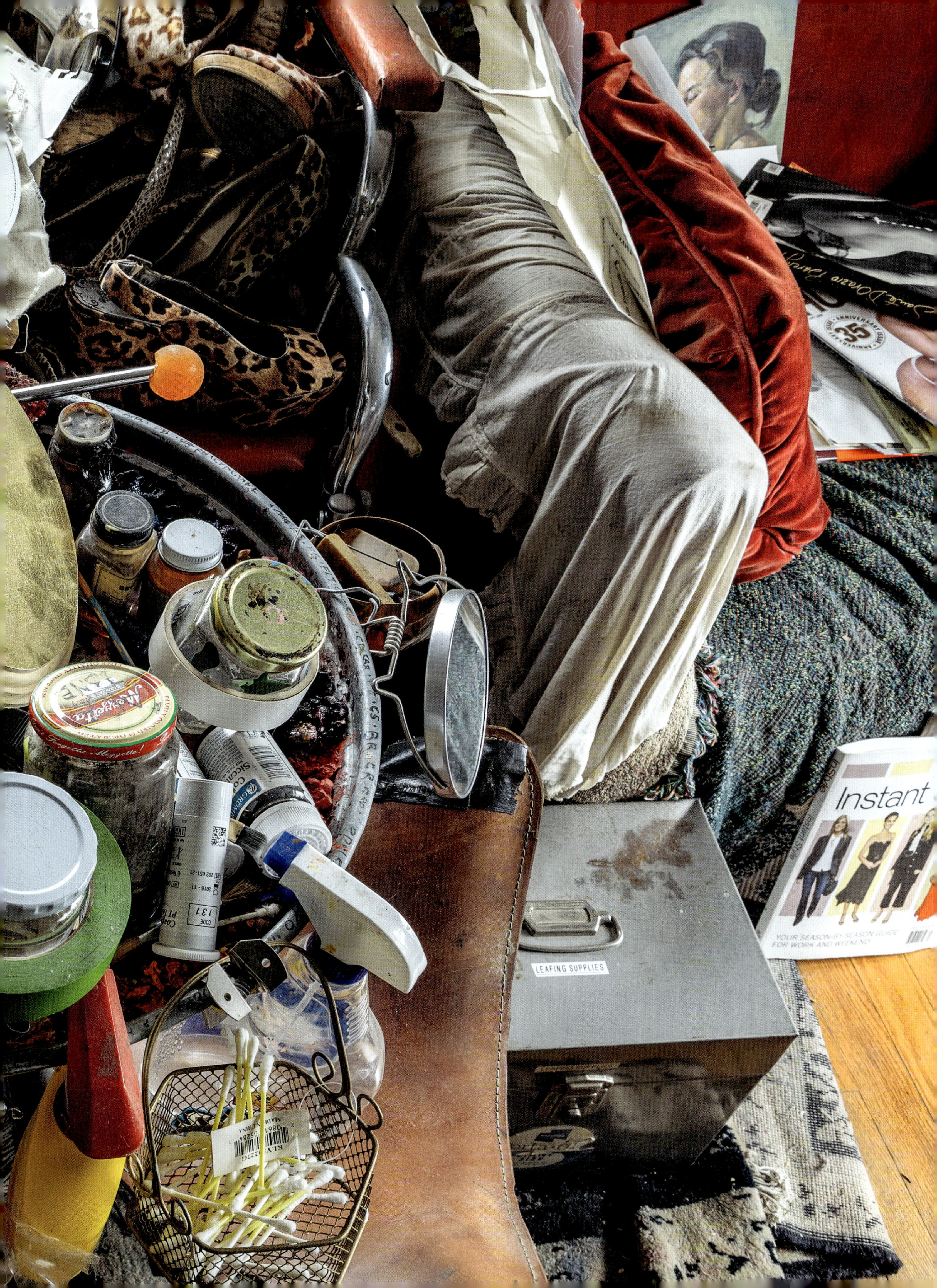
LEAFING SUPPLIES
Instant
YOUR SEASON-BY-SEASON GUIDE
FOR WORK AND WEEKEND

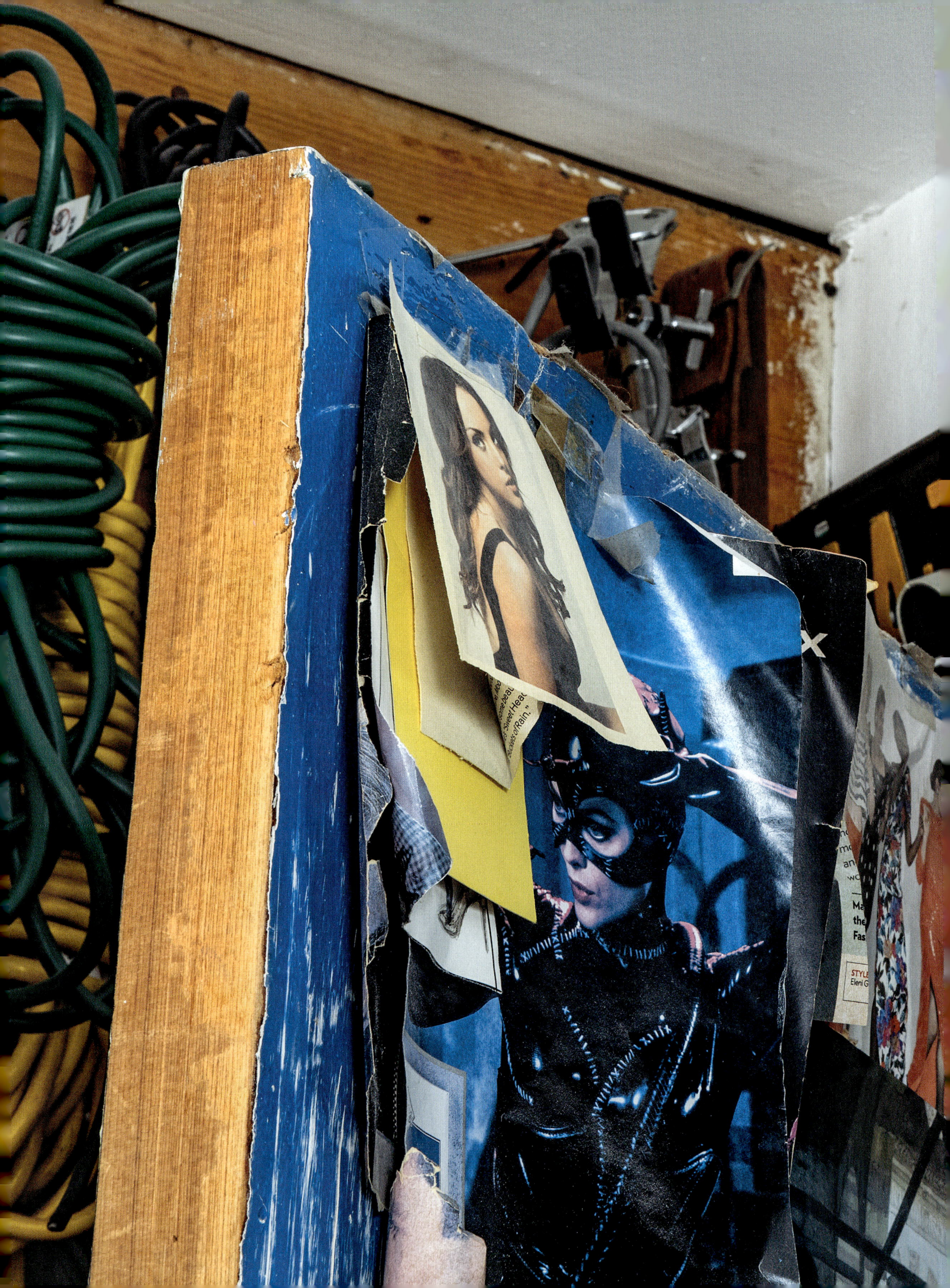

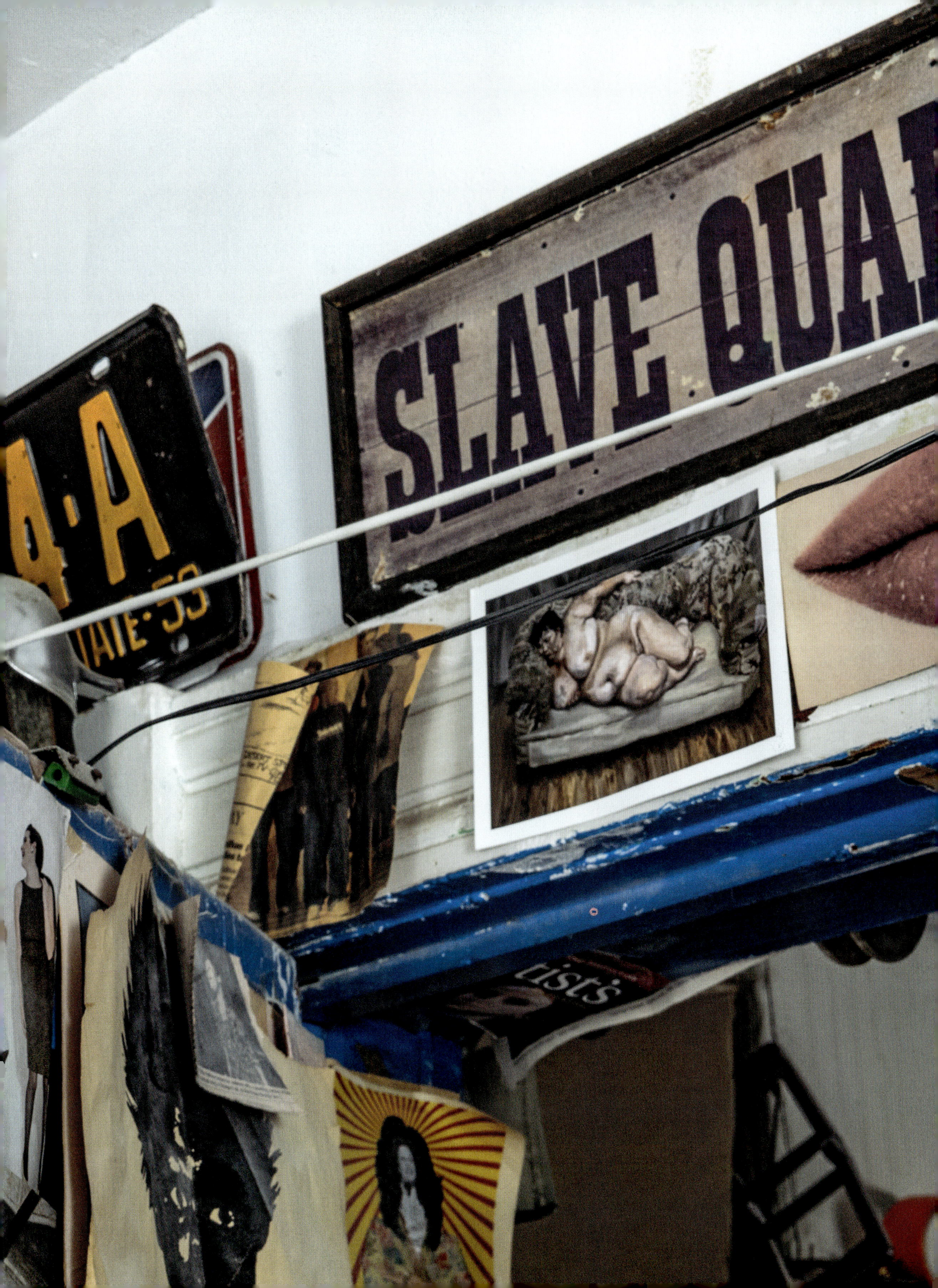
SLAVE
4-A
53

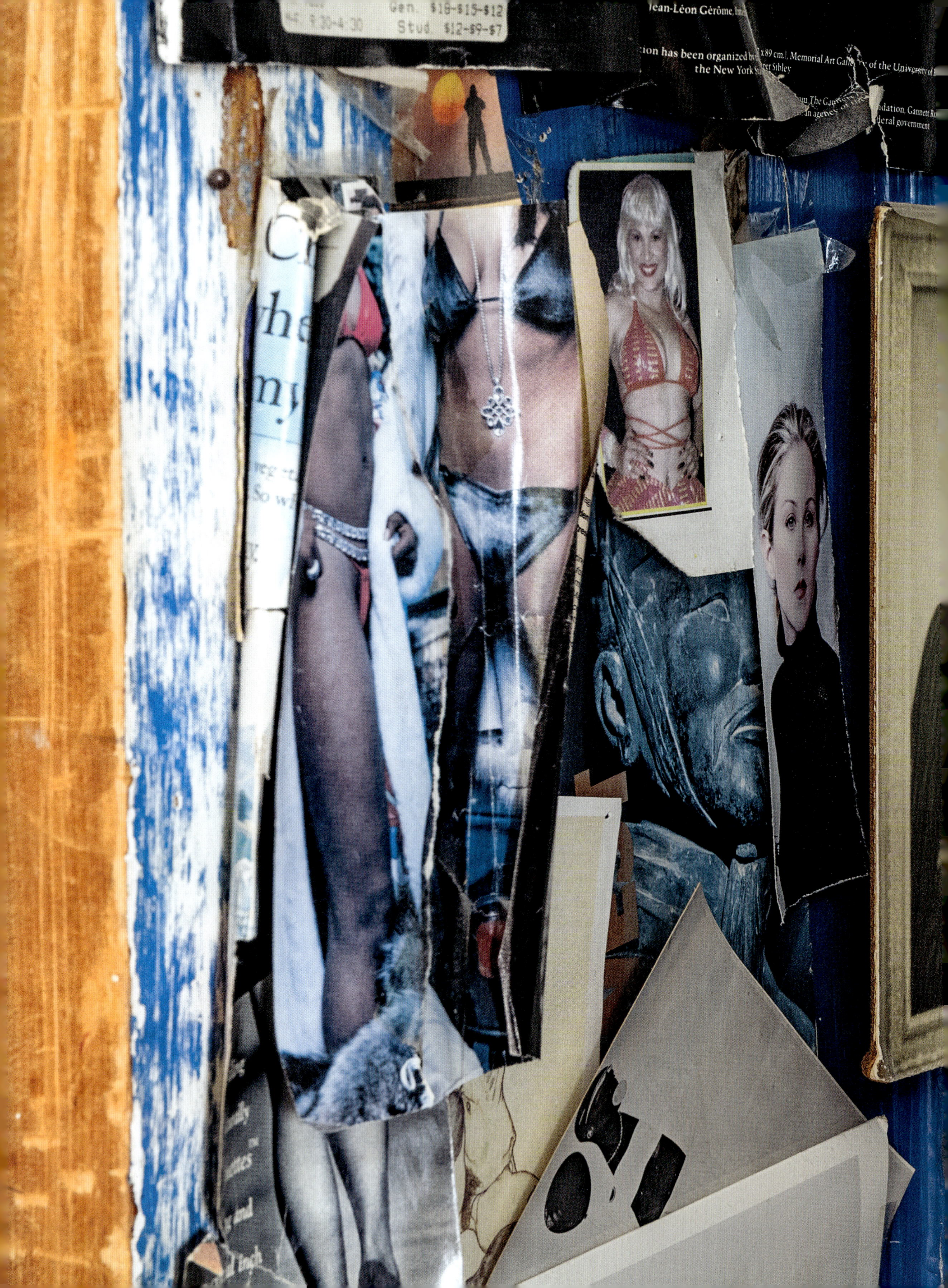

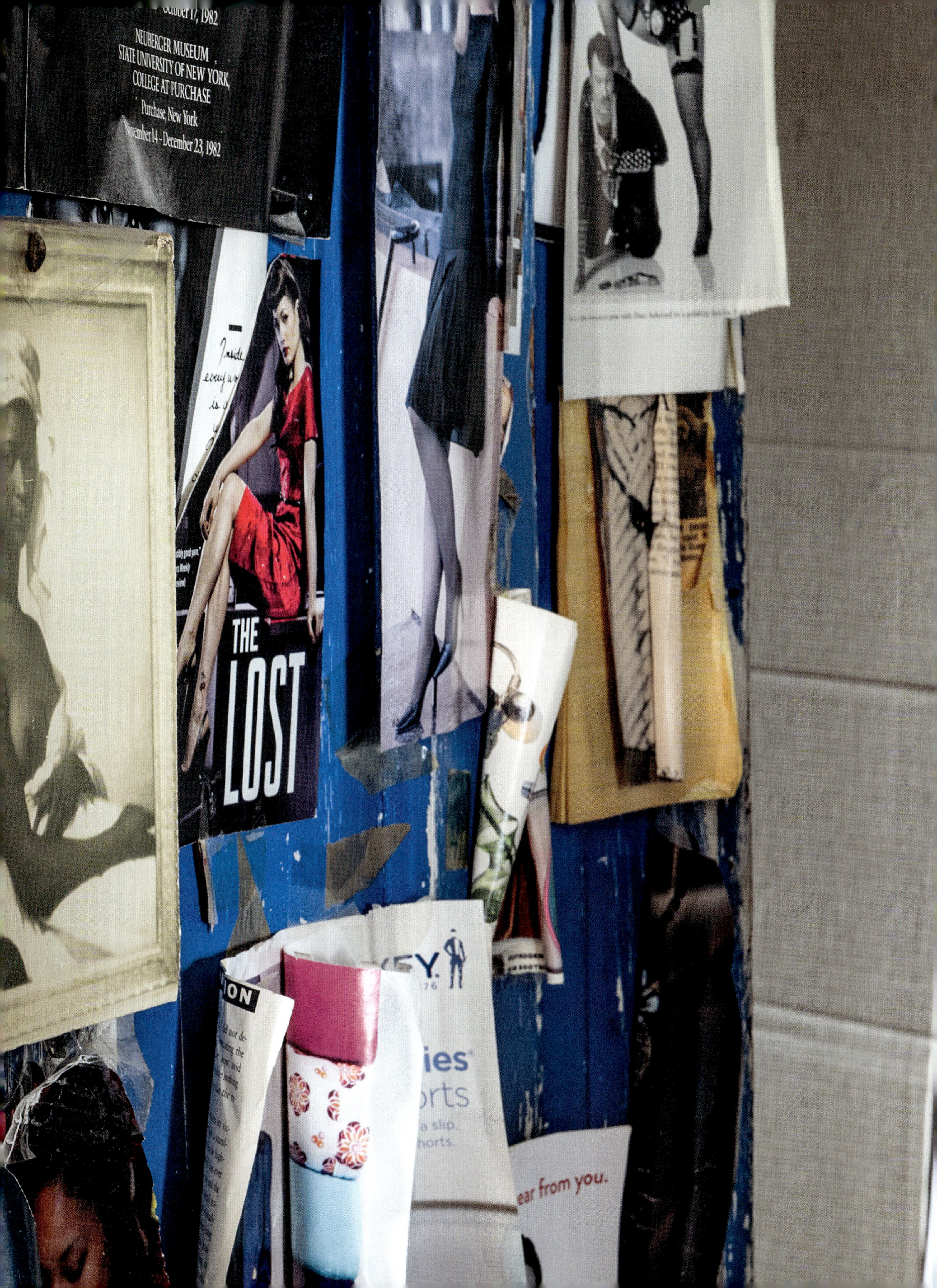

October 17, 1982
NEUBERGER MUSEUM
STATE UNIVERSITY OF NEW YORK,
COLLEGE AT PURCHASE
Purchase, New York
November 14 – December 23, 1982
THE
LOST
ear from you.

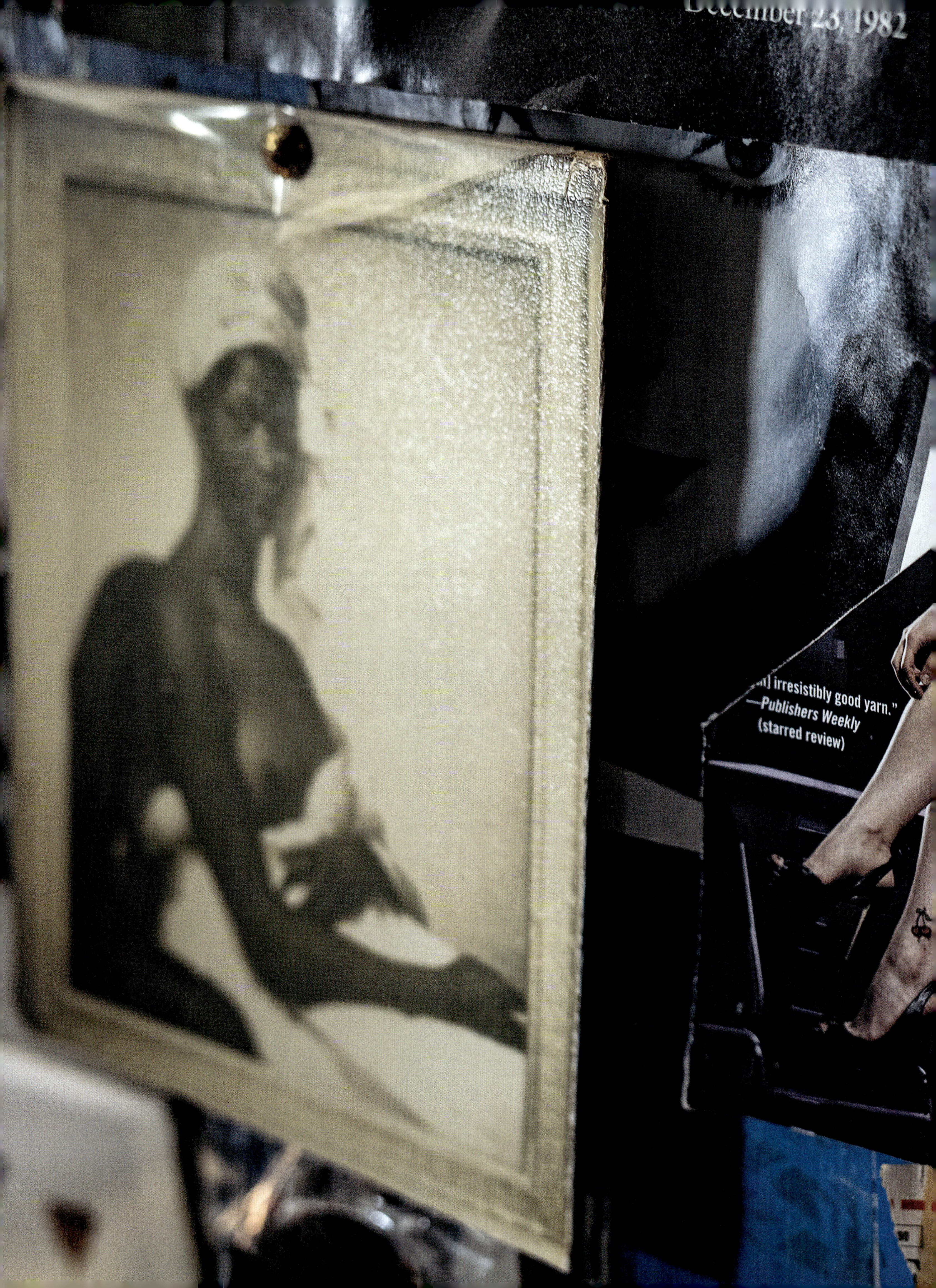
December 23, 1982
irresistibly good yarn."
—Publishers Weekly
(starred review)

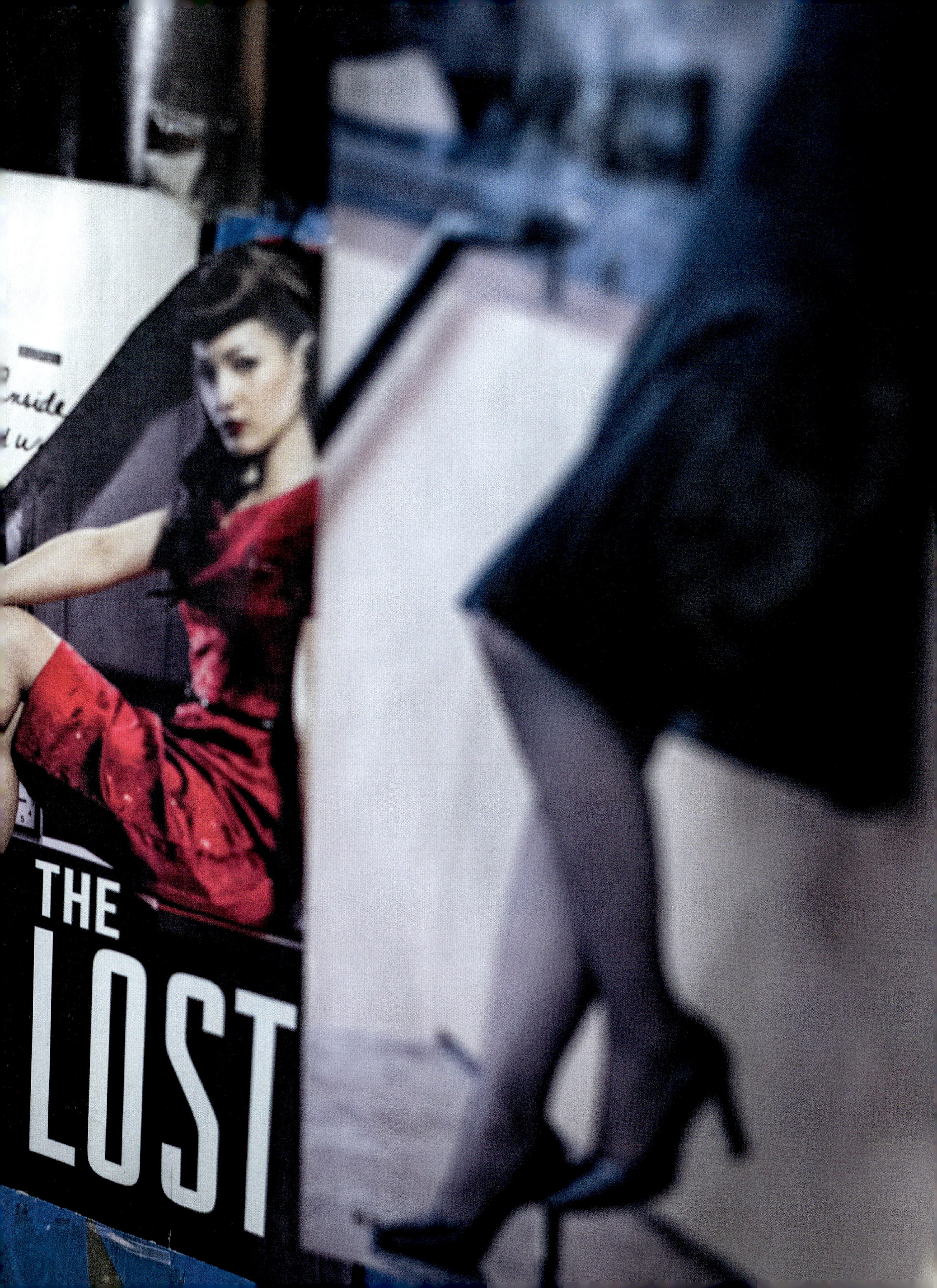
THE
LOST

**Is there a difference between slickness and elegance. Of course there is, yet in my mind I find the things most people call slick, elegant. The so called "slick" fashion models, I find quite elegant.**

"SLICKNESS VS ELEGANCE," Feb 19, 1978 (see p. 237)

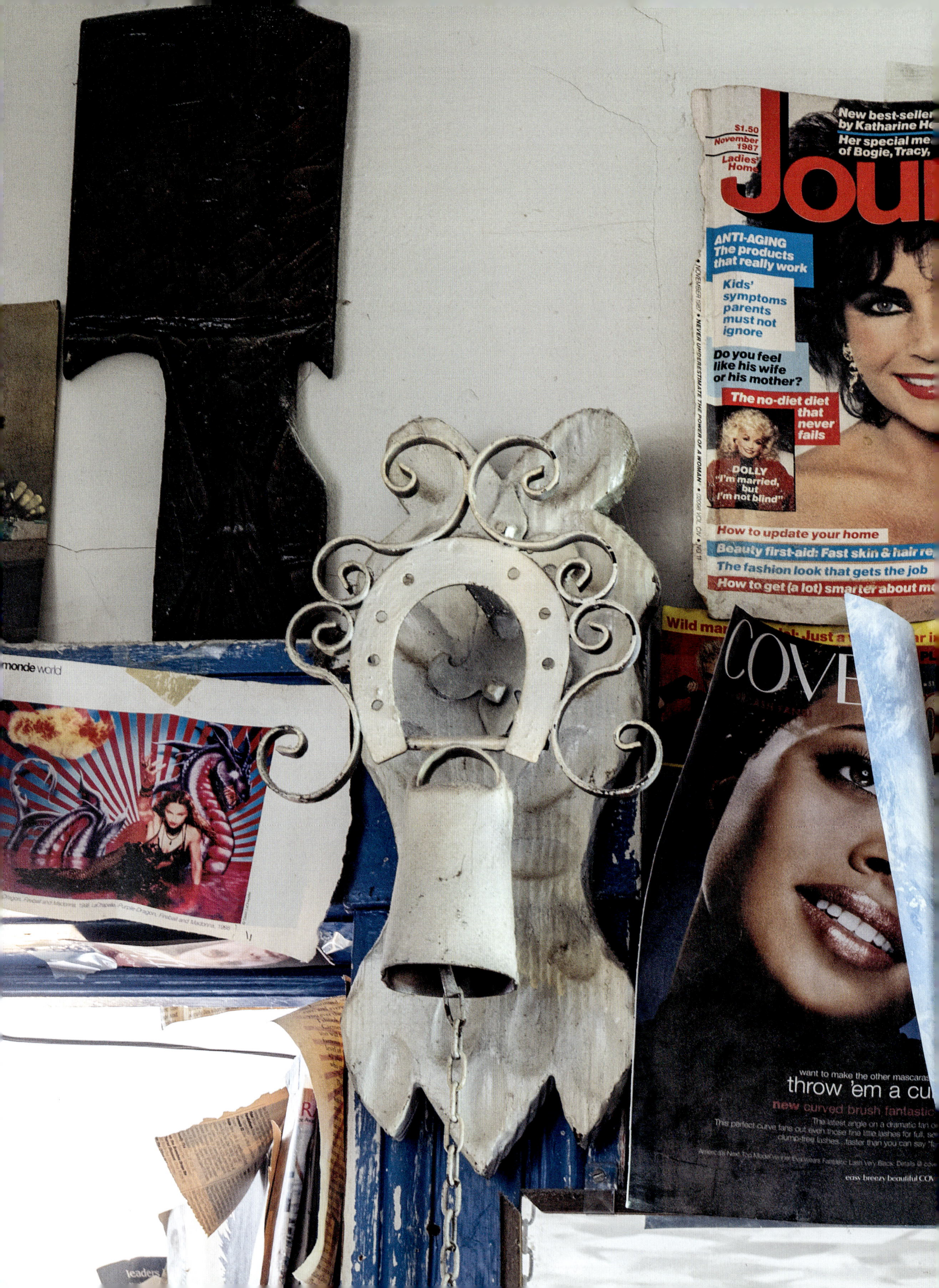

$1.50
November
1987
Ladies'
Home
Jou
New best-seller
by Katharine He
Her special me
of Bogie, Tracy,
ANTI-AGING
The products
that really work
Kids'
symptoms
parents
must not
ignore
Do you feel
like his wife
or his mother?
The no-diet diet
that
never
fails
DOLLY
"I'm married,
but
I'm not blind"
NEVER UNDERESTIMATE THE POWER OF A WOMAN
How to update your home
Beauty first-aid: Fast skin & hair re
The fashion look that gets the job
How to get (a lot) smarter about me
monde world
COVE
want to make the other mascaras
throw 'em a cu
new curved brush fantastic
easy breezy beautiful COV

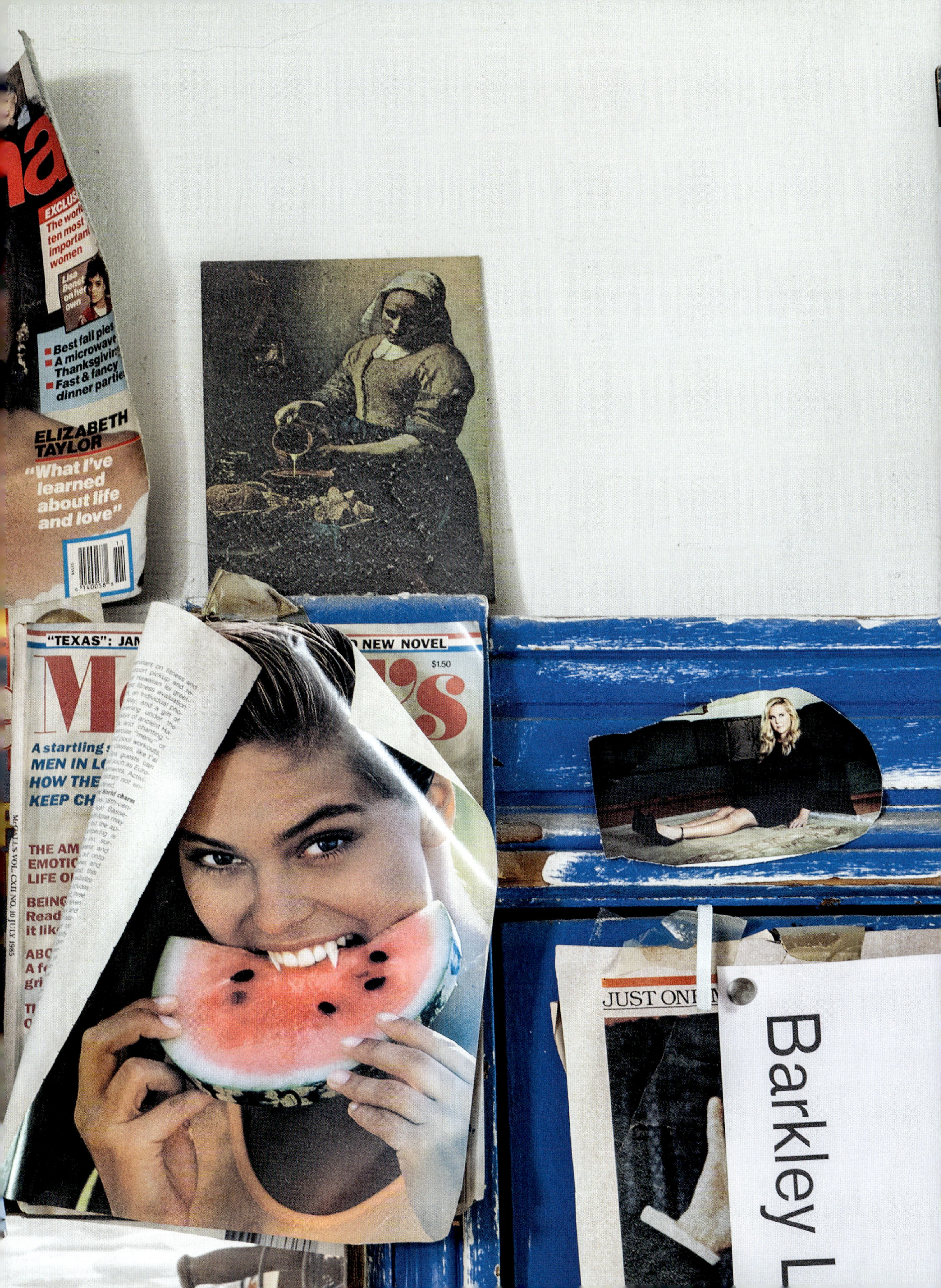

EXCLUS
The worl
ten most
importan
women
Best fall ple
A microwave
Thanksgivin
Fast & fancy
dinner partie
ELIZABETH TAYLOR
“What I've learned about life and love”
“TEXAS”: JAN
NEW NOVEL
$1.50
A startling
MEN IN LO
HOW THE
KEEP CH
THE AM
EMOTIO
LIFE OF
BEING
Read
it lik
JUST ON
Barkley L

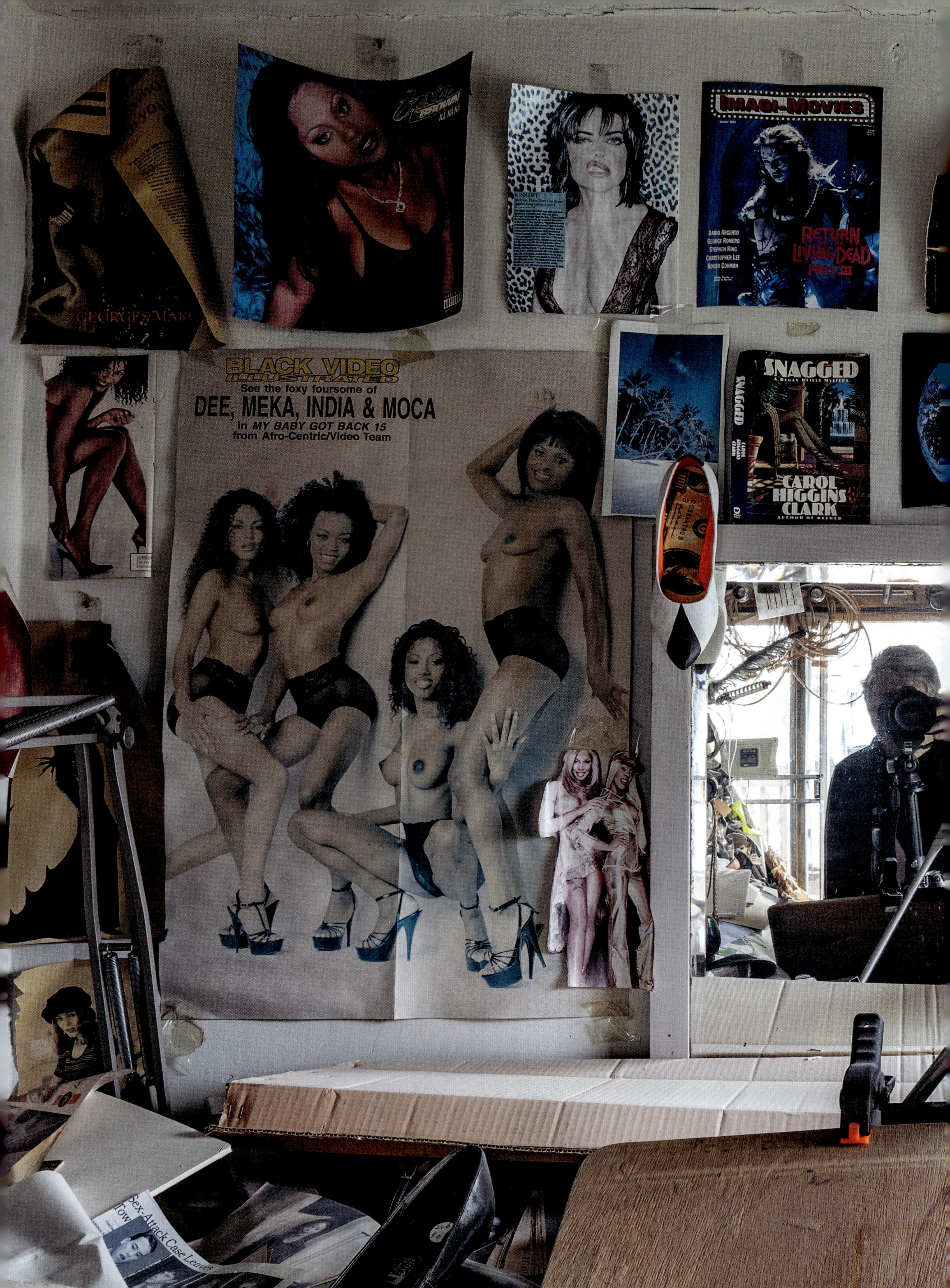
GEORGES MARC
IMAGI-MOVIES
DARIO ARGENTO
GEORGE ROMERO
STEPHEN KING
CHRISTOPHER LEE
ROGER CORMAN
RETURN LIVING DEAD PART III
BLACK VIDEO ILLUSTRATED
See the foxy foursome of
DEE, MEKA, INDIA & MOCA
in MY BABY GOT BACK 15
from Afro-Centric/Video Team
SNAGGED
CAROL HIGGINS CLARK
Sex-Attack Case Leaves

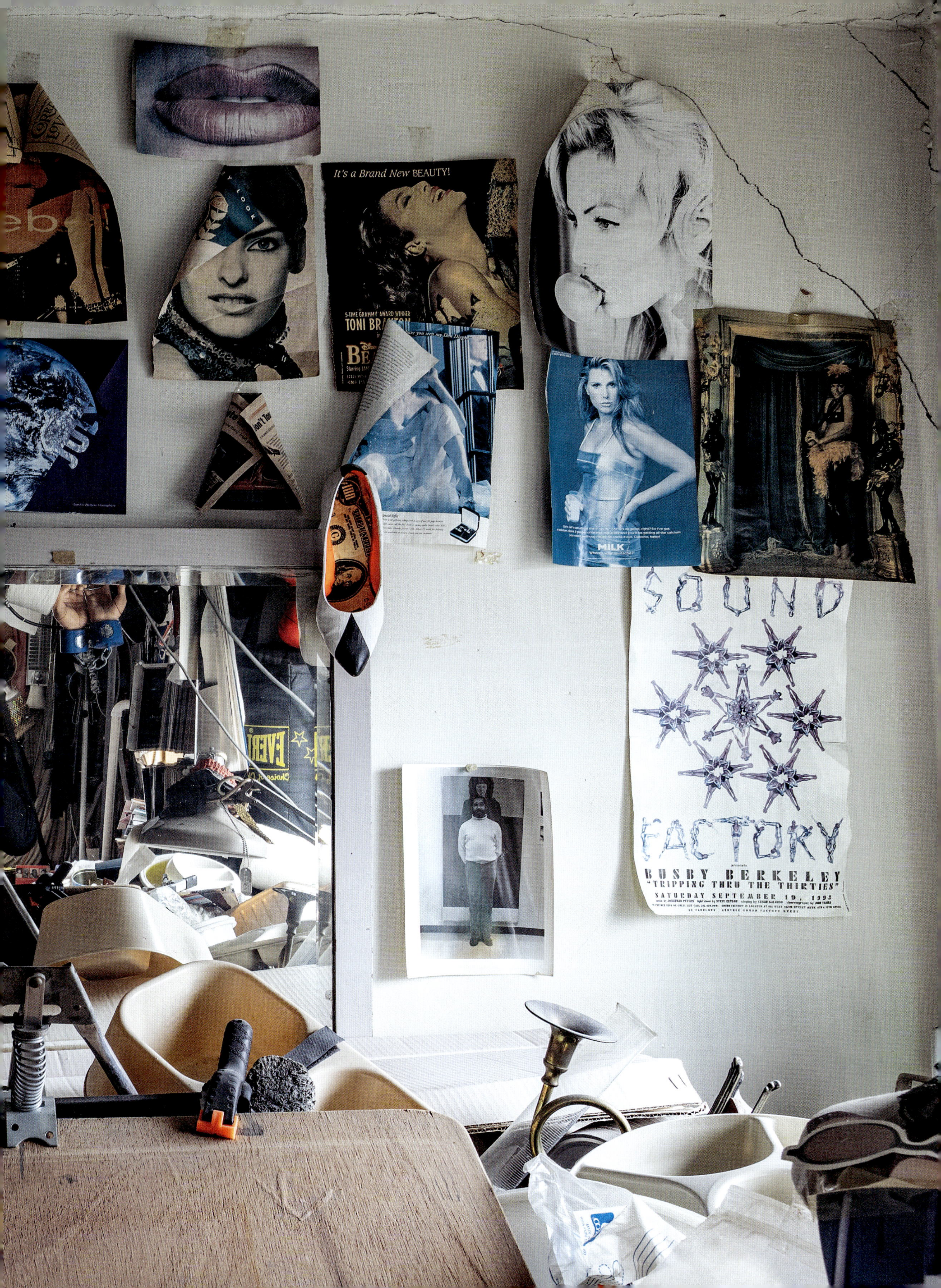
It's a Brand New BEAUTY!
TONI BRAXTON
MILK
SOUND
FACTORY
presents
BUSBY BERKELEY
"TRIPPING THRU THE THIRTIES"
SATURDAY SEPTEMBER 19, 1998

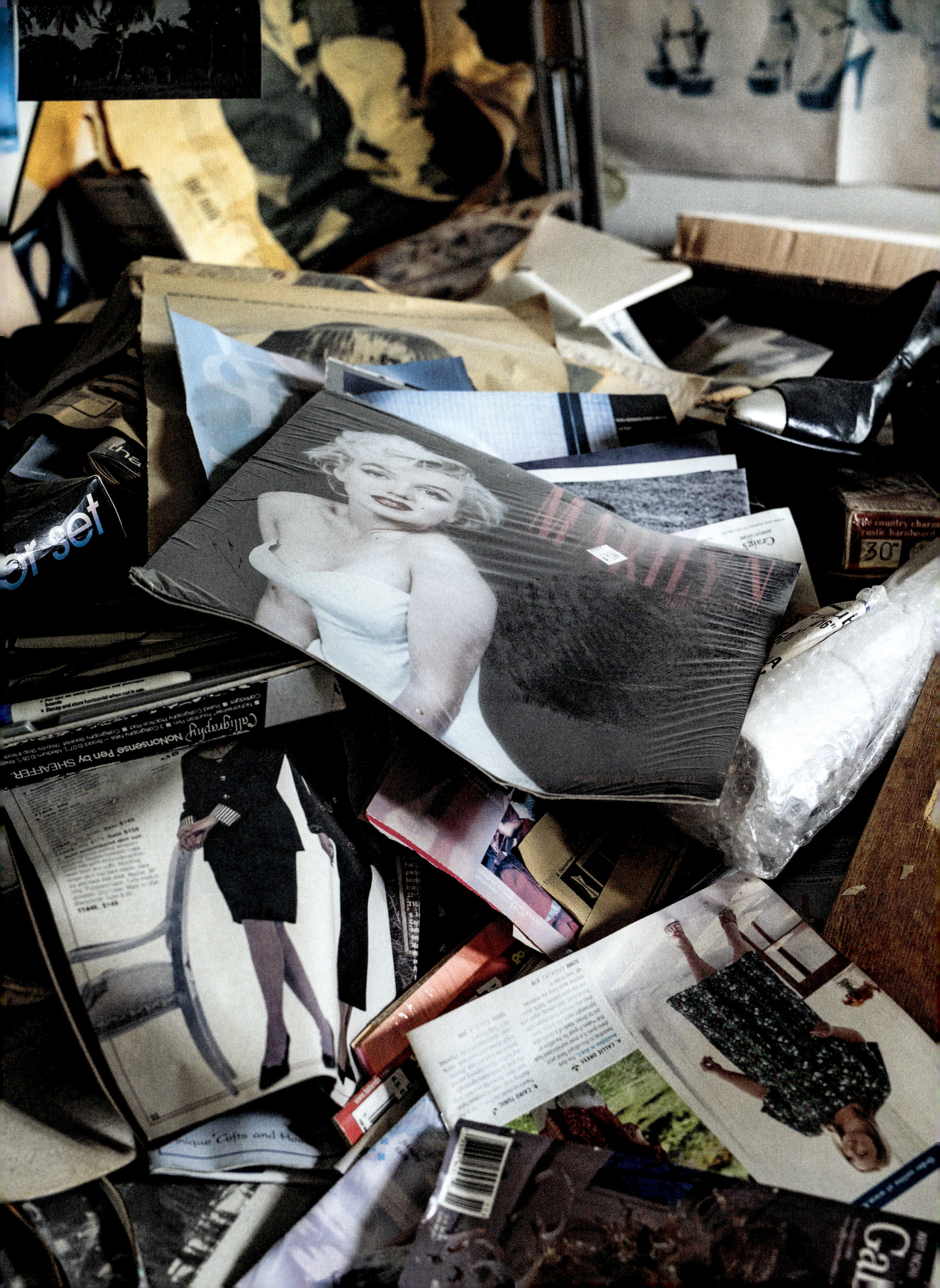
Calligraphy
NoNonsense Pen by SHEAFFER

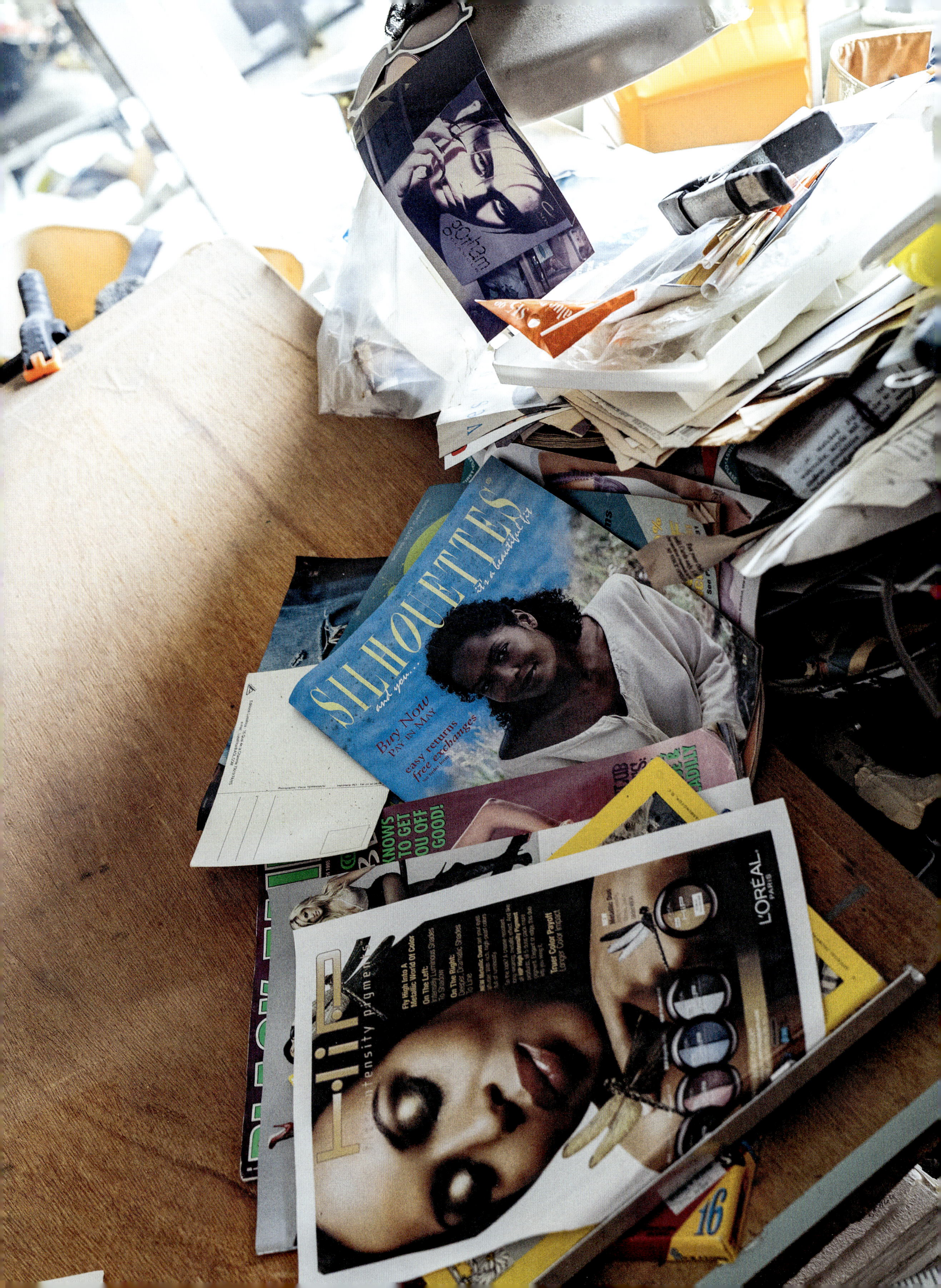
SILHOUETTES
it's a beautiful fit
and you...
Buy Now
PAY IN MAY
easy returns
free exchanges
L'OREAL
PARIS
intensity pigments
16

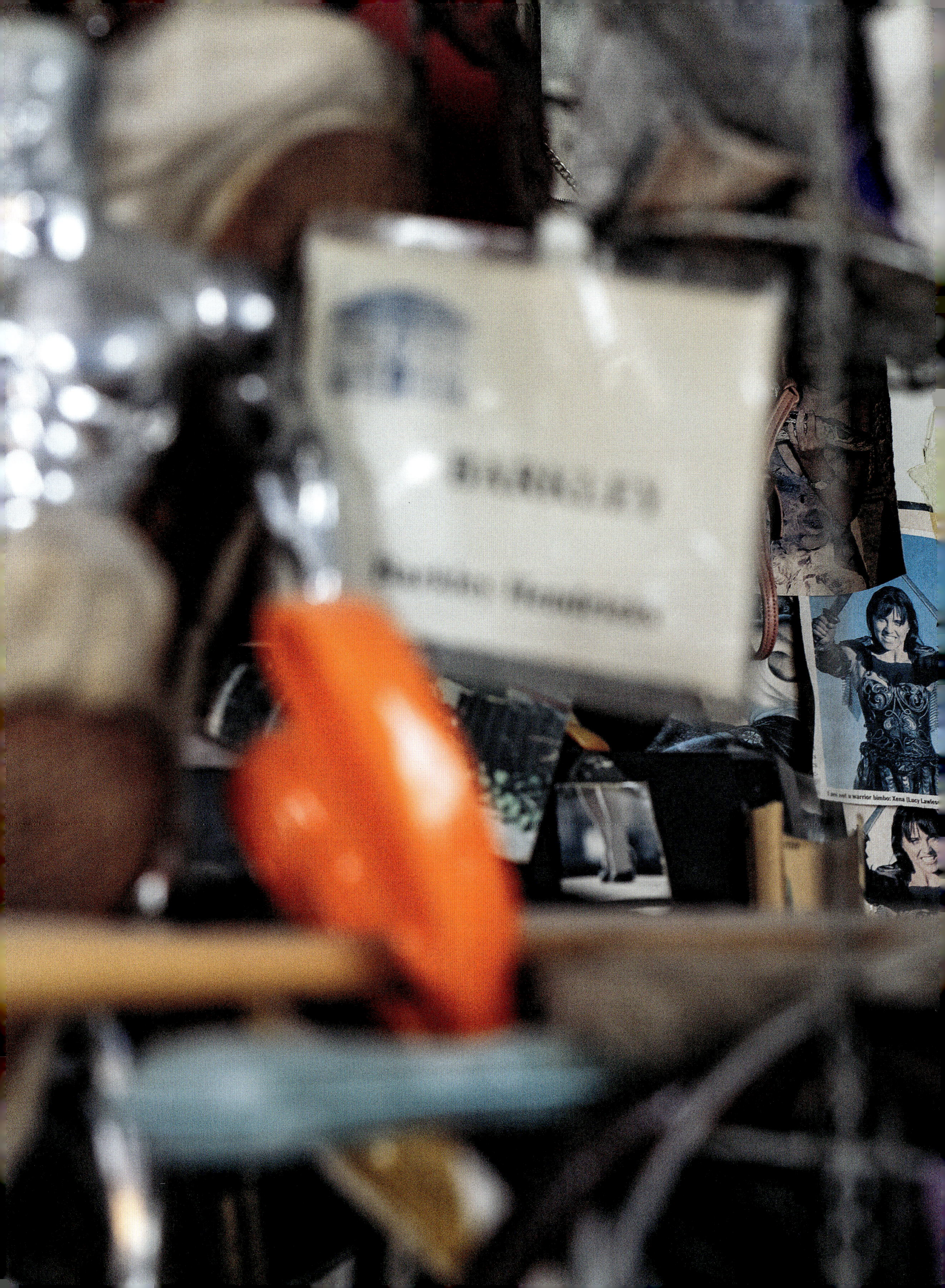
I am not a warrior bimbo: Xena (Lucy

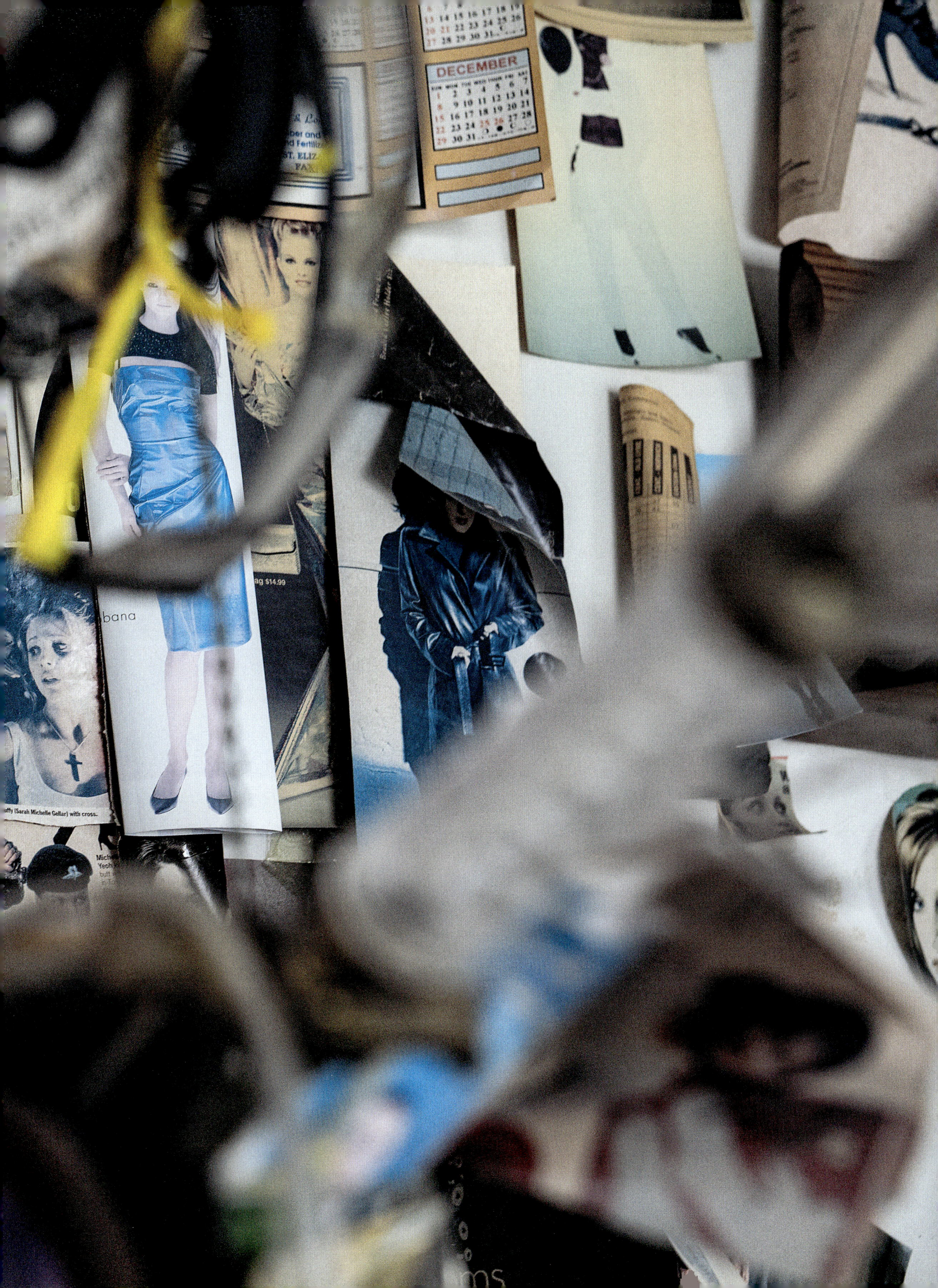
DECEMBER
bana
ag $14.99
uffy (Sarah Michelle Gellar) with cross.

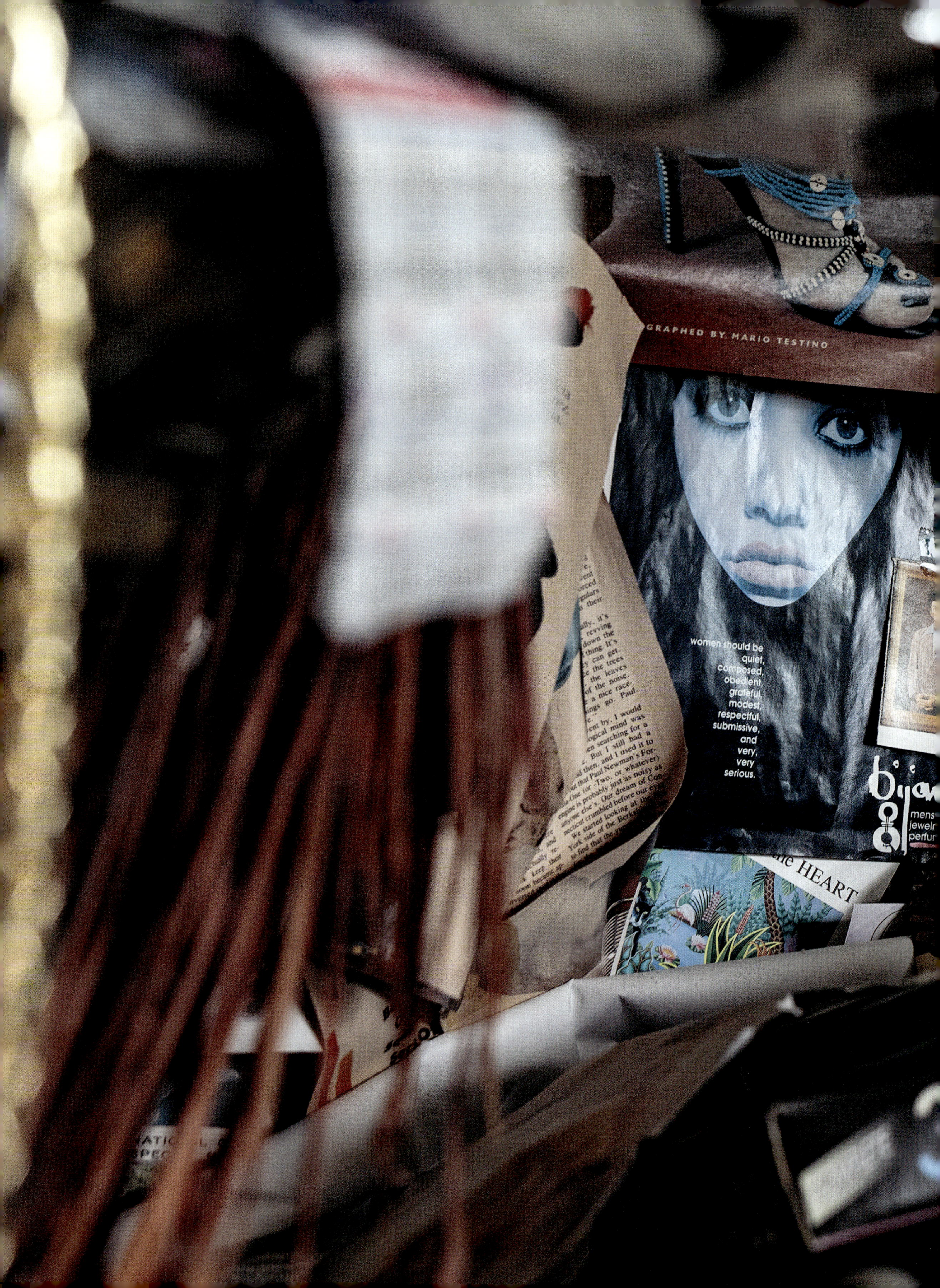
GRAPHED BY MARIO TESTINO
women should be
quiet,
composed,
obedient,
grateful,
modest,
respectful,
submissive,
and
very,
very
serious.
HEART

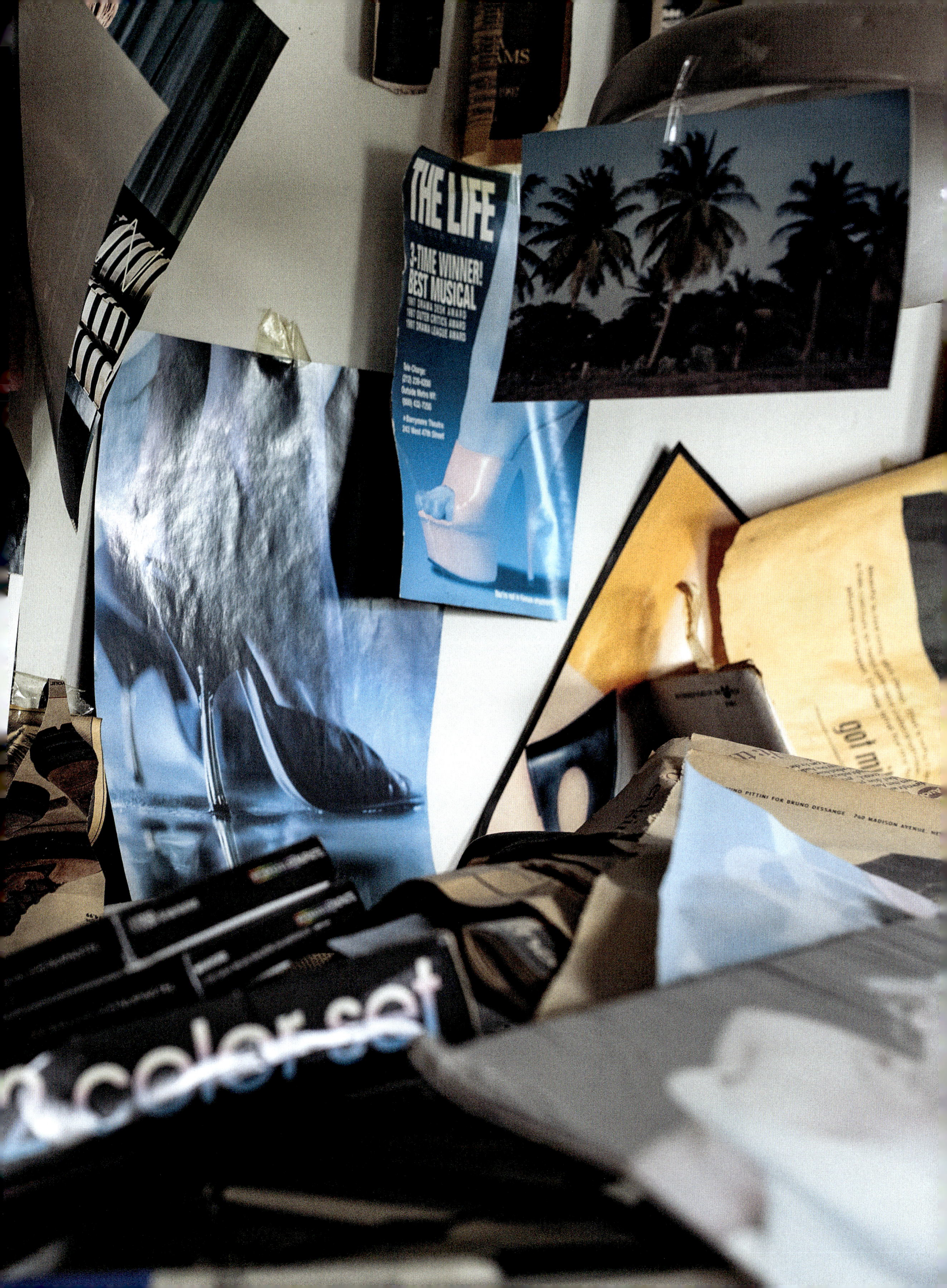
THE LIFE
3-TIME WINNER!
BEST MUSICAL
color set

# There has been the odd critic or writer that has referred to my work as "cool." I wonder do they know about cool: or what is their definition of cool.

"COOL/KOOL," March 23, 1978 (see p. 236)

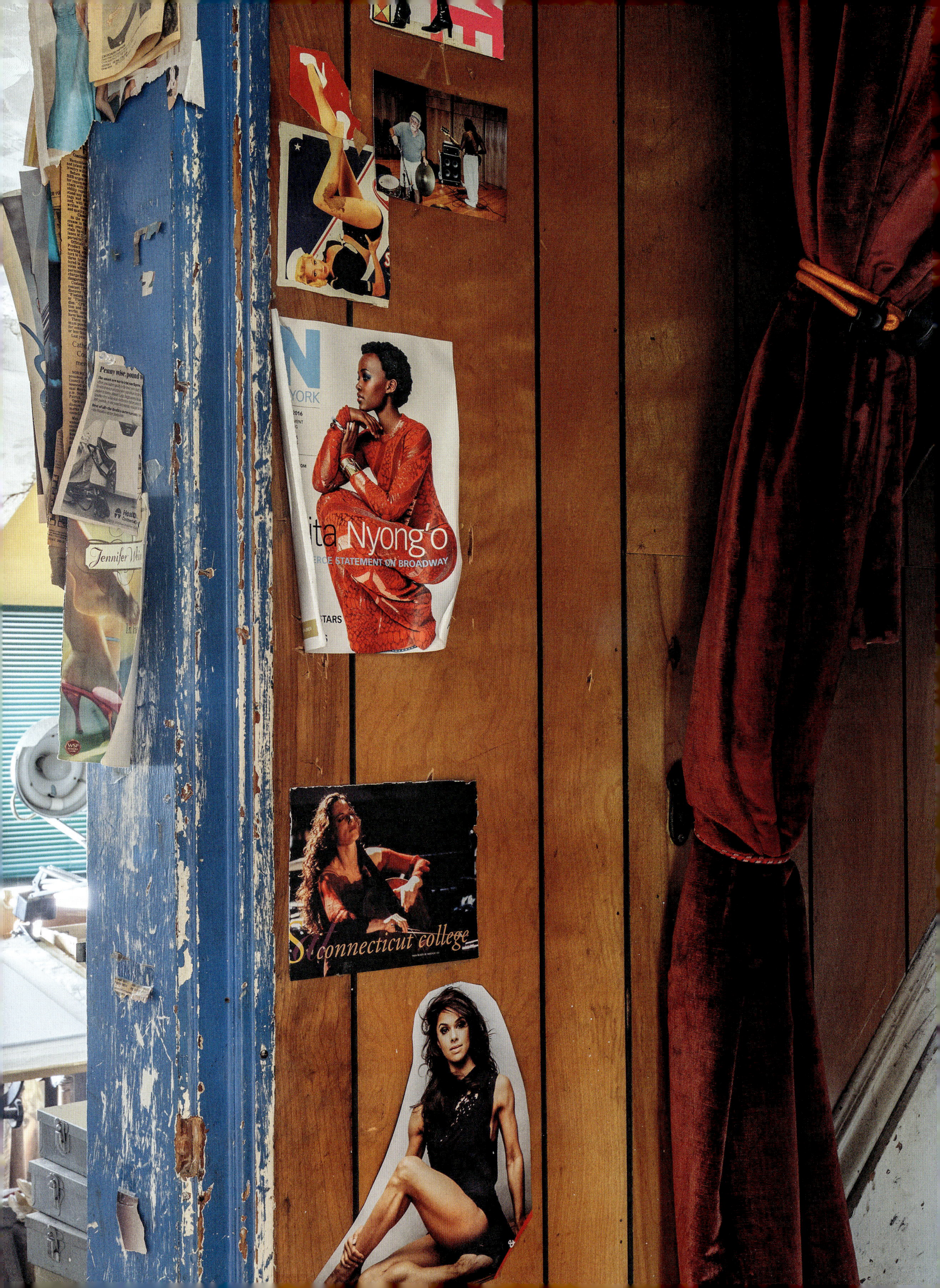

YORK
ita Nyong'o
STATEMENT ON BROADWAY
STARS
connecticut college

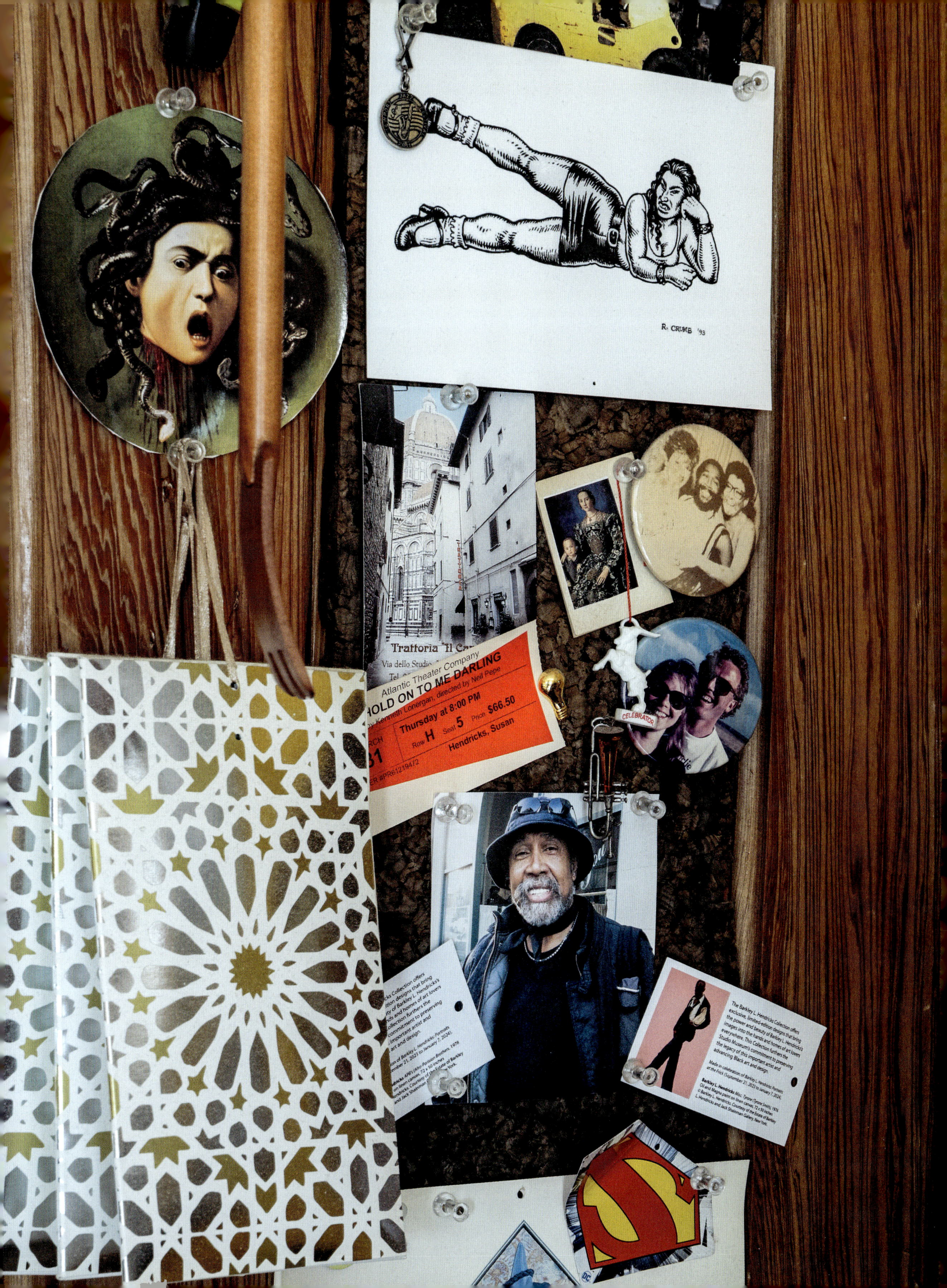
R. CRUMB '93
Atlantic Theater Company
HOLD ON TO ME DARLING
Thursday at 8:00 PM
Row H Seat 5 Price $66.50
Hendricks, Susan
CELEBRATOR

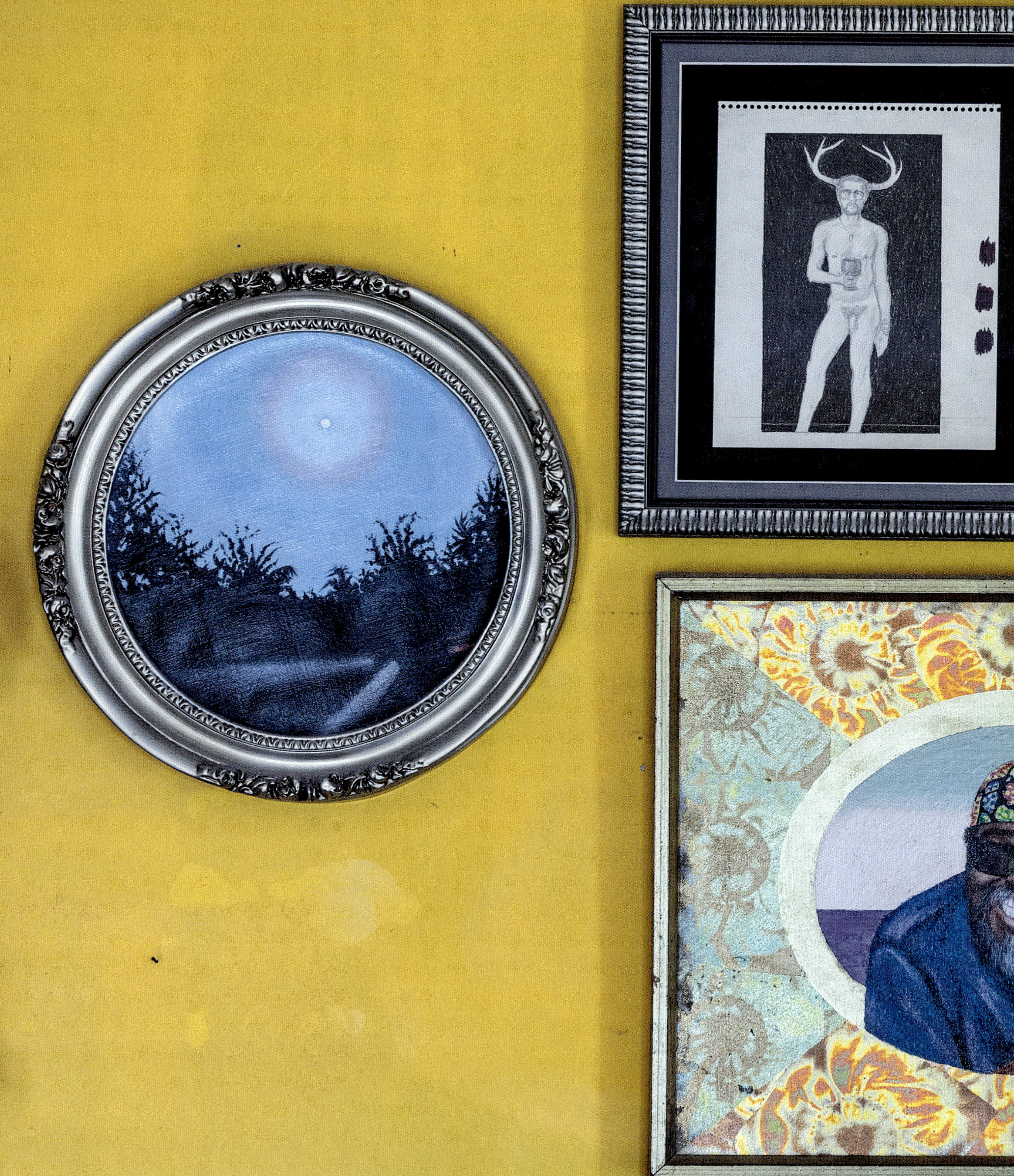

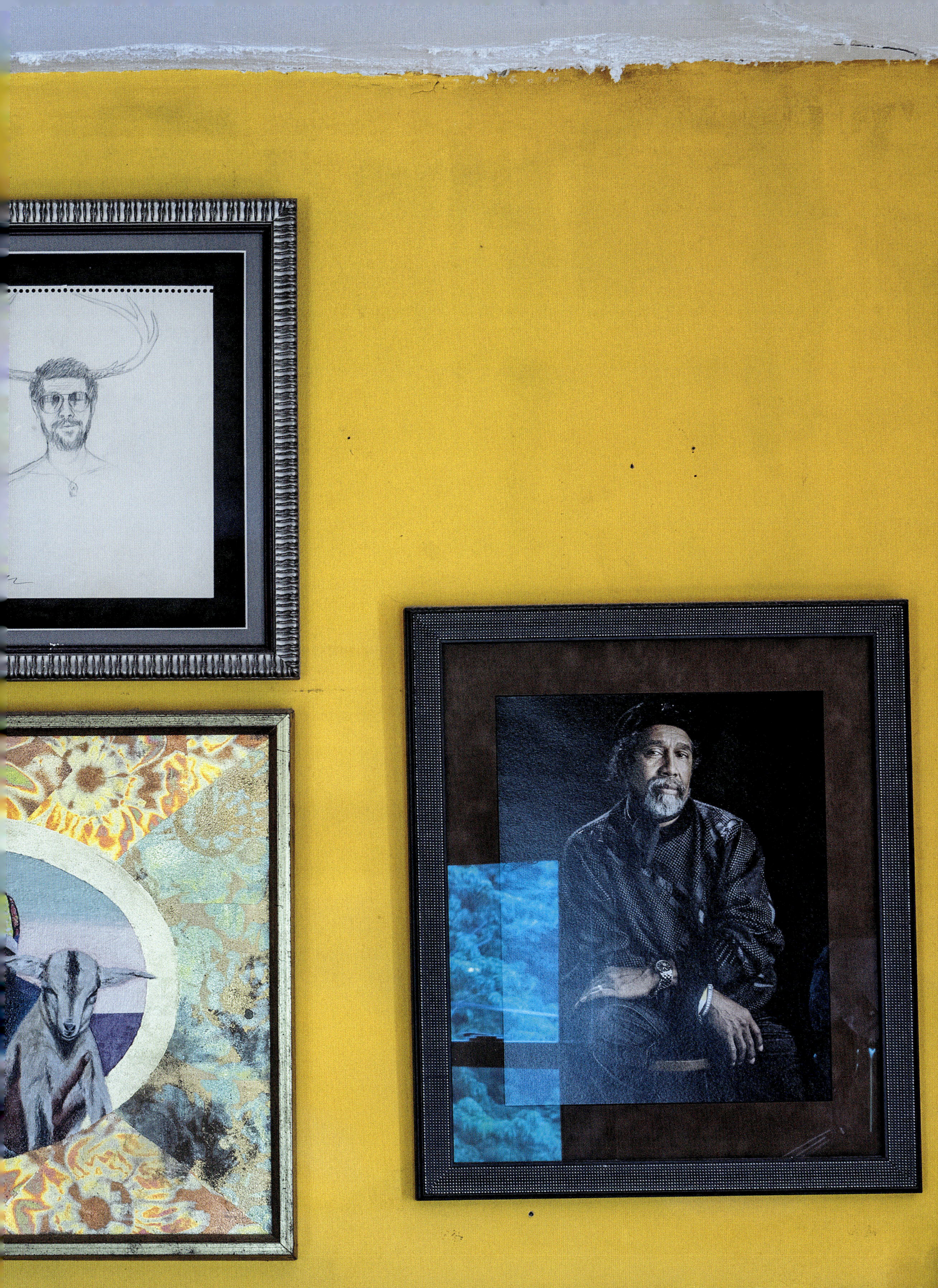

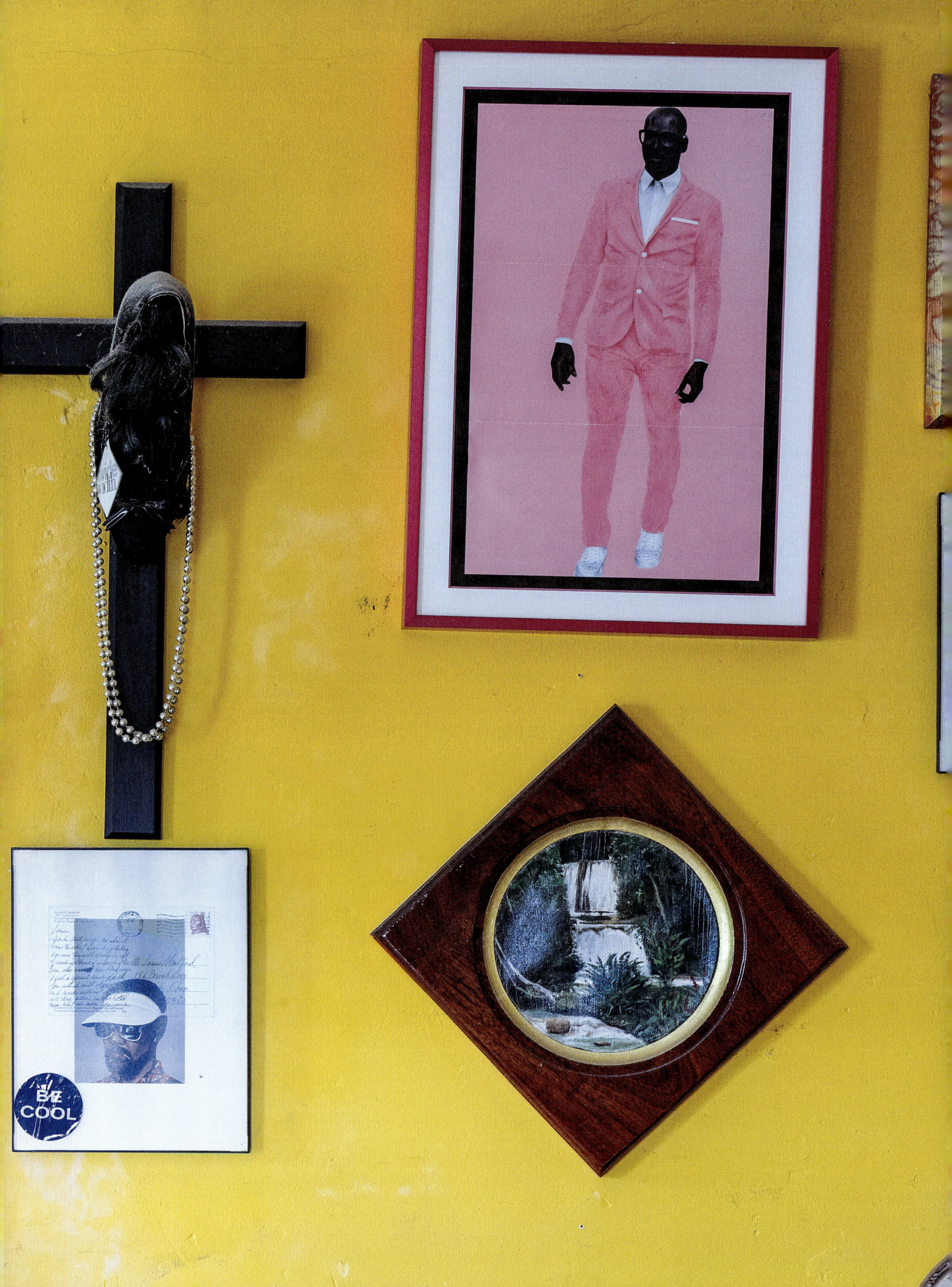
BE
COOL

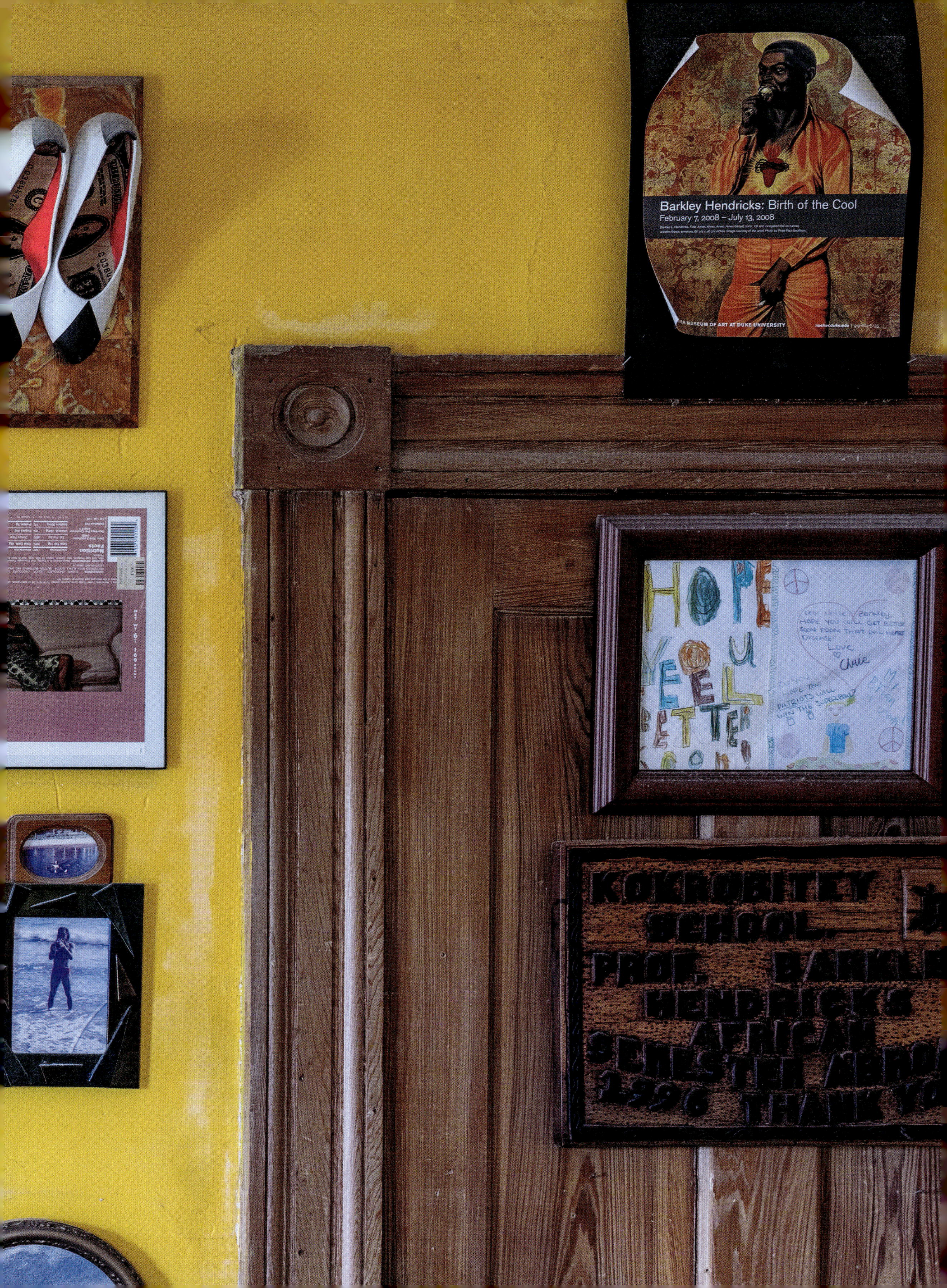

Barkley Hendricks: Birth of the Cool
February 7, 2008 – July 13, 2008
HOPE
KOKROBITEY
SCHOOL.
PROF. BARKLE
HENDRICKS
AFRICAN
SEMESTER ABRO
1996 THANK YO

# There is an inner vision which does little to make clear those areas of grey often found in cultures and humans who seek to describe our world in black and white terms.

ARISTOTLE, DATE: Unknown (see p. 254)

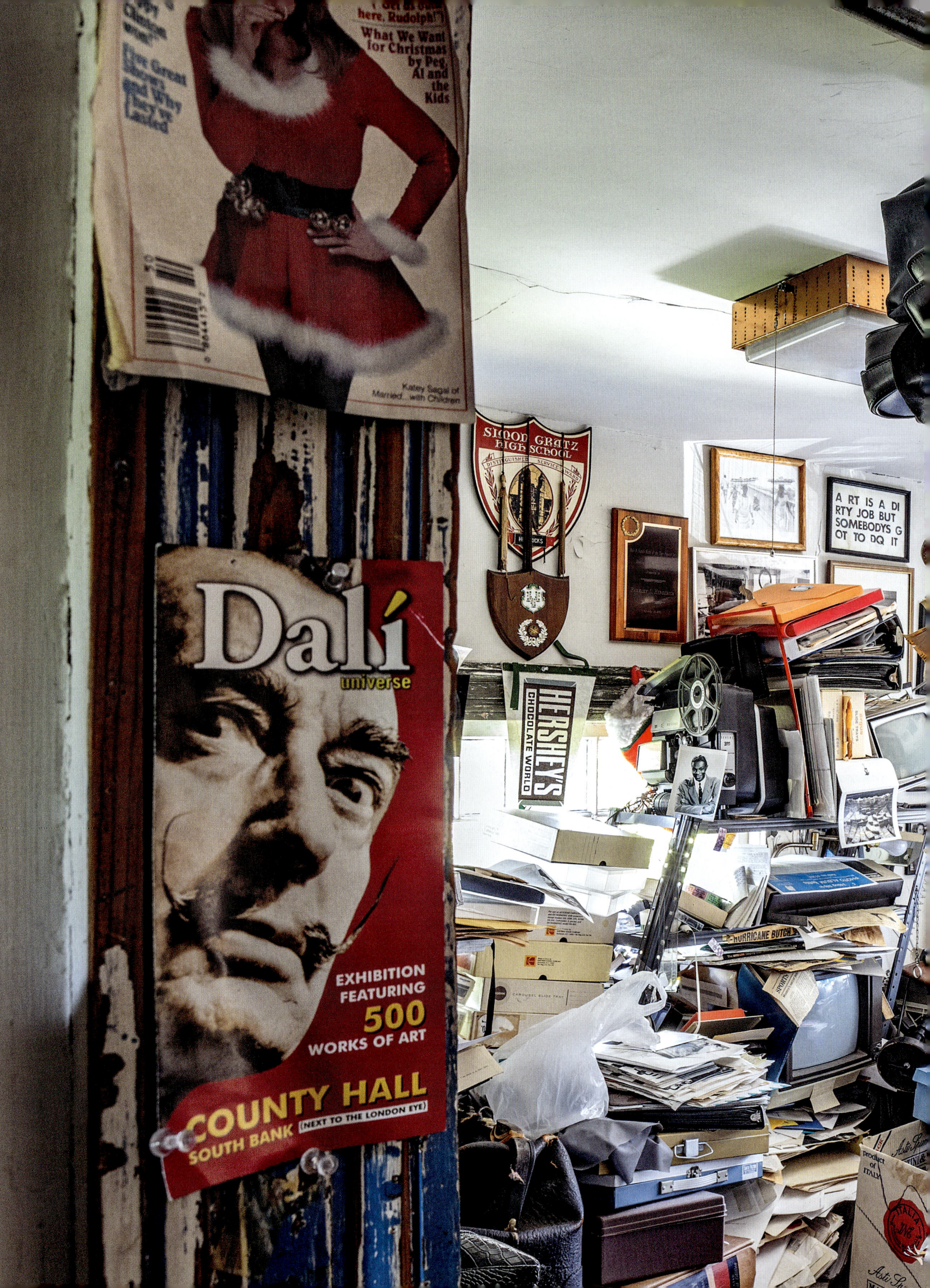

here, Rudolph!"
What We Want for Christmas by Peg, Al and the Kids
Five Great Shows and Why They've Lasted
Katey Sagal of Married...with Children
SIMON GRATZ HIGH SCHOOL
DISTINGUISHED SERVICE AWARD
A RT IS A DI
RTY JOB BUT
SOMEBODYS G
OT TO DO IT
HERSHEY'S
CHOCOLATE WORLD
Dalí
universe
EXHIBITION
FEATURING
500
WORKS OF ART
COUNTY HALL
SOUTH BANK
(NEXT TO THE LONDON EYE)
HURRICANE BUTCH
CAROUSEL SLIDE TRAY

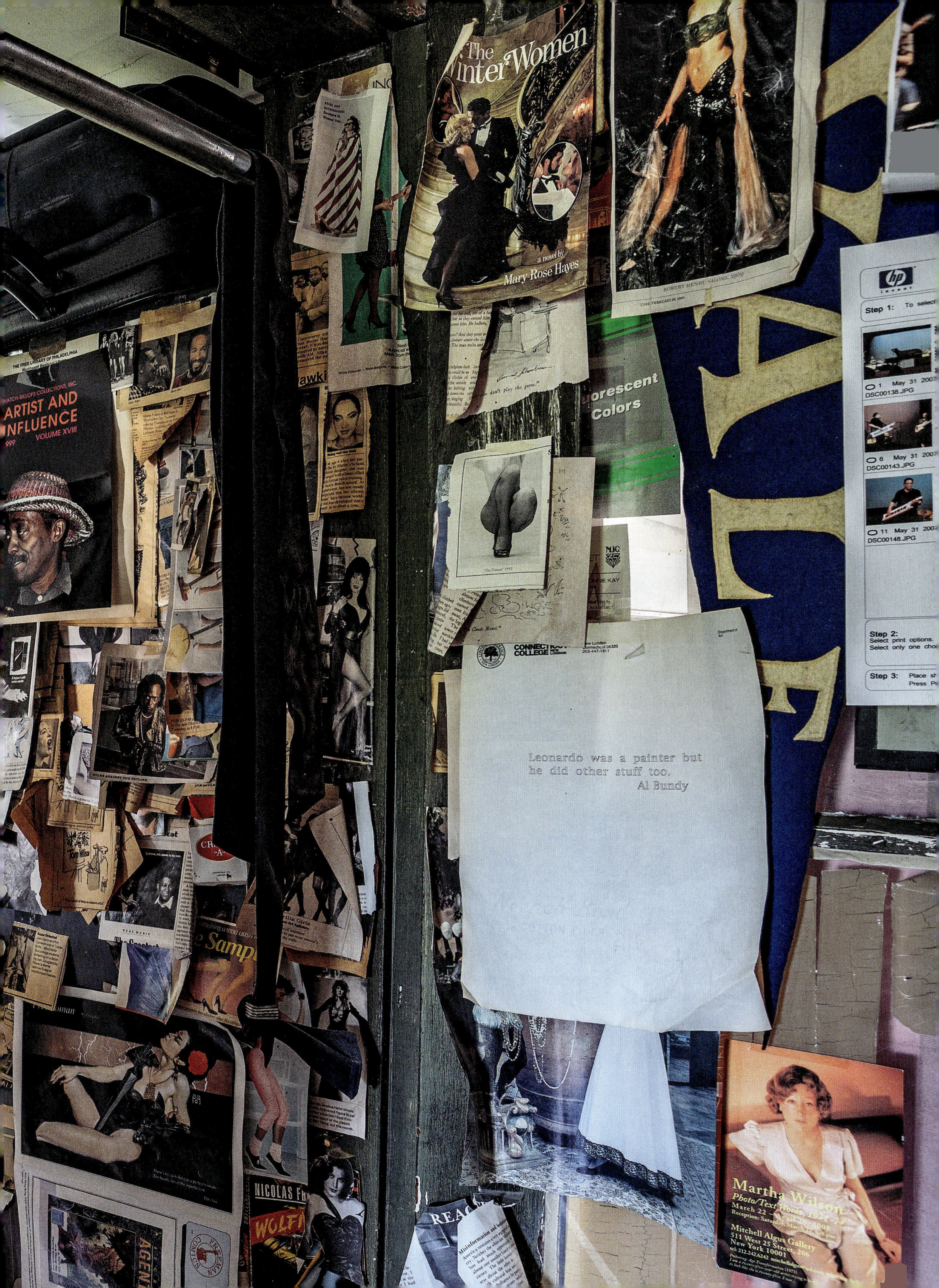

The Winter Women
a novel by
Mary-Rose Hayes
ARTIST AND
INFLUENCE
VOLUME XVIII
orescent
Colors
Leonardo was a painter but
he did other stuff too.
Al Bundy
CONNECTICUT
COLLEGE
Step 1:
DSC00138.JPG
DSC00143.JPG
DSC00148.JPG
Step 2:
Select print options.
Step 3:
Martha Wilson
Photo/Text Works
Mitchell Algus Gallery
511 West 25 Street
New York 10001
NICOLAS

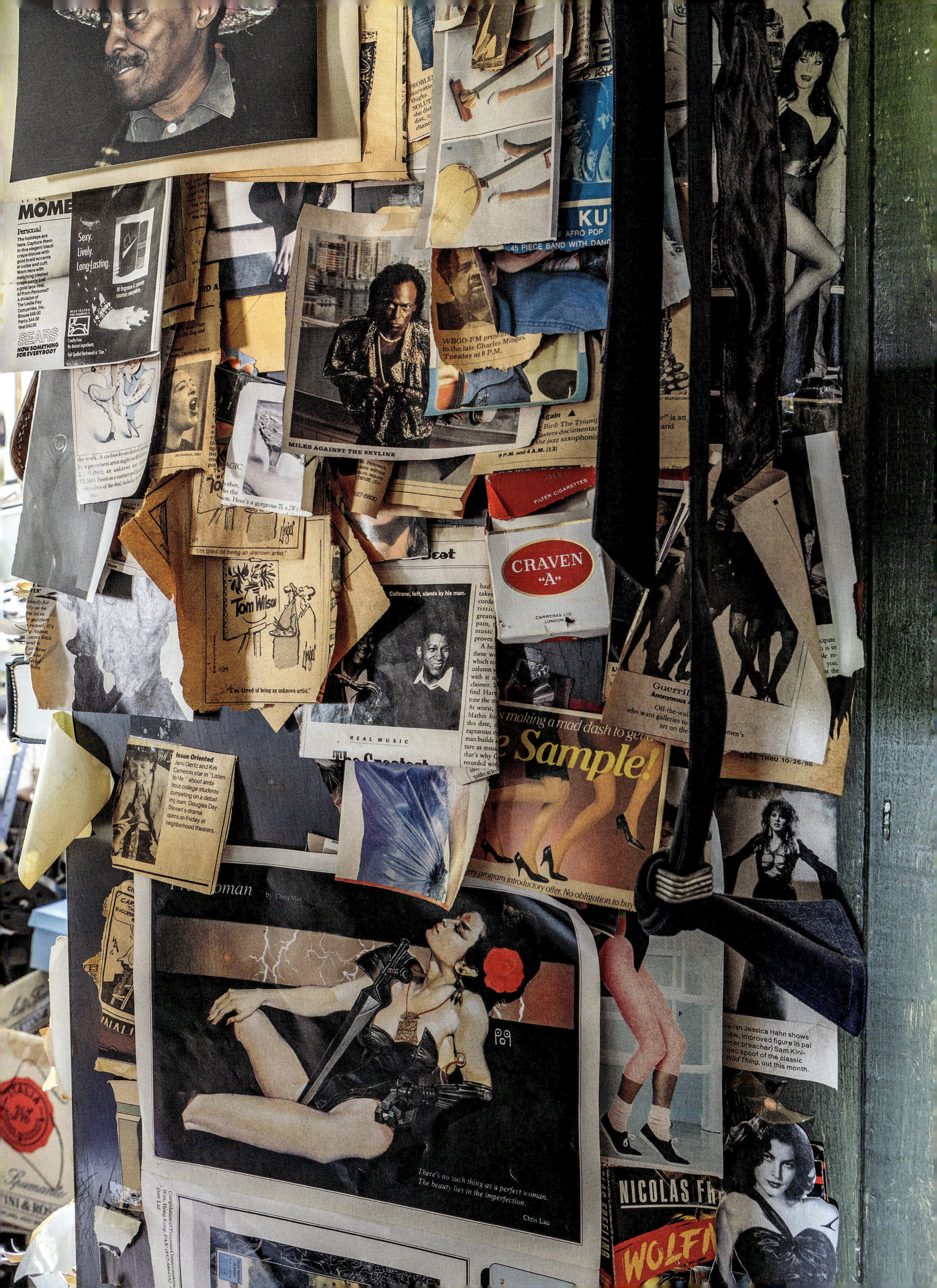
Sexy.
Lively.
Long-Lasting.
SEARS
NOW SOMETHING FOR EVERYBODY
MILES AGAINST THE SKYLINE
FILTER CIGARETTES
CRAVEN "A"
CARRERAS LTD LONDON
Tom Wilson
"I'm tired of being an unknown artist."
REAL MUSIC
Sample!
Issue Oriented
Jami Gertz and Kirk Cameron star in "Listen to Me," about ambitious college students competing on a debating team. Douglas Day Stewart's drama opens on Friday at neighborhood theaters.
SALE THRU 10/26/88
There's no such thing as a perfect woman. The beauty lies in the imperfection.
Chris Lau
NICOLAS

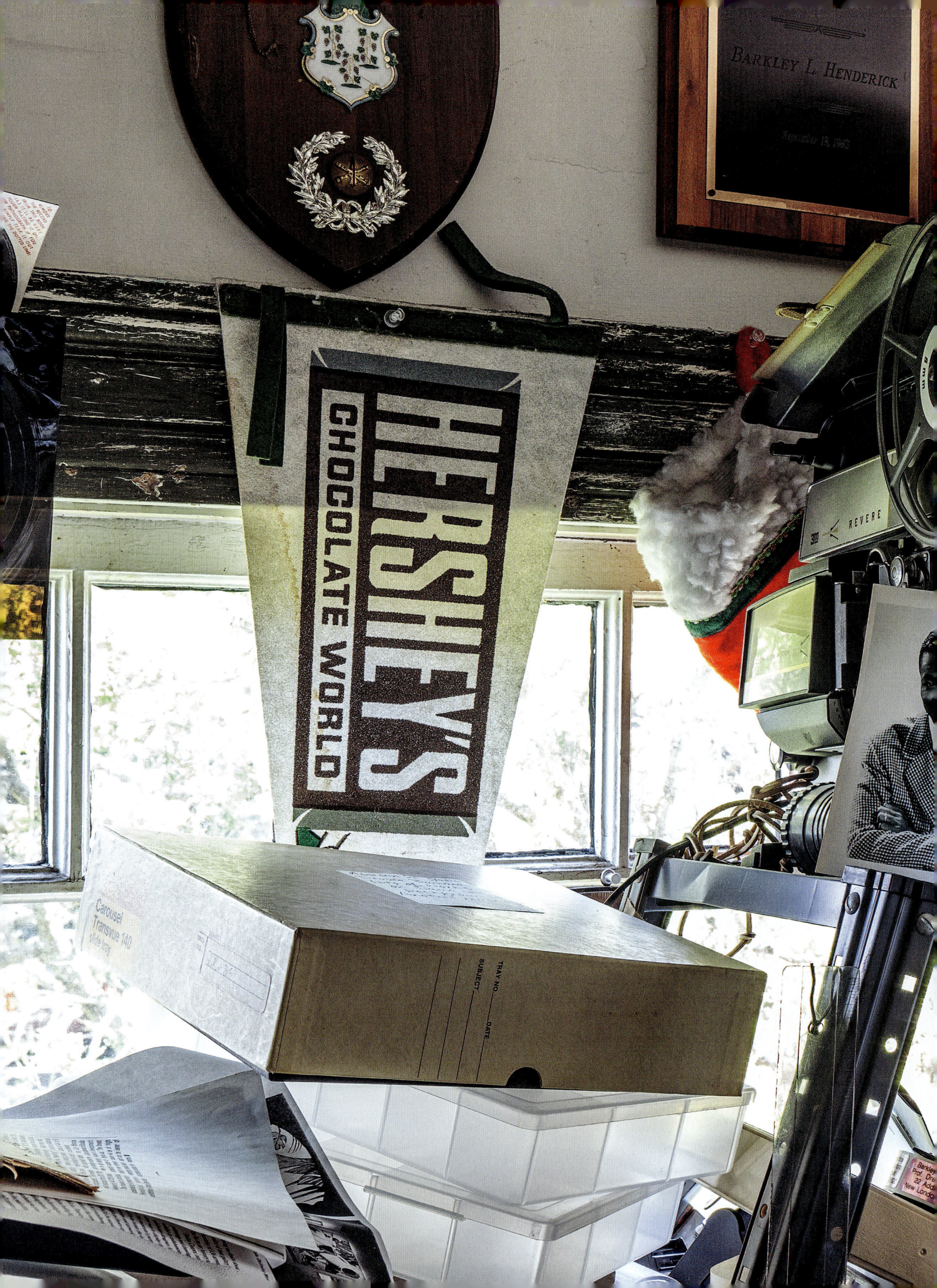
BARKLEY L. HENDERICK
HERSHEY'S
CHOCOLATE WORLD
Carousel
Transvue 140
slide tray
TRAY NO.
DATE
SUBJECT
REVERE

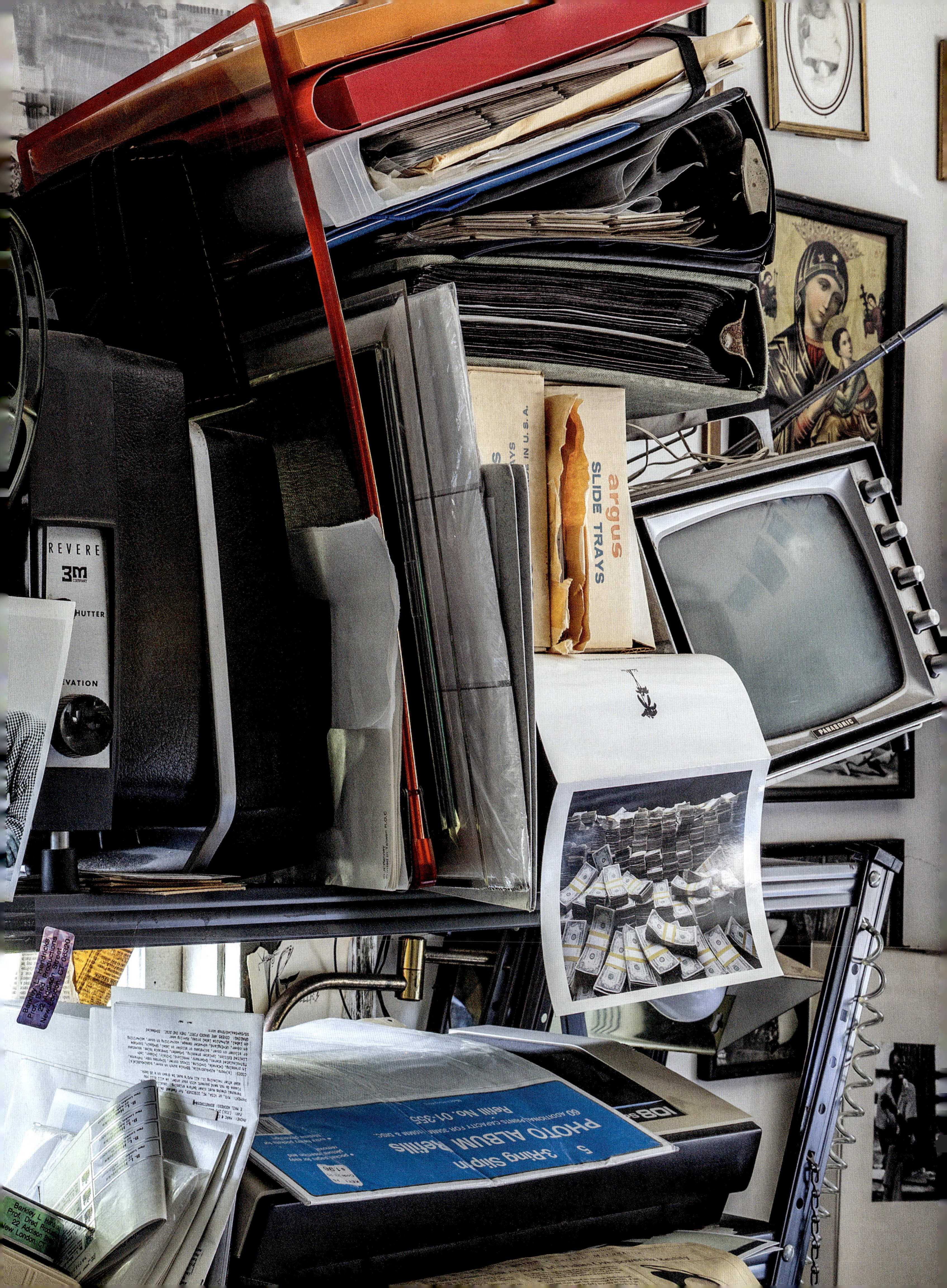
REVERE
3M
argus
SLIDE TRAYS
PHOTO ALBUM Refills

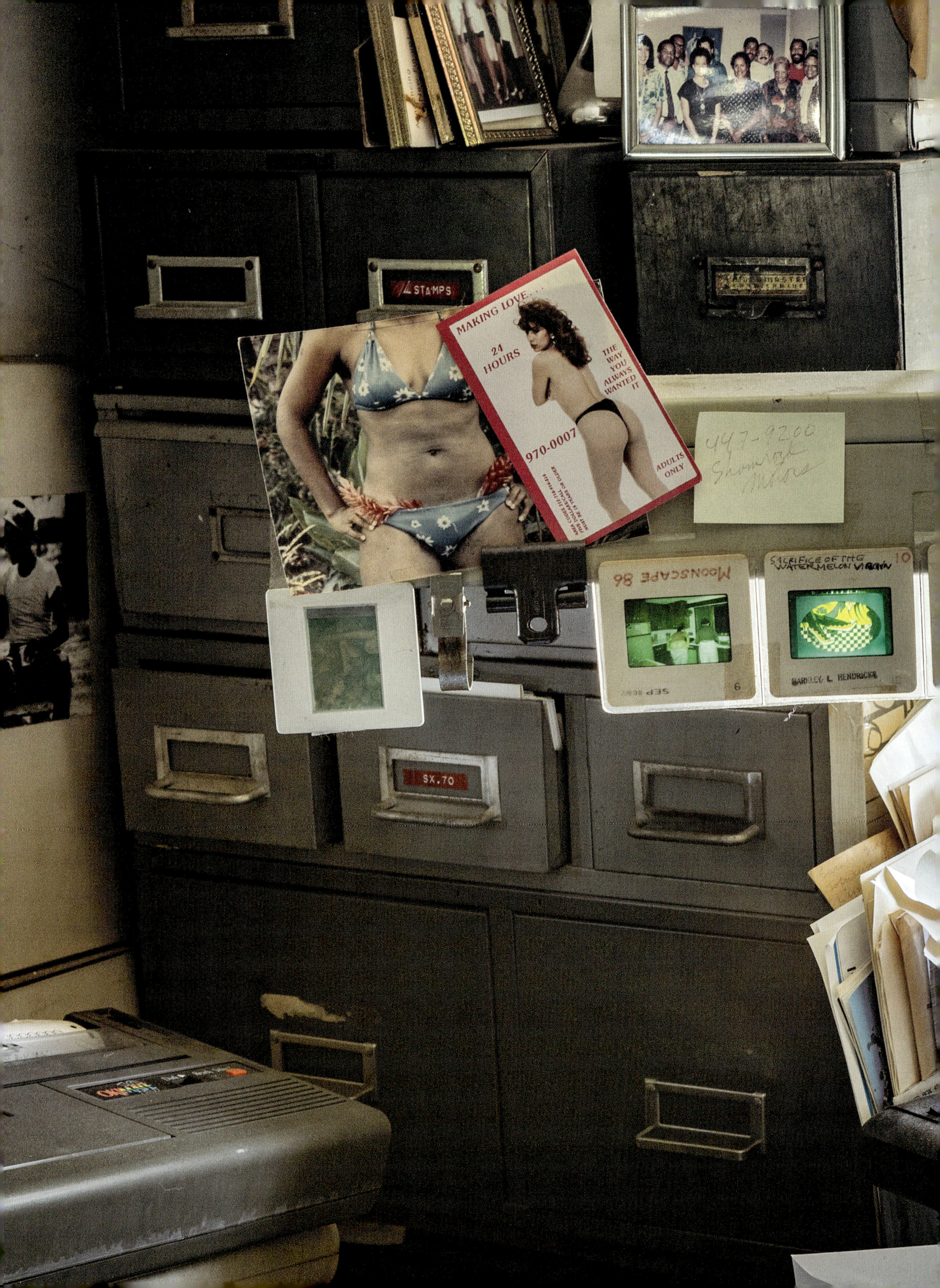
STAMPS
MAKING LOVE...
24 HOURS
THE WAY YOU ALWAYS WANTED IT
970-0007
ADULTS ONLY
447-9200
MOONSCAPE 86
SACRIFICE OF THE WATERMELON VIRGIN
10
BARKLEY L. HENDRICKS
SX.70

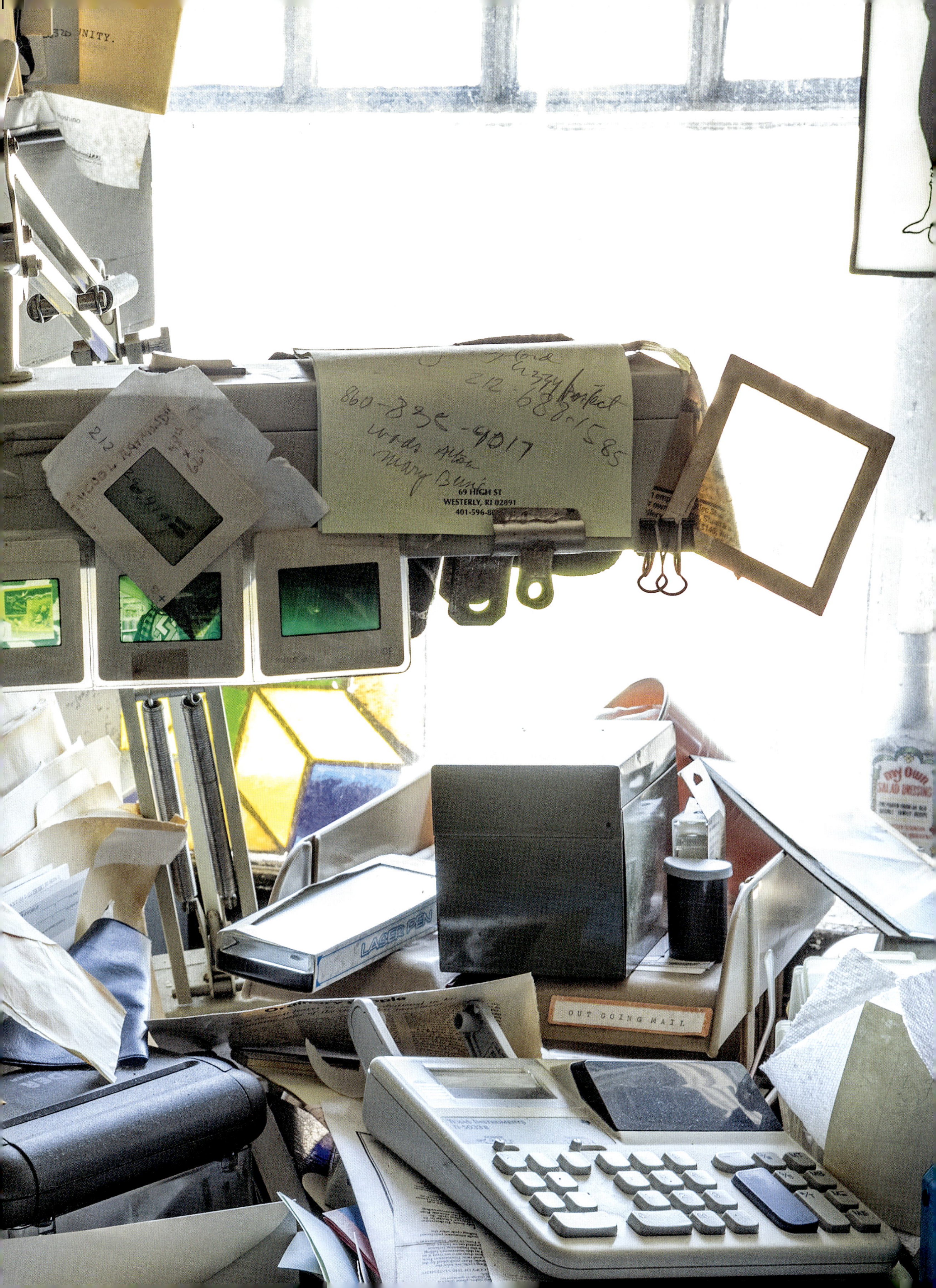
860-835-9017
212-688-1585
69 HIGH ST
WESTERLY, RI 02891
LASER PEN
OUT GOING MAIL

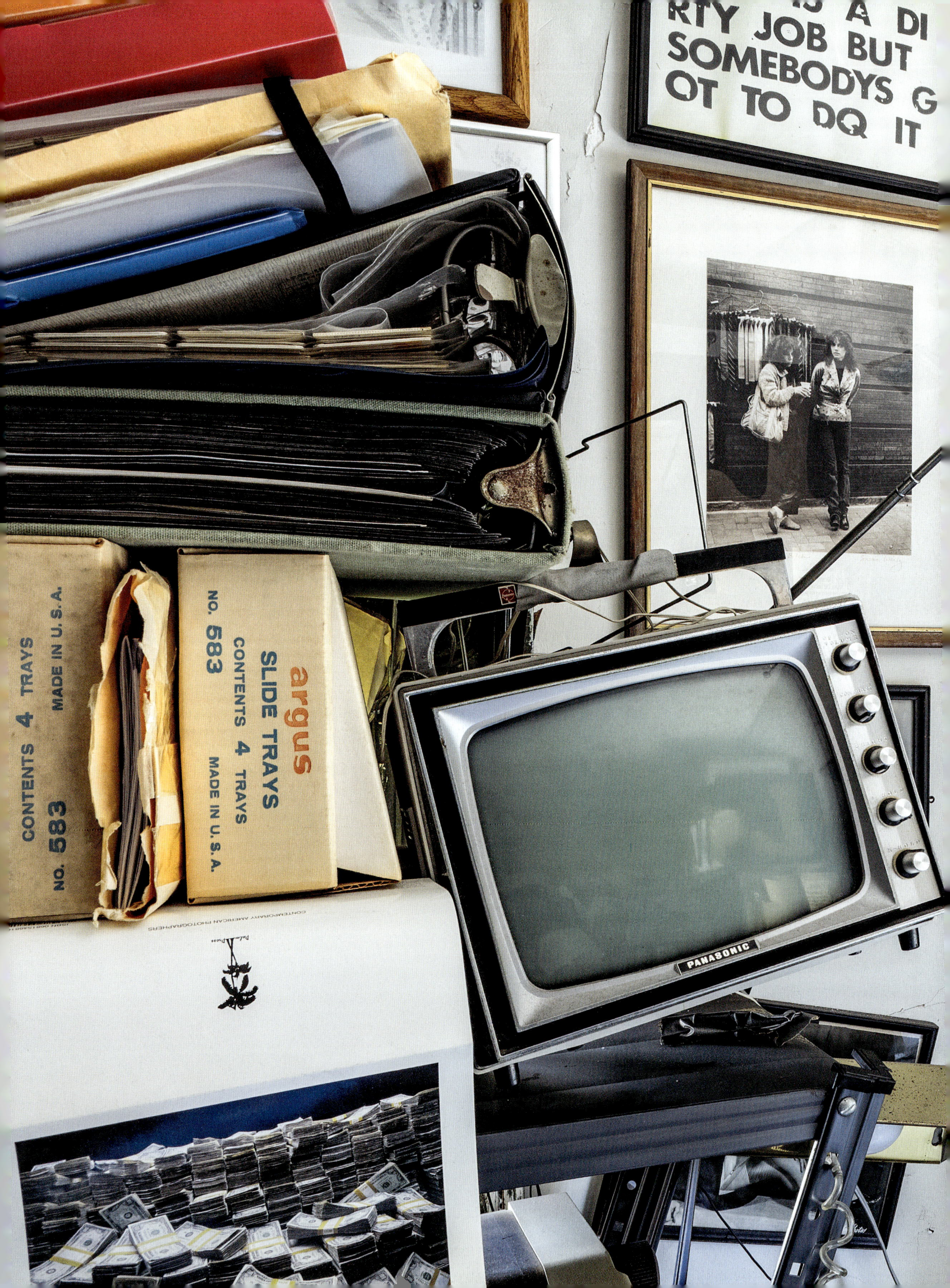
RTY JOB BUT
SOMEBODYS G
OT TO DO IT
NO. 583
CONTENTS 4 TRAYS
MADE IN U.S.A.
argus
SLIDE TRAYS
CONTENTS 4 TRAYS
NO. 583
MADE IN U.S.A.
PANASONIC

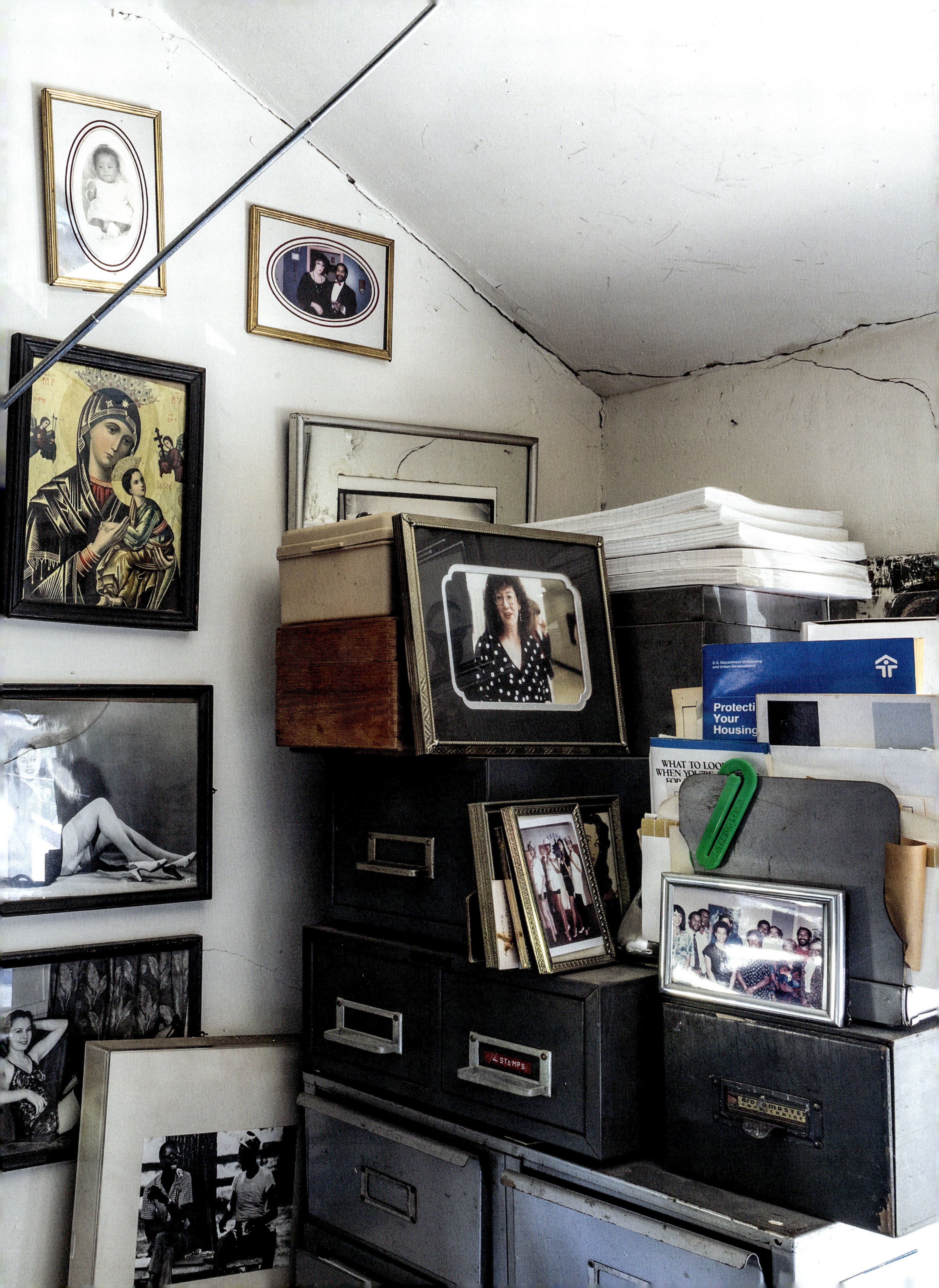

Protecti
Your
Housing
WHAT TO LOO
STAMPS

**I have used the camera in a "creative" capacity for a little over ten years. Three years prior, it was restricted to providing a record of my paintings.**

**Even in that subordinate role I realized it was love at first sight (No pun intended)**

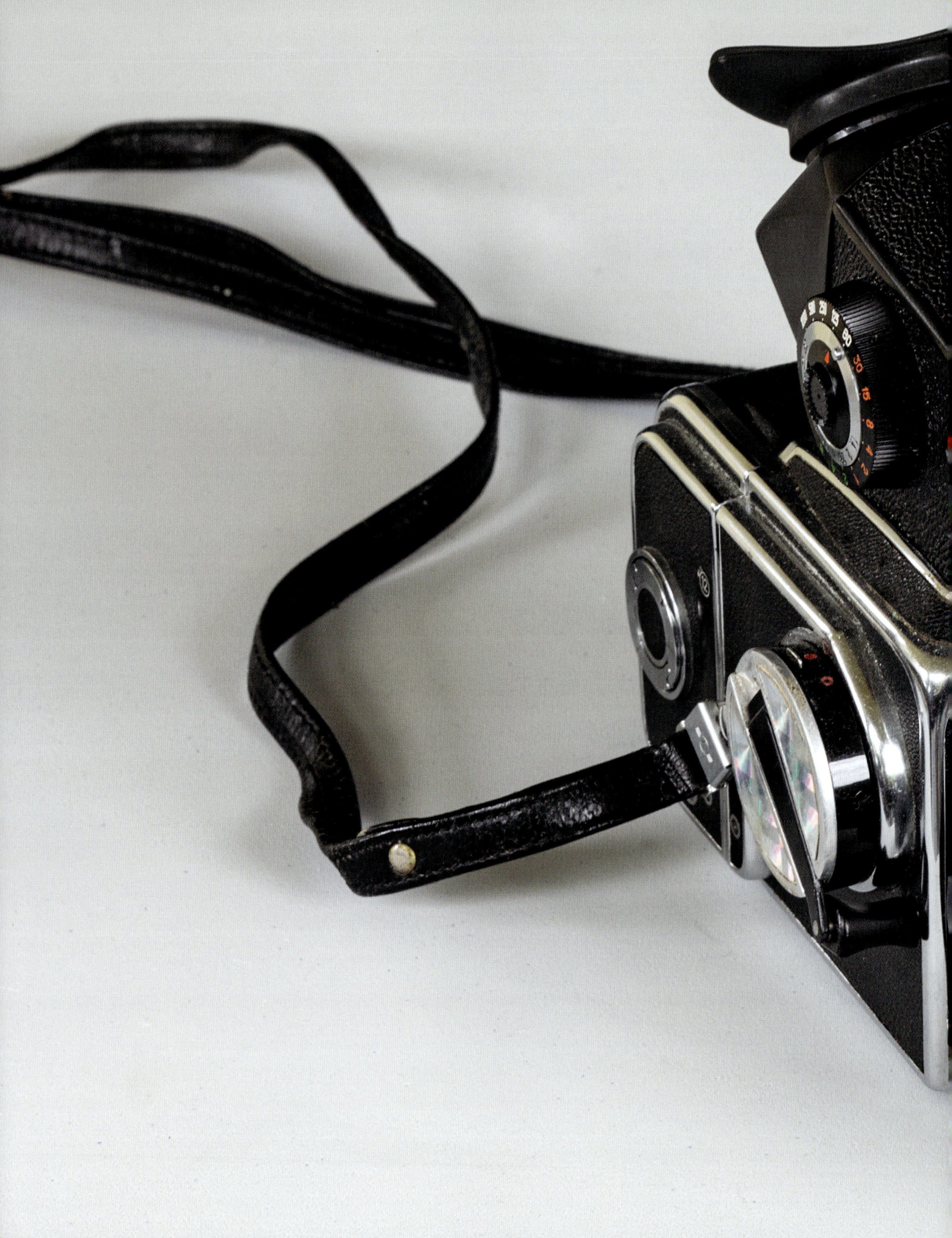

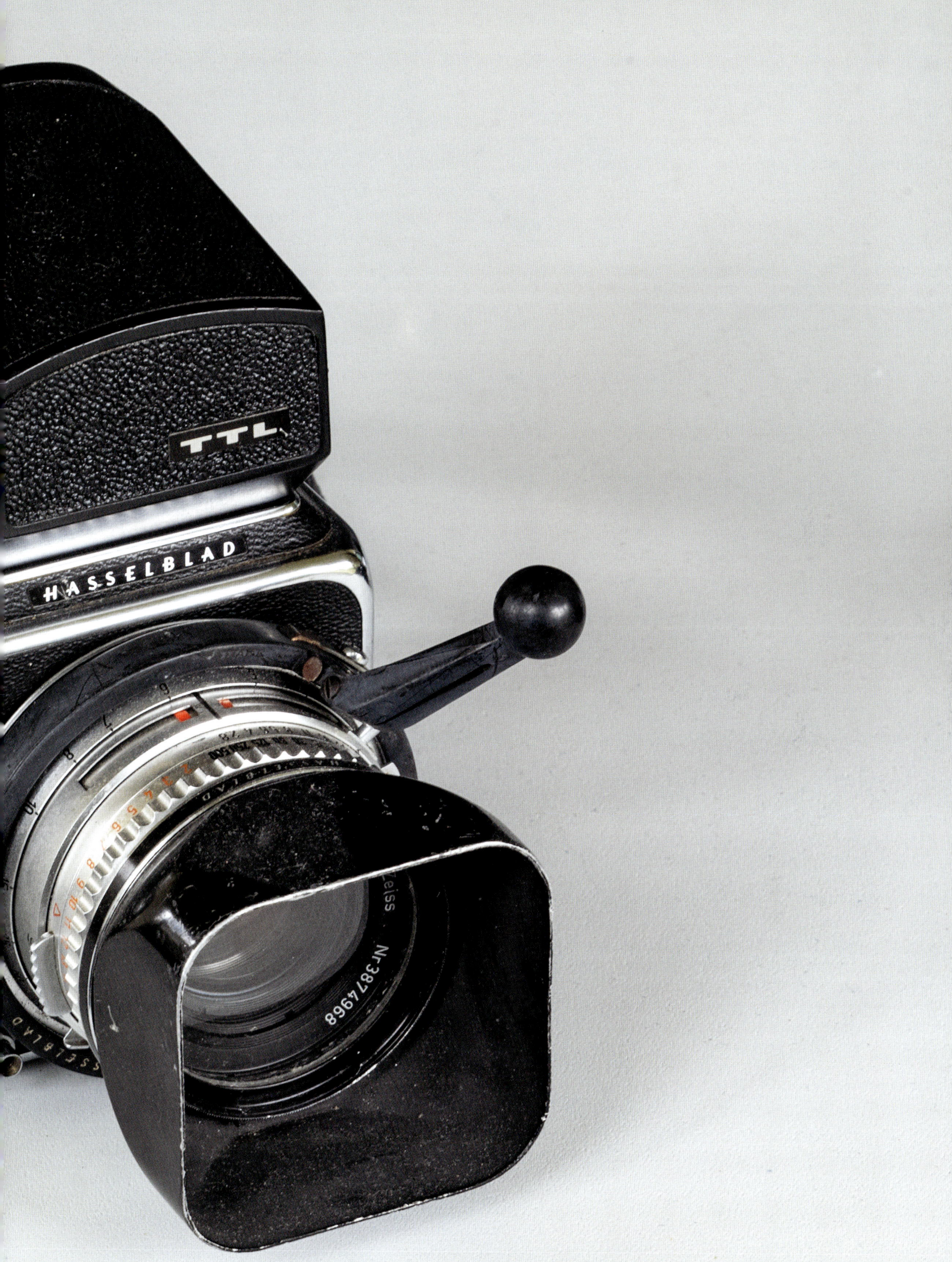
TTL
HASSELBLAD
Nr 3874968

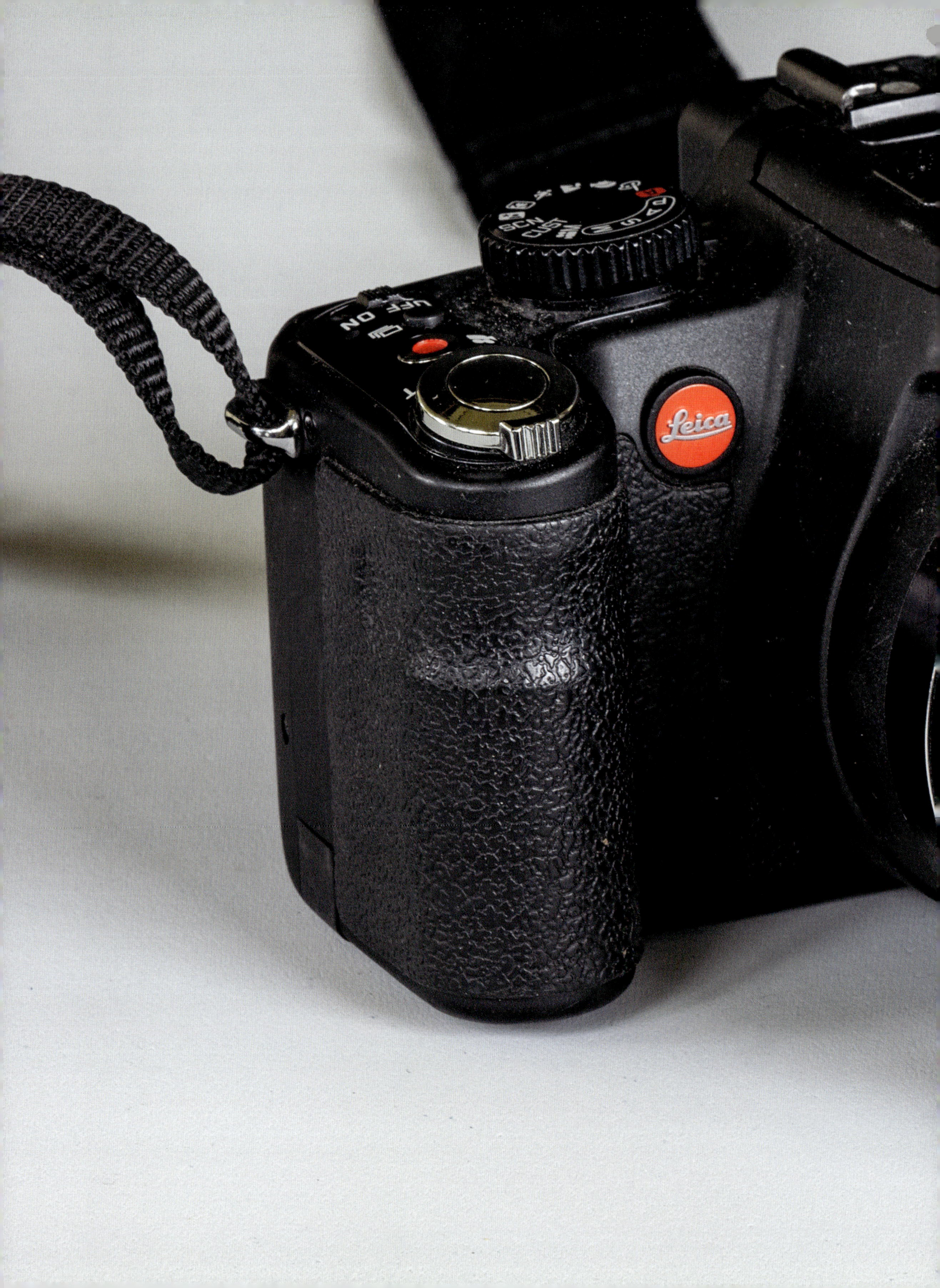
Leica

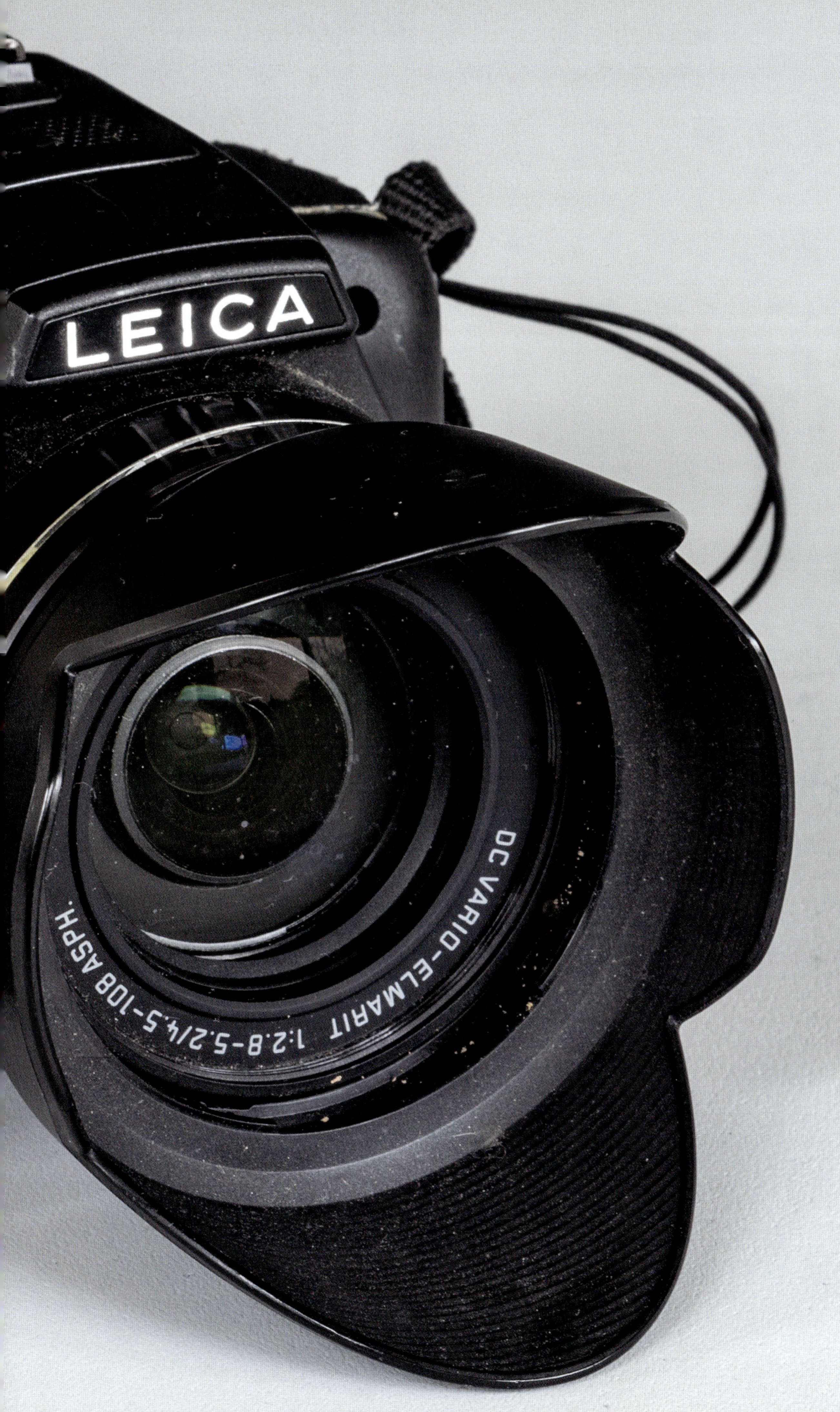
LEICA
DC VARIO-ELMARIT 1:2.8-5.2/4.5-108 ASPH.

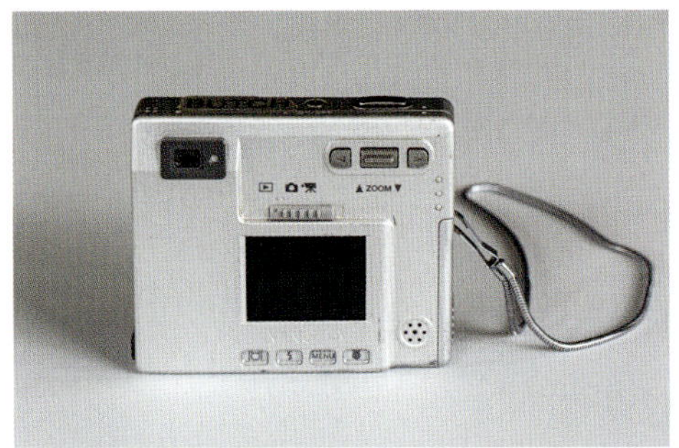

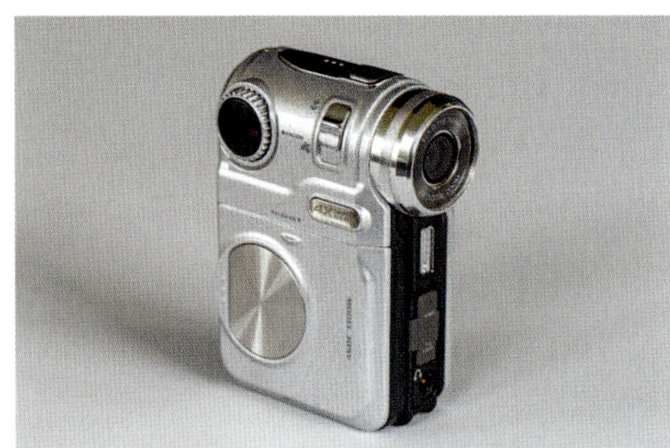

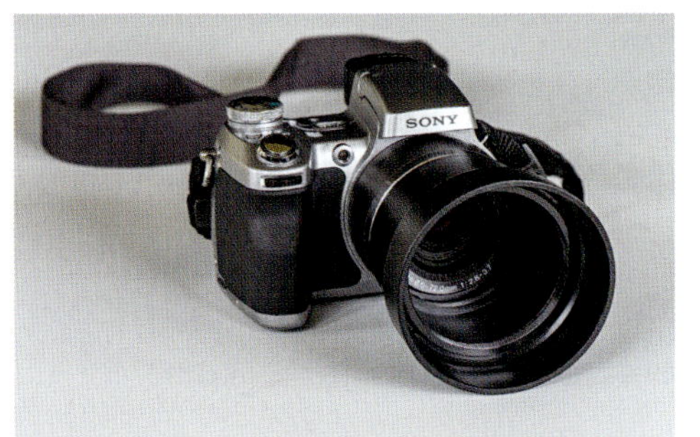
SONY

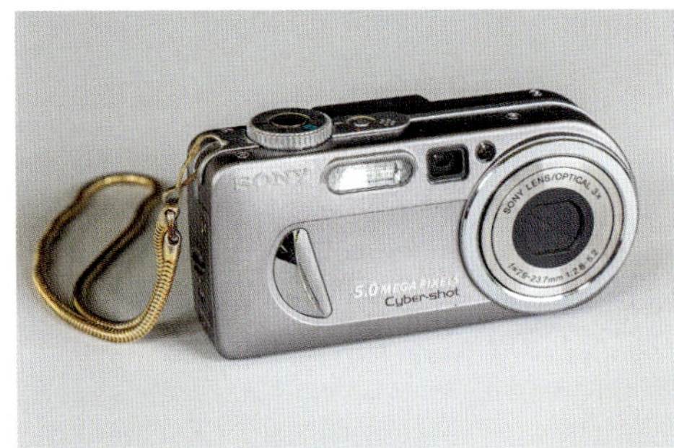
SONY
Cyber-shot

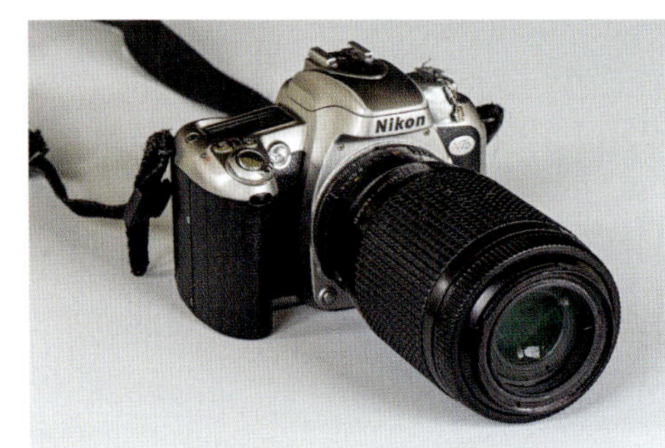
Nikon

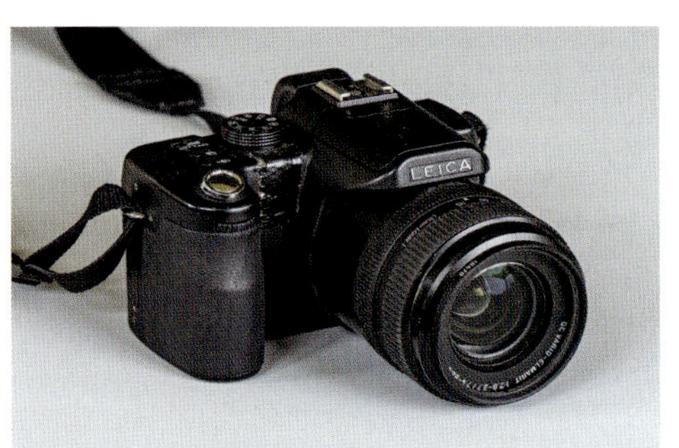
LEICA

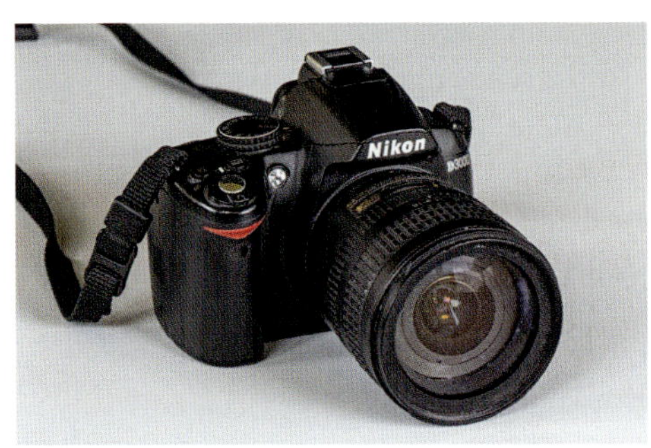
Nikon

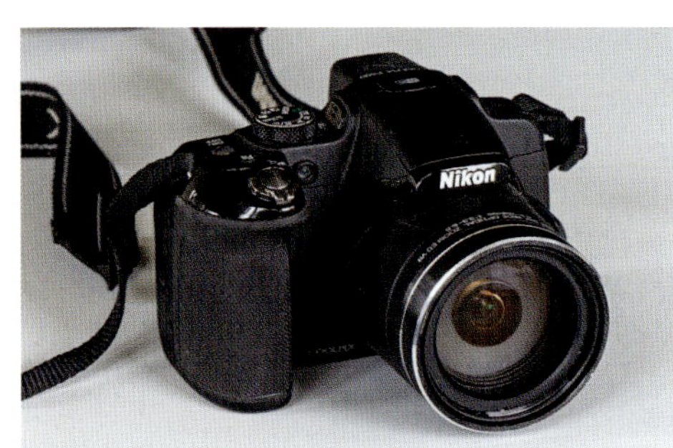
Nikon

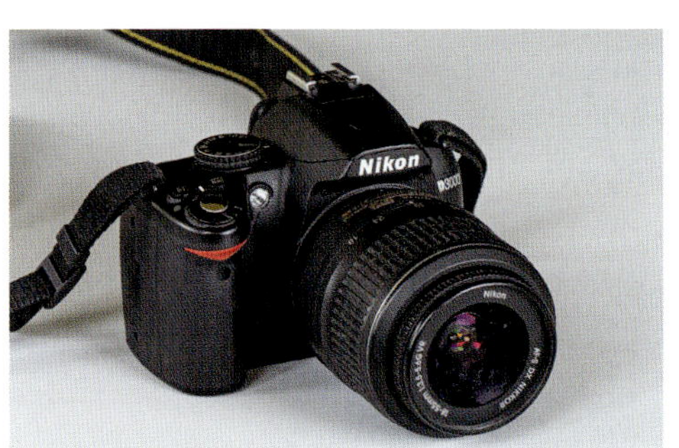
Nikon

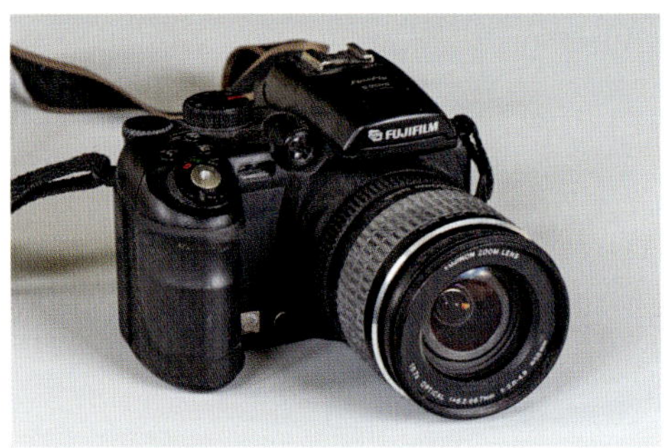
FUJIFILM

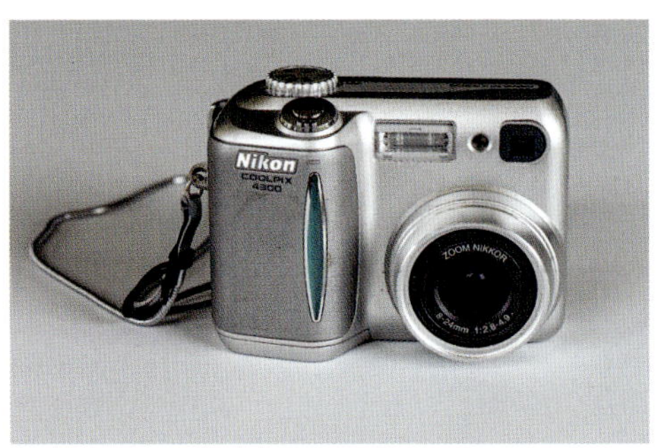
Nikon
COOLPIX
4300

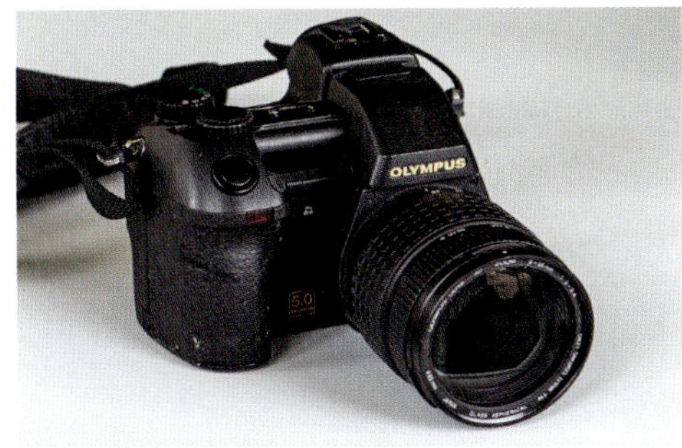
OLYMPUS
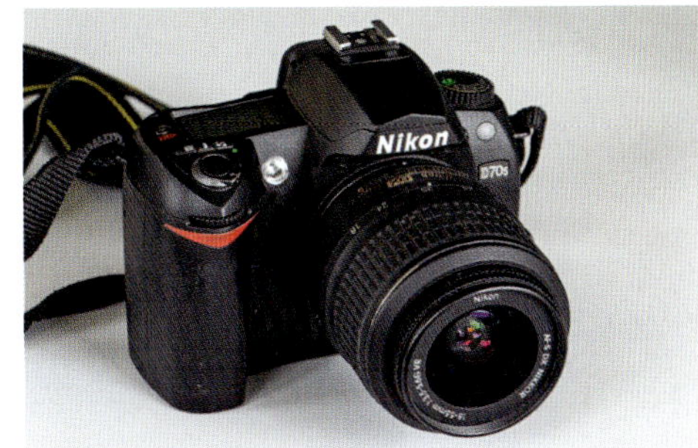
Nikon
D70s
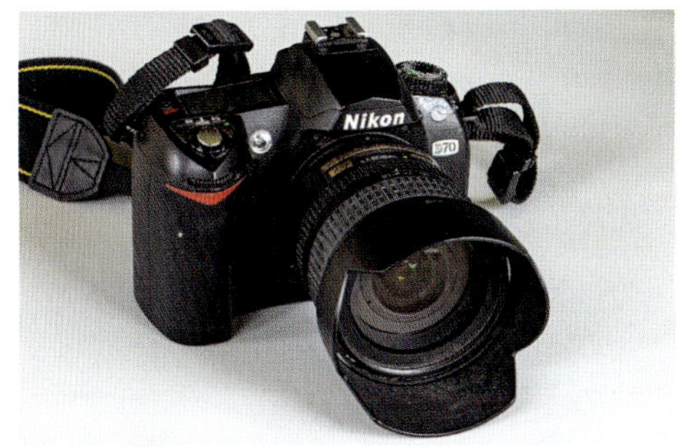
Nikon
D70
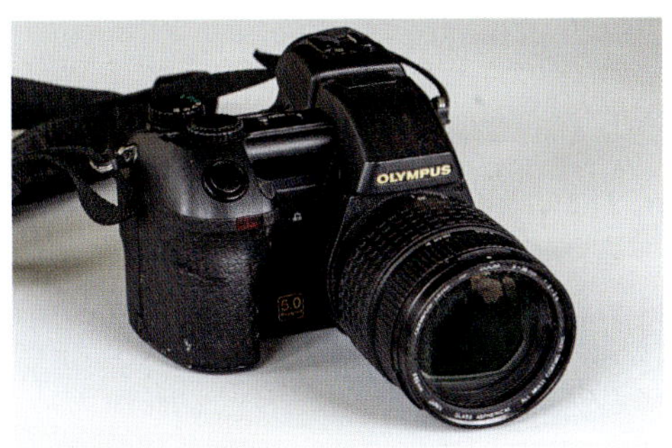
OLYMPUS
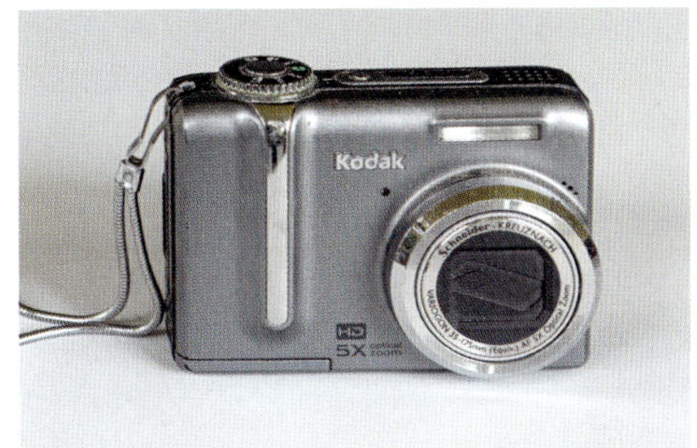
Kodak
5X
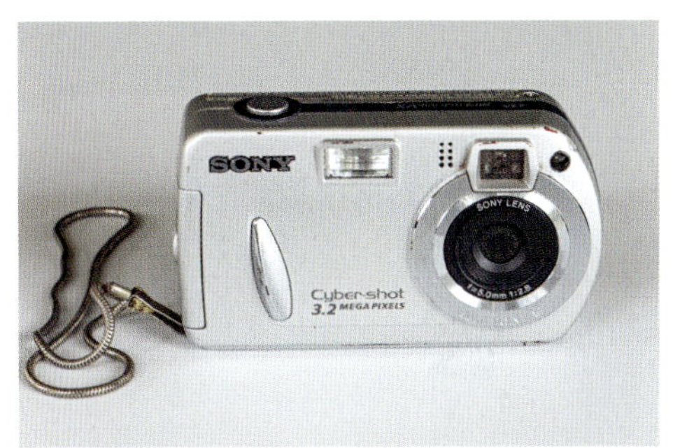
SONY
Cyber-shot
3.2 MEGA PIXELS
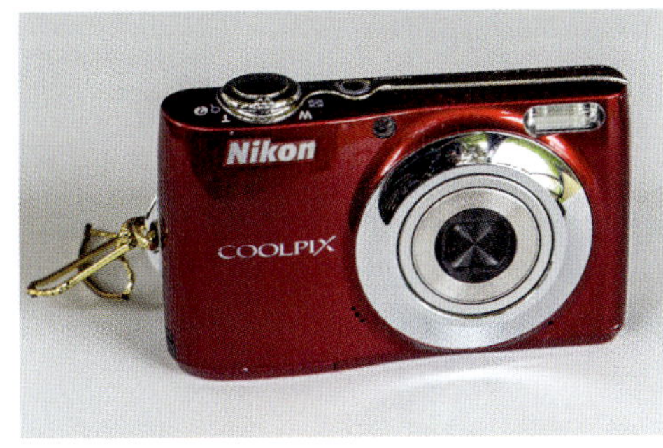
Nikon
COOLPIX
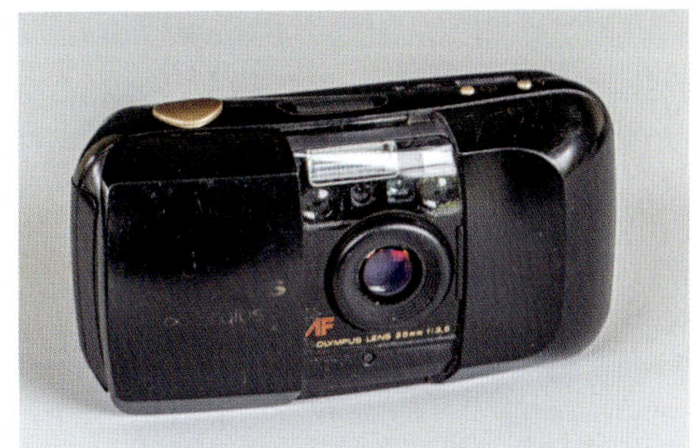
AF
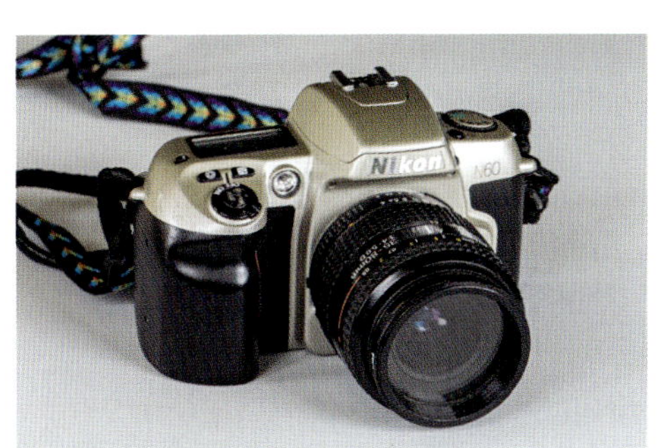
Nikon
N60
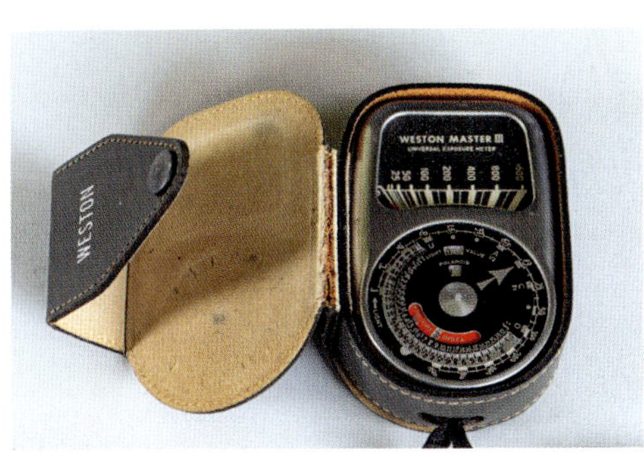
WESTON
WESTON MASTER

# 3rd Floor

# Darkroom

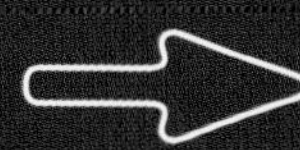

**On the date above I got a buzz on and dug some poems by Langston Hughes. I love that mans works.**

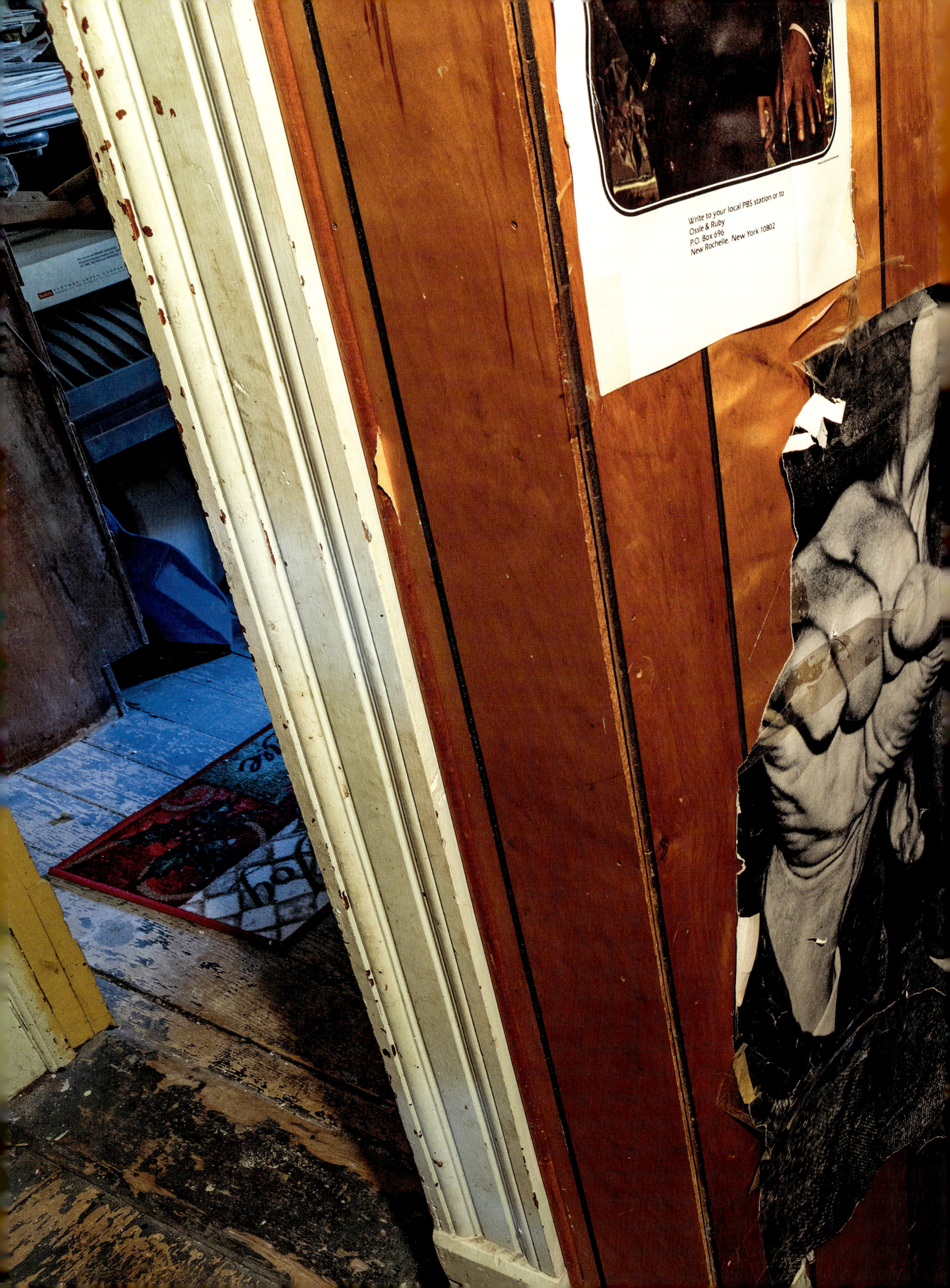

Write to your local PBS station or to
Ossie & Ruby
P.O. Box 696
New Rochelle, New York 10802

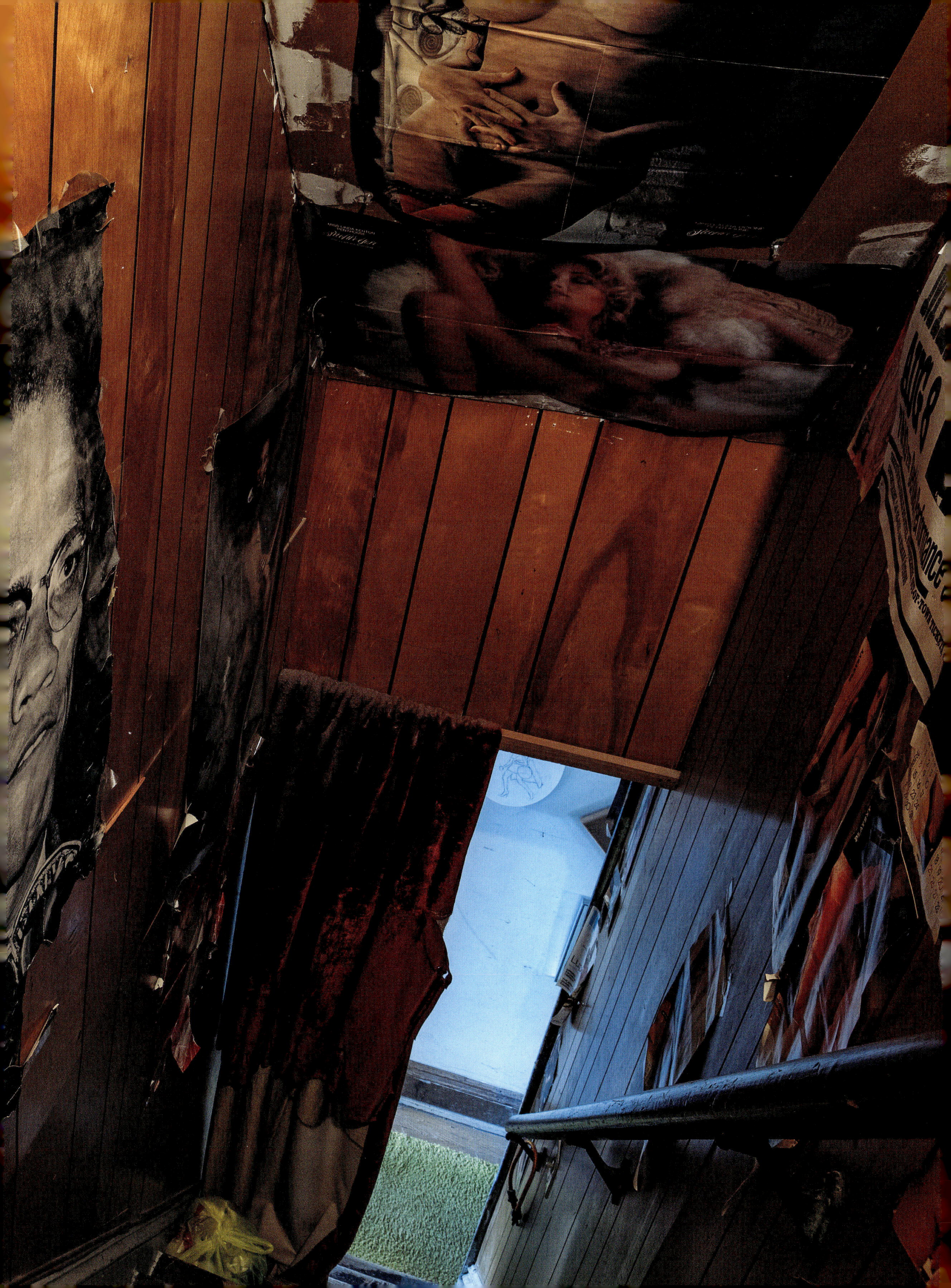

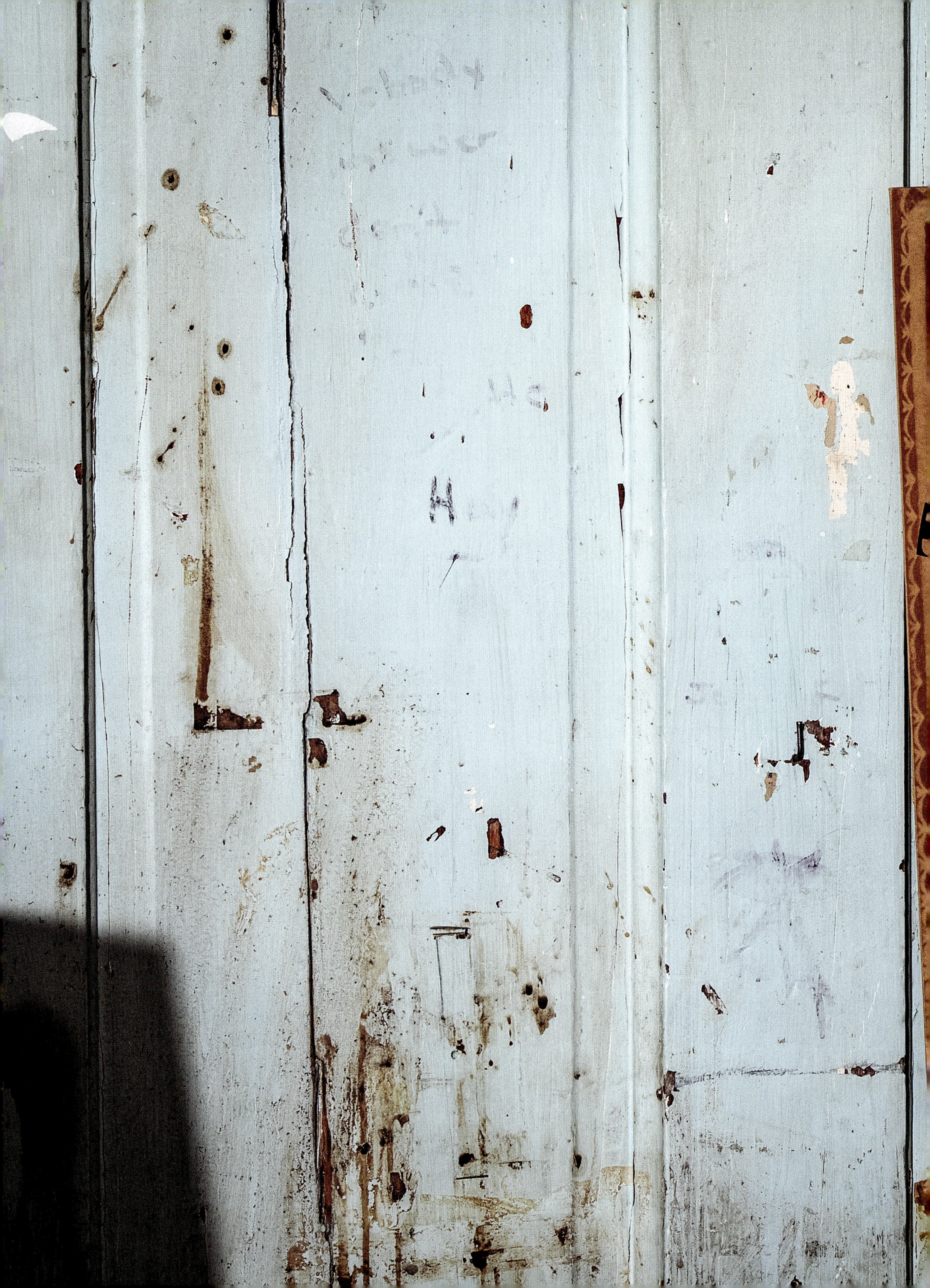

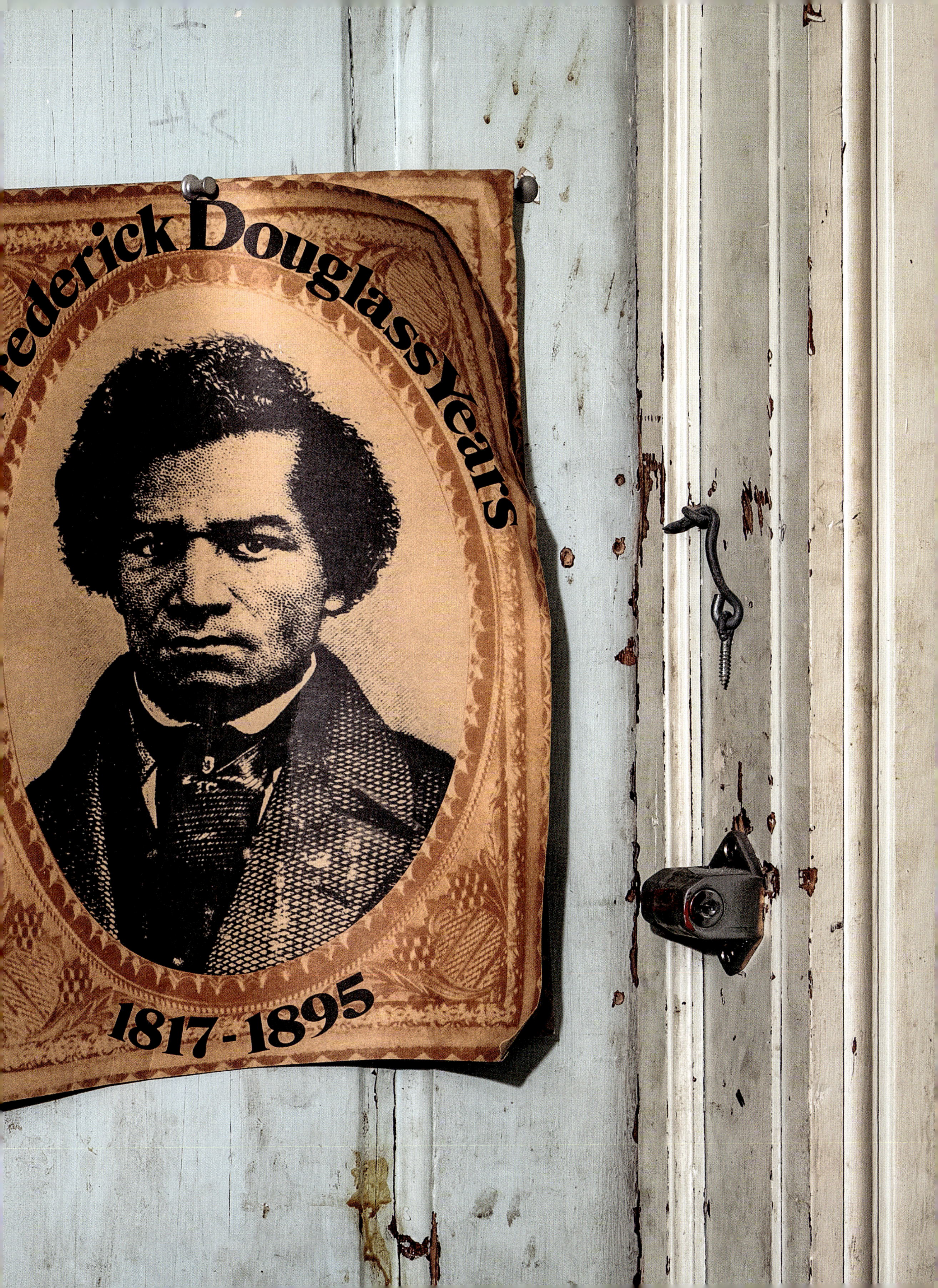
rederick Douglass Years
1817 - 1895

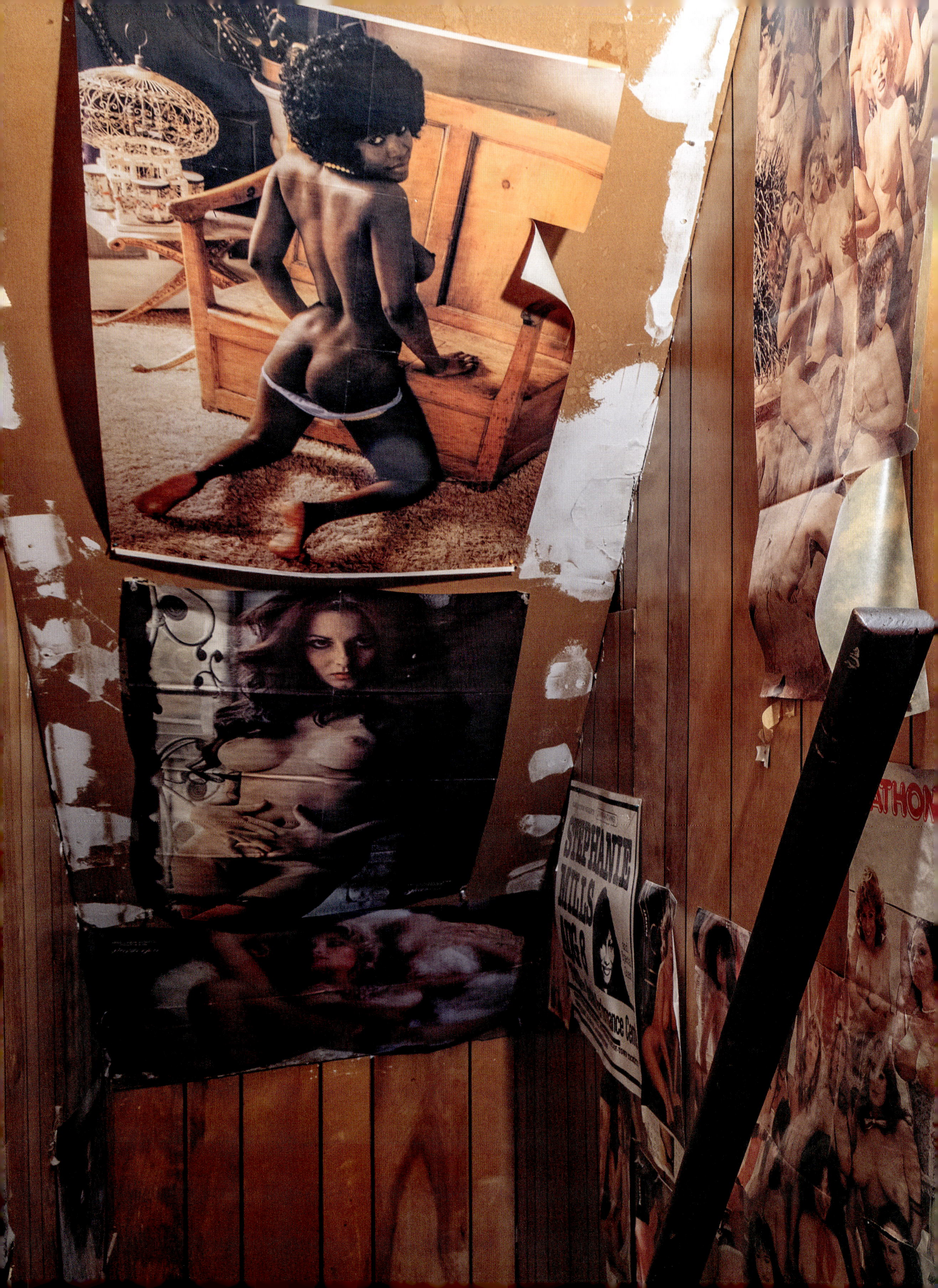
STEPHANIE
MILLS

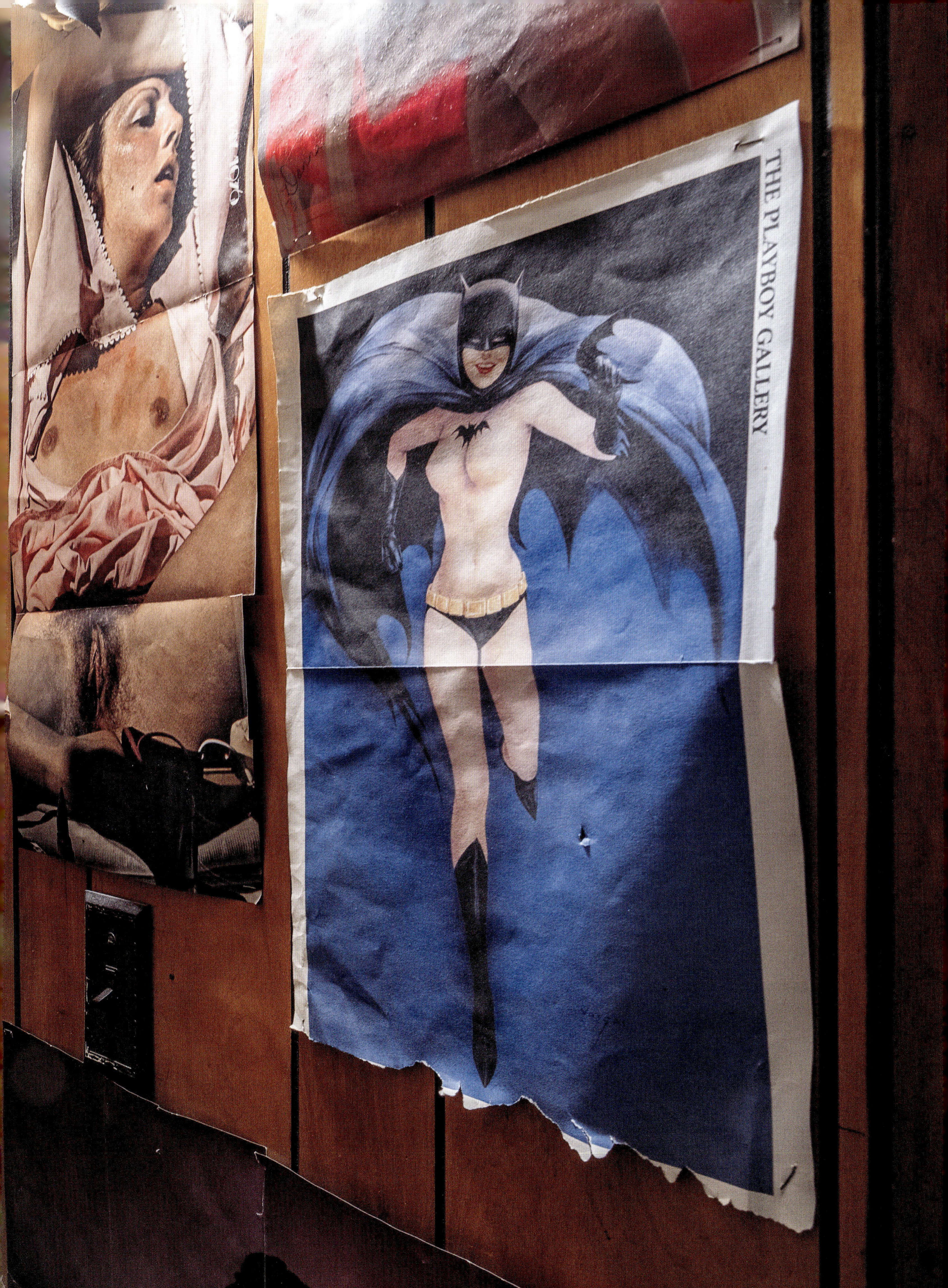
THE PLAYBOY GALLERY

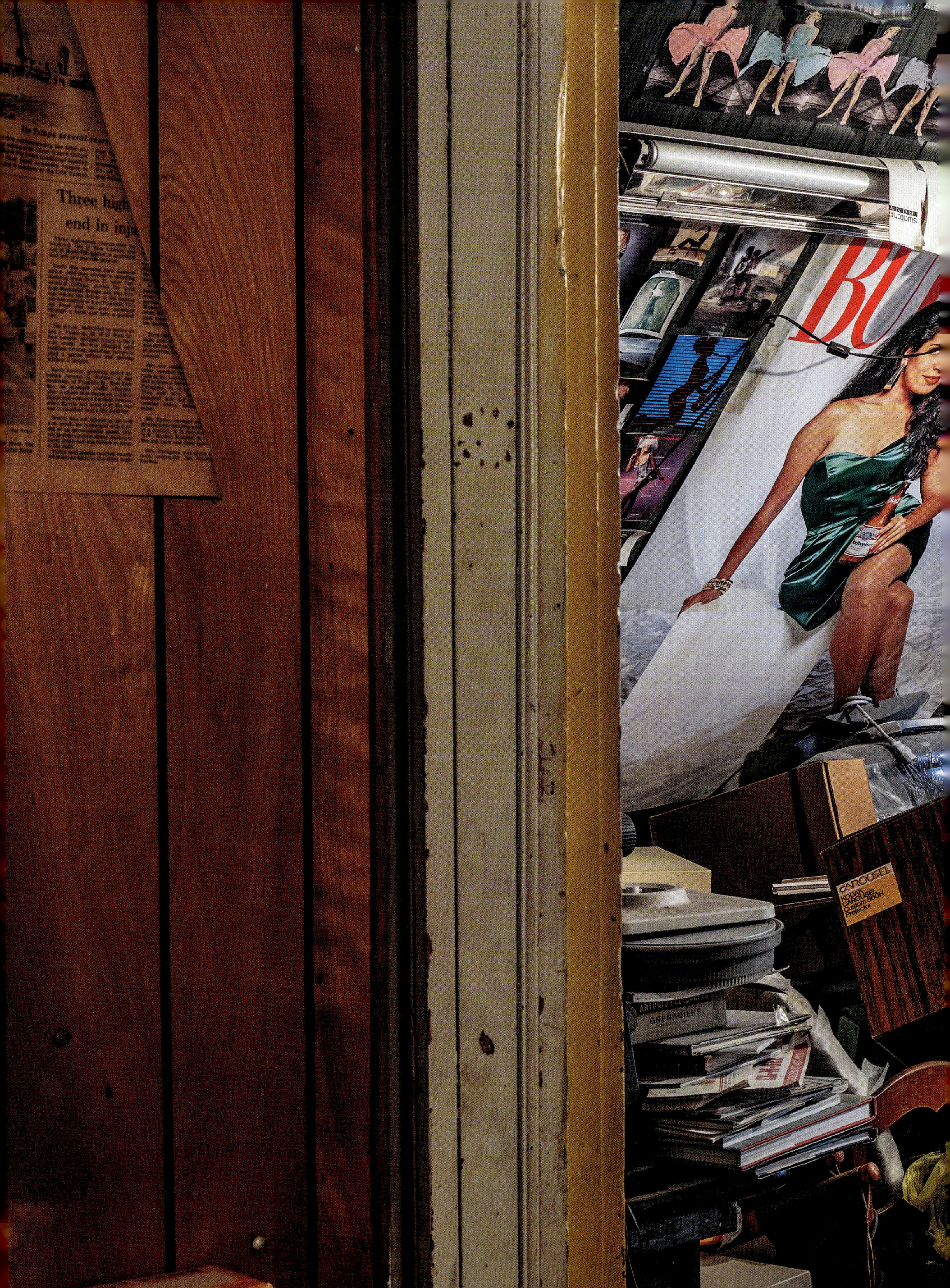
Three high
end in inju
CAROUSEL
KODAK
CAROUSEL
Custom 860H
Projector
GRENADIERS

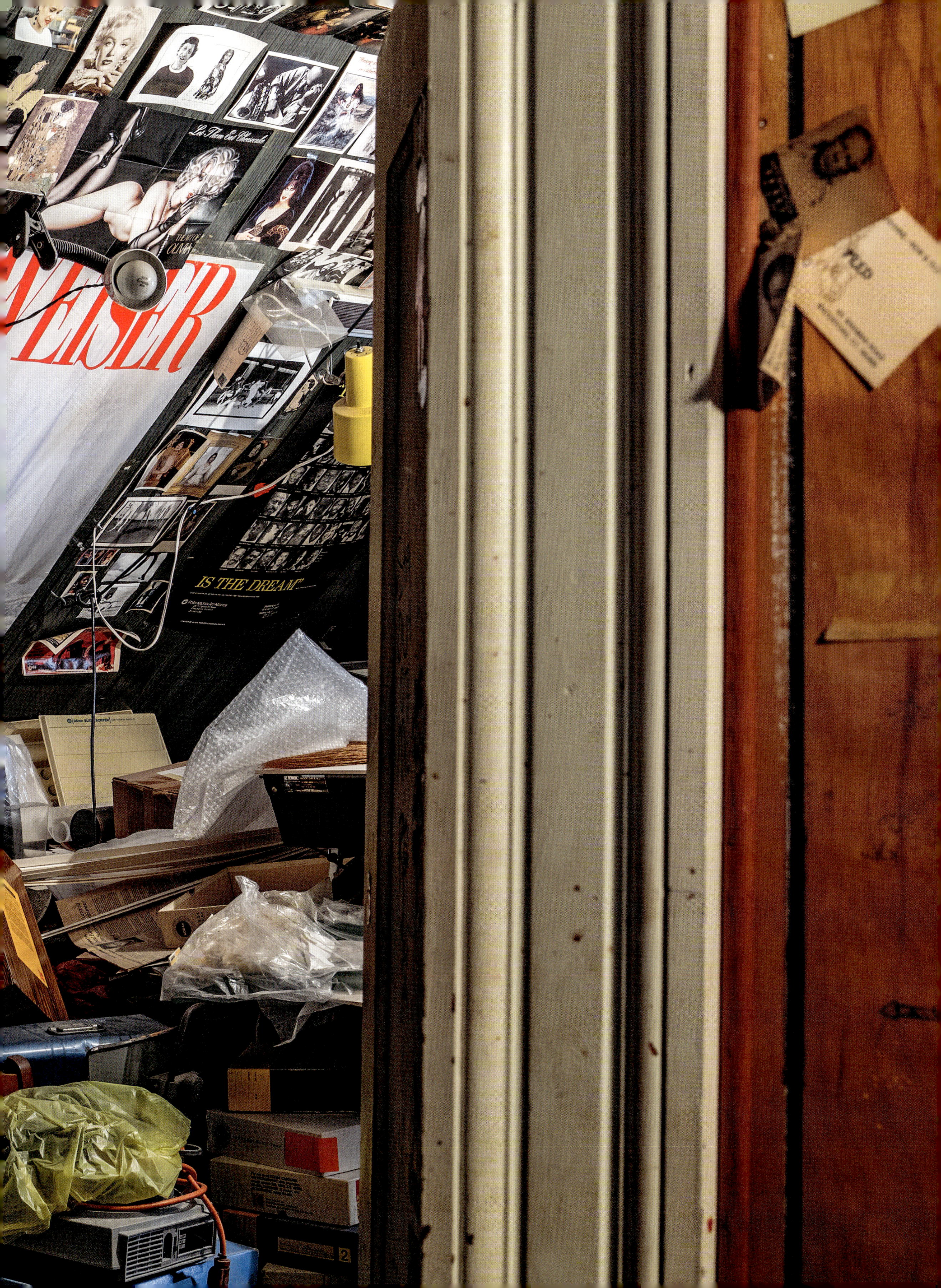
IS THE DREAM

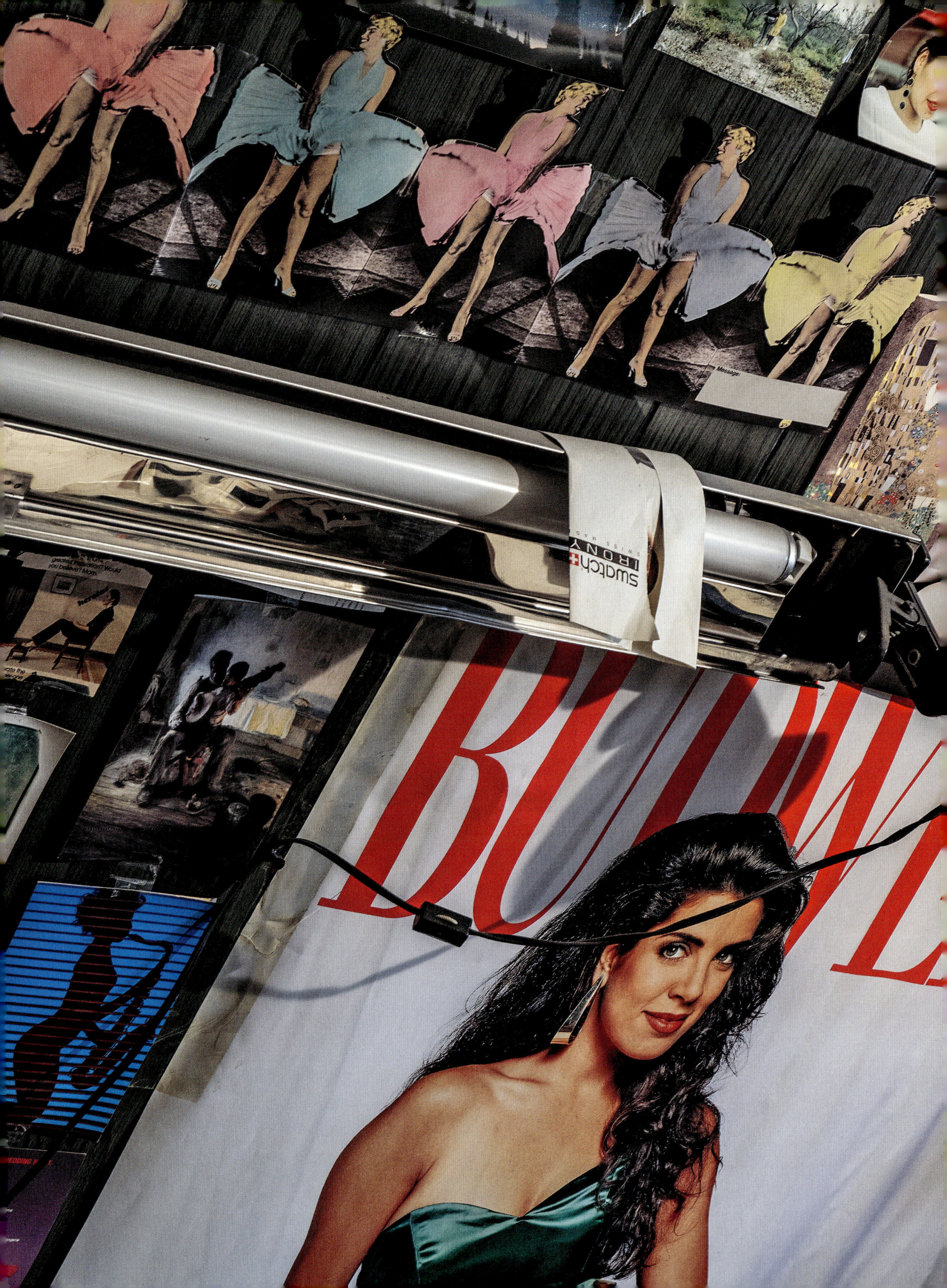
Message:
swatch
IRONY

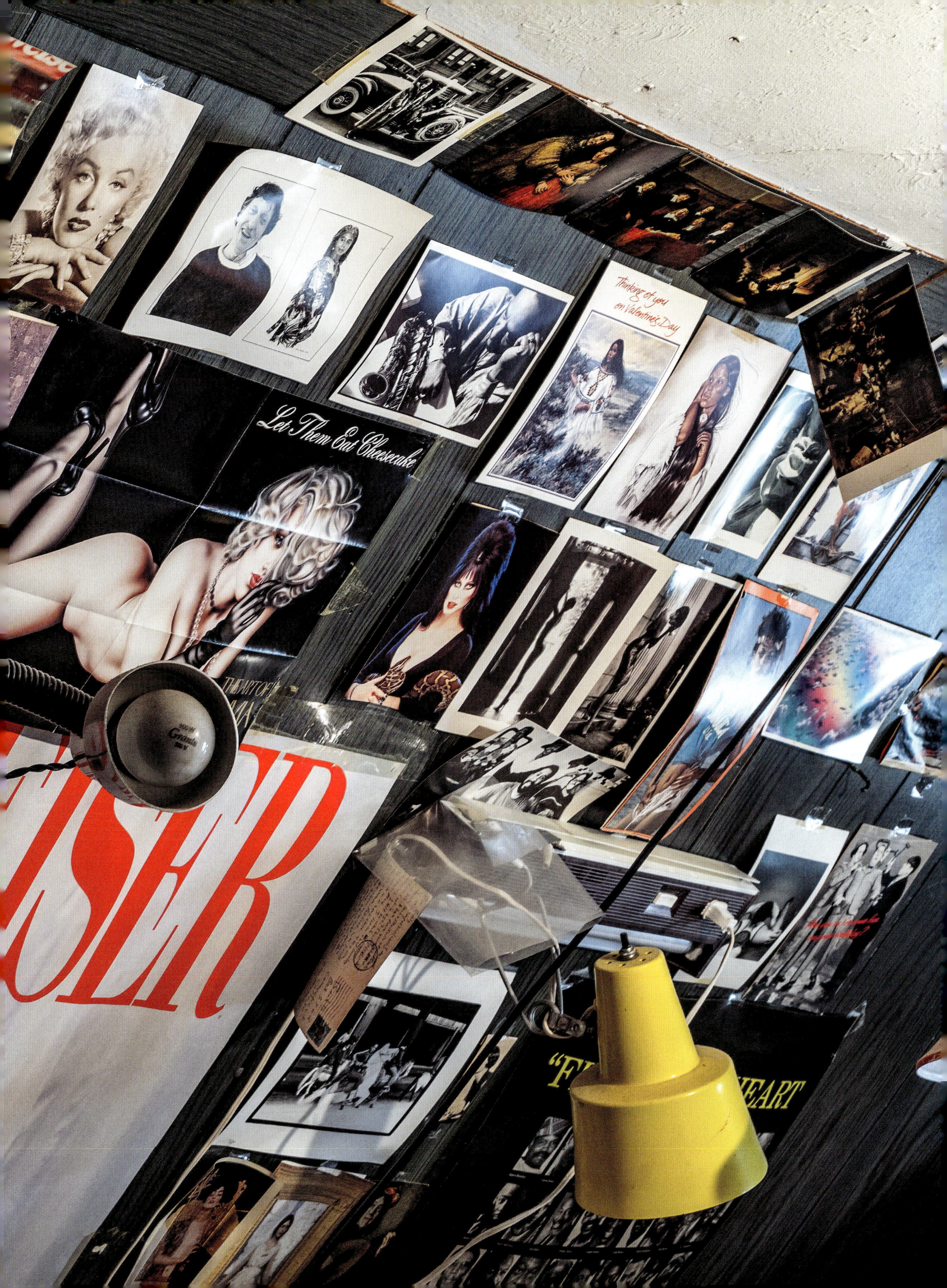
Let Them Eat Cheesecake
Thinking of you on Valentine's Day

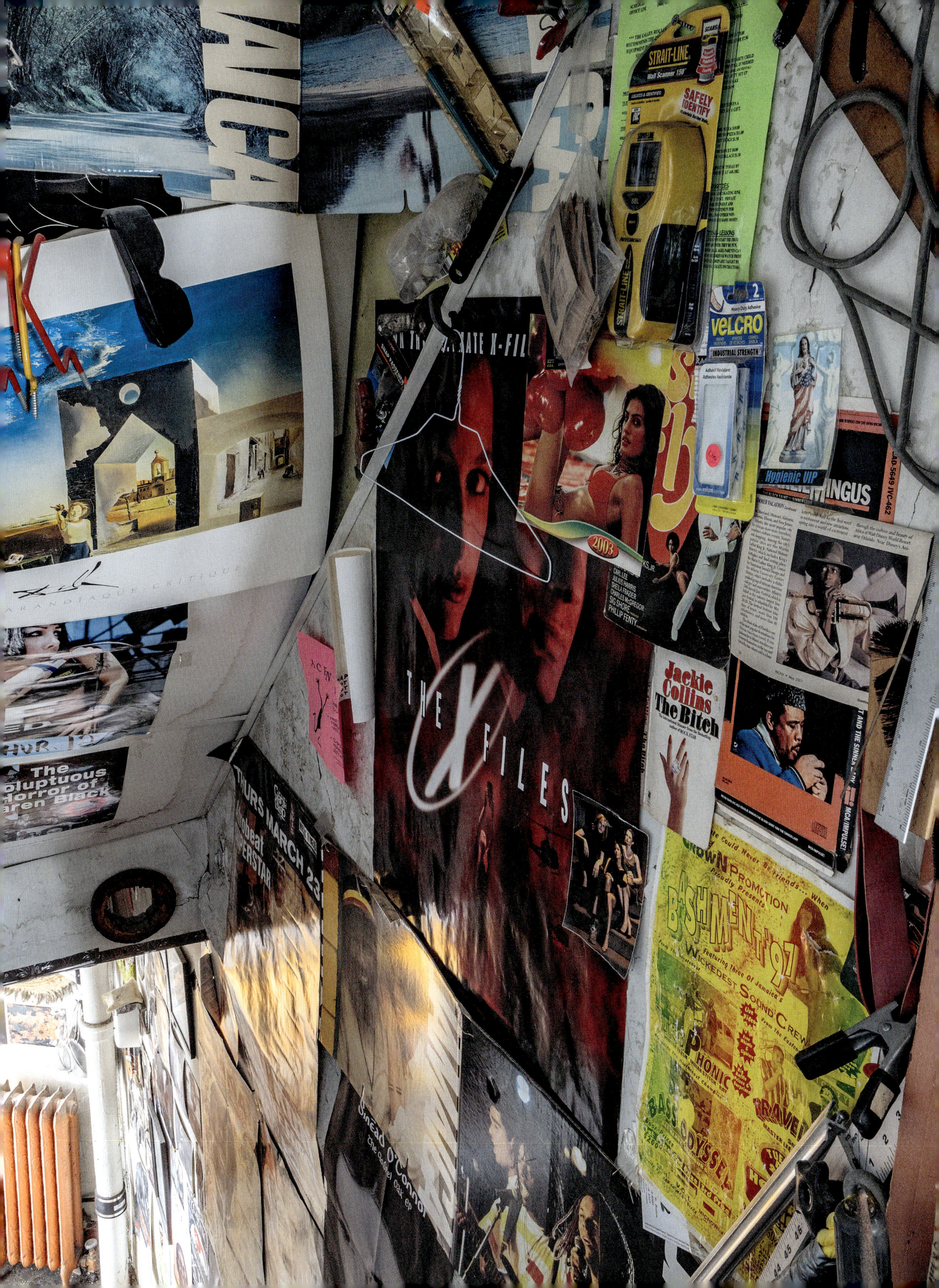

STRAIT-LINE
SAFELY IDENTIFY
VELCRO
INDUSTRIAL STRENGTH
Hygienic VIP
2003
THE X FILES
Jackie Collins
The Bitch
The
oluptuous
orror of
aren Black
THURS MARCH 23
Sinead O'Connor
CROWN PROMOTION

# As I wait through a painting problem my mind drifted to my Sunday journal. The idea or concept of putting my thought on paper is still quite new to me.

Portraits of Ma

I find myself yet a
composer and musical
piano, Charles Mingu
my subjects from also
or should I say min
said about the beauty
are allowed our feeble
her wonder and ma
must be done no matt
our results all are. Fo
in depth to the artis
the odds

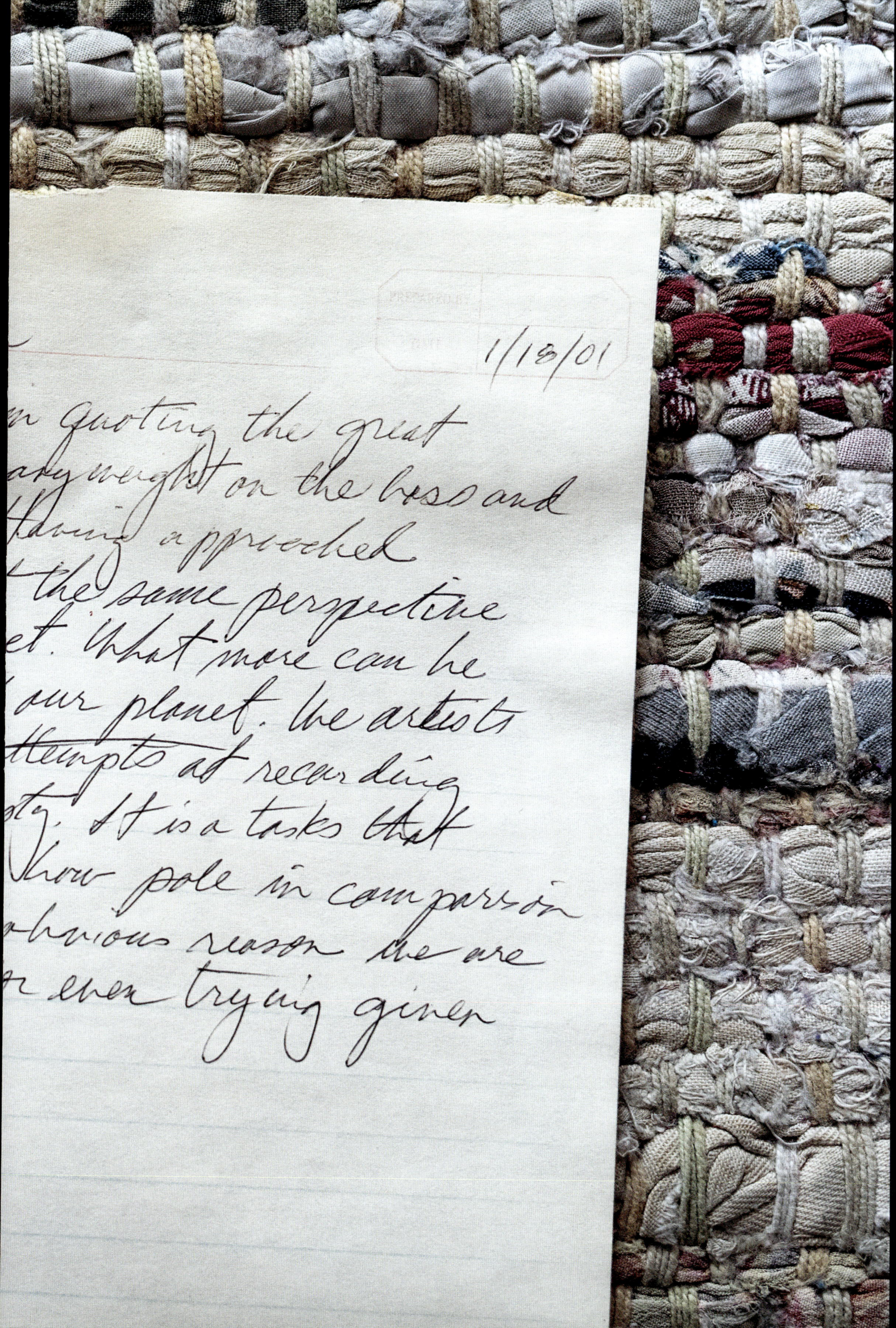

PREPARED BY

DATE 1/18/01

n quoting the great
ary weight on the boss and
having approached
t the same perspective
et. What more can be
our planet. We artists
ttempts at recording
sty. It is a tasks that
Those pale in comparison
obvious reason we are
r even trying given

3/17/78

I have used the camera in a "creative" capacity for a little over ten years. Three years prior, it was restricted to providing a record of my paintings. Even in that subordinate role I realized it was love at first sight. (No pun intended) The directness I found in the medium merged perfectly with ~~the~~ attitudes I had about my images. No other medium has been so totally supportive of my paintings, yet, so totally independent. It is this dual role I find so stimulating, addictive and boundless in its creative potential. Initially, I'm recognized as a painter. That I am. But to be only "a painter" would be very limiting, confusing and downright stupid. Photography responded to a basic need and I in turn am responding to its creative magnetism. I have little to say about my images, other than they excite me and I like them.

On a number of occasions I have refered to my camera as a mechanical sketchbook. Therefore on this auspicious occasion I have torn from its binder 39 pages for you to view. Please enjoy.

Peace

Barkley L. Hendricks

Education: The institution of higher learning historically have approached the subject of how to educate mankind from many perspective – like every thought and deed some were good some were not. Be that as it may I equate my education with my musical input, ~~an input which is rich in the music~~ ~~and culture~~ I have learned to trust my visual senses more ~~and~~ more each ~~year~~ time I venture out beyond my nest. I am apart of a very fascinating drama which I record in the chambers of my desire. My very small view of this magnificent drama, with is our day to day interaction helps me to stop the action (so to speak) for a longer look. That longer look provides me with the means necessary for a more harmonious relationship between that which I am and that and those ~~others~~ who are also on the stage. I want to watch from the audience as the same time act in the drama. Though my act of recording some simultaneously expressions are very delightful and important. The important is the education which takes when study is allowed to run its course of personally satisfaction, without too much interference from me.

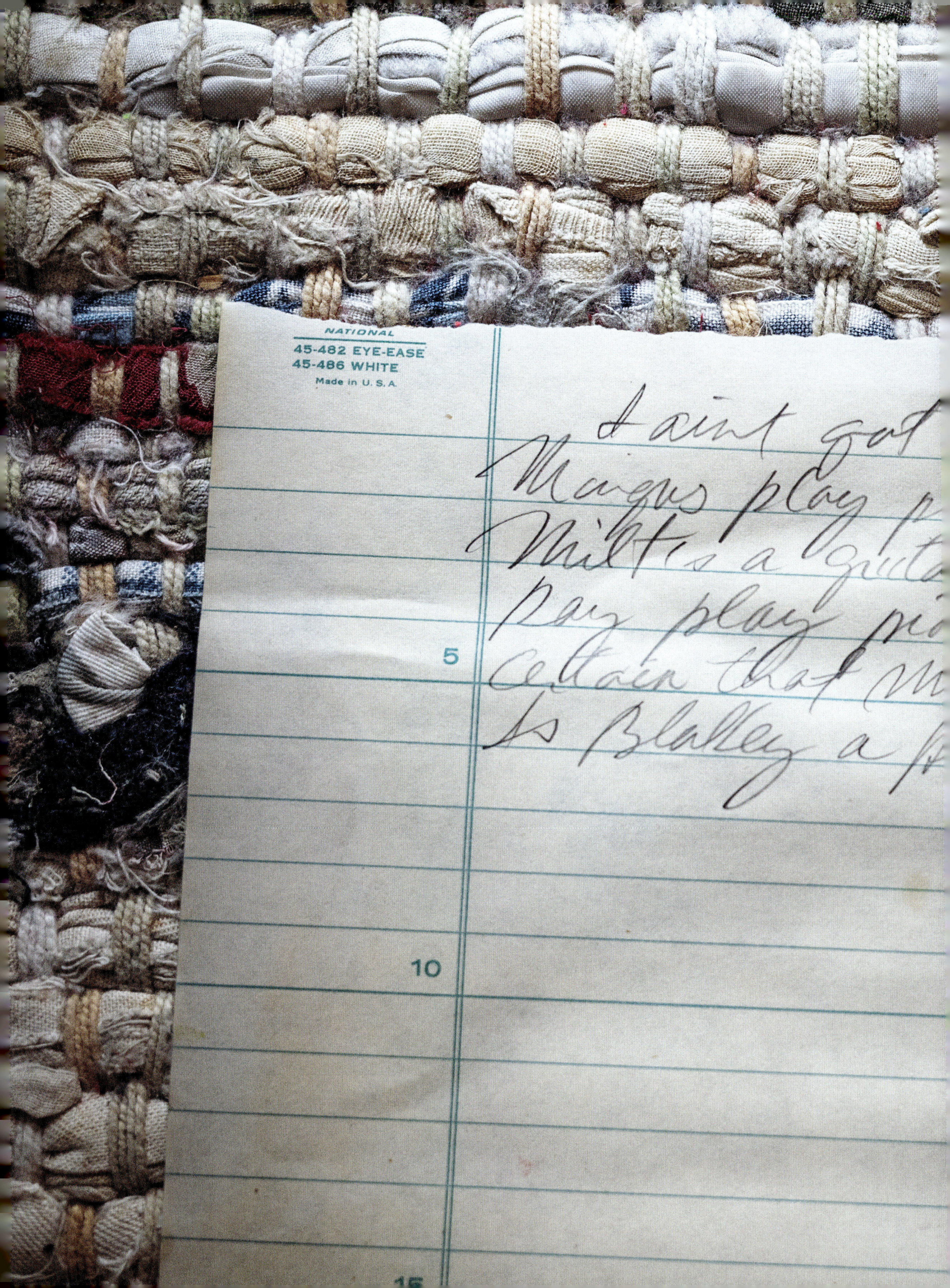

NATIONAL
45-482 EYE-EASE
45-486 WHITE
Made in U.S.A.

I aint got
Margus play p
Milt's a guita
Ray play pia
certain that M
Is Blakey a p

othin to Lose
ns or does he play both?
ost or a singer. Does
g or alto? Can it be
es plays only the piano.
ain't only

" "
April 23, 1978

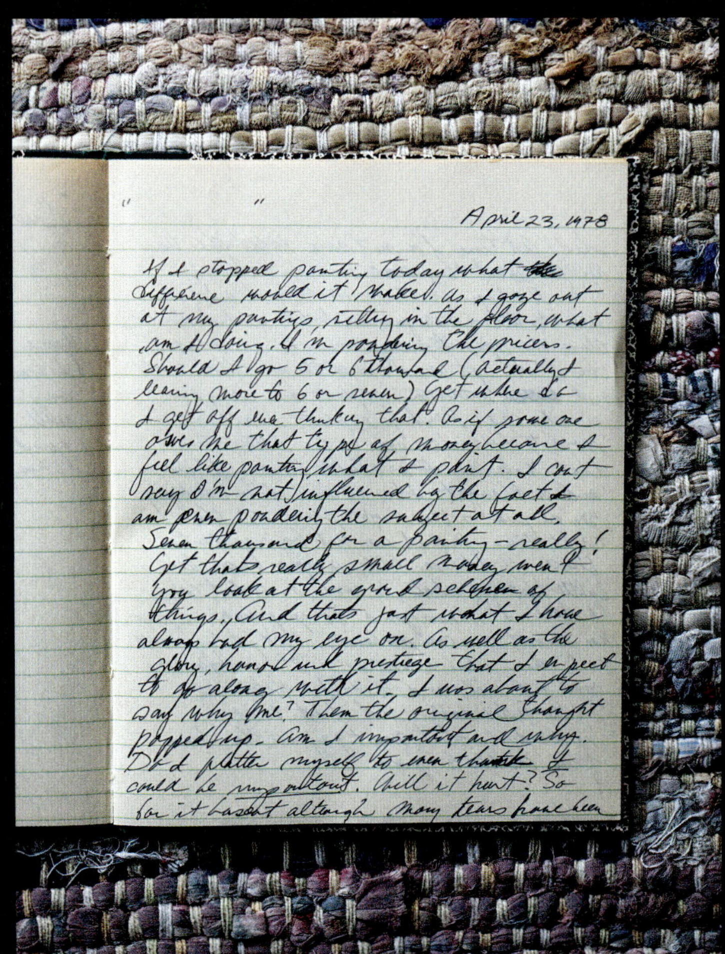
" " April 23, 1978

If I stopped painting today what ~~the~~ difference would it make? As I gaze out at my paintings sitting on the floor, what am I doing. I'm pondering the prices. Should I go 5 or 6 thousand (actually I leaning more to 6 or seven) Yet where do I get off even thinking that. As if some one owes me that type of money because I feel like painting what I paint. I can't say I'm not influenced by the fact I am even pondering the subject at all. Seven thousand for a painting – really! Yet that's really small money when you look at the grand scheme of things. And that's just what I have always had my eye on. As well as the glory, honor and prestige that I expect to go along with it. I was about to say why me? Then the original thought popped up. Am I important and why. Did I flatter myself to even ~~think~~ I could be important. Will it hurt? So far it hasn't although many tears have been

"COOL/KOOL"
March 23, 1978

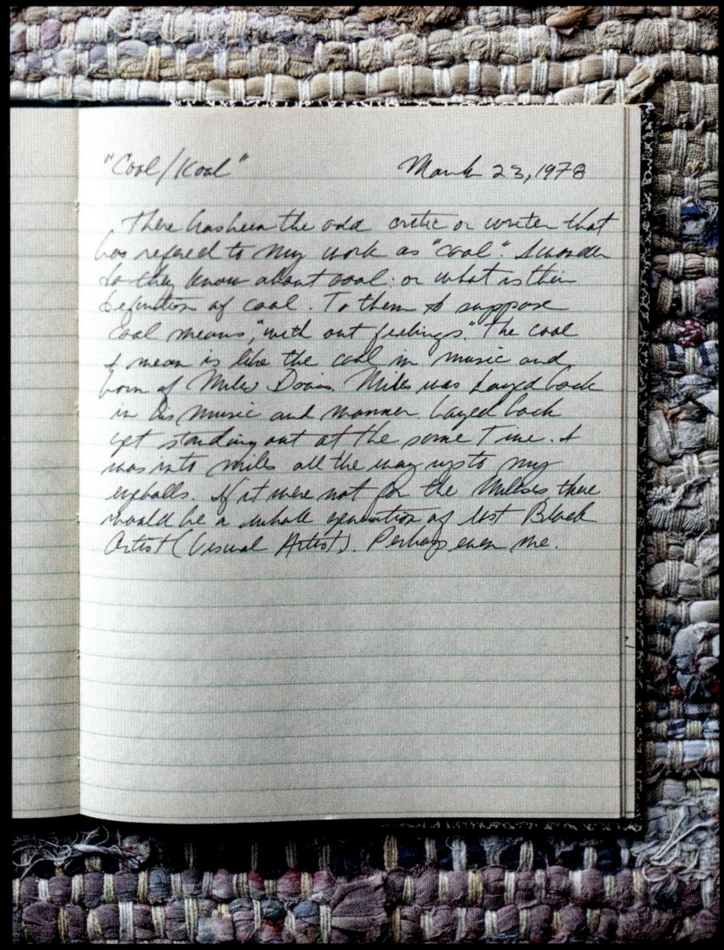
"Cool/Kool" March 23, 1978

There has been the odd critic or writer that has refered to my work as "cool". I wonder do they know about cool; or what is their definition of cool. To them I suppose cool means, "with out feelings." The cool I mean is like the cool in music and form of Miles Davis. Miles was layed back in his music and manner. Layed back yet standing out at the same time. I was into Miles all the way up to my eyeballs. If it were not for the Miles there would be a whole generation of lost Black Artist (Visual Artist). Perhaps even me.

"SLICKNESS VS ELEGANCE"
February 19, 1978

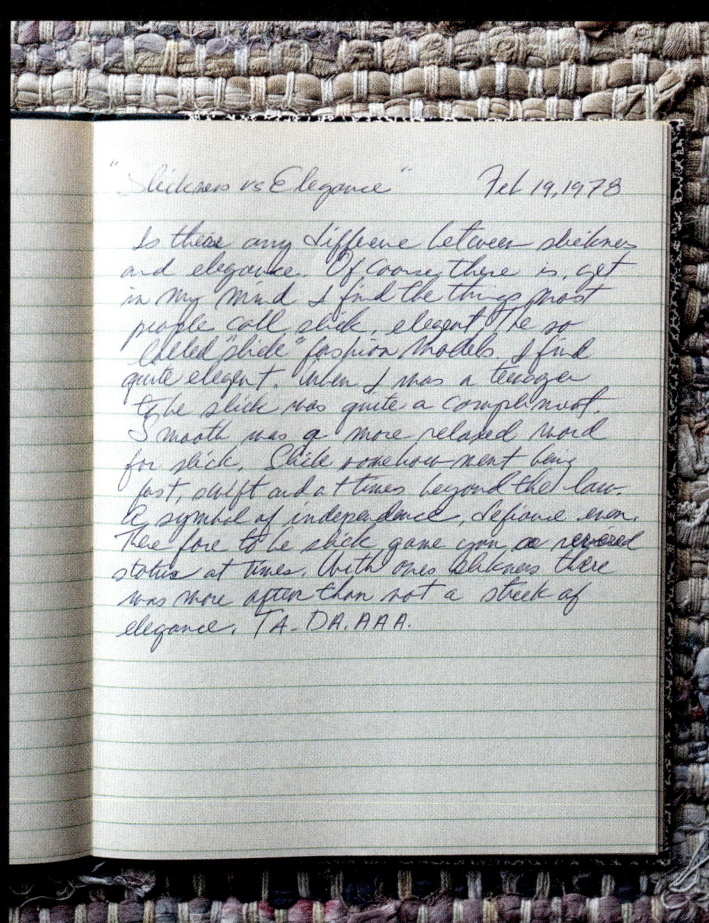
"Slickness vs Elegance" Feb 19, 1978

Is there any differene between slickness and elegance. Of course there is, yet in my mind I find the things most people call slick, elegant. The so labeled "slick" fashion models I find quite elegant. When I was a teenager to be slick was quite a compliment. Smooth was a more relaxed word for slick. Slick somehow meant being fast, swift and at times beyond the law. A symbol of independance, defiance even. There fore to be slick gave you a revered status at times. With ones slickness there was more often than not a streak of elegance. TA-DA.AAA.

"TROPHIES"
July 22, 1978

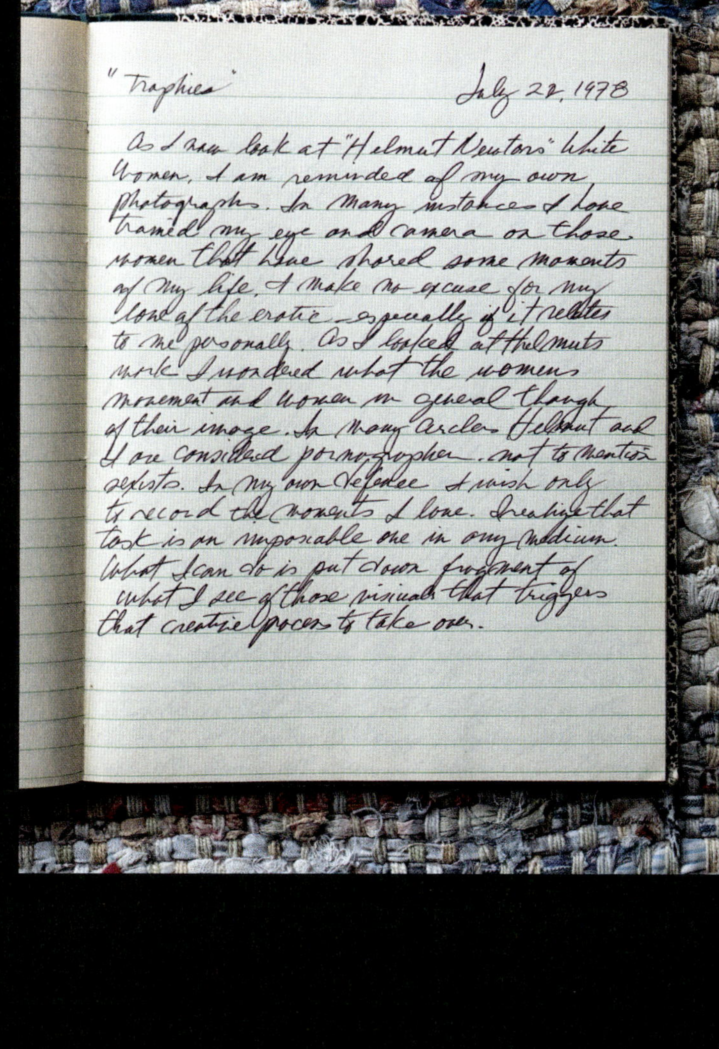
"Trophies" July 22, 1978

As I now look at "Helmut Newtons" White Women, I am reminded of my own photographs. In many instances I have trained my eye and camera on those women that have shared some moments of my life. I make no excuse for my love of the erotic – especially if it relates to me personally. As I looked at Helmuts work I wondered what the womens movement and women in general thought of their image. In many circles Helmut and I are considered pornographers, not to mention sexists. In my own defense I wish only to record the moments I love. Realize that task is an imposable one in any medium. What I can do is put down fragment of what I see of those visuals that triggers that creative process to take over.

with the rest of us to Big Youths version of "Every Nigger is Star," or hip hop to the provocation and poignant lyrics of Niggaz With Attitudes. They are not alone in the deconstruction and liberation of the N word.

After photographing the KKK in Connecticut, I wrote a companion page of thoughts for publication relating to the event. When I mentioned not once did the Grand Wizard/Dragon/Cyclopes mention the word

which rhymed with the name
of Roy Rodgers horse. One of my
former students upon reading the
dissertation looked at me in a
puzzeled state and admitted
she had no clue what the
name of that legendary steed
was. She was well aware of
the N word. Happy Trails.

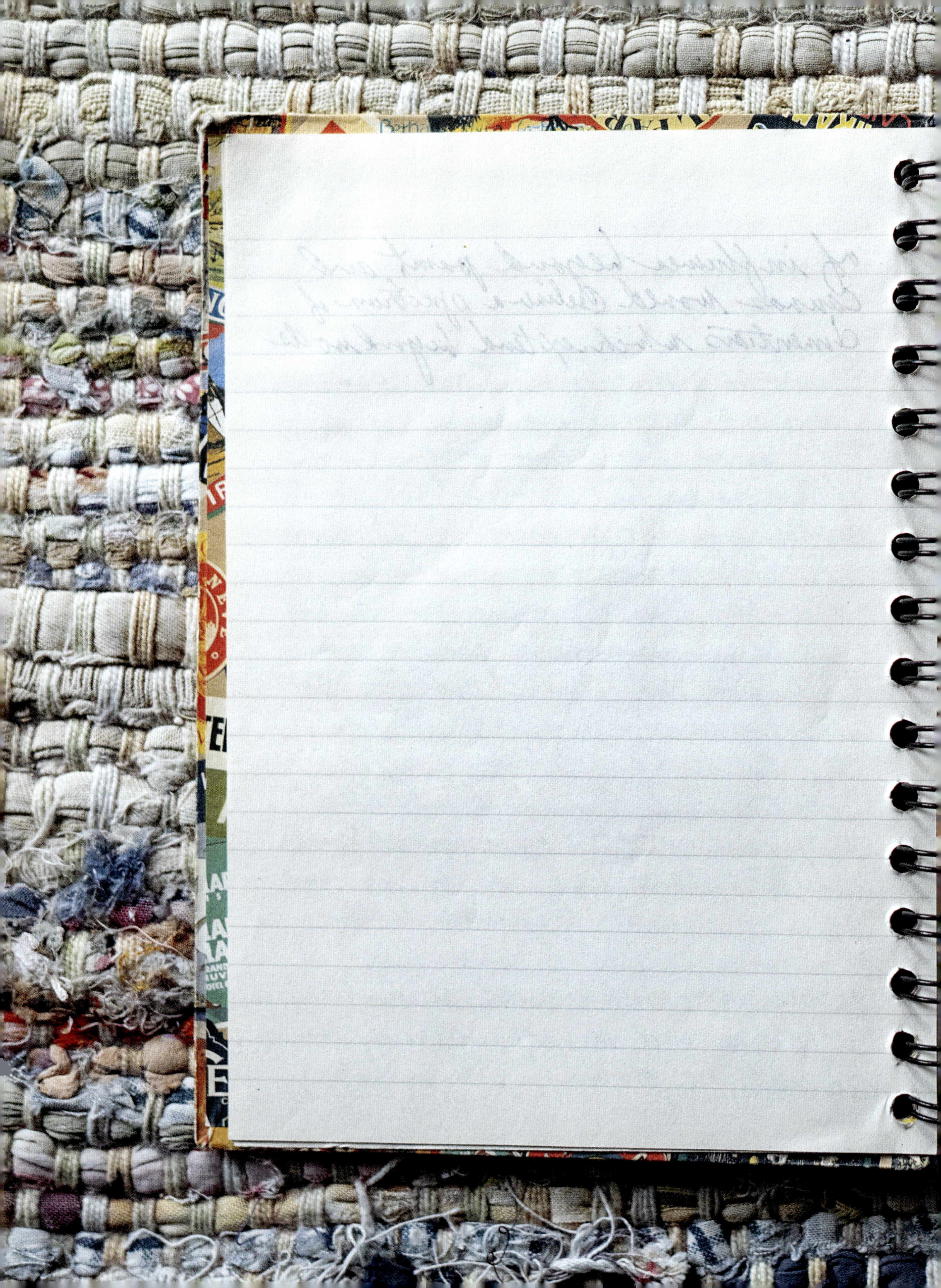

Great Benny at Great Bay 1/4/07

The wind is to strong for my aluminum easel for me to paint. So after a vigorous swim chillin out in the shade of small leafed tree I decided to watch the wind toss the waves to the shore with the power to create spray that stood for seconds like vertical water people. It is a time like this that nature mandates me to look and absorb. It does however make me want to try and capture instanious water configurations and freeze several in oil with my trusty fan brush. I am reminded by my last conversation with Benny (Andrews). He said I was bold and courageous to do and exhibit works which were not figures specifically Black figures. Our painterly

**The more I learn how to employ words to convey thoughts and ideas the less I know what to say about my own work—at least in the written form.**

5 123456789

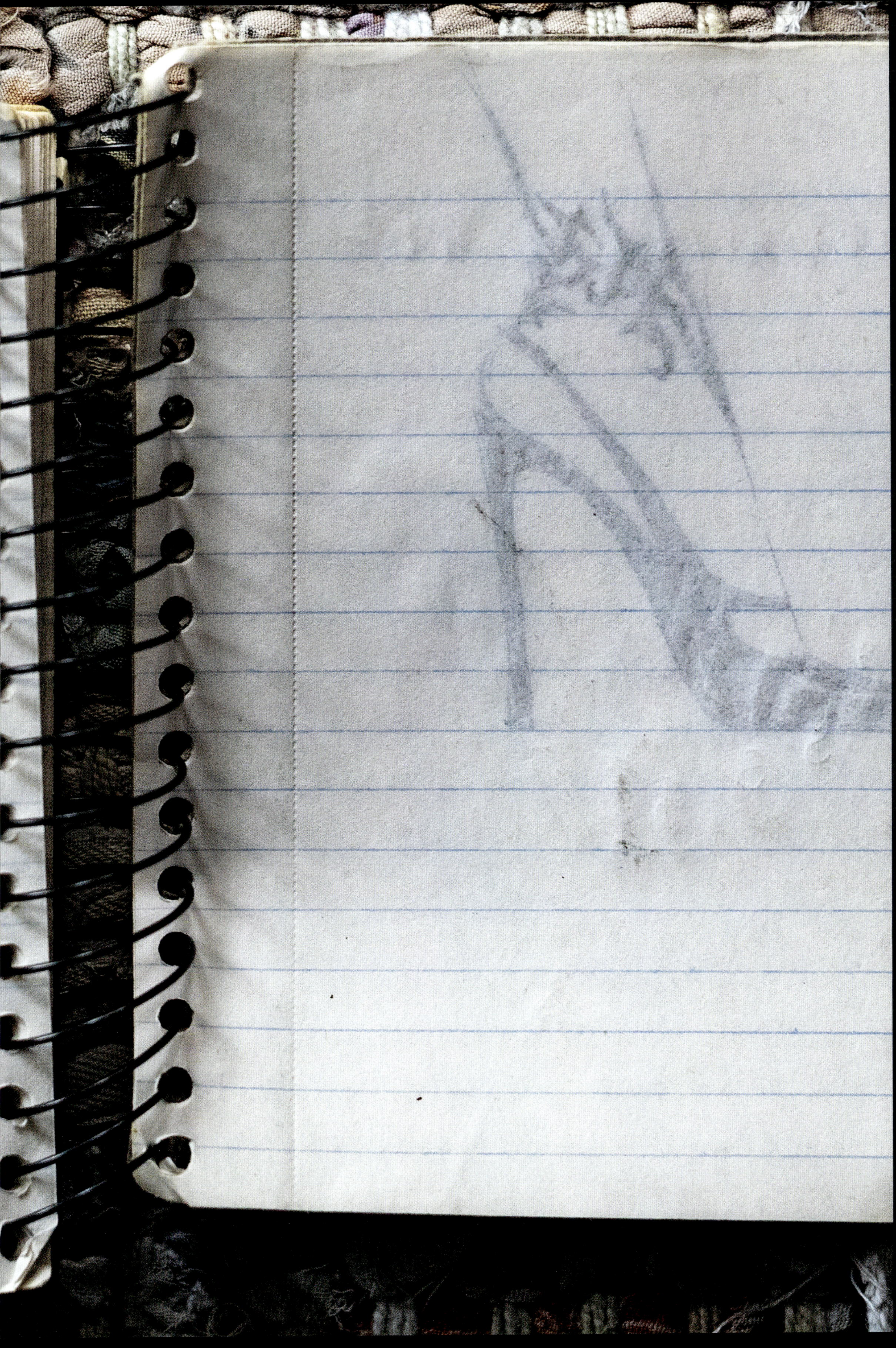

UNTITLED

DATE: Unknown

"Almost the next day"

I just thought of something: I may not paint every day, but I listen to music almost everyday.

I also just thought of this. I feel something good is going to burst open with my work in New York City. It should put me in the top ten good painters in the United States, the white art U.S.A. I will begin to make some bucks. It will be heavy. You will get close to cracking open, in fact you will see inside, really inside. It will be beautiful and terrifying at the same time. After that things will be cool. Really laid back. For a long, long time. Maybe not till I die, but a long time. I will have really enjoyed it all. No regrets. Just complete love for it all, and all people. You will be one proud little Mothafucka.

"Friday" Dec 15, 1978

As I wait through a painting problem my mind drifts to my Sunday journal. The idea or concept of putting my thought on paper is still quite new to me. I have yet to gain total confidence in this art form. I'm trying, for what it may be worth. This morning started out with a bit of sun. I am close to completing my last (maybe) banana tree. There may be actual possession of my creative energies when those plants entered 58 State, they have provided me many hours of study. The only difficulty encountered was when I really didn't feel like something was not right with the set up angle or mental frame of mind this is the lesson one faces to look and paint. Perhaps this is why I paint. Words fall all too short when it comes to providing the image I need planted in my brain. I should like to become skilled with the use of English language so the paint would be satisfied on the level of my paintings and photographs.

Jan 20, 1976

"Old times - Pre Bop"

Tonight as I paint it feels like old times in my studio. I have been in a post-Bop mood. My Studio has been filled with sounds of Horace Silver and Art Blakey. Its been a long time since my diet has called for an evening with these gentlemen. There is a warm and contented feeling floating around my studio. As I paint I feel happy. I'm happy about what I am working on, and the music seem to go right with that feeling. The old days in my other studios were happy ones too, so nice is this feeling it is almost like I have been transported back. Or time as stood still. These are very familiar friends on my turntable, and it is good to make their aquaintance again. They helped me through many, many hours of solitude. I was alone but not lonely.

"Hello Mile"

Sept 6, 1976

Hello Mile, hello "Cannonball" hello Bill, hello John, hello Jimmy, hello Wynton and hello Paul. Its good to hear you again. Fond memories are conjured up with the help of your music. My taste in music has become broader with the arrival of the [illegible], at one time you occupied the only space in my mind and record shelfs. Now with the change the electric sound has crept in. Fear not - you are still number one, my main squeeze, so to speak. Nothing has replaced the sensuous sound you gentlemen seem to capture my way [illegible].

For many years your creations were the steady diet of many young black men. We would gather around our hi-fi set to be transported to distant places by your sounds. We would sit spell bound in some lit room and float to where-ever you cared to take us. "Kind of Blue" was our only passport. Today I still float, and "Kind of Blue" is still my only visa

"Much too late to specula

Which is what I have
lately. Or have I?

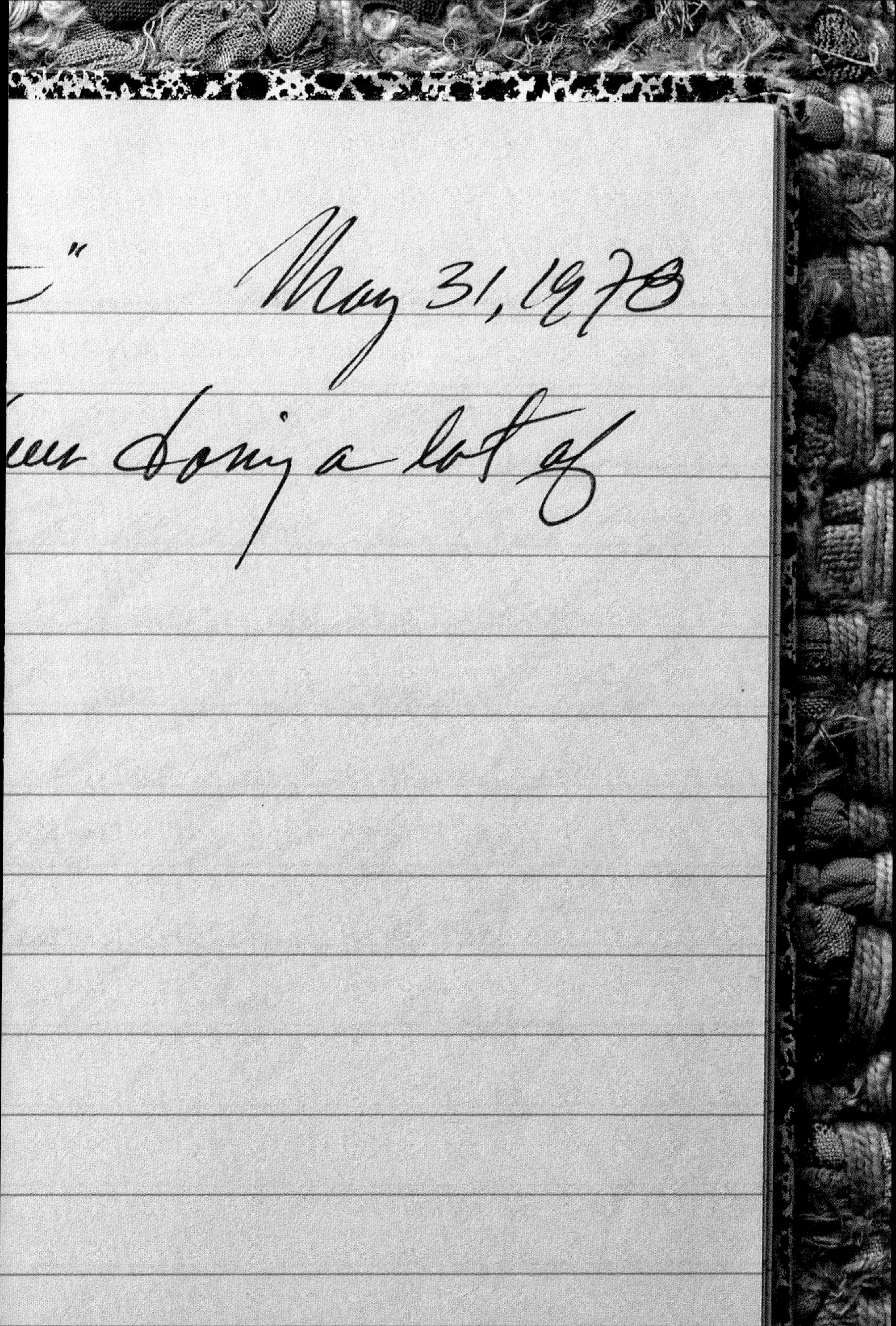

e”     May 31, 1978

een doing a lot of

"Moonburns" Jan 18, 1979

I have been feeling strange about starting this new painting that has been on my mind for the last few days. I just knew something would happen with "Brilliantly Endowed" (?) at the National Academy of Design – it got rejected (smile) I was at the crossroads of a new nude self portrait, another difficult piece to handle. No naked Niggahs!

"Lagos & Paris" Sunday Sept 25, 1977

This morning I arose to the sound of Fela.
My visuals ~~was~~ supplied by Atget.
This year Lagos and Paris has been embedded
in my mind so I guess Fela and Atget
are symbolic of my desire to return to
their ~~native~~ country. Their creations have
have inspired me to ~~[illegible]~~ greater hight

"Octopus"

I feel one of those
inhabit the deep,
the fellow with the
feel a bit like him
my life. I feel
more arms than I
Energy! Energy! E

Sept 28, 1977

creatures that
you know the one!
many arms. I
at this time in
into everything.
me, all reaching.
energy!

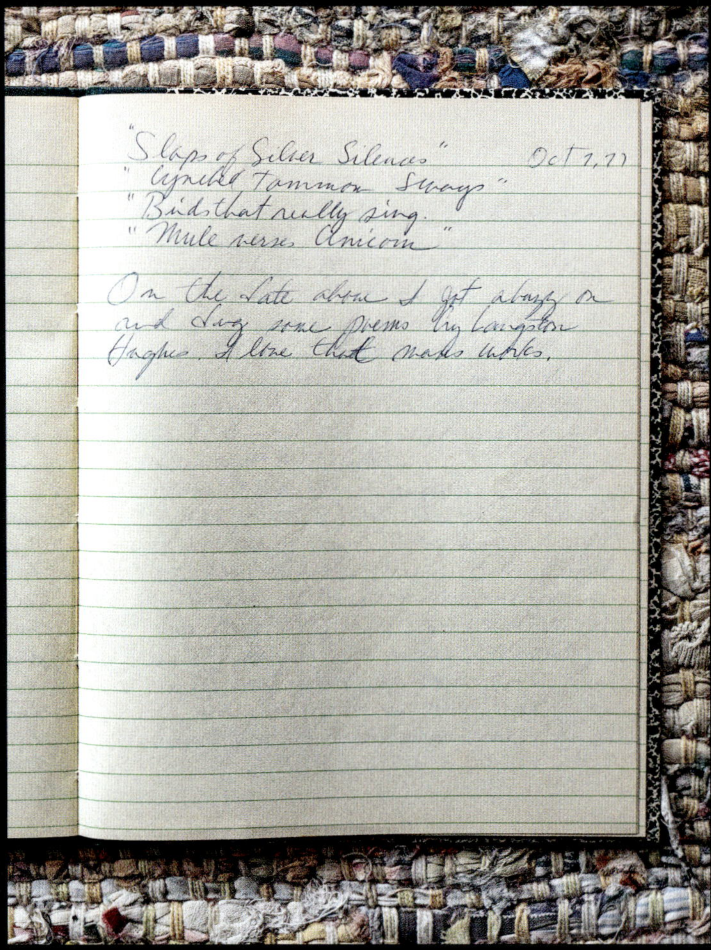

"Slaps of Silver Silences" Oct 1, 77
"Wicked Tammon Sways"
"Birds that really sing.
"Mule verses Unicorn"

On the Late show I got a buzz on and sang some poems by Langston Hughes. I love that man's works.

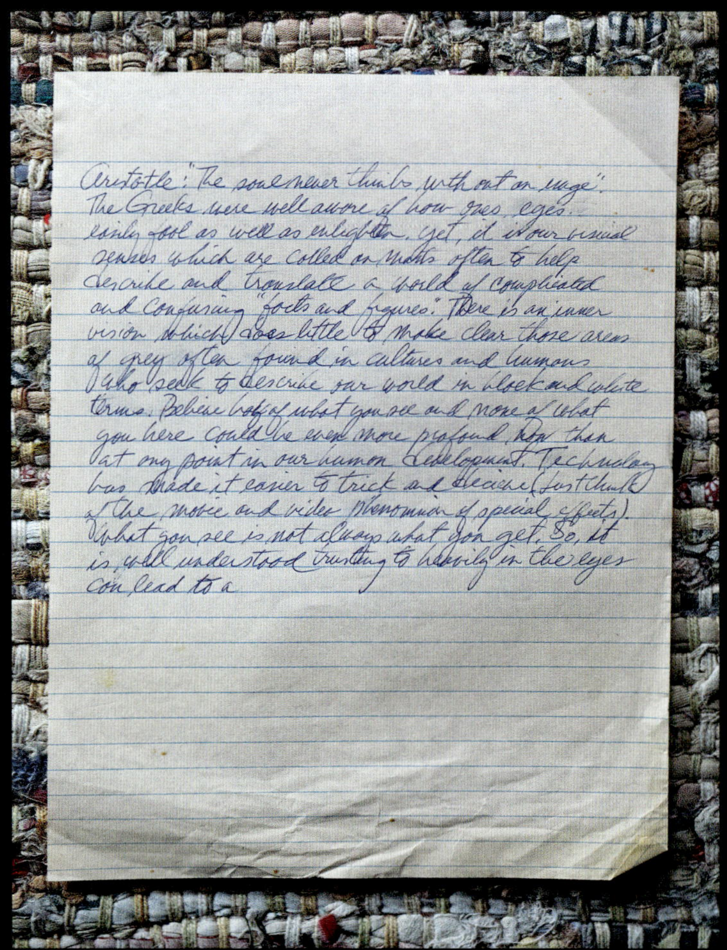

Aristotle: "The soul never thinks without an image".
The Greeks were well aware of how eyes, eyes easily fool as well as enlighten. Yet, it is our visual senses which are called on most often to help describe and translate a world of complicated and confusing "facts and figures". There is an inner vision which does little to make clear those areas of grey often found in cultures and humans who seek to describe our world in black and white terms. Believe half of what you see and none of what you hear could be even more profound now than at any point in our human development. Technology has made it easier to trick and deceive (just think of the movie and video phenomenon of special effects). What you see is not always what you get. So, it is well understood trusting to heavily in the eyes can lead to a

UNTITLED
DATE: Unknown

Put on your red lace undies and those pointy
high heel shoes

Put on your red lace undies and those pointy
high heel shoes

I need some sexual stimulation to chase
away these blues

Fetch those Jimmy Choos from the closet
and strap them on real tight

Fetch those Jimmy Choos from the closet
and strap them on real tight

That magenta toe nail polish
will make me feel alright, ~~tonight~~.

Fruit Painter

at times I feel I'm destined to live the very life style and principals I was staunchly defending while I was at Fed tac. My position was: the value of an artist to the society cannot and should not be measured in capital gains or anointing by the lords of words; the very fact the artist was committing the art of painting was in itself the primary contribution to a better world". Well this concept went over like a Tylenol capsule at an orgy. My fellow artist did not grasp that point till a bit later (for some nutty reason they held out for a long spell).

"Eating pussy and smoking dope" Mar. 6, 1980

Two more weeks til spring. What next? I guess I should start thinking about getting my ass over to 22 Addison. I was thinking earlier about things change. Yes indeed! Papa Lamont. What can I say about that little baron? Well I'm cruising high on good vibes from my show – I wish there was some money with all those good words; got an offer for October Gone, good night though. Tommorrow is "the Day" good old Hilton is supposed to do his thing: If its going to be on the street tommorrow it should be done by now. Anyways, I'm surprising myself again on this new couple. Another knock out – wow!

The more I learn how to employ words
to convey thoughts and ideas the less
I know what to say about my own
work - at least in written form. There
is something to be said for the old
standby - "the work speaks for itself". I have
tried for weeks to come up with a coherent
string of words and ideas which I hope
would make sense to the both of us -
Then moments ago I was enlightened
about my foolishness: My work does not
depend on the written word for creditability.
So I will not try to squeeze my foot into
a shoe that's proves itself to be too tight.
All the words I have ever used to describe
my work ~~knows~~ that somewhere within
me sit a ~~boiling~~

No sooner that it took for the words to leave
my lips I'm ~~aware~~ ~~some part of that~~
(for me at least) there is no way words
will describe what I want to create humanity
color, and design -

"Honky Dory" May 2, 1983

In a conversation with my wife
I said, in response to dialogue

Mr John.

John Floyd was a good
hearted man who loved
his liquor. On the weekends
he would don his sunday
bests and snort vast
amounts of his favorite
blends. He would then
sit on his front porch
and watch the day
go by. He would
occasionally treat us
to his state of the art
Polaroid Camera. That
was when I really

caught the camera germ
Mr. John would be a
bit too buzzed to remember
just how to make his
machine take the photos
he knew it could.
Thats where I come
in. Needless to say
I was drawn to that
silver and grey instrument
He would hand it to
me and let me
shoot up some film
on those days when he
found it difficult

make his drink get
out the way of his actions
"Here Butch," he would
say, as he made him-
self take a seat and
let me operate his
wonder Machine. It
was indeed a machine
of wonderful wonders.
It caught on fast to
its operations and
recorded many images
of him and those who
were nearby. It most
certainly started something.

No Singles

A man with a pistol, stuck it in the face of a bank teller and demanded money. He told the person between him and the cash: "This is a holdup. I have AIDS and I have nothing to live for. Do you? Put all your cash in the bag — No Singles." What would you do if you were the teller? What would you do if you were the robber? What do you think about the whole situation? Well, when I heard it, I thought another wild story from the naked city. What else can you think given the nature of these strange times which we find ourselves in.

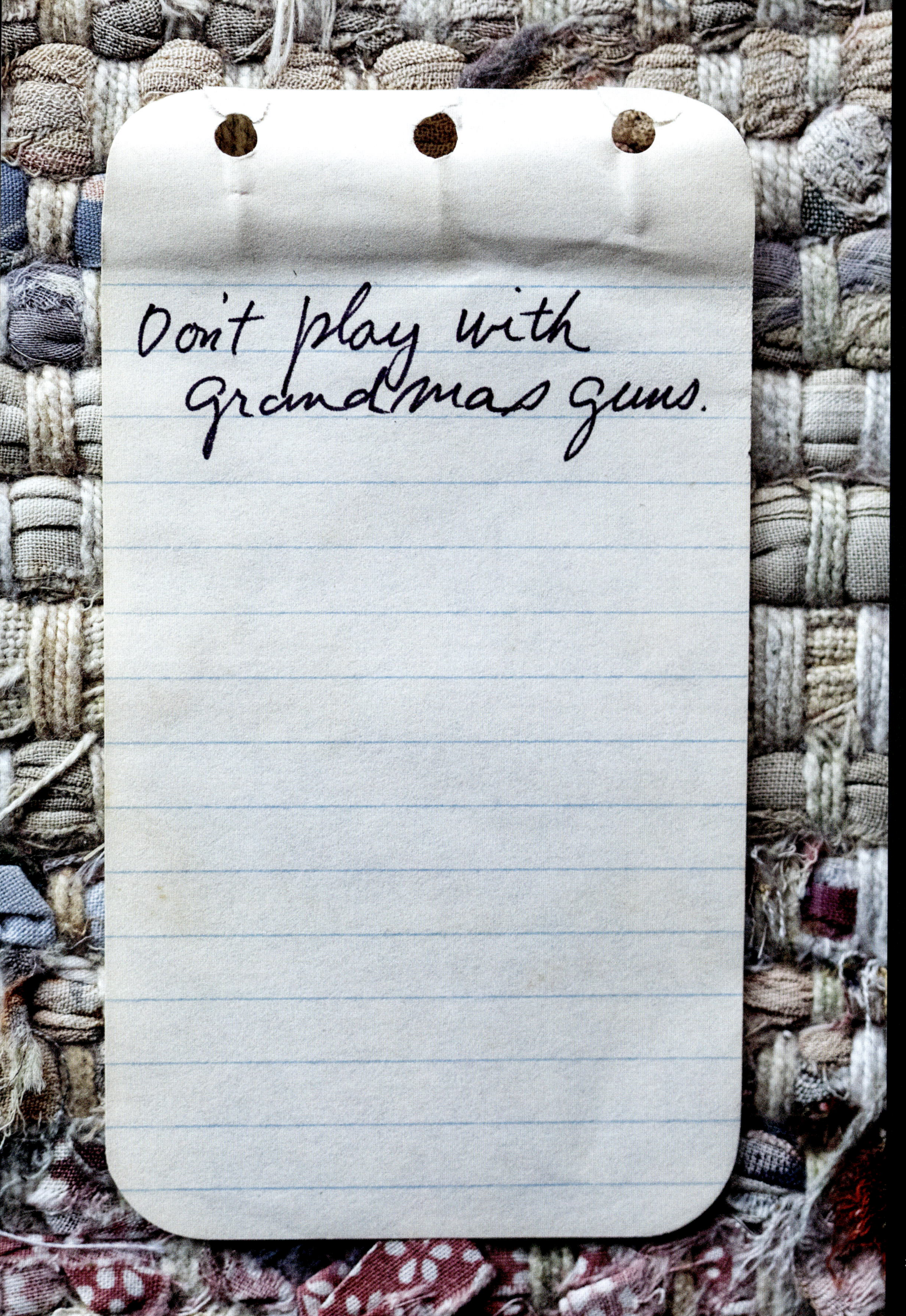




DATE: Unknown

6

Is it possible to forcast ones own insanity? If so, if so? if so shit! I wanted all of you to know what is being done to me at this time. I am tuned into <u>Good</u> music, food, and smoke.

What does all this mean. Why are you all flashing through my mind Why are you all important — at all. Too many things flying too fast for me to put down on paper — I too damn slow.

Fela is in Istanbul in front of the Blue Masque. Fela just jumped into Venice. Now Fela ends his trip. Now Herbie takes us through Italy — our Maiden Voyage

Wayne builds to a all time high inside the De Medici Dome

Freddie is in Venice in the middle of St. Marks square. Waking the man beat the bell.

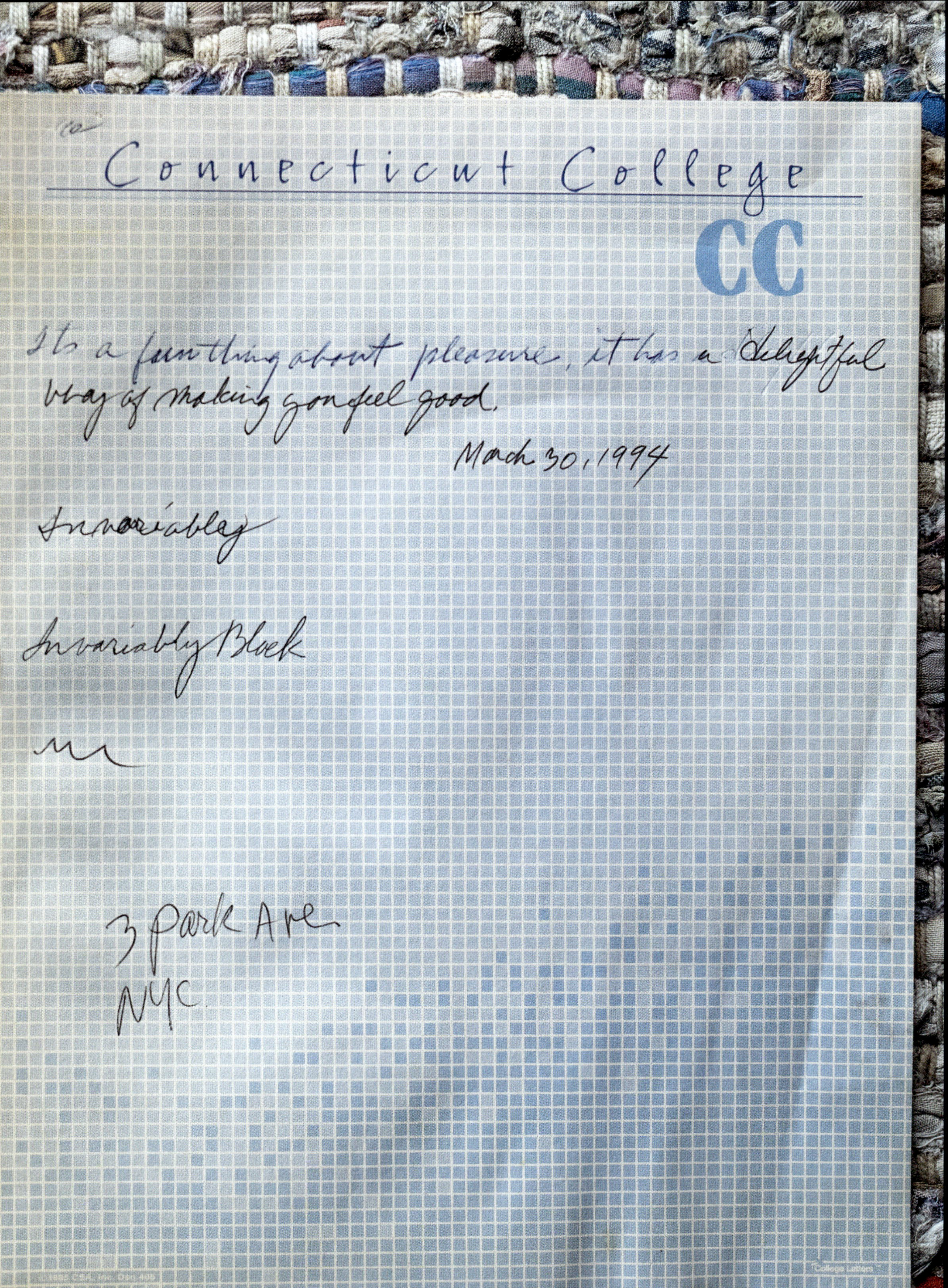

Connecticut College

CC

It's a fun thing about pleasure, it has a delightful way of making you feel good.

March 30, 1994

Invariably

Invariably Black

3 Park Ave
NYC

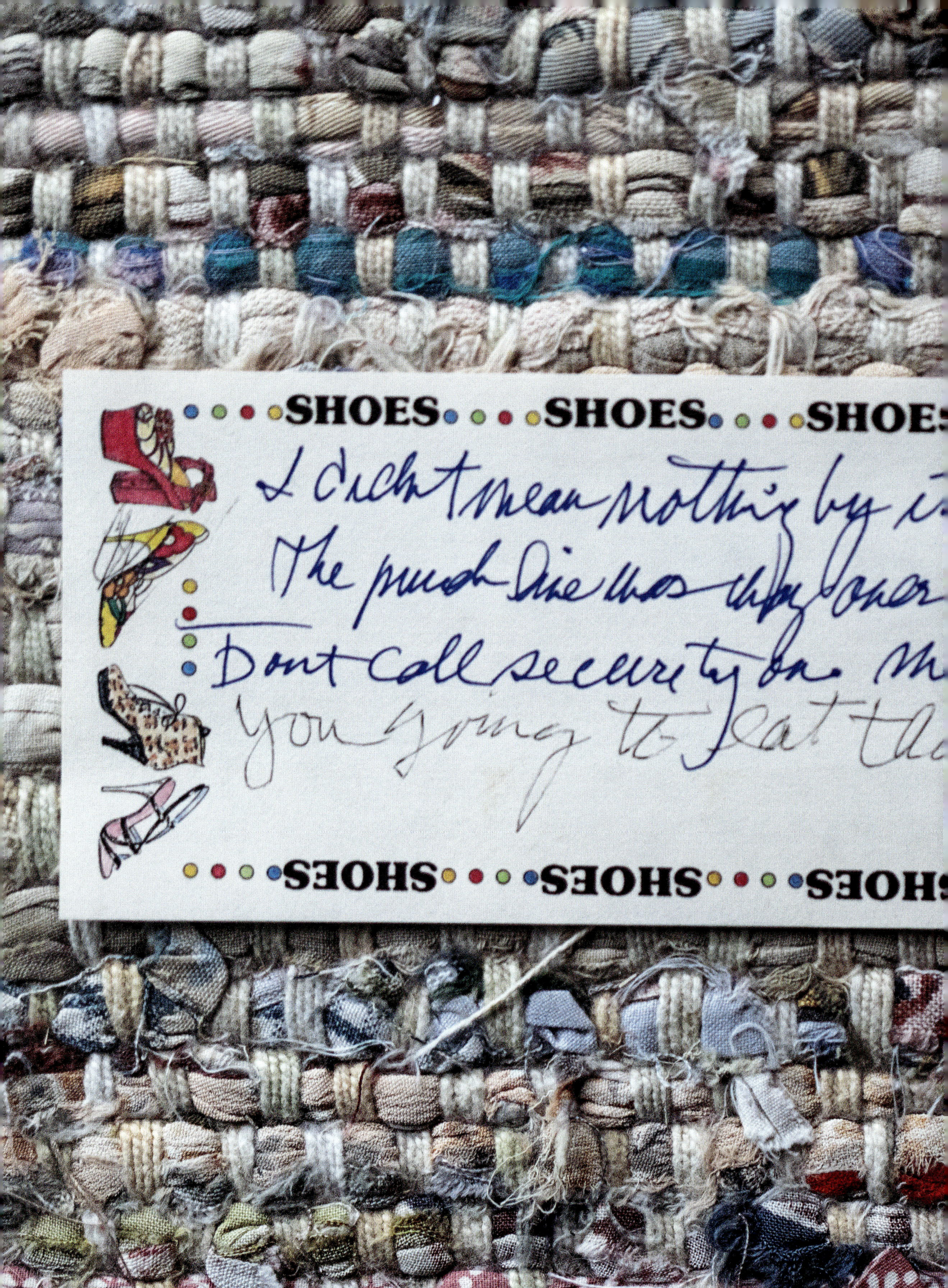
SHOES SHOES
I didnt mean nothing by
The punch line was way
Dont call security on
You going to

DATE: Unknown

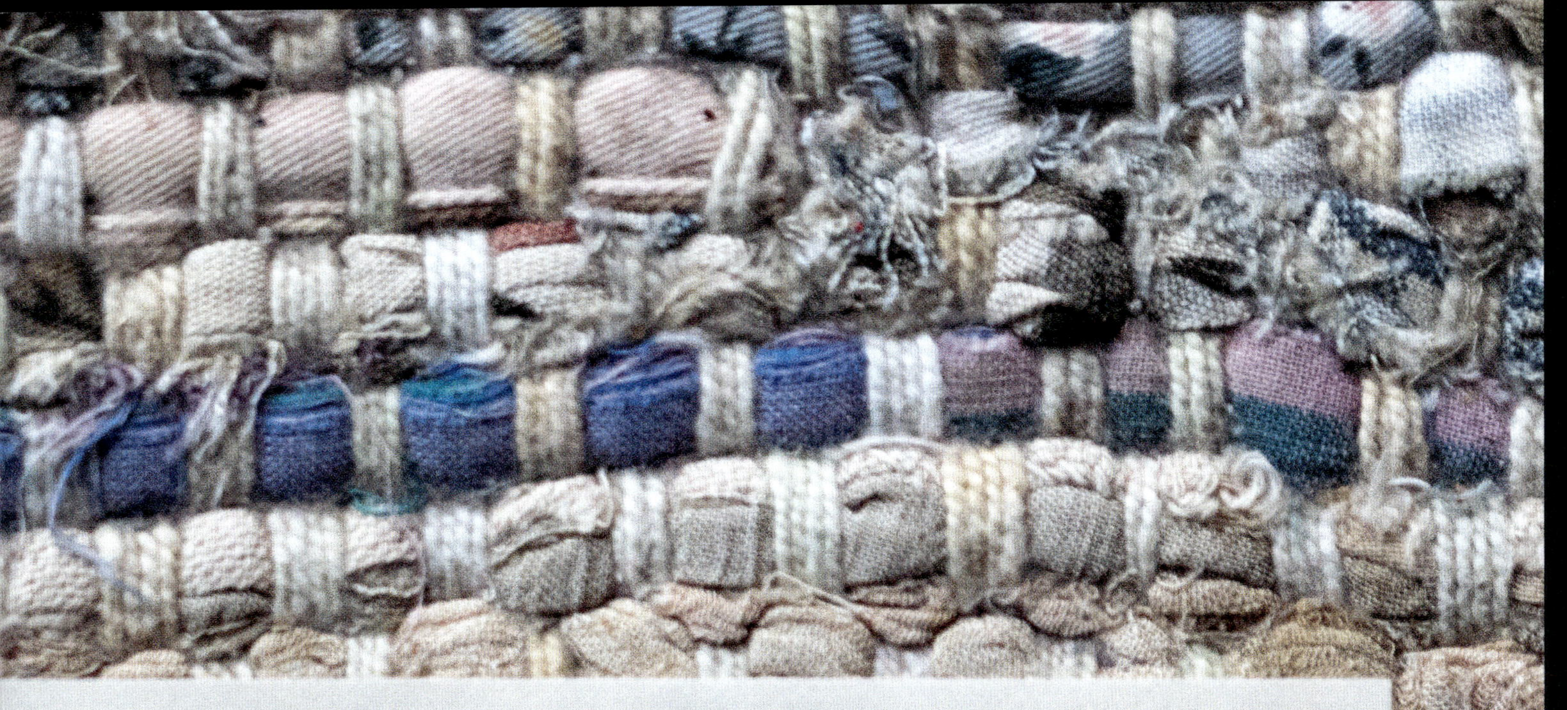

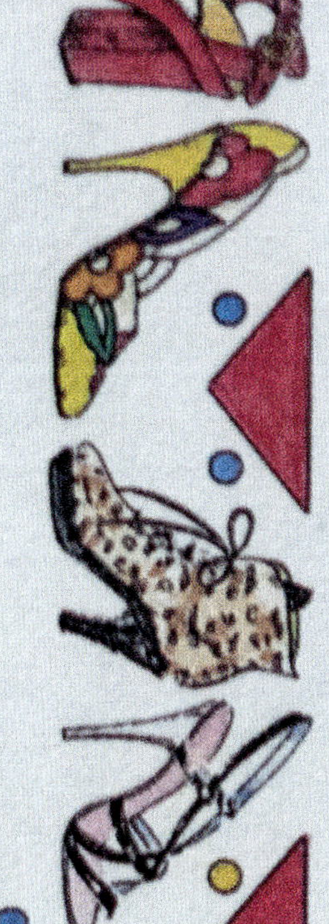


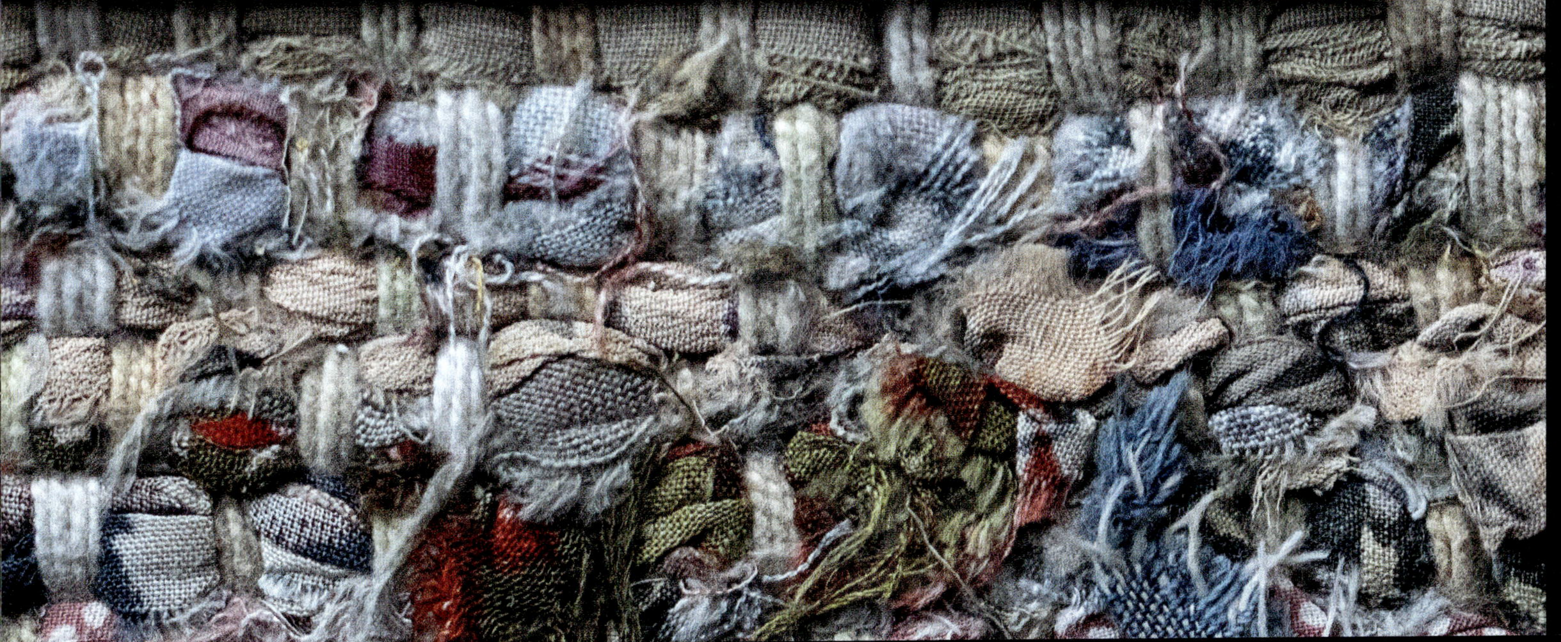

**What does all this mean. Why are you all flashing through my mind. Why are you all important— at all.**

# Contributors

**Barkley L. Hendricks**

Barkley L. Hendricks (b. Philadelphia, PA, 1945; d. New Haven, CT, 2017) was an American painter and photographer who revolutionized portraiture through his realist and post-modern oil paintings of Black Americans living in urban areas, beginning in the 1960s and 1970s.

He attended the Pennsylvania Academy of the Fine Arts and earned both his BFA and MFA from Yale University in 1972. He was Professor of Art at Connecticut College from 1972 to 2010. Hendricks lived and worked in New London, Connecticut, for most of his lifetime.

Throughout his career, Hendricks refused to be boxed into a medium, and his practice was commanding, bold, and without limitations to media or form. He was first a photographer before taking up painting, and he consistently refused to tether himself to just one form of artistic expression. Beyond his portraiture, he also created distinct works on paper and painted landscapes and still lifes, including an early series of basketball paintings that explored abstraction and color theory.

Recent solo exhibitions include *Barkley L. Hendricks: Portraits at the Frick* (The Frick Collection, New York, NY, in 2023–2024), *Barkley L. Hendricks in New London* (Lyman Allyn Art Museum, New London, CT, in 2023), and *My Mechanical Sketchbook - Barkley L. Hendricks & Photography* (Rose Art Museum, Waltham, MA, in 2022).

Barkley L. Hendricks' work is included in numerous public collections, including the Museum of Modern Art (New York, NY); Whitney Museum of American Art (New York, NY); National Gallery of Art (Washington, DC); Tate Modern (London, UK); Los Angeles County Museum of Art (Los Angeles, CA); The Studio Museum in Harlem (New York, NY); Philadelphia Museum of Art (Philadelphia, PA); Nasher Museum of Art at Duke University (Durham, NC); and Harvard Art Museums (Cambridge, MA).

**Susan Hendricks**

Susan Hendricks is the Managing Director of the Estate of Barkley L. Hendricks.

Under her stewardship, the Estate of Barkley L. Hendricks has continued to honor the artist's iconic portrayal of African American life, identity, and culture, while expanding his reach through engagement with museums, galleries, and cultural institutions.

With a deep commitment to preserving the legacy and work of her late husband, Susan is dedicated to ensuring that Hendricks' groundbreaking contributions to contemporary art remain accessible to future generations and are recognized for their profound impact on both art history and social discourse.

**David Katzenstein**

New York based fine arts photographer David Katzenstein has traveled throughout the world on his lifelong artistic journey as a visual chronicler of humanity. Using subject, light, and composition to create visual dynamism, he sets the stage for the viewer to be in the moment with him. His goal is to allow viewers to experience a scene through his eyes—as if they were standing there beside him. Steeped in the tradition of documentary photography, Katzenstein imbues his work with immediacy, emotional engagement, and a deep respect for his subjects.

Katzenstein studied photography at Connecticut College with Barkley L. Hendricks, and he is currently the managing editor of the Barkley L. Hendricks Photography Archive. To date, Katzenstein has published three monographs with Hirmer Verlag: *Ritual* (2022), *Distant Journeys* (2024), and *Brownie* (2025).

# Acknowledgments

**DK:** Well, Susan, we did it! We managed to complete this book project without killing each other! Just kidding. It has been a wonderful, rewarding experience to work with you over these past few years to create this book that will now serve as a visual tribute to Barkley's legacy.

**SH:** **What a wild, marvelous journey it has been, my friend. From those nascent days just weeks after Barkley passed so unexpectedly to—well, yesterday—when we were discussing the finer details about the book's cover.**

**It's been a bold visual reckoning as you and I have ventured throughout and documented the home where Barkley created and where he and I lived together. Barkley was an extremely private person, especially where his work and studio were concerned. We were private as a couple—few visitors, no studio space sharing. So for you to suggest, and then undertake with such precision and determination, the photographic documentation of our home and Barkley's studio, well, this had simply never been done.**

**DK:** Now that we're looking back on the process of bringing this book to fruition, let us take a moment to thank those who have been so instrumental.

**SH:** **First and foremost, I have to acknowledge Barkley L. Hendricks: my husband, partner, and source of constant inspiration, without whom this book would not have been possible. The phrase *piles of inspiration everywhere* is something Barkley often said about his/our environs, and it really reflects how he interacted with the space he created around himself—around both of us, really.**

**I was so fortunate to have lived in this house with Barkley for 35 years, every moment of which was a profound daily visual, aural, and spatial adventure. Even though he has now passed on, in many ways that adventure is ongoing as I continue to inhabit the space we shared.**

**DK:** Susan, besides my gratitude for our partnership in this project, I'd like to give a shout out to my wife Sherrie Nickol, a consummate photographer in her own right, who has been supportive of my work since we met almost 40 years ago, and who still laughs at my jokes.

**SH:** **I am deeply grateful to you, David. Our partnership working on this book together has been revelatory. Without your persistence, let's face it—your pestering—this book would not exist. Now I'm kidding. But without your effort, we would not be sharing with the world the joyful, visual cacophony that was Barkley's life and creative work.**

**DK:** I would also like to reiterate the impact that Barkley had on my own development as an artist. Our professor/student relationship began when we were both young, and over the years stayed constant with deep respect on both sides. I only wish that future young artists have the opportunity to be mentored as I was, and to understand that creativity in its pure form is universal. I hope that they are as fortunate as I was to get to participate in the creative process with a true master. I therefore take this opportunity to acknowledge the importance of Barkley's guidance and presence in my own life as an artist.

**SH:** **And of course, we want to acknowledge our brilliant graphic designers, Tracey Shiffman and James Ihira, to whom we are so grateful.**

**This book project is unique because it is not about an artist's work but about how and where he created it. As you and I have discussed several times, we have been consistently amazed by how deep Tracey and James' inherent understanding has been—of not only the artwork placed in their hands, but of the underlying themes that they create as they ingest the materials.**

**DK:** I couldn't have said it better. This really has been a true collaboration with Tracey and James.

**SH:** **I—we, for I know you share my sentiments on this, David—are immensely grateful for their brave wandering down the difficult path of reading, deciphering, and understanding Barkley's words and writings taken from his journals.**

**With this completed book, I am so pleased to offer readers the rare opportunity to experience Barkley's "natural habitat" where he mused and created.**

# Well this concept went over like a Tylenol capsule at an orgy.

FRUIT PAINTER, DATE: Unknown (see p. 256)